Romantic Rebels

Romantic Rebels

ESSAYS ON SHELLEY AND HIS CIRCLE

Kenneth Neill Cameron, Editor

Harvard University Press   Cambridge, Massachusetts   1973

FOREWORD

If the rebels represented in this volume were "romantic" in the form of their rebellion, the matters against which they were rebelling were real and the solutions they proposed were, on the whole, practical. When Mary Wollstonecraft published her pioneer work *A Vindication of the Rights of Woman* in 1792 women were excluded from the professions and the universities, were denied the vote, and were legally discriminated against in regard to property and other rights. In the following year, William Godwin, Mary Wollstonecraft's husband, protested in *Political Justice* against war, economic inequality, political dictatorship, restrictive marriage and divorce laws, the prison system, and a criminal code that imposed the death penalty for petty theft. Byron's maiden speech in the House of Lords was an eloquent plea for justice to the "frame-breaking" factory workers. His death was the result of his participation in the Greek war for independence. Shelley campaigned in Ireland for Irish separation and wrote pamphlets on parliamentary reform, protesting a franchise based on narrow property rights. In *Prometheus Unbound* he envisioned an egalitarian world without nations, classes, or war. Leigh Hunt, the first radical, crusading journalist, battled week after week in *The Examiner* against all forms of injustice from child labor to army flogging. Among Thomas Love Peacock's heroes were Thomas Jefferson and William Cobbett, and in his lively, satiric novels he excoriated all forms of sham and humbug. Mary Shelley, daughter of Mary Wollstonecraft and William Godwin, produced in *Frankenstein* not only the first science fiction novel but also one of the first novels to introduce radical social and antireligious views.

The rebellion, as today also, extended into personal matters and life style. Mary Wollstonecraft had an affair with the American adventurer Gilbert Imlay, and bore his child Fanny. After her death William Godwin published her letters to Imlay, feeling that they showed an aspect of the personality of a great woman and should be published regardless of the moral condemnation of the age. Byron's love affairs were conducted in public and celebrated in his poetry. Shelley and Mary Godwin eloped and lived openly together while he was still married to Harriet Westbrook. His humanitarian philosophy extending to include animals, he became a vegetarian. Like Byron and Keats he favored opened-necked shirts and long hair.

The rebels paid for their rebellion. Shelley was deprived of his children, Byron was driven by persecution into exile, Hunt was imprisoned. If all this has a modern ring, it is because the earlier period uniquely anticipated the present. The years 1790 to 1820 saw the rise of the first industrial civilization; the first great national revolutions, the American and the French; the first modern-type war, the Napoleonic Wars; the first major development of both a city middle class and an industrial working class. The rebellion of the 1920's, reflected in literature in Joyce, Lawrence, O'Casey, Kafka, O'Neill, Sinclair Lewis, is remarkably parallel to that of the 1790's, which included Blake, Wordsworth, and Coleridge. And the second wave of the rebellion, with Shelley, Keats, Byron, Hazlitt, and Hunt, is similar to that of today, with Ginsberg and Lowell, the "new left," and the revolt of the young. The romantic rebels of the past speak more directly to the rebels of today than any other group of writers of the past.

The essays in this book appeared first in volumes one to four of *Shelley and his Circle,* an edition of the manuscripts in The Carl H. Pforzheimer Library,* which contains the largest collection of Shelley manuscripts next to that in the Bodleian Library at Oxford University. The essays on Shelley, Byron, Wollstonecraft, Godwin, Hunt, Peacock, and Mary Shelley were used in those volumes to introduce their letters and other manuscripts. The essay on the suicide of Harriet Shelley, the discussion of the letters of Mary Shelley to Shelley's friend Thomas Jefferson Hogg, and "Another Shelley Family Elopement" are primarily biographical, that on manuscript provenance is bibliographical—an attempt to trace the history and present whereabouts of the manuscripts of Shelley and others. As the *Shelley and his Circle* volumes are large and expensive these essays have not been easily available to students or the general reading public. It is to make them available that they are here presented.

K. N. C.

*<i>Shelley and his Circle,</i> 1773–1822, ed. Kenneth Neill Cameron, Harvard University Press, vols. I–II, 1961, vols. III–IV, 1970.

CONTENTS

PERCY BYSSHE SHELLEY

(August 4, 1792–July 8, 1822)

PRINCIPAL WORKS

EARLY LIFE

THE family connections of Mr. Shelley," wrote Leigh Hunt in his *Autobiography*, "belonged to a small party in the House of Commons, itself belonging to another party. They were Whig Aristocrats, voting in the interests of the Duke of Norfolk."[1] The family, however, had been neither aristocrats nor Whigs until the rise of Shelley's grandfather, Sir Bysshe Shelley. Sir Bysshe, born in Newark, New Jersey, in 1752, established the family fortunes by two marriages and made a political alliance with the Duke of Norfolk whereby his son Timothy, father of the poet, became a Member of Parliament. To this seat Timothy's son was intended to succeed. Politics, the Duke informed young Percy Bysshe, "are the proper career for a young man of ability and of your station in life."[2] But the "young man," born in a year in which Godwin was writing *Political Justice* and the French Revolution was rising to its

1. Hunt, *Autobiography*, II, 28.

2. Hogg, *Shelley*, I, 129. Hogg does not name the "duke" who gave Shelley this advice but the context shows that it was Norfolk.

heights, had other plans. He had soon passed beyond the Whigs into republicanism and beyond republicanism into Godwinian egalitarianism. He wished not to sit in Parliament but to reform it, and ultimately to do away with it.

The influence of Shelley's grandfather upon him is an interesting and puzzling question. That the influence is there is certain. Sir Bysshe, his grandson informs us, was "a complete Atheist."[3] His talk was largely of politics and liberally flavored, one would gather, with denunciations of "bigots" and "tyrants."[4] He was a flamboyant and dominating character, living in a small house in Horsham instead of in his castle, Castle Goring, and mingling in a democratic way — perhaps a relic of his American birth and American mother — with the town folk "in the tap-room of the Swan Inn."[5] But the influence must have been rather indirect than direct for we hear of little contact between grandfather and grandson beyond a story that the grandfather paid for the printing of the grandson's first volume of verses.

Of Sir Bysshe's son Timothy, later Sir Timothy, *The Gentleman's Magazine* wrote that he "possessed, in a high degree, the best qualities of the English country gentleman"; and we have a picture of him by a visitor to the family estates (at Field Place near Horsham in Sussex) as "clad in his yeoman-like garb and tanned leather gaiters."[6] His letters are in accord with the picture. They reveal a man of solid common sense, with a good head for practical detail and the management of affairs, but with little imagination or capacity for abstract reasoning. "Never read a book, Johnnie," he told his second son, "and you will be a rich man."[7] The advice, however, was given only in the bitterness of the disasters attending the first son, disasters which Timothy attributed in large part to reading. Timothy himself had read books — he was an M.A. of Oxford University — and had at first taken a good deal of pride in the talented Percy Bysshe. "My son here," he told Henry Slatter, bookseller of Oxford, "has a literary turn; he is already an author, and do pray indulge

3. Shelley to Elizabeth Hitchener, Jan. 26, 1812.

4. Shelley to Sir Bysshe Shelley, Oct. 13, 1811.

5. [Joseph Gibbons Merle], "A Newspaper Editor's Reminiscences," *Fraser's Magazine*, XXIII (June 1841), 702. See also Medwin, *Shelley*, p. 11.

6. Quoted in White, *Shelley*, I, 14, 12.   7. Quoted, *ibid.*, p. 12.

him in his printing freaks."[8] Father and son, although never deeply intimate, were fond of each other; Shelley's sisters tell of his standing vigil anxiously outside his father's door when the good squire was down with an attack of the gout.

Of Shelley's mother surprisingly little is known. Although she is said to have been a gifted letter writer (her sister, wife of John Grove of Fern, Wiltshire, was a painter), her letters do not seem to have survived. From Shelley's accounts of her in his letters she seems to have been an intelligent and liberal-minded woman who had the confidence of her son and who was strongly devoted to him. "Mrs. Shelley often spoke to me of her son," wrote a later visitor to Field Place, "her heart yearned after him with all the fondness of a mother's love."[9] Yet, in all the years of his exile from home, and in his personal troubles — the suicide of Harriet, the deaths of his children — there is no record of Shelley's writing to his mother or receiving a letter from her.

Although Shelley never fulfilled the ambition of his father that he succeed him in Parliament he was brought up in the expectation that he would do so. He was, that is to say, brought up in the Whig creed, and the Whig creed, during these years of war with France, was a surprisingly liberal one: sympathy for the principles of the American and French revolutions; the extension of the franchise (out of a population of 11,000,000 only 11,000 had the vote); the abolition of the rotten boroughs (300 out of 513 members owed their seats to individual "proprietors"); the championing of the cause of the Irish (who were represented by Protestants in an English parliament); a faith that the "mighty changes of the rising world" (to quote Thomas Erskine) would bring about "a happy and glorious consummation."[10] An imaginative youngster imbibing these ideas had not far to step to get to republicanism and Tom Paine or from republicanism to Godwinian egalitarianism. And the young Shelley made both steps.

The seeds of religious dissent were present at Field Place also. "Indeed, his religious opinions were also very lax," wrote Shelley's

8. Henry Slatter to Robert Montgomery, Dec. 13, 1833, Robert Montgomery, *Poetical Works* (London, 1854), p. 442.

9. Captain Kennedy, quoted in Hogg, *Shelley*, II, 152.

10. *Hansard*, XXXIII (1797-1798), 661.

cousin, Thomas Medwin, of Timothy, ". . . he possessed no true devotion himself, and inculcated none to his son and heir."[11] He subscribed to a book of Unitarian sermons, signing himself: "A friend to religious liberty."[12]

Shelley's subsequent views were not, therefore, as is often stated, the result of a rebellion against a conservative home. On the contrary the basis for them was laid in that home. Radical views on political subjects and deistic views in religion are present in his earliest works, in the novel *Zastrozzi* and the book of verses, *Original Poetry*, both written before he went to Oxford or had studied *Political Justice*.

His first taste of some of the consequences that might follow such views came when he was little more than an Eton schoolboy. He and his cousin, Harriet Grove, had long been attracted to each other, and had reached an "understanding" approved by both families. The understanding was broken off, we are informed by Harriet's brother Charles, because of "the tone of his letters on speculative subjects," letters which Harriet showed to her father.[13]

At Oxford Shelley met Thomas Jefferson Hogg, son of a northern landowner, who later became his biographer, and who has left us a vivid picture of their first meeting:

At the commencement of Michaelmas term, that is, at the end of October in the year 1810, I happened one day to sit next to a freshman at dinner: it was his first appearance in hall. His figure was slight, and his aspect remarkably youthful, even at our table, where all were very young. He seemed thoughtful and absent. He ate little, and had no acquaintance with anyone. I know not how it was that we fell into conversation, for such familiarity was unusual, and, strange to say, much reserve prevailed in a society where there could not possibly be occasion for any. We have often endeavoured in vain to recollect in what manner our discourse began, and especially by what transition it passed to a subject sufficiently remote from all the associations we were able to trace. The stranger had expressed an enthusiastic admiration for poetical and imaginative works of the German school. I dissented from his criticisms. He upheld the originality of the German writings. I asserted their want of nature.

'What modern literature', said he, 'will you compare to theirs?'

I named the Italian. This roused all his impetuosity; and few, as I soon discovered, were more impetuous in argumentative conversation. So eager was

11. Medwin, *Shelley*, p. 13.   12. Dowden, *Shelley*, I, 5 fn.
13. Charles Grove to Hellen Shelley, Feb. 16, 1857, Hogg, *Shelley*, II, 155.

our dispute that when the servants came to clear the tables, we were not aware that we had been left alone.[14]

Hogg, like Shelley, had questioned the tenets of orthodox religion. From his own and Hogg's writings on the subject Shelley put together and had printed a little pamphlet entitled *The Necessity of Atheism,* by which they did not mean that atheism was necessarily true but that certain arguments logically ("of necessity") seemed to point toward it. These they modestly requested their theological betters to answer. The sequel is also told by Hogg:

It was a fine spring morning on Lady Day, in the year 1811, when I went to Shelley's rooms: he was absent; but before I had collected our books he rushed in. He was terribly agitated. I anxiously inquired what had happened.

'I am expelled,' he said, as soon as he had recovered himself a little, 'I am expelled! I was sent for suddenly a few minutes ago; I went to the common room, where I found our master and two or three of the fellows. The master produced a copy of the little syllabus, and asked me if I were the author of it. He spoke in a rude, abrupt, and insolent tone. I begged to be informed for what purpose he put the question. No answer was given; but the master loudly and angrily repeated, "Are you the author of this book?" If I can judge from your manner, I said, you are resolved to punish me, if I should acknowledge that it is my work. If you can prove that it is, produce your evidence; it is neither just nor lawful to interrogate me in such a case and for such a purpose. Such proceedings would become a court of inquisitors, but not free men in a free country. "Do you choose to deny that this is your composition?" the master reiterated in the same rude and angry voice.' Shelley complained much of his violent and ungentlemanlike deportment, saying, 'I have experienced tyranny and injustice before, and I well know what vulgar violence is; but I never met with such unworthy treatment. I told him calmly, but firmly, that I was determined not to answer any questions respecting the publication on the table. He immediately repeated his demand; I persisted in my refusal; and he said furiously, "Then you are expelled; and I desire you will quit the college early to-morrow morning at the latest." One of the fellows took up two papers and handed one of them to me; here it is.' He produced a regular sentence of expulsion, drawn up in due form, under the seal of the college.

Shelley was full of spirit and courage, frank and fearless; but he was likewise shy, unpresuming, and eminently sensitive. I have been with him in many trying situations of his after-life, but I never saw him so deeply shocked and so cruelly agitated as on this occasion. A nice sense of honour shrinks from the

14. Hogg, *Shelley*, I, 46.

most distant touch of disgrace — even from the insults of those men whose contumely can bring no shame. He sat on the sofa, repeating, with convulsive vehemence, the words, 'Expelled, expelled!' his head shaking with emotion, and his whole frame quivering.[15]

As does not seem to have been noted, Shelley could not answer the Master's question because he had not alone written the pamphlet. Hogg had written part of it. And to answer would have been to implicate his friend. Immediately on hearing the news from Shelley, Hogg also went before the college dons and also was expelled.

The angry and troubled air of men, assembled to commit injustice according to established forms, was then new to me; but a native instinct told me, as soon as I entered the room, that it was an affair of party; that whatever could conciliate the favour of patrons was to be done without scruple; and whatever could tend to impede preferment was to be brushed away without remorse.

The next day Shelley and Hogg left for London on the stagecoach and a long period of negotiations between Shelley and his father began, Timothy Shelley being upset almost to the point of distraction by the disgrace of expulsion. Even as these negotiations were going on, however, a more serious crisis was in the making. Shelley had become interested in a school friend of his sister Hellen's, Harriet Westbrook, the daughter of a wealthy coffee house owner; in August they eloped to Scotland.

Following the elopement Shelley went to Ireland to assist in the movement for Catholic Emancipation and the severing of the Act of Union between Great Britain and Ireland (a union which Byron referred to as "the union of the shark with his prey").[16] He there addressed a large public meeting at which Daniel O'Connell was the principal speaker, published *An Address to the Irish People*, and established contacts with various Irish nationalists. These experiences moved him from an obsessive anticlericalism toward social reform. The first product of the change, *A Letter to Lord Ellenborough* (1812), was a vigorous plea for freedom of the press. The second, his poem *Queen Mab* (1812–1813), surveyed the social evils of the past and present and depicted a "gradual renovation"[17]

---

15. *Ibid.*, pp. 168–169. Hogg's account is colored by his concept of Shelley and needs to be compared with others (as given, for instance, in Edmund Blunden's "Shelley Is Expelled," *On Shelley*, Oxford University Press, 1938). But there is, as usual, a certain core of truth in Hogg's narrative and it has the virtue of dramatic vividness.

16. *Hansard*, XXII (1812), 651.   17. *Queen Mab*, VIII, 143.

in the future (not, as is usually stated, a sudden change to the millennium; Shelley, no more than did Godwin, believed in social miracles).

It was while writing *Queen Mab* that Shelley first became acquainted with Godwin (in October 1812). It was nearly two years later (July 28, 1814) that he eloped with Godwin's daughter Mary; and it was more than two years after this elopement that Harriet Shelley committed suicide (November 8, 1816). The following March, although he and Mary were then married, he was deprived by law of the custody of his children by Harriet (Charles and Ianthe), and the following year he left England for Italy.

In Italy his life was comparatively uneventful. After a year and more of wandering, during which he and Mary lost two children, Clara and William, and a third, Percy Florence, was born, they settled in Pisa. There they were joined by Byron, Trelawny, Jane and Edward Williams, and others to make a brilliant intellectual circle, Byron writing on *Don Juan*, Shelley writing *Epipsychidion*, *Adonais*, and *Hellas*. It was as a result of his efforts to have Byron establish a new journal — *The Liberal* — to battle the Tory *Quarterly* that Shelley met his death. He had brought Leigh Hunt to Italy to assist in the scheme and while returning from an editorial conference with Hunt and Byron was drowned in the Bay of Spezzia (July 8, 1822) along with Edward Williams. He was twenty-nine years of age. No other English poet had by so early an age produced such a body of work. Had Shakespeare died at twenty-nine, he would have been known only as one of the most promising Elizabethans, inferior to Marlowe or Jonson, but somewhat above Greene and Lyly.

POET AND THINKER

Although in the nineteenth century such Shelley admirers as George Bernard Shaw, Thomas Hardy, H. Buxton Forman, H. S. Salt, and William Michael Rossetti regarded Shelley as an intellectual poet, the concept of him as a pure lyricist later grew to dominate the scene and fed the complaints of the "new critics" (who attack Shelley because he fails to write in the style of John Donne). Now it is true, of course, that Shelley wrote lyrics, in fact, some of the finest lyrics in the language, including "To a Skylark" and "Ode to the West Wind." But to describe him as a "lyric poet" and leave it at that would be like describing

Shakespeare as a sonneteer. Shelley was not primarily a lyric poet but a philosophical poet — as Carl Grabo pointed out more than two decades ago in *The Magic Plant: The Growth of Shelley's Thought*:

An overstress of emotion has been the curse of Shelleyan criticism. Shelley the thinker is distorted and obscured in the haze of emotional speculation. He is thereby wholly falsified, for if ever a man lived the intellectual life and was less the victim of unreason and blind emotion it was Shelley. He thought passionately. For him a beautiful idea was as exciting as is a beautiful woman or the thought of an illicit amour to some of his critics. Impassioned thinkers constitute but a small part of the human race, the part of greatest importance to be sure, but misunderstood, derided, hated, and crucified by the rest of mankind. It will be incomprehensible to many people that Shelley was not chiefly preoccupied with clouds, skylarks, and beautiful dream maidens; that he spent vastly more time and thought upon questions of practical politics, and upon the problems of good and evil, and of free will and determinism. Shelley's was a poetic mind but also a philosophic mind, realizing that ideal of poet-philosopher which he most admired in the great minds of the past.[18]

Both Shelley's range as a "poet-philosopher" and the "modern" applicability of his thought are greater than is commonly supposed. This underestimation is due partly to that "overstress of emotion" which characterizes the textbook and anthology accounts and partly to a neglect of Shelley's prose works.

Central to his thinking, as to that of Hunt and Godwin, is the humanitarianism of the period, a humanitarianism the spirit of which is concentrated in the two famous lines in *Julian and Maddalo* —

Me — who am as a nerve o'er which do creep
The else unfelt oppressions of this earth —

and which found expression in his philosophy of love. This philosophy anticipates in some respects such modern psychological theories as Freud's on the libido; for Shelley conceives of love as a unifying force with widely variant manifestations, biological, psychological, and social — sexual love, romantic love, friendship, love of humanity, love of nature:

Man is in his wildest state a social being: a certain degree of civilization and refinement ever produces the want of sympathies still more intimate and complete; and the gratification of the senses is no longer all that is sought in sexual connexion. It soon becomes a very small part of that profound and complicated sentiment, which we call Love, which is rather the universal thirst

18. Grabo, *The Magic Plant*, p. vii.

for a communion not merely of the senses, but of our whole nature, intellectual, imaginative and sensitive; and which, when individualised, becomes an imperious necessity, only to be satisfied by the complete or partial, actual or supposed, fulfilment of its claims. This want grows more powerful in proportion to the developement which our nature recieves [*sic*] from civilization; for man never ceases to be a social being. The sexual impulse, which is only one, and often a small part of those claims, serves, from its obvious and external nature, as a kind of type or expression of the rest, as common basis, an acknowledged and visible link. Still it is a claim which even derives a strength not its own from the accessory circumstances which surround it, and one which our nature thirsts to satisfy.[19]

This is an extraordinary passage to have been written in the early nineteenth century. Shelley does not make the dichotomy customary at least since the troubadours, and first openly challenged in the present century by D. H. Lawrence, among others, between the biological and romantic aspects of love. The "sexual impulse" is "a type or expression of the rest." In another passage he speaks of the sexual act as "the act which ought always to be the link and type of the highest emotions of our nature."[20] If Shelley differs from some modern psychologists in regarding the biological aspect of love as subordinate to the total love pattern, others (for instance, Erich Fromm) are turning toward this concept.

Love, for Shelley, however, extends beyond sexual and even beyond all individual personal relationships:

Thou demandest what is love? It is that powerful attraction towards all that we conceive, or fear, or hope beyond ourselves, when we find within our own thoughts the chasm of an insufficient void, and seek to awaken in all things that are, a community with what we experience within ourselves . . . This is Love. This is the bond and the sanction which connects not only man with man, but with every thing which exists.[21]

> That Light whose smile kindles the Universe,
> That Beauty in which all things work and move,
> That Benediction which the eclipsing Curse
> Of birth can quench not, that sustaining Love
> Which through the web of being blindly wove
> By man and beast and earth and air and sea,
> Burns bright or dim, as each are mirrors of

19. *A Discourse on the Manners of the Antient Greeks Relative to the Subject of Love*, Notopoulos, *Platonism*, pp. 408–409.

20. *Ibid.*, p. 410.   21. *On Love*, Shelley, *Complete Works*, VI, 201.

> The fire for which all thirst; now beams on me,
> Consuming the last clouds of cold mortality.[22]

The "eclipsing Curse of birth" is death; the great counter to death is love, love which is part of the "web of being," both in man and in nature.

This philosophy of love did not blind Shelley to present evils. On the contrary, it gave him more insight by holding up a vision of the possible as against the actual. His general views on these matters, his social philosophy, received their most complete expression in his long prose work, *A Philosophical View of Reform*. Like Godwin — and Rousseau — he did not believe that evil was inherent in humanity but that it arose from corrigible social causes. Like Godwin — and Condorcet — he believed that this evil had been diminishing, that society had been progressing, and that it would progress further. He did not, however, view this progress, as did Godwin, primarily as the result of "reason." History, he believed, had been dominated by a struggle between despotism and liberty; in this struggle, liberty, although many times defeated, had always arisen again, and arisen stronger than before. There had been a clear line of progress since "the dissolution of the Roman Empire": the Italian city states, the Puritan revolution in England, the American revolution:

> The system of government in the United States of America was the first practical illustration of the new philosophy. Sufficiently remote, it will be confessed, from the accuracy of ideal excellence is that representative system which will soon cover the extent of that vast Continent. But it is scarcely less remote from the insolent and contaminating tyrannies under which, with some limitation of these terms as regards England, Europe groaned at the period of the successful rebellion of America. America holds forth the victorious example of an immensely populous, and as far as the external arts of life are concerned, a highly civilized community administered according to republican forms.[23]

Following the American revolution came the French, an even greater upheaval:

> The just and successful Revolt of America corresponded with a state of public opinion in Europe of which it was the first result. The French Revolution was the second.

22. *Adonais*, lines 478–486.

23. *A Philosophical View of Reform*, Shelley, *Complete Works*, VII, 10-11.

Connected with these political upheavals were social and economic phenomena of a new and complex kind (thrown into relief by the economic crisis following the Napoleonic wars):

The mechanical sciences attained to a degree of perfection which, though obscurely foreseen by Lord Bacon, it had been accounted madness to have prophesied in a preceding age. Commerce was pursued with a perpetually increasing vigour, and the same area of the Earth was perpetually compelled to furnish more and more subsistence. The means and sources of knowledge were thus increased together with knowledge itself, and the instruments of knowledge. The benefit of this increase of the powers of man became, in consequence of the inartificial forms into which society came to be distributed, an instrument of his additional evil. The capabilities of happiness were increased, and applied to the augmentation of misery. Modern society is thus a[n] engine assumed to be for useful purposes, whose force is by a system of subtle mechanism augmented to the highest pitch, but which, instead of grinding corn or raising water acts against itself and is perpetually wearing away or breaking to pieces the wheels of which it is composed.

Following the French Revolution, liberty had again been restricted — by Napoleon, first, then by Castlereagh and Metternich with their Quadruple Alliance. But now, in his own day, a new rise of liberty was beginning, in Germany, Spain (1819), Italy (1820), and Greece (1821).

We find the same concepts also in the poetry; for instance, in the Chorus to liberty in *Hellas*:

From age to age, from man to man,
  It lived; and lit from land to land
  Florence, Albion, Switzerland.
Then night fell; and, as from night,
Re-assuming fiery flight,
From the West swift Freedom came,
  Against the course of heaven and doom,
A second sun array'd in flame,
  To burn, to kindle, to illume.
From far Atlantis its young beams
Chased the shadows and the dreams.
France, with all her sanguine steams,
  Hid, but quench'd it not; again
  Through clouds its shafts of glory rain
  From utmost Germany to Spain.

[11]

The new resurgence of liberty would surpass the American and French revolutions even as they had surpassed the Puritan revolution (a prediction partially fulfilled in 1830 and 1848). In time the (continuing) expansion of liberty would result in the egalitarian society envisaged by Godwin:

> Thrones, altars, judgment-seats, and prisons; wherein
> And beside which, by wretched men were borne
> Sceptres, tiaras, swords, and chains, and tomes
> Of reasoned wrong, glozed on by ignorance,
> Were like those monstrous and barbaric shapes,
> The ghosts of a no more remembered fame . . . .
> The loathsome mask has fallen, the Man remains, —
> Sceptreless, free, uncircumscribed, — but man:
> Equal, unclassed, tribeless and nationless,
> Exempt from awe, worship, degree, the King
> Over himself.[24]

This evolutionary vision of history provided the inspiration for Shelley's first major poem, *Queen Mab*, and supplied the frame on which was hung the lengthy narrative of *The Revolt of Islam*. It animated alike his masterpiece, *Prometheus Unbound*, and the three great odes, "Ode to Liberty," "Ode to Naples," and "Ode to the West Wind."

Shelley, like his own favorite philosophical poets, Dante and Milton, was ever consumed by the mysteries of Man's relations to the universe; and these, too, he converted into poetry, in "Hymn to Intellectual Beauty" —

> The awful shadow of some unseen Power
>   Floats tho' unseen among us —

in *The Triumph of Life*, in "Mont Blanc," in "The Cloud," in *The Sensitive Plant*, in *Adonais*:

> The One remains, the many change and pass;
> Heaven's light forever shines, Earth's shadows fly;
> Life, like a dome of many-coloured glass,
> Stains the white radiance of Eternity,
> Until Death tramples it to fragments.

24. *Prometheus Unbound*, III, iv, 164–169; 193–197.

In other poems, *Alastor, Julian and Maddalo, Epipsychidion*, he searched into his own mind and life, hoping there to find truths for other men also —

> Mind from its object differs most in this:
> Evil from good; misery from happiness;
> The baser from the nobler; the impure
> And frail, from what is clear and must endure.
> If you divide suffering and dross, you may
> Diminish till it is consumed away;
> If you divide pleasure and love and thought,
> Each part exceeds the whole.

As is insufficiently recognized he produced narrative verse with an extraordinary range of effects and styles, from the intensity of the final passage of *Epipsychidion* or the Madman's soliloquy in *Julian and Maddalo* to the supple ease of the *Letter to Maria Gisborne* with its realistic vignettes:

> But what see you beside? A shabby stand
> Of Hackney-coaches — a brick house or wall
> Fencing some lonely court, white with the scrawl
> Of our unhappy politics; — or worse —
> A wretched woman reeling by, whose curse
> Mixed with the watchman's, partner of her trade,
> You must accept in place of serenade.

In the year 1819 Shelley tried a new medium, the drama. His play *The Cenci*, declared by Leigh Hunt to be "the greatest dramatic production of the day," failed to find a producer (although as a book it went into a second edition). In the present century, however, it has begun to come into its own and has been produced in Europe (Paris, Moscow, Prague), in the United States, and in London:

Although the performance lasted three solid hours, with only one short break, the audience listened with rapt attention from start to finish, and, exhausted as it must have been by the effort required to grasp Shelley's magnificent imagery, it would not leave until everybody had been called again and again, and Miss Thorndike, looking positively worn out after playing the long trying part of Beatrice, had come forward to make a speech.[25]

25. *The Graphic*, Nov. 18, 1922, quoted in Kenneth N. Cameron and Horst Frenz, "The Stage History of Shelley's *The Cenci*," *PMLA*, LX (December 1945), 1085.

In 1821 Shelley attempted still another field, that of literary philosophy. Although not a professional critic, as were Hunt and Hazlitt, he had previously written some criticism (in reviews and prefaces), but with *A Defence of Poetry* he entered the realm of Wordsworth's Preface to *Lyrical Ballads* and Coleridge's *Biographia Literaria* — the analysis not so much of individual works as of the nature of literature itself. This analysis he continued also in his Prefaces, for instance, in that to *Prometheus Unbound*, where, perhaps most concisely, he discusses the relationship of literature to history:

> The peculiar style of intense and comprehensive imagery which distinguishes the modern literature of England, has not been, as a general power, the product of the imitation of any particular writer. The mass of capabilities remains at every period materially the same; the circumstances which awaken it to action perpetually change. If England were divided into forty republics, each equal in population and extent to Athens, there is no reason to suppose but that, under institutions not more perfect than those of Athens, each would produce philosophers and poets equal to those who (if we except Shakespeare) have never been surpassed. We owe the great writers of the golden age of our literature to that fervid awakening of the public mind which shook to dust the oldest and most oppressive form of the Christian religion. We owe Milton to the progress and development of the same spirit: the sacred Milton was, let it ever be remembered, a republican, and a bold inquirer into morals and religion. The great writers of our own age are, we have reason to suppose, the companions and forerunners of some unimagined change in our social condition, or the opinions which cement it.

The range of Shelley's prose is essentially the same as that of the poetry: social philosophy, history, metaphysics, ethics, narrative. One large group revolves around social and political subjects: another parliamentary reform essay in addition to *A Philosophical View of Reform*: three works of protest against social injustice: *A Letter to Lord Ellenborough* (a plea for freedom of the press); a defense of the prosecuted radical publisher, Richard Carlile, in the form of an open letter to *The Examiner*; *Address to the People on the Death of the Princess Charlotte*, which protested the execution of three workmen who had been incited to Luddite violence by the government labor spy known as Oliver (a work of extraordinary vigor of style):

> So soon as it was plainly seen that the demands of the people for a free representation must be conceded if some intimidation and prejudice were not

conjured up, a conspiracy of the most horrible atrocity was laid in train. It is impossible to know how far the higher members of the government are involved in the guilt of their infernal agents. It is impossible to know how numerous or how active they have been, or by what false hopes they are yet inflaming the untutored multitude to put their necks under the axe and into the halter. But thus much is known, that so soon as the whole nation lifted up its voice for parliamentary reform, spies were sent forth. These were selected from the most worthless and infamous of mankind, and dispersed among the multitude of famished and illiterate labourers. It was their business if they found no discontent to create it. It was their business to find victims, no matter whether right or wrong. It was their business to produce upon the public an impression, that if any attempt to attain national freedom, or to diminish the burthens of debt and taxation under which we groan, were successful, the starving multitude would rush in, and confound all orders and distinctions, and institutions and laws, in common ruin. The inference with which they were required to arm the ministers was, that despotic power ought to be eternal.[26]

Another group of works deals with philosophical questions: *A Refutation of Deism; On a Future State; On the Devil and Devils; On Life*:

Life and the world, or whatever we call that which we are and feel, is an astonishing thing. The mist of familiarity obscures from us the wonder of our being. We are struck with admiration at some of its transient modifications, but it is itself the great miracle. What are changes of empires, the wreck of dynasties, with the opinions which supported them; what is the birth and the extinction of religious and of political systems, to life? . . . We are born, and our birth is unremembered, and our infancy remembered but in fragments; we live on, and in living we lose the apprehension of life.[27]

In *Speculations on Metaphysics* he ventures into the problems of the identity and analysis of the self:

If it were possible that a person should give a faithful history of his being, from the earliest epochs of his recollection, a picture would be presented such as the world has never contemplated before. A mirror would be held up to all men in which they might behold their own recollections, and, in dim perspective, their shadowy hopes and fears, — all that they dare not, or that daring and desiring, they could not expose to the open eyes of day. But thought can with difficulty visit the intricate and winding chambers which it inhabits. It is like a river whose rapid and perpetual stream flows outwards; — like one in dread

26. Shelley, *Complete Works*, VI, 79–80.   27. *Ibid.*, pp. 193–194.

who speeds through the recesses of some haunted pile, and dares not look behind.[28]

Still another group of works discusses ethical and religious questions: *Essay on Christianity; Speculations on Morals; A Discourse on the Manners of the Antient Greeks Relative to the Subject of Love,* which contains one of Shelley's most eloquent passages on the social status of women:

Among the antient Greeks the male sex, one half of the human race, recieved [*sic*] the highest cultivation and refinement; whilst the other, so far as intellect is concerned, were educated as slaves . . . The gradations in the history of man present us with a slow improvement in this respect. The Roman women held a higher consideration in society, and were esteemed almost as the equal partners with their husbands in the regulation of domestic economy and the education of their children. The practices and customs of modern Europe are essentially different from and incomparably less pernicious than either, however remote from what an enlightened mind cannot fail to desire as the future destiny of human beings.[29]

The notorious homosexuality of the ancient Athenians, he believed, was not primarily psychological but was the consequence of the social subordination of women: "Among the Greeks these feelings, being thus deprived of their natural object, sought a compensation and a substitute."

In reading Shelley's prose, even more than in reading his poetry, one feels that of all the great English poets of the past (not excluding Blake or Byron) he was the most modern in his social thinking. It has been said that he was neglected by his age; but as Newman White pointed out, it was not so much that his age neglected him as that it was afraid of him. In Shelley's day as in ours there were those who wished to have certain problems regarded as settled and others as taboo; but Shelley regarded little as settled and nothing as taboo. He questioned everything: political and parental authority, marriage and divorce laws, Christian theology, the relation of sex to love, the nature of the self. Such questioning was profoundly disturbing to a still largely feudal society which tolerated rotten boroughs, approved of paternal absolutism, had virtually no divorce procedures, nodded benignly at romantic love but considered sex unmentionable, barred from the government, the universities, and the professions all except members of the Established Church, and

28. *Ibid.*, VII, 64.   29. Notopoulos, *Platonism*, p. 409.

preferred to keep psychological analysis on a purely sentimental level. Shelley's questions were all the more disturbing because he reached out beyond the immediate issue. The limitations of the franchise led him to consider the uses of government in general; the marriage and divorce laws provoked inquiries into the nature of marriage; and everything drove his mind to the problem of the meaning of history, until, as George Bernard Shaw commented, we find him "anticipating also the modern view that sociological problems are being slowly worked out independently of the conscious interference of man."[30] It was this desire to seek out regardless of consequence the final value and nature of things that led Shelley to anticipate later trends of interest and thought. The things that he refused to consider as settled are, after all, still with us — and still unsettled. His thinking does not, of course, always run along the same lines as ours, but it is surprising how frequently it does; and his suggestions — even when he is wrong — are often startling in their individual insights. Furthermore, he was able to express his philosophy not only in the reasoned analysis of prose but also, and primarily, in the imaginative synthesis of poetry.

30. *Note Book of the Shelley Society* (London, 1888), p. 31.

WILLIAM GODWIN

(March 3, 1756–April 7, 1836)

PRINCIPAL WORKS

LIFE

WILLIAM GODWIN's father and grandfather were Dissenting ministers and as a young man Godwin followed their path. Born in the little town of Wisbeach in Cambridgeshire on March 3, 1756, he was sent to a small private school, the master of which was famed as "the best, or second best, penman in the county of Norfolk," and whose influence is to be seen in the extreme clarity of Godwin's hand ("legible as print," writes Kegan Paul gratefully after having savored also of other hands preserved among the Abinger Manuscripts).[1] In 1773 Godwin was sent to one of the leading Dissenting theological academies, that at Hoxton near London, where two of the outstanding scholars of the day, Andrew Kippis and Abraham Rees, editor of *Rees' Encyclopedia*, were among the teachers. Kippis and Rees, however, were not only noted scholars, they were also noted liberals. The tradition of religious dissent was a tradition also of political dissent. And it was out of this tradition that William Godwin arose. It was not too far a step from the political views of Andrew Kippis to those of Thomas Paine. Godwin, however, at first resisted the liberalizing influences of Kippis

1. Paul, *Godwin*, I, 9.

[18]

and others at Hoxton, going, in fact, stubbornly in the opposite direction; but the seeds had been planted:

A little time before the period of my entering the Dissenting College at Hoxton, I had adopted principles of toryism in government, by which I was no less distinguished from my fellow-students than by my principles of religion. I had, however, no sooner gone out into the world than my sentiments on both these points began to give way; my toryism did not survive above a year, and between my twenty-third and my twenty-fifth year my religious creed insensibly degenerated on the heads of the Trinity, eternal torments, and some others.[2]

Even before his graduation from Hoxton, Godwin had done some preaching during his summer vacations. After his graduation he became a minister at Stowmarket in Suffolk. He was, in spite of the doubts mentioned above, devoted to his profession and wished to remain in it. But "in consequence of a dispute with my hearers on a question of Church discipline" he was forced to leave Stowmarket, and the following year left the ministry also.

With his expulsion from Stowmarket a new chapter opened in Godwin's life. At a loss to know where to turn, he went to London, and there for the next ten years he earned a precarious living by his pen:

I resided during the rest of the year [1782] at a lodging in Holborn, and by the persuasions of [Joseph] Fawcet and another friend was prevailed on to try my pen as an author. I drew up proposals for a periodical series of English Biography, but having set down first to the Life of Lord Chatham, I found it grow under my hands to the size of a volume, which I completed by the end of the year. . . . My principal employment was now [1783-1784] writing for the 'English Review,' published by Murray in Fleet Street, at two guineas a sheet, in which employment it was my utmost hope to gain twenty-four guineas per annum. . . . Notwithstanding these resources, for the most part I did not eat my dinner without previously carrying my watch or my books to the pawnbroker to enable me to eat.

He was relieved from this poverty by the intervention of his old tutor, Dr. Kippis, who in 1785 introduced him to George Robinson, publisher of *The New Annual Register*, a rival — with liberal overtones — to *The*

2. Paul, *Godwin*, I, 16. Godwin, at various periods in his life, wrote autobiographical essays and fragments which he may have thought of using as the basis for an actual autobiography. It is from these that Paul quotes.

Annual Register, both of which gave a summary of the major happenings of each year, in politics, literature, international affairs, and so forth, and reviewed past history also. Godwin was appointed to write these historical accounts, a task at which he earned an uncongenial living for some six years. In the year 1789 he was deeply moved by the French Revolution — "this was the year of the French Revolution. My heart beat high with great swelling sentiments of Liberty" — and the following year his mind caught the vision of a great work, one to transcend the political and moral principles of the republicans. In 1791 he was enabled to write this work through the generosity of George Robinson, who (rare among publishers) agreed to advance his living expenses and relieve him of all work until he finished the task.

> This year was the main crisis of my life. In the summer of 1791 I gave up my concern in the New Annual Register, the historical part of which I had written for seven years, and abdicated, I hope for ever, the task of performing a literary labour, the nature of which should be dictated by anything but the promptings of my own mind. I suggested to Robinson the bookseller the idea of composing a treatise on Political Principles, and he agreed to aid me in executing it. My original conception proceeded on a feeling of the imperfections and errors of Montesquieu, and a desire of supplying a less faulty work. . . . It was my first determination to tell all that I apprehended to be truth, and all that seemed to be truth, confident that from such a proceeding the best results were to be expected.

With the publication of *An Enquiry concerning the Principles of Political Justice, and its Influence on General Virtue and Happiness* in February 1793 Godwin emerged from his comparative obscurity to become almost overnight the leading radical social philosopher of the age. "No work in our time," wrote William Hazlitt more than thirty years later, "gave such a blow to the philosophical mind of the country as the celebrated Enquiry concerning *Political Justice*. Tom Paine was considered for the time as a Tom Fool to him; Paley an old woman; Edmund Burke a flashy sophist. Truth, moral truth, it was supposed, had here taken up its abode; and these were the oracles of thought. 'Throw aside your books of chemistry,' said Wordsworth to a young man, a student in the Temple, 'and read Godwin on Necessity.'"[3]

3. Hazlitt, "William Godwin," *The Spirit of the Age, Complete Works*, XI, 17.

Coleridge wrote a sonnet on Godwin as one "form'd t'illumine a sunless world forlorn"; Southey "all but worshipped" the book; Crabb Robinson wrote of it as a work "which directed the whole course of my life."[4] When Godwin visited Warwickshire in the year following its publication he found that "there was not a person almost in town or village who had any acquaintance with modern publications that had not heard of the 'Enquiry concerning Political Justice,' or that was not acquainted in a great or small degree with the contents of that work. I was nowhere a stranger."

Nor was Godwin known as a philosophical radical only. The "great swelling sentiments of Liberty" engendered by the French Revolution drove him to protest against all practical as well as theoretical violations of "political justice." In the very year in which the book was published, two Scottish parliamentary reformers, Thomas Muir, an advocate (M.A. of Edinburgh University), and Thomas Palmer, a Unitarian minister, were sentenced respectively to fourteen and twelve years' deportation on charges of sedition. The case was brought — to no avail — before Parliament; and Godwin wrote a letter to the liberal *Morning Chronicle*, beginning:

> The situation in which Messieurs Muir and Palmer are at this moment placed is sufficiently known within a certain circle, but is by no means sufficiently adverted to by the public at large. Give me leave, through the channel of your paper, to call their attention to it.
>
> All the consolations of civilized society are pertinaciously refused to them. Property, whether originally their own or the gift of their friends, is to be rendered useless. Supplies of clothing, it seems, have been graciously received on board the vessels; but stores of every kind and *books* have constantly been denied admission. The principle which has been laid down again and again by the officers of Government is — *they are felons like the rest*.[5]

The following year an even more important trial took place, this time not of Scottish but of English parliamentary reformers, among

4. Brown, *Godwin*, p. 62.

5. Quoted in Paul, *Godwin*, I, 121. When the ship bearing Muir and Palmer to exile in Australia was at Woolwich, Godwin visited them. We find the following entry in his Journal for December 7, 1793: "Walk to Woolwich, with Fenwick; visit Muir and Palmer." On December 17 Godwin "dined" with Muir at Woolwich.

them one of Godwin's oldest friends, Thomas Holcroft, novelist and playwright, and John Horne Tooke, one of the leading scholars of the day.

The year 1794 was memorable for the trial of twelve persons, under one indictment upon a charge of high treason. Some of these persons were my particular friends; more than half of them were known to me. This trial is certainly one of the most memorable epochs in the history of English liberty. The accusation, combined with the evidence adduced to support it, is not to be exceeded in vagueness and incoherence by anything in the annals of tyranny. . . . Holcroft immediately surrendered himself, and was committed to Newgate: he wrote me word of his situation, and requested my presence. I left Dr Parr on Monday the 13th, and reached town on that evening. Having fully revolved the subject, and examined the doctrines of the Lord Chief Justice's charge to the grand jury, I locked myself up on Friday and Saturday, and wrote my strictures on that composition, which appeared at full length in the *Morning Chronicle* of Monday, and were transcribed from thence into other papers. During the progress of these trials I was present at least some part of every day.

Godwin's "strictures" appeared not only in *The Morning Chronicle* and other papers, but also as a separate work, and were generally considered to have had an important influence in securing a verdict of acquittal. Godwin writes with vigor and indignation:

An association for Parliamentary Reform may desert its object, and be guilty of High Treason. True: so may a card club, a bench of justices, or even a cabinet council. Does Chief Justice Eyre mean to insinuate that there is something in the purpose of a Parliamentary Reform, so unhallowed, ambiguous, and unjust, as to render its well wishers objects of suspicion, rather than their brethren and fellow subjects? What can be more wanton, cruel, and inhuman, than thus gratuitously to single out the purpose of Parliamentary Reform, as if it were of all others most especially connected with degeneracy and treason? . . . But the authors of the present prosecution probably hope that the mere names of Jacobin and Republican will answer their purposes, and that a Jury of Englishmen can be found who will send every man to the gallows without examination, to whom these appellations shall once have been attributed![6]

In the same month that the trials began, a new fame came to Godwin with the success of his novel *Caleb Williams*. "Few books," wrote Hazlitt, "have made a greater impression than *Caleb Williams* on its first appearance. It was read, admired, parodied and dramatized. . . . It was a new

6. *Cursory Strictures on the Charge delivered by Lord Chief Justice Eyre to the Grand Jury, October 2, 1794. First Published in the Morning Chronicle, October 21* (London, 1794), pp. 22–23.

and startling event in literary history for a metaphysician to write a popular romance. Mr. Godwin was thought a man of very powerful and versatile genius; and in him the understanding and the imagination reflected a mutual and dazzling light upon each other."

In 1797 London intellectual society was startled by the news that William Godwin had married Mary Wollstonecraft, whose *Vindication of the Rights of Woman* (1792) and *Historical and Moral View of the Origin and Progress of the French Revolution* (1794) had earned her a reputation almost as extensive as Godwin's. But within a few short months Mary was dead and Godwin was left with two small children on his hands, Mary, named after her mother, and Fanny Imlay, the child of Mary Wollstonecraft and Gilbert Imlay.

The popularity of *Political Justice*, Godwin believed, was due to the fact that its doctrines "coincided in a great degree with the sentiments then prevailing in English society." They did not coincide for long. The Pitt government, temporarily thwarted by the acquittal of Holcroft, Tooke, and the other defendants in 1794, soon began to take the offensive. A time of war, of the life and death struggle with Napoleon, was not one to breed liberalism. Habeas Corpus was suspended, trade unions were declared illegal, Ireland was subdued by armed force, the leaders of a mutiny in the fleet were summarily executed, the committee of the London Corresponding Society was arrested, the editor of *The Courier* — then a liberal, later a Tory paper — was imprisoned (for slandering the Czar of Russia), the Act of Union between Great Britain and Ireland was made into law. As a result of these measures English liberal opinion had by 1800 either been suppressed or converted into Tory opinion. A flight to safety began. Coleridge broke his "baby trumpet of sedition," Wordsworth began to wrestle with moral problems "in vain" and forget about political problems, Southey became — as Byron later called him — a renegade and within a few years was writing for *The Quarterly Review*. The Whig leaders, Grey, Fox, Sheridan, fought a hopeless rear-guard action and at last boycotted the House of Commons. In the House of Lords, the Duke of Norfolk (friend and patron of Timothy Shelley), stripped of some of his honors as a result of an antiroyalist toast to "the Majesty of the people," lapsed into silence.

With the change in the climate of opinion Godwin ceased to be widely read. By 1800 the decline which Hazlitt protested in 1825 had already begun:

> Mr. Godwin's person is not known, he is not pointed out in the street, his conversation is not courted, his opinions are not asked, he is at the head of no cabal, he belongs to no party in the State, he has no train of admirers, no one thinks it worth his while even to traduce and vilify him, he has scarcely friend or foe, the world makes a point . . . of taking no more notice of him than if such an individual had never existed.

Hazlitt is, for dramatic effect, exaggerating. Godwin was, in fact, still known although to a more restricted audience. In the year prior to that in which Hazlitt is writing there had appeared the first volume of Godwin's four-volume *History of the Commonwealth of England* (1824–1828), and several of his novels were still quite widely read. Moreover, he retained a certain intimate circle of admirers. (John Forster, later the biographer of Charles Dickens, made a hero-worshipping pilgrimage to his home in 1832 — but four years before his death: "He sits in his little library in Gower Place surrounded by musty folios Quartos & octavos in plentiful abundance. Indeed his library is large in its number of books — books too not less venerable than the philosopher himself who sits there writing away still — 'still in his old age' lives his wonted fire. His face is singularly fine — with a mixture of earnest intellectual expression and dignity to a degree I never saw before. . . . He is all intellect — you *feel that* in looking at him — and the slightest word he says *fixes* your attention — for you feel *raised* by his presence."[7])

There is, however, a certain essential truth to Hazlitt's picture. Godwin's great fame did fade. London society became afraid of him and of association with him, even intellectual association. He did not, as did Southey, acquire a new fame by abandoning his principles; and his condemnation of the political apostasy of Wordsworth and Southey was blunt: "We must look elsewhere than in the naked convictions of the understanding, for the principles of their conduct."[8]

Although Godwin, as he himself correctly contended, did not change

7. ALs, John Forster to James Whiteside, Dec. 31, 1832. (The Carl H. Pforzheimer Library.)

8. *Thoughts Occasioned by the Perusal of Dr. Parr's Spital Sermon, Preached at Christ Church, April 15, 1800, Being a Reply to the Attacks of Dr. Parr, Mr. Mackintosh, the Author of An Essay on Population, and Others* (London, 1801), pp. 7–8.

his principles, he retired from activity. When Sir Francis Burdett was imprisoned in 1810 and Daniel Isaac Eaton put in the pillory in 1812 he raised no voice in their defense. Even the horror of Peterloo (which inspired Shelley's *The Masque of Anarchy*) failed to rouse him. He followed parliamentary elections with great interest, writing detailed accounts of them in his letters, but he took no part in them. The result was that when the liberal movement began to revive between 1810 and 1816 and new audiences were provided for political opinion — *Cobbett's Political Register* sold 50,000 copies a week — Godwin neither joined the movement nor found the audience. He was ignored by the Tories and made no effort to seek out the new liberals.

In his verse *Letter to Maria Gisborne* (1820) Shelley wrote of Godwin —

> You will see
> That which was Godwin, — greater none than he
> Though fallen — and fallen on evil times —

perhaps hinting that Godwin (unlike Milton) had "fallen on evil times" because he had first himself "fallen." The name of William Godwin was still a great name — "greater none than he" — and the new movement of Burdett and Cobbett and Leigh Hunt and, later, the Whig reformers would have welcomed him. As it was he was remembered with admiration and affection, and when in 1808 he appealed for a subscription, the names of the subscribers included those of Grey, Holland, and Kinnaird, and in 1833 with the passage of the Reform Bill, Grey awarded him a sinecure of £200 a year. But Godwin from about 1798 on, in spite of his adherence to his principles, gives one the impression of a man in retreat, socially and psychologically. Out of this retreat grew that deterioration of character which — exaggerated out of all proportion — has been used to build up the caricature of Godwin as a shuffling borrower. Godwin's character did deteriorate; he did borrow; he did not always pay back what he borrowed; he became both insistent and — as Francis Place discovered — not always completely frank in his borrowing. But this is not the essential Godwin. "The author of *Political Justice* and *Caleb Williams*," wrote Hazlitt, "can never die, his name is an abstraction in letters; his works are standard in the history of intellect." "Though fallen," yet "greater none than he"

                              to stand
      Among the spirits of our age and land,
      Before the dread tribunal of *to come*
      The foremost.

We have to remember, too, that Godwin faced real financial burdens. In 1801 he remarried. His second wife, Mary Jane Clairmont, came to him with two children, Charles and Jane, and she and Godwin had a son, William, born in 1803. From this time on Godwin had to support a household with five small children. The task of educating these children was, in itself, a tremendous burden; how great, some of his letters reproduced in *Shelley and his Circle* show.

Nor did Godwin by any means live mainly through borrowing. He continued to earn a good deal of money by his books (as some of his contracts with publishers reveal) and after 1805 he had a source of income for some years in the Juvenile Library. The Juvenile Library was, in fact, an enterprise of some importance. One of the first publishing houses of children's books in England to maintain high literary standards, its most famous venture was the *Tales from Shakespear* of Charles and Mary Lamb. Both Godwin and his wife, who managed the enterprise, worked hard, but their expenses were high, and their inexperience in business finally drove them to the wall.

When on January 5 or 6, 1812, Godwin received a letter beginning — "You will be surprised at hearing from a stranger. . . . The name of Godwin has been used, to excite in me feelings of reverence and admiration" — and signed Percy B. Shelley, he replied without delay, requesting further information, although the name was unknown to him. A second letter arrived on January 12 or 13, giving the history of his correspondent, his expulsion from Oxford, his interest in Godwin's books and theories, his writing of novels and poems, his future literary aspiration and containing, almost incidentally, the sentence: "It will be necessary, in order to elucidate this part of my history, to inform you that I am heir by entail to an estate of £6,000 per annum." The lives of Godwin and Shelley were joined. Shelley eloped with and later married Mary Godwin. Jane Clairmont left the Godwin household to live with them; apparently rebuffed by Shelley she entered into a disastrous affair with Byron:

Thou too, O Comet beautiful and fierce,
Who drew the heart of this frail Universe
Towards thine own; till, wrecked in that convulsion,
Alternating attraction and repulsion,
Thine went astray and that was rent in twain.[9]

Fanny Imlay committed suicide. Charles Clairmont left home for Vienna where he became a successful teacher of languages. With the death of Shelley, Mary — already the author of *Frankenstein* — returned to England and became a well-known novelist but lived in virtual retirement, always in fear of the revival of the scandal of the past. And in 1832 Godwin's son William, himself a beginning novelist,[10] died. When in 1834, Godwin felt that he himself had not much longer to live, he looked back over the journal which he had kept, almost day by day, for more than forty-five years and wrote a final entry. In 1836 when he knew himself to be dying he placed the entry at the end:

With what facility have I marked these pages with the stamp of rolling weeks and months and years — all uniform, all blank! What a strange power is this! It sees through a long vista of time, and it sees nothing. All this at present is mere abstraction, symbols, not realities. Nothing is actually seen: the whole is ciphers, conventional marks, imaginary boundaries of unimagined things. Here is neither joy nor sorrow, pleasure nor pain. Yet when the time shall truly come, and the revolving year shall bring the day, what portentous events may stamp the page! what anguish, what horror, or by possibility what joy, what Godlike elevation of soul! Here are fevers, and excruciating pains 'in their sacred secundine asleep.' Here may be the saddest reverses, destitution and despair, detrusion and hunger and nakedness, without a place wherein to lay our head, wearisome days and endless nights in dark and unendurable monotony, variety of wretchedness; yet of all one gloomy hue; slumbers without sleep, waking without excitation, dreams all heterogeneous and perplexed, with nothing distinct and defined, distracted without the occasional bursts and energy of distraction. And these pages look now all fair, innocent, and uniform. I have put down eighty years and twenty-three days, and I might put down one hundred and sixty years. But in which of these pages shall the pen which purposes to record, drop from my hands for ever, never again to be resumed?

9. Shelley, *Epipsychidion*, lines 368–372. On the identification of the Comet as Jane (Claire) Clairmont, see White, *Shelley*, II, 266; Kenneth Neill Cameron, "The Planet-Tempest Passage in *Epipsychidion*," *PMLA*, LVIII (September 1948), 953.

10. *Transfusion; or The Orphans of Unwalden* (London, 1835).

WRITER AND THINKER

Hazlitt's essay on Godwin occurs, appropriately, in *The Spirit of the Age*, for Godwin was one of the shapers of that spirit. His works, however, did not only help to shape the spirit of the age; they were also an expression of it, and of its history.

The essence of that history was the rise and decline of a socio-economic revolution. A feudal-mercantile economy changed into an industrial economy. The social revolution was described by the great Oriental scholar, Sir William Jones, as early as 1799:

> There has been a continued war in the constitution of *England* between two jarring principles; the evil principle of the feudal system with his dark auxiliaries, ignorance and false philosophy; and the good principle of increasing commerce, with her liberal allies, true learning and sound reason.[11]

This "war" existed not only in England but in all Europe and in North and South America. It lay behind the American and the French revolutions, the Napoleonic wars, and the English movement for the reform of Parliament. The remarks of Sir William Jones were, in fact, part of a speech on parliamentary reform (i.e., the abolition of the rotten boroughs and the extension of the franchise).

It was the first tide of this movement that inspired alike Paine and Jefferson, Mary Wollstonecraft and Godwin. Paine, following his experiences in the American Revolutionary War, became one of the leaders in European republican thinking. In *The Rights of Man*, he attacked feudalism, its succession of great landed property, its search for further property as leading to war and political oppression: "But I might go further, and place also foreign wars, of whatever kind, to the same cause. It is by adding the evil of hereditary succession to that of monarchy, that a permanent family interest is created, whose constant objects are dominion and revenue."[12]

The feudal interests in their control of government had invaded the realm of society as a whole and severed man from nature: "All the great laws of society are the laws of nature." "Government is no further neces-

11. "Speech on the Reformation of Parliament," *Works* (London, 1799), VI, 719.

12. Thomas Paine, *The Rights of Man, The Life and Works of Thomas Paine* (New Rochelle, New York, 1925), VII, 15.

sary than to supply the few cases to which society and civilization are not conveniently competent." As a result the age was in turmoil, and revolutions "may be considered as the order of the day." The solution was to set up republican and democratic forms of government. In such governments, however, although the abuses of feudalism may be curbed, "the right to property" is "inviolable and sacred."[13]

It was largely because of Godwin's feeling that this republican philosophy contained inadequacies that he wrote *Political Justice* (1793). The book, as we have seen, was an immediate sensation.

Republicanism was inadequate, Godwin argued, because it failed to see that the great evils of society flow not from political oppression but from economic inequality. "However great and extensive are the evils that are produced by monarchies and courts, by the imposture of priests and the iniquity of criminal laws, all these are imbecil and impotent, compared with the evils that arise out of the established system of property."[14] Political oppression may deprive people of their political rights but economic oppression corrupts the moral fabric of the nation:

> The spirit of oppression, the spirit of servility, and the spirit of fraud, these are the immediate growth of the established system of property. These are alike hostile to intellectual and moral improvement. The other vices of envy, malice and revenge are their inseparable companions.[15]

These evils cannot be eliminated by political reform but only by economic transformation, the full development of the economy, and a sharing of its "bounties":

> In a state of society where men lived in the midst of plenty, and where all shared alike the bounties of nature, these sentiments would inevitably expire. The narrow principle of selfishness would vanish. No man being obliged to guard his little store, or provide with anxiety and pain for his restless wants, each would lose his own individual existence in the thought of the general good. No man would be an enemy to his neighbour, for they would have nothing for which to contend; and of consequence philanthropy would resume the empire

13. *The Life and Works of Thomas Paine*, VI, 243, 241, 235, 149.

14. *An Enquiry concerning Political Justice, and its Influence on General Virtue and Happiness* (London, 1793), II, 799. In the 2nd edition (1796) "Morals" was substituted for "General Virtue" in the title and retained in the 3rd edition (1798).

15. *Political Justice* (1793), II, 810.

which reason assigns her. Mind would be delivered from her perpetual anxiety about corporal support, and free to expatiate in the field of thought which is congenial to her. Each man would assist the enquiries of all.[16]

In such a society bureaucratic government would vanish and democracy triumph:

In reality the constitution of a state governed either in whole or in part by a political monopoly, must necessarily be complicated. But what need of complexity in a country where the people are destined to govern themselves?[17]

Thus Godwin differed from the republicans in proposing economic and not political reform as the basic problem of society. He did not, however, we should note, have in mind the socialistic society which Robert Owen — with whom he was acquainted — was to envisage a few years later, a society based on state regulation of an industrialized economy. Godwin wanted not more government but less.

It has been stated that Godwin expected his new society to come about rapidly. But this is not so. It was an ultimate goal, still far in the reaches of time. But he did believe that it was inevitable. And here again Godwin attempted to delve deeper than the republicans. Revolutions were "the order of the day." But why were they the order of the day? Was there perhaps some force in history itself which decided such things, a force of which they and the present were but fragments? Were there laws governing the development of history? If there were such laws were they unique to history alone or were they somehow connected with the laws of nature? Were nature and history somehow fundamentally one? What of mind, was it, too, subject to laws beyond itself?

The conclusion to which Godwin came was that there was indeed universal law, that it applied to nature, to history, and to the mind of man. The workings of this law were as omnipresent as they were inexorable: "This view of things presents us with an idea of the universe as connected and cemented in all its parts, nothing in the boundless progress of things being capable of happening otherwise than it has actually happened."[18]

If one looked back over the whole sweep of history one could see the working of this law. History was not cyclical but developmental.

16. *Ibid.*　　　　17. *Ibid.*, p. 660.　　　　18. *Ibid.*, I, 305.

There had been a steady ascent of mankind and this ascent would continue:

> First, there is a degree of improvement real and visible in the world. This is particularly manifest, in the history of the civilised part of mankind, during the three last centuries. . . . And, as improvements have long continued to be incessant, so there is no chance but they will go on.[19]

Why had the ascent begun, why would it continue? The answer was to be found in the nature of the human mind itself. Mind is essentially developmental: "The inherent tendency of intellect is to improvement."[20] This improvement has not been steady. It has been driven back by the countertides of "barbarism." But in the end the intellect has its way, reason has always, in the long run, triumphed; and it will be so in the future also. Eventually, in the course of the generations the new society must arrive:

> Undoubtedly, this state of society is remote from the modes of thinking and acting which at present prevail. A long period of time must probably elapse, before it can be brought entirely into practice. All we have been attempting to establish is, that such a state of society, is agreeable to reason, and prescribed by justice; and that, of consequence, the progress of science and political truth among mankind, is closely connected with its introduction.[21]

Godwin's fame rested chiefly on *Political Justice* but he achieved a striking success also with *Caleb Williams* (1794), the first psychological novel:

> Its influence was extensive. Within three years five translations had appeared, in French and German; in the continental libraries, according to Mackintosh, later a friendly critic of it, it was *Caleb Williams* that needed most frequently to be replaced. It influenced the work of Charles Brockden Brown in America, thus affording, to those interested in such matters, fine speculation on the philosopher's influence, through Brown and Nathaniel Hawthorne, on Henry James. Walter Scott read it with interest, commenting particularly on the skill with which Godwin kept up his story by nowhere revealing the contents of Falkland's mysterious iron chest; and it was thought in their time to have affected the style and method of Bulwer-Lytton, Ainsworth and Dickens. In

19. This passage was added in the 2nd edition. See *Political Justice* (Priestley ed.), I, 450–451, III, 175.

20. *Ibid.*, II, 475, III, 216. (In the first edition, I, 6, Godwin wrote: "Mind must go forward.")

21. *Political Justice* (Priestley ed.), II, 475.

George Colman's dramatisation of it as *The Iron Chest* Edmund Kean found one of his most powerful characterisations as the Falkland of the play; Talma was noted for his performance of the same part in the French version, and in America it was one of Thomas Cooper's finest rôles.[22]

Godwin's total work covers a remarkable range. In addition to *Caleb Williams* there were five other novels: *St. Leon* (1799); *Fleetwood* (1805), the manuscript of which is in The Carl H. Pforzheimer Library; *Mandeville* (1817); *Cloudesley* (1830), the manuscript of which is also in this library; *Deloraine* (1833). He wrote an important work of history, the full value of which has been obscured, as Allibone notes, by the intrusion of political bias among its critics, a four-volume *History of the Commonwealth of England* (1824-1828). He wrote essays — *The Enquirer* (1797), *Thoughts on Man* (1831), *Essays* (published posthumously in 1873) — and political and scholarly biography — *The Life of Chatham* (1783), *The Life of Geoffrey Chaucer* (in four volumes, 1803), *The Lives of Edward and John Philips, Nephews and Pupils of Milton* (1815). He wrote one of the great personal biographies of English literature, a moving and powerful tribute to his dead wife: *Memoirs of the Author of a Vindication of the Rights of Woman* (1798). He wrote one of the most impassioned pleas for liberty and condemnation of tyranny since Milton's *Areopagitica*, his *Cursory Strictures on Lord Chief Justice Eyre's Charge to the Grand Jury* (1794).

Yet in spite of the richness and versatility of his work and the great impact his views had on the England of the reflected turmoil of the French Revolution, Godwin was until recent years almost a forgotten figure, remembered, when remembered at all, as the father-in-law of Shelley, and, even then, through the savage caricature of him both as man and thinker by Sir Leslie Stephen. But in time the Godwinian spirit of Reason began to assert itself in the matter of its master's reputation. Fresh and penetrating studies have begun to turn the tide.

"In recent years," writes Professor F. E. L. Priestley in the Introduction to his excellent edition of *Political Justice* (1946), "apart from the works already mentioned as brought into being by Maurois' *Ariel*, a tendency is at last apparent to re-examine Godwin and to give him his

22. Brown, *Godwin*, pp. 86–87. Cooper was brought up by Godwin and later became a leading dramatic actor in the United States.

rightful place among the moulders of democratic thought. The most important single effort has been that of Mr. Middleton Murry, who has recently (1938) included Godwin among his *Heroes of Thought*. The inclusion of an article by H. N. Brailsford on Godwin in Barrett Brown's *Great Democrats* is also symptomatic. It is to be hoped that travesties of Godwin as the 'ridiculous philosopher' will no longer gain public acceptance. It is over a century since Mackintosh wrote that 'the moment for doing full justice will come.' If it has now come, it is time for us to echo another sentence of Mackintosh's: 'He has thus, in our humble opinion, deserved the respect of all those, whatever may be their opinions, who still wish that some men in England may think for themselves, even at the risk of thinking wrong; but more especially of the friends of liberty, to whose cause he has courageously adhered.'"[23]

23. Since Priestley wrote, the number of studies has increased and includes the following books: George Woodcock, *William Godwin, a Biographical Study* (London, [1946]); David Fleisher, *William Godwin, a Study in Liberalism* (London, 1959); A. E. Rodway, *Godwin and the Age of Transition* (London, 1952); D. H. Monro, *Godwin's Moral Philosophy* (Oxford, 1953); Rosalie Glynn Grylls (Lady Mander), *William Godwin & his World* (London, 1953).

MARY WOLLSTONECRAFT

(April 27, 1759–September 10, 1797)

PRINCIPAL WORKS

1787 Thoughts on the Education of Daughters

1788 Mary, a Fiction

1788 Original Stories from Real Life

1790 A Vindication of the Rights of Men

1792 A Vindication of the Rights of Woman

1794 An Historical and Moral View of the French Revolution

1796 Letters Written during a Short Residence in Sweden, Norway, and Denmark

1798 Posthumous Works

EARLY LIFE

MARY WOLLSTONECRAFT was born in London, the second of six children of Edward John Wollstonecraft, a master weaver who came into a small fortune,[1] and his first wife, Elizabeth Dickson.[2] At some time during her fourth year her father moved his family to a farm in Epping Forest, the beginning of an attempted transition — never successful — to gentleman farmer. The parents seem to have said little to their children of these earlier years in London, and Mary was never to be certain whether she was born in London or Epping Forest. "Her earliest recollection of residence was in an old mansion, with a court yard before

---

1. Mary's birthplace and her father's vocation have not previously been known; they were evidently not known to Godwin, whose *Memoirs of the Author of a Vindication of the Rights of Woman* (London, 1798) has been the primary source for all subsequent biographers. Godwin tells of Mary's uncertainty as to where she was born (p. 6, 1st ed.; all subsequent references are to this edition). For some reason, Paul concluded that she was born at Hoxton (Paul, *Wollstonecraft*, p. vii). Wardle (*Wollstonecraft*, p. 3), picking up Godwin's statement that "her paternal grandfather was a respectable manufacturer in Spitalfields, and is supposed to have left to his son a property of about 10,000 *l*," searched the parish records of Christchurch, Spitalfields, but without success (see p. 342, fn. 3). Wardle correctly translated "Spitalfields manufacturer" by weaver but took too literally Godwin's doubt (p. 5) "whether the father of Mary was bred to any profession." The Books of The Weavers' Company (Guildhall Library, Ms 4656/7) show that on "2ᵈ May 1757. Edwᵈ John Wollstonecraft son of Edwᵈ Woolstonecraft Citizen and Weaver of London bound Appᵗce 2ᵈ April 1750 to his sᵈ father is made free by servitude on the Testimony of John Stanley the Beadle" (quoted by permission of the Librarian, the Guildhall Library). For documentation of Mary's birth, see below, fn. 5.

2. Godwin spells it *Dixon* in his *Memoirs of the Author of a Vindication of the Rights of Woman* (1798); it is Dickson, however, in the Wollstonecraft papers, Abinger Manuscripts. A copy of the second edition of the *Memoirs* once belonging to William Allingham, with his autograph notes, is now in The Carl H. Pforzheimer Library. On the right margin of page 5, opposite *Dixons*, he has written: "properly Dicksons — WA" and on the lower margin notes speculating on the probability of his being related to Mary Wollstonecraft through his own Dickson connections.

it, in Epping Forest, near the Whalebone, where she continued till five years of age."[3]

Early London directories supply the essential clues to the mystery: *Kent's Directory for the Year 1759* lists "Wollstonecraft Edward-John, Weaver, *Primrose-street Bishopsgate-street* without." *The Universal Directory . . . for 1763*, which breaks down its listings for occupation and further subdivides these "as to articles manufactured," lists under Weavers, "Wollstonecraft, Edward John, Handkerchief, Primrose Street, Bishopsgate-street." In the *Complete Guide to . . . the City of London*, sixth edition (for 1755), Edward Wollstonecraft, the grandfather, appears; in the eighth and ninth editions (1760 and 1763 respectively), Edward John Wollstonecraft appears — in each case at Primrose Street, Bishopsgate Street, Without.[4]

Primrose Street falls within the jurisdiction of the City as Spital Square, directly across Bishopsgate Street, does not, although both contained the houses of master weavers. Residents of Primrose Street who were members of the Established Church (as Mary continued to be throughout her life) were parishioners of St. Botolph, Bishopsgate. The Parish Registers show that Mary was baptized at St. Botolph's on May 20, 1759, and the next Wollstonecraft child, her sister Elizabeth, on July 24, 1763.[5] The baptismal registrations, together with the evidence

3. Elizabeth Ogborne, *The History of Essex, from the earliest period to the present time . . . with Biographical Notices of the most distinguished and remarkable Natives* (London, 1814), p. 161. According to the *DNB*, this volume — the date of the imprint to the contrary — did not appear (and thus was not available to students) until 1817. It has not been mentioned by the biographers of Mary Wollstonecraft. Mrs. Ogborne's story was drawn from talk with and at least one letter from Godwin (Sept. 21, 1815) which is in The Carl H. Pforzheimer Library. In September 1796 (*Memoirs*, pp. 13–14) Godwin and Mary made a pilgrimage to the old Wollstonecraft mansion "near the Whalebone" — quite likely the "Sun & Whalebone Public House" three miles beyond Epping village and the turn-off for Chelmsford (shown in Carey's *Survey of the High Roads from London*, 1810, Plate 40). See also William Addison, *Epping Forest* (London, 1945), p. 155.

4. *Without* means beyond London Wall. Only a remnant of Primrose Street now remains, just north of the Liverpool Street Station. A copy of *Kent's Directory* for 1759 is in The Carl H. Pforzheimer Library. *A Complete Guide to . . . the City of London* was consulted at Bishopsgate Institute, London, and *The Universal Director; or, the Nobleman and Gentleman's True Guide* at the Guildhall Library. No Wollstonecraft appears in the guides for 1765, which would have been printed before the end of 1764.

5. Parish Registers of St. Botolph, Bishopsgate; Christenings & Burials 1753–1779 (Guildhall Library Ms. 4517/2), quoted by permission of the Librarian, the Guildhall Library.

of the directories, would suggest that the Wollstonecrafts did not leave Primrose Street for Epping Forest until 1763, when Mary was four years of age and her brother Edward six or seven.

About a year later Edward John Wollstonecraft moved his family to Barking, also in Essex, and in 1768 to Beverley, in Yorkshire. He had, in fact, proved to be ill-equipped for farming by both aptitude and training, and his family drifted across England in his restless wake. In the course of this wandering three more children were born: Everina, perhaps before the family left Epping Forest; James, baptized February 23, 1768, at Barking;[6] and Charles, probably born in Yorkshire. The family spent six years on a farm near Beverley before moving back again to the London area. Mary was then fifteen and a half.

Mary Wollstonecraft was an active, responsive child and highly observant. She acquired a close knowledge of rural and village England and of yeoman farmers, journeymen, and small tradesmen. She was not, as a child, inclined either to solitude or books. "The principal part of her school-education passed during this [Yorkshire] period; but it was not to any advantage of infant literature, that she was indebted for her subsequent eminence; her education in this respect was merely such, as was afforded by the day-schools of the place."[7] Edward was prepared for the law and Mary herself, years later, saw that James had enough training to fit him for a Navy commission, but there was no thought of preparing the Wollstonecraft daughters for a vocation.

Mr. Wollstonecraft seems always to have been harsh and autocratic; as his fortunes worsened he became quarrelsome, often openly violent towards his wife. Mary rebelled against his despotism, protecting her mother against physical abuse when she could and beginning to dream of her own escape from the improvident, discordant household.

About Michaelmas 1774 Edward John Wollstonecraft moved his family to Hoxton, a village on the northern outskirts of London. Near the Wollstonecrafts on Queens Row, Hoxton, lived the Reverend Mr. Clare and his wife, who opened their home to Mary. She spent many hours, sometimes days, with the Clares. Quiet, scholarly Mr. Clare

6. W. Clark Durant, ed. *Memoirs of Mary Wollstonecraft Written by William Godwin* (London, 1927), p. xiv.

7. Godwin, *Memoirs*, p. 15.

talked with her and directed her reading; Godwin believed that to him "she was probably in some degree indebted for the early cultivation of her mind."[8] Through Mrs. Clare's efforts she gained a friend and model, Frances Blood, who was two years her senior. Less venturesome and resilient, Fanny Blood was at that time more disciplined than Mary; she was accomplished in drawing and penmanship and was a great reader. The two girls were no doubt drawn together at first by their painfully similar family circumstances (as later described by Mary in her first novel, *Mary, a Fiction*).

It was during this period that William Godwin was studying at the Dissenting academy at Hoxton. Many years later, when he was writing his *Memoirs* of Mary, he indulged in the speculation of "what would have been the amount of the difference in the pursuits and enjoyments of each party, if they had met, and considered each other with the same distinguishing regard in 1776, as they were afterwards impressed with in the year 1796. The writer had completed the twentieth, and Mary the seventeenth year of her age."[9] As Godwin so brilliantly demonstrates in the succeeding pages of the *Memoirs*, Mary at seventeen was only beginning that intellectual and personal development which contributed to the "distinguishing regard" which she and Godwin were to feel for each other.

In the spring of 1776, shortly after Mary had turned seventeen, the Wollstonecrafts moved to Laugharne in Wales, only to move back again to the London area in April 1777. A year later, without her parents' consent, she took a position as companion to Mrs. Dawson, a wealthy widow who lived at Bath. As Mrs. Dawson also made periodic visits to Southampton and Windsor, Mary now added to her experience wide contact with the world of fashion. "I have spent a very agreeable summer," she wrote to a Yorkshire friend,

S——n is a very pleasant place in every sense of the word — The situation is delightful; and, the inhabitants polite, and hospitable. I received so much civility that I left it with regret. . . .

I am quite agree [*sic*] with you in admiring Bath, it is a delightful place — . . . the buildings here are the most regular and elegant I have ever seen. I cannot say that I should chuse a large town for my constant residence, if I was

8. Godwin, *Memoirs*, p. 17.   9. *Ibid.*, pp. 16-17.

my own mistress, as I am fond of the country; but if I was obliged to fix in one — in point of situation Bath would be as agreeable to me as any.

The family I am with here is a very worthy one, Mʳˢ Dawson — has a very good understanding — and she has seen a great deal of the World, I hope to improve myself by her conversation, and I endeavor to render a circumstance (that at first was disagreeable,) useful to me.[10]

This was Mary's first experience at earning her living in the various types of remunerative work then open to respectable but indigent females — she was to try her hand at them all. She served as a companion for two years, until she was called home to nurse her dying mother. After Mrs. Wollstonecraft's death in 1780, Edward — then working at the law in London[11] — took the youngest of the girls, Everina, into his home as housekeeper; eighteen-year-old Eliza married a Mr. Bishop;[12] James, twelve, went to sea; Charles lived for a time with Edward in London and then with his father, who had married again. Mary found haven with the Bloods, assisting Mrs. Blood with the needlework which, with Fanny's drawing, augmented the uncertain income of the family.

Eliza's marriage turned out to be no refuge; it was as unhappy as her mother's had been, in part because she herself was immature and quick-tempered, with a strong sense of grievance. After the birth of a child in the autumn of 1782[13] her reason became temporarily affected and

10. Mary to Miss Arden, [at] Sir Mordant Martin's bart., Bronham, Norfolk [autumn 1778]. (Abinger Manuscripts, Pforzheimer Microfilm, reel IX.)

11. Edward was then about 23 years of age. His first child, also named Edward, was born in 1783, at which time he lived at "No 1 St Katherine's Street, Tower." Mary's letters to Everina in January 1783 (see below, fn. 14) were sent in care of "Mr Wollstonecraft"; writing in May 1787 from Dublin Mary addressed her letter in care of "Mr Wollstonecraft's, Attorney at Law, No 2 King's Street, Tower-hill." Clarke's *New Law List* for 1806 shows Edward Wollstonecraft at 12 Circus, Minories·

12. Paul (*Wollstonecraft*, pp. ix–x) could not "discover what position in life Mr. Bishop held," but had "some notion he was a clergyman." When writing the *Memoirs* Godwin queried Everina on this point. She replied from Dublin on November 24, 1797: "My sister's husband was not a clergyman — the Mr Bishop a clergyman whose name you have probably seen in some of poor Fanny's letters was Master of Merchant-taylor's school and a person whom F—— and Mary met at Mr Clare's." (Abinger Manuscripts, Pforzheimer Microfilm, file 6.)

13. Godwin is quite clear about this date (*Memoirs*, p. 29); Paul (*Godwin*, I, 166–171) dates the events of this winter, 1783–1784, a year too late. His error can be explained: Mary often failed to date letters, especially in this period, and since most of these letters were sent by messenger, there is little help to be had from postmarks. Some later hand (possibly Lady Shelley's) penciled in dates on these letters — dates which Paul followed. His transcripts not always being entirely accurate, references here are from the originals, now among the Abinger Manuscripts.

Mary was called to nurse her. At first Mary gave little credence to Eliza's complaints of brutal treatment: "her mind is in a most unsettled state," she wrote Everina. "She seems to think she has been very ill used."[14] In the ensuing weeks Mary became well acquainted with Mr. Bishop's mercurial temperament. On January 6, 1783, she wrote Everina that

misery haunts this house in one shape or other — How sincerely do I join with you in saying that if a person has *common sense* they cannot make one completely unhappy. But to attempt to lead or govern a weak mind is impossible . . . — My spirits are harried with listening to pros and cons . . . — I cannot insult him with advise [*sic*] — which he would never have wanted if he was capable of attending to it. May my habitation never be fixed among the tribe that can't look beyond the present gratification — [15]

Perhaps in her desire to mitigate Eliza's immediate distress she did not realize that her actions could break up the marriage; she was later to insist, in her own defense, that she held "the marriage vow sacred." How soon Mary determined on flight is difficult to say. She had evidently discussed some part of her plan with Everina — perhaps also with her brother Edward. "I would do anything to rescue her from her present situation," she wrote:

do you think Edward will receive her do speak to him — . . . she declares she had rather be a teacher then [*sic*] stay here — I must again repeat it you must be secret nothing can be done till she leaves the house — For his friend Ward very justly said that he was either a "lion or a spanniel" — I have been some time deliberating on this — for I can't help pitying B. . . . [but] those who would save Bess must act and not talk.[16]

In the middle of January[17] Mary acted; with the help of Fanny Blood she got Eliza away, changing coaches en route to Hackney and taking

14. [November 1782], sent by messenger, addressed: Miss Averina [*sic*] Wollstonecraft| Mr Wollstonecraft| No 1 St Katherine's Street| Tower|. (Abinger Manuscripts, Pforzheimer Microfilm, reel IX.)

15. To Averina [*sic*] Mon a.m. [postmarked Jan. 7, a Tuesday]. (Abinger Manuscripts, Pforzheimer Microfilm, reel IX.)

16. [January 1783]. This letter was sent by messenger. The penciled date is December 1783 and Paul prints this as a December letter, but the content seems to follow rather than precede that of January 6. (Abinger Manuscripts, Pforzheimer Microfilm, reel IX.)

17. In the letter written Monday, January 6, and mailed on Tuesday (see above, fn. 15) Mary writes "I expect Fanny next Thursday," — most likely January 16, the Thursday of the following week. This would place the day of flight between January 16 and 18 (Mary's first distraught letter from Hackney; see Paul, *Godwin*, I, 169) and January 19, a Sunday, when Mary wrote again from Hackney.

another name at her lodgings there to prevent discovery. Even those who sympathized with Eliza censured Mary, who found herself

the *shameful incendiary* in this shocking affair of a woman's leaving her bed-fellow — they "thought the strong affection of a sister *might* apologize for my conduct, but that the scheme was by no means a good one" — In short 'tis contrary to all the rules of conduct that are published for the benefit of new married Ladies by whose advice Mrs Brook was actuated when she with grief of heart gave up my friendship — [18]

Mary accepted the responsibility she had, in effect, brought upon herself and began looking about for some employment which would permit her and Eliza to support themselves. At first she planned "a school or a little shop" in Ireland, but "the *monies* did not answer."[19] She wrote to Edward in February that Fanny would join them and they would earn their living by painting and needlework, but Fanny demurred. Her drawing could bring in no more than half a guinea a week, and with needlework Mary and Eliza together could not earn more than a like sum even if they had constant employment. The solution was found in a day school, to be located in the suburbs north of London. In 1783

By the advice of Mrs Burgh, a friend of Dr Price's, and Mr Church her nephew, they [Mary and her sister Eliza, now legally separated from Bishop] in concert with Fanny Blood took lodgings at Islinton [*sic*] with the expectation of establishing a school, but meeting with no success, Mrs Burgh persuaded them to remove to Newington-Green, where she herself lived, and there through her exertions they in the course of two or three weeks obtained near twenty scholars.[20]

Mary Wollstonecraft had many friends among famous Dissenters then living at Newington Green, notably Dr. Richard Price, Mrs. James

18. Mary to Everina [late January 1783, from Hackney]. (Abinger Manuscripts, Pforzheimer Microfilm, reel IX.)

19. Mary to Everina [January-February 1783]. (Abinger Manuscripts, Pforzheimer Microfilm, reel IX.)

20. Everina Wollstonecraft to Godwin, Nov. 24, 1797. (Abinger Manuscripts, Pforzheimer Microfilm, file 6.) Despite the duplication in names, somewhat less than a quarter of Newington Green lies in the parish of Stoke Newington, and as a consequence "the parish of Stoke Newington has very little interest in Newington Green, which forms a square of respectable houses, chiefly inhabited by gentlemen and merchants; three sides of the square, with the inclosed ground in the centre, are in the parish of Islington; the north side, comprising about ten or twelve houses, with the meeting-house belonging formerly to the Presbyterian dissenters, but now to the Socinian Independents, only being in this parish. The centre was railed in and brought to its present state about the year 1745." (William Robinson, *The History and Antiquities of the Parish of Stoke Newington in the County of Middlesex*, London, 1842, 2nd ed., p. 11.)

Burgh, the Rogers family, and John Hewlett.[21] Their role in her development belongs properly to the discussion (below) of her ideas and works.

The school prospered during its first two years. Then Fanny Blood married and went to Portugal. Expecting a child, she pleaded with Mary to be with her. Mary made the voyage, but Fanny did not survive the birth of her child, and when Mary returned to Newington Green it was to find the school in difficulties from which it was never to recover. Portugal — with its exploitation of women and oppression of the lower classes — remained a vivid memory later to be drawn on for her *Vindication of the Rights of Woman*.

While the loss of her dearest friend was the most severe, it was only one of Mary Wollstonecraft's personal troubles. At some time between 1778 at Bath and 1786 when she left Newington Green, she had been unhappily in love with the Reverend Joshua Waterhouse, thirteen years her senior. He was a handsome, well-educated man, smooth of manner and smartly dressed. The son of a yeoman farmer, he had been at St. Catherine's College, Cambridge, since 1771, engaged in taking three leisurely degrees and relieving the tedium of college life by excursions to Bath and Bristol Hot Wells. Waterhouse was awarded the Baccalaureate in Sacred Theology in 1786 (he was forty) and was granted a fellowship at St. Catherine's, which included the living in a nearby parish. In his arrogance and ambition he overreached himself and was exiled to a country parsonage where he became an ill-kempt, miserly recluse and was finally murdered in the kitchen of his own rectory.[22]

But when Mary fell in love with him, Waterhouse was at the peak of fashion and stood, so he must have thought, at the beginning of a most promising career. Whether, after a time, Mary came to know his faults — she had had considerable experience with vain, weak, selfish men — and refused him, or whether he had had from the first no serious intentions toward a girl with neither family nor means is not known. In a letter to George Blood written in July 1786, Mary seems to imply the source of discord: "Give my love to your father and mother — and

21. Godwin, *Memoirs*, pp. 32–36; P. W. Clayden, *The Early Life of Samuel Rogers* (London, 1887).

22. This attachment, which came to light in 1827, was never widely known and soon forgotten. It was rediscovered by Professor Elizabeth Nitchie; see "An Early Suitor of Mary Wollstonecraft," *PMLA*, LVIII (March 1943), 163–169; the article includes a full bibliography.

you may give the same to Neptune. I have done with all resentments — and perhaps I was as much to blame in expecting too much as he in doing too little."[23]

The school at Newington Green had been closed in the late spring of 1786, Everina returning to her brother's home in London and Eliza going to Leicestershire to teach. Although her spirits were low, Mary had set to work on a book, encouraged by her friend John Hewlett. She called her work *Thoughts on the Education of Daughters*.[24] Hewlett sold the manuscript during the summer to his friend Joseph Johnson, the radical publisher;[25] the £10 it realized was given to Mr. and Mrs. Blood to help them get to Dublin where they could be cared for by their son George. Now twenty-seven, Mary turned reluctantly to the idea of re-entering private service. Through her friend Dr. Richard Price she had become acquainted with Mr. and Mrs. Prior of Eton, who had been commissioned to find a governess for the three elder daughters of Robert King, Viscount Kingsborough.[26] During the late summer she corresponded with Mrs. Prior and in the autumn spent some time with the Priors until the King family was ready to travel to Ireland. There a new chapter in her life opened.

23. Mary to George Blood, July 6, 1786. (Abinger Manuscripts, Pforzheimer Microfilm, reel IX.) Wardle (*Wollstonecraft*, p. 42) deduces "Neptune" from *Water*house.

24. An interesting sequence of titles suggests Mary's familiarity with James Burgh's educational theory and also — directly, or indirectly through Burgh or Price — with John Locke: Locke's *Some Thoughts Concerning Education* (1673) is recalled in the title of Burgh's *Thoughts on Education* (1747) and Mary's *Thoughts on the Education of Daughters* (1787).

25. For Johnson see *Shelley and his Circle*, I, 67-71.

26. Robert King (1754-1799) married his cousin, Caroline FitzGerald (1754-1823), in December 1769. Her fortune included Mitchelstown and extensive estates surrounding it. Seven sons and five daughters were born to them. Mary Wollstonecraft wrote to her sister Eliza Bishop on November 5, 1786: "I have committed to my care three girls, the eldest fourteen." (Abinger Manuscripts, Pforzheimer Microfilm, reel IX.) Her charges were Margaret (later Lady Mount Cashell), Caroline, and Mary Elizabeth, who could not have been much more than six at the time. Mary Wollstonecraft based her book *Original Stories from Real Life* on the Irish year. In this volume Mrs. Mason, the governess, is in charge of two girls, fourteen-year-old Mary and twelve-year-old Caroline. (*DNB*; *Complete Peerage*; J. Bernard Burke, *Landed Gentry of Ireland*, London, 1912; Arthur Young, *A Tour in Ireland*, Dublin, 1780, pp. 375-382, and *Autobiography of Arthur Young*, ed. M. Bentham-Edwards, London, 1898, Chapter IV. See also Edward C. McAleer, *The Sensitive Plant: A Life of Lady Mount Cashell*, University of North Carolina Press, 1958 — a study published after the above biographical research had been completed.)

IDEAS AND WORKS

Mary Wollstonecraft's active writing life occupied but one decade, during which she produced seven original works and a number of translations in addition to doing routine reviewing and editing for *The Analytical Review*. The manuscript draft of one of her reviews is in The Carl H. Pforzheimer Library and we know that she assigned reviews to other writers as well. In the fall of 1796 she asked Mary Hays to review *The Gossip's Story* by Mrs. Jane West;[30] on March 17, 1797, she wrote to Godwin: "There is a good boy, write me a review of Vaurien. I remember there is an absurd attack on a Methodist preacher, because he denied the Eternity of future punishments."[31] (This is tongue-in-cheek, for Godwin also figured in the book as "Mr. Subtile, the greatest philosopher of the world."[32])

She continued to plan and write books until shortly before her death at the early age of thirty-eight. Among the papers from which Godwin fashioned the four volumes of *Posthumous Works* were a number of works-in-progress which suggest that, had she lived, she would have continued to do substantial work in her middle years.

During her brief life she had a remarkably diverse series of experiences, in a number of countries, and became personally acquainted with some of the finest minds of her age — Price, Paine, Godwin, Fuseli, Blake, Brissot, the Rolands, Madame de Genlis. Her mode of being was

30. *The Love-Letters of Mary Hays*, ed. A. F. Wedd (London, 1925), pp. 240–241. See also Ralph M. Wardle, "Mary Wollstonecraft, Analytical Reviewer," *PMLA*, LXII (December 1947), 1000–1009.

31. Abinger Manuscripts, Pforzheimer Microfilm, reel IX. Printed in part also by Paul, *Godwin*, I, 244.

32. Brown, *Godwin*, pp. 31–32, 161. *Vaurien: or, Sketches of the Times: exhibiting Views of the Philosophies, Religions, Politics, Literature, & Manners of the Age*, written by Isaac D'Israeli, was published anonymously in 1797. So far as we can determine, no one has followed the clue of Mary's letter to the pages of *The Analytical Review*, where in the April 1798 issue (XXVII, 425–428) *Vaurien* is reviewed in unmistakably Godwinian periods. The review may have been completed soon after Mary's request in March 1797 (it quotes "Mrs. Wollstonecraft"), being held over by Johnson. It is clear that Godwin is not amused by the book. He pronounces obviously false the author's "asseveration in the advertisement, that his volumes contain not a single individuality, and that the attack has only been personal where the person is named." He is even more severe in his strictures against putting into the mouth of an identifiable character speeches of radical, even treasonous, content: "Such a representation, we cannot help thinking, is highly injurious; it may be attended with infinite danger to the individual; and, in sketching the present character, if our author has shown any superior talent, to use his own expression, 'it lies towards the sarcastic, the caustic, and malicious.'"

essentially empirical. To a remarkable degree hers was a mind shaped by personal experience, by contact with actual individuals, by involvement in events. To the philosophical concepts of the English radicals she could bring direct knowledge of a wide range of English, Welsh, and Irish life, of Portugal, revolutionary France, and the Scandinavian countries. More than any other member of her group except Thomas Paine she knew the tyrannies against which the male radicals protested; she knew also with what special, additional tyrannies women had to cope, "the misery and oppression, peculiar to women, that arise out of the partial laws and customs of society."[33] In her earliest writing she was concerned almost entirely with these special tyrannies, but as her acquaintance with the philosophical bases of radicalism grew — first at Newington Green and later among the Johnson coterie in London — she saw the struggle of the middle-class Englishwoman in its larger context, as part of the universal struggle of the individual against institutionalized social and intellectual oppression. Moreover, she came to see that the injustices against which womankind struggled could be alleviated or eliminated only if men could be made to see the problem as one aspect — and a vital one — of the universal struggle for *human* rights. "She had the insight to perceive," wrote H. N. Brailsford, "that the first task of the pioneer was to raise the whole broad issue of the subjection of her sex."[34]

In style and in their major themes her original works reveal a straight line of development. Even the choice of her most important translation, C. G. Salzmann's *Elements of Morality* (1790), was determined by its correspondences to her point of view. Beginning the translation as an exercise in German, she found that

the writer coincided with me in opinion respecting the method which ought to be pursued to form the heart and temper, or, in other words, to inculcate the first principles of morality. . . . All the pictures are drawn from real life, and that I highly approve of this method, my having written a book on the same plan*, is the strongest proof.[35]

33. Wollstonecraft, "Author's Preface" to *The Wrongs of Woman, Posthumous Works*, I, [xiv].

34. H. N. Brailsford, *Shelley, Godwin and Their Circle* (London, 1949), p. 207.

35. Wollstonecraft, trans. *Elements of Morality*, by C. G. Salzmann (London, 1792), I, i-ii, iv. The asterisk is Mary's own and calls attention to a footnote which reads: "*Entitled, Original Stories

Mary drew much of her material from her own life, and some of the autobiographical elements in her work have been taken into account by her biographers. But there is more involved than the use of characters or incidents from her own experience. Her mode, her style, is intensely personal. There was the belief, upon which her practice was founded, that truth was to be discovered, or validated, by searching into one's own experiences and thoughts upon the meaning of those experiences. In this she anticipated much of the attitude and tone of the Romantic period, to which Shelley and her daughter belonged. Because the personal mode was so firmly established by this following generation we tend to overlook the innovations in Mary Wollstonecraft's work. She stated her position in the Preface to her second book, *Mary, a Fiction:*

> Those compositions only have power to delight, and carry us willing captives, where the soul of the author is exhibited, and animates the hidden springs. . . . These chosen few, wish to speak for themselves, and not to be an echo — even of the sweetest sounds — or the reflector of the most sublime beams.[36]

She is aware from the beginning of speaking as a woman, although somewhat shy of making the point overtly. The Preface of *Mary* continues:

> In an artless tale, without episodes, the mind of a woman, who has thinking powers is displayed. . . . Without arguing physically about *possibilities* — in a fiction, such a being may be allowed to exist; whose grandeur is derived from the operation of its own faculties, not subjugated to opinion; but drawn by the individual from the original source.

Three years later she extended her declaration to include her non-fictional works (in the Advertisement to *Elements of Morality*, quoted above).[37] In *A Vindication of the Rights of Men* her argument for "the liberty of reason" (based on freedom of conscience and inquiry) is characterized by a confident, almost audacious use of the first person singular:

I war not with an individual when I contend for the *rights of men* and the liberty of reason. You see I do not condescend to cull my words to avoid the

from Real Life." While Mary's name did not appear on the title of *Elements*, she signed the Advertisement. *Original Stories* had been published anonymously.

36. *Mary, a Fiction* (London, 1788), pp. [vi–viii].

37. Although published early in 1788, *Mary, a Fiction* was written during the summer of 1787. The first volume of *Elements of Morality* appeared late in 1790, slightly ahead of *A Vindication of the Rights of Men*, which was one of the first replies to appear after Burke's *Reflections* was published in November 1790.

invidious phrase . . . . Reverencing the rights of humanity, I shall dare to assert them.[38]

(It should be noted here that she equates "rights of men" with "rights of humanity," implying the position of her second *Vindication*.) In the following passage from the first *Vindication* the first person plural serves to include herself, a woman, as an inheritor of the rights of humanity:

Is it necessary to repeat, that there are rights which we received, at our birth, as men, when we were raised above the brute creation by the power of improving ourselves — and that we receive these not from our forefathers, but from God?

My father may dissipate his property, yet I have no right to complain; — but if he should attempt to sell me for a slave, or fetter me with laws contrary to reason; nature, in enabling me to discern good from evil, teaches me to break the ignoble chain.[39]

In her second *Vindication* she was no longer to imply but openly to plead that women be allowed

to participate [in] the inherent rights of mankind. Make them free, and they will quickly become wise and virtuous, as men become more so; for the improvement must be mutual, or the injustice which one half of the human race are obliged to submit to, retorting on their oppressors, the virtue of men will be worm-eaten by the insect whom he keeps under his feet.[40]

Letters Written during a Short Residence in Sweden, Norway, and Denmark is one of her most appealing books, largely because of the quiet intimacy in which she tells about people and customs. Here she is more urbane, less self-conscious, less impatient:

A person has a right, I have sometimes thought, when amused by a witty or interesting egotist, to talk of himself when he can win on our attention by acquiring our affection. Whether I deserve to rank amongst this privileged num-

38. *A Vindication of the Rights of Men, in a Letter to the Right Honourable Edmund Burke; Occasioned by His Reflections on the Revolution in France* (London, 1790), p. 2. The italics are Mary's. She took "the invidious phrase" (the *rights of men*) from the resolution adopted by the Constituent Assembly in Paris in August 1789.

39. *A Vindication of the Rights of Men*, p. 21. For some reason, she revised this passage in the second edition, casting it in the third person and removing personal references, which seems to imply exclusion, although the revisions may have been dictated by prudence — the allusions to her own father's fecklessness being rather too obvious.

40. *A Vindication of the Rights of Woman* (London, 1792), p. 406.

ber, my readers alone can judge — and I give them leave to shut the book, if they do not wish to become better acquainted with me.[41]

That truth was to be discovered by examining oneself and revealing one's own experience became an article of faith for her, and to Godwin's stringent criticism of her last work-in-progress, *The Wrongs of Woman*, she replied:

I am compelled to think that there is something in my writings more valuable than in the productions of some people on whom you bestow warm elogiums — I mean more mind — denominate it as you will — more of the observations of my own senses, more of the combining of my own imagination — the effusions of my own feelings and passions than the cold workings of the brain on the materials procured by the senses and imagination of other writers.[42]

The philosophical basis for this attitude toward the validity of one's own experience was laid at Newington Green, long a leading center of Dissent, where Mary lived from 1783 to 1786. In the last half of the eighteenth century the exploration of the secular aspects of liberty occupied many of the leading thinkers among the Dissenters, but their political liberalism was firmly grounded in their religious conviction of the "natural" right of freedom of conscience.[43]

In general the residents of Newington Green were people of middle rank — retired statesmen, merchants, scientists, and the families of London business and professional men such as Dr. John Aikin and Thomas Rogers, London banker and father of Samuel Rogers (who as a boy saw Mary Wollstonecraft at church in Newington Green and as an older man knew her daughter, Mary Shelley). For well over a hundred years Newington Green had been one of the intellectual centers of the Dissenting interest. During the first century following the Restoration and the Test and Corporation Acts, which forbade Dissenters a university education, a series of academies had been located there.[44] Ashley Smith, sum-

---

41. *Letters Written during a Short Residence in Sweden, Norway, and Denmark* (London, 1796), pp. [iii–iv].

42. Mary to Godwin, Sept. 4, 1796. (Abinger Manuscripts, Pforzheimer Microfilm, reel IX.)

43. Anthony Lincoln, *Some Political and Social Ideas of English Dissent: 1763–1800* (Cambridge University Press, 1938).

44. Following The Act of Uniformity in 1662, "Newington-green became one of the strongholds of dissent, several of the ejected clergy making it their place of abode and . . . [they] eventually suc-

marizing the effect of the various Dissenting academies on the curriculum, states that at Newington Green "unorthodox text books," practical science, and political theory were introduced.[45] The interest in political theory continued. James Burgh (1714–1775), whose widow became the staunch friend of Mary Wollstonecraft, lived at the Green from 1750 to 1775. Burgh was primarily concerned with the franchise — with "public errors, defects, and abuses" of representation — and he had compiled three volumes of statistics which were published in 1774–1775 as *Political Disquisitions* and became a reformer's handbook. Godwin knew it; Price cited it in his *Observations on Civil Liberty* (1776).[46]

Richard Price (1723–1791), Mary's "first" friend, was primarily concerned to establish philosophically the inherent right to freedom of inquiry — civil as well as religious.[47] After finishing his studies under John Eames at the Dissenting academy in Moorfields, London, he had served as a private chaplain at Stoke Newington before being called to the Meeting-house on Newington Green in 1758. At the Green he was visited by his friends Joseph Priestley, Andrew Kippis, and Benjamin Franklin. His first work, *A Review of the Principal Questions in Morals*, was published in 1758. A decade later *Observations on Reversionary Payments, Annuities, &c.* brought him to the attention of Pitt, who made use of his concepts of the management of debt. In February 1776 — a month after Paine's *Common Sense* — Price published his "philosophic examination of the foundations of the American problem," a pamphlet entitled *Observations on the Nature of Civil Liberty, the Principles of Government, and*

ceeded in the establishment of a succession of academies." Thomas Coull, *The History and Traditions of Islington* (London, 1861), pp. 54–55. See also Irene Parker, *Dissenting Academies in England* (Cambridge University Press, 1914), pp. 58, 137–143; J. W. Ashley Smith, *The Birth of Modern Education* (London, 1954), pp. 44–46, 56–61. Among the tutors and students at the Newington Green academies were Theophilus Gale (1628–1677), Daniel Defoe, and Charles Morton (1627–1698), who later became a tutor at Harvard College. On the relationship between Newington Green, Stoke Newington, and Islington, see above, fn. 20. Among the schools at the Green were a "Charity School established by the Dissenting Ladies" for fourteen poor girls and one, supported by needlework, for daughters of Quakers. (Robinson, *History of Middlesex*, p. 209.)

45. Smith, *Modern Education*, p. 61.

46. *Memoirs*, pp. 35–36; Price, *Observations*, p. 10. S. Maccoby cites Burgh in *English Radicalism: 1762–1785* (London, 1955), p. 520, as does Anthony Lincoln, *English Dissent*, p. 142.

47. Lincoln, *English Dissent*, Chapter IV, "Richard Price"; Roland Thomas, *Richard Price: Apostle of Liberty* (London, 1924); D. Daiches Raphael, ed., "Preface" to Price's *Review of the Principal Questions in Morals* (Oxford University Press, 1948).

the Justice and Policy of the War with America. (Sixty thousand copies were sold in the first year and reprints were issued in Philadelphia, Boston, and New York.) In 1783, the increasing invalidism of his wife, together with his own poor health, made it advisable for him to resign the pastorate at the Green. He continued to live there, however, until 1786. In the years of Mary's association with him he was working on the revisions for the third edition (published in 1787) of his *Review of the Principal Questions in Morals.* The *Review* laid the groundwork for extension of the "natural" rights of religious freedom into a rationale for political freedom. "All his works written subsequently . . . are applications of, footnotes to, his moral theory. . . . his translation of his moral into a political philosophy was both important and original."[48] In common with other intellectuals of the period, outside as well as within the Dissenting interest, Price joined discussion clubs, one of them the Revolution Society — to which the reverend doctors Priestley, Kippis, Rees, and Morgan also belonged (Burke called it a "Club of Dissenters"). It was around the Three Resolutions of the Revolution Society that Price built the famous Old Jewry sermon of November 1789 — thereby furnishing the immediate provocation for Burke's *Reflections on the French Revolution.*

The continuity of Price's thought is clear. In the *Review,* discussing *"the Nature and Essentials of* Virtue in Practice," he wrote: *"practical* virtue supposes LIBERTY. . . . The *liberty* I here mean is the same with the power of *acting* and *determining*: And it is self-evident, that where such a power is wanting, there can be no moral capacities."[49] In *Observations on the Nature of Civil Liberty* (1776) he enumerated four aspects of liberty — physical, moral, religious, and civil — "And I have placed *Civil* Liberty last, because I mean to apply to it all I shall say of the other kinds of liberty. . . . In general, to be *free* is to be guided by one's own will; and to be guided by the will of another is the characteristic of *Servitude.*" Returning in this work to the "self-evident" correlation examined in the *Review* between liberty and morality, he declared that "licentiousness and despotism are more nearly allied than is commonly imagined."[50] This concept appeared in Mary Wollstonecraft's *Vindica-*

48. Lincoln, *English Dissent,* pp. 114, 145.   49. Price, *Review,* ed. Raphael, pp. 177–181.
50. Price, *Observations,* pp. 3, 11, 13.

tion of the Rights of Men and became a major premise of her *Vindication of the Rights of Woman.*

In the *Memoirs* Godwin was chiefly concerned with the influence of Price as a religious thinker, making the point that Price strengthened the nondoctrinaire tendencies of Mary Wollstonecraft. The first full-length study of Mary Wollstonecraft's thought, the first attempt to place her in the long tradition of English political thinkers (rather than in the more restricted group of women writers on woman), was made by Emma Rauschenbusch Clough, in a work begun as a doctoral dissertation at Heidelberg and published in England as *A Study of Mary Wollstonecraft and the Rights of Woman* (1898). Mrs. Clough corrects Godwin's interpretation of the influence of Price (page 49) and points up a number of parallels in the position of Price and of Mary (pages 53, 87, 231), with specific reference to Price's *Review of the Principal Questions in Morals.* She does not, however, fully explore the Newington Green milieu, thus missing its germinal effect and assigning — as Godwin does — proportionally too much weight to the London period.

It is difficult to assess the influence on Mary Wollstonecraft of James Burgh or his wife. Mary could have known Burgh only through his three-volume *Political Disquisitions.* Although he had died nearly ten years before Mary came to the Green, his widow was a vigorous advocate of his opinions,[51] and while Mary Wollstonecraft nowhere specifically cites the *Disquisitions* she evidently read and understood them, eventually extending Burgh's view on parliamentary representation to include women:

I may excite laughter, by dropping an hint, which I mean to pursue, some future time, for I really think that women ought to have representatives, instead of being arbitrarily governed without having any direct share allowed them in the deliberations of government.

But, as the whole system of representation is now, in this country, only a convenient handle for despotism, they need not complain, for they are as well represented as a numerous class of hard working mechanics, who pay for the support of royalty when they can scarcely stop their children's mouths with bread.[52]

51. Andrew Kippis, biographical account of James Burgh in the second edition of *Biographia Britannica.*

52. Wollstonecraft, *A Vindication of the Rights of Woman,* p. 335.

Mary had known a number of older women whom she admired and who appeared in one guise or another in her books. Mrs. Clare of Hoxton and the gentle, semi-invalid Mrs. Price probably suggested such amiable wives of clergymen as Mrs. Trueman of *Original Stories*. But the figure who most closely resembles what we know of Mrs. Burgh — her cultivation, self-discipline, and benevolence — the "first, and most amiable virtue" — is Mrs. Mason of *Original Stories*.[53] Mary's early ideas on charity and poverty — evidently those of Mrs. Burgh — belonged to the Lady Bountiful tradition. In *Thoughts on the Education of Daughters* she notes (page 37) that much money "is squandered away, which if saved for charitable purposes, might alleviate the distress of many poor families, and soften the heart of the girl who entered into such scenes of woe." Again (page 139): "some part of the money that is allowed [girls] for pocket-money, they should be encouraged to lay out this way, and the short-lived emotions of pity continually retraced 'till they grow into habits.'" The heroine of *Mary, a Fiction* learned (pages 26–27)

the luxury of doing good; and the sweet tears of benevolence frequently moistened her eyes . . . . The warmth of her compassion often made her so diligent, that many things occurred to her, which might have escaped a less interested observer. In like manner, she entered with such spirit into whatever she read, and the emotions thereby raised were so strong, that it soon became a part of her mind.

However, there is a hint in this book (page 135) of some small degree of awareness of "the misery that rises from poverty and the want of education." And in *Original Stories* (page 177) Mrs. Mason demonstrates to her charges how often the rich, by failing to pay their bills, reduce "the poor trades-people" to penury.

Only after her association, in the Johnson coterie in London, with the philosophical radicals did Mary see poverty as an evil to be eradicated rather than to be endured (by the poor) or alleviated (by the rich, who

53. In the same book, Mary Wollstonecraft modeled the schoolmistress, Anna Lofty, on herself. The identification of Mary as Mrs. Mason — most lately advanced by Edward C. McAleer in *The Sensitive Plant: A Life of Lady Mount Cashell* — does not hold up. While it is true that Mary and the character she created for *Original Stories* are both governesses, here the likeness ends; in personality and temperament Mrs. Mason resembles Mrs. Burgh. The name "Mrs. Mason" was later assumed by the eldest of the little girls in Mary's charge, Margaret King (Lady Mount Cashell). She was so known to Shelley and Mary during their Italian years and is thought to have served Shelley as the model for the lady in *The Sensitive Plant* (White, *Shelley*, II, 180).

were thereby trained in compassion and sensibility). In her first *Vindica-tion* — *A Vindication of the Rights of Men* — she stated emphatically (page 11) that "charity is not a condescending distribution of alms, but an intercourse of good offices and mutual benefits, founded on respect for humanity." Benevolence she described as

a very amiable specious quality; yet the aversion which men feel to accept a right as a favour, should rather be extolled as a vestige of native dignity, than stigmatized as the odious offspring of ingratitude. The poor consider the rich as their lawful prey; but we ought not too severely to animadvert on their ingrati-tude. When they receive an alms they are commonly grateful at the moment; but old habits quickly return, and cunning has ever been a substitute for force.[54]

In her last, unfinished novel there are two heroines — Maria, whose misfortunes illustrate the wrongs done the rich woman, and Jemima, who has suffered the outrages known to the very poor and the abandoned. In the handling of Jemima's story Mary Wollstonecraft most nearly approaches the modern sociological point of view, that the poor are the victims of the social order, not to be held morally accountable for acts done in the attempt simply to survive. Cruelty, depravity, irresponsi-bility toward children[55] and all helpless persons — these "wrongs" are to be fought by eliminating institutionalized inequality and by educating the mind and heart of both men and women, of all classes. The right she is most concerned to vindicate, then, is the right to become a rational, responsible, independent adult.

For a time after the success of *A Vindication of the Rights of Men* — by which she meant, as has been noted above, the rights of all humanity — Mary Wollstonecraft must have thought her point made. But as Mary Beard has recently demonstrated, there is contained in the terms *man*, *men*, and even *mankind* "an ambiguity amounting to double talk or half talk," and Mary Wollstonecraft's thesis ran afoul of the ancient ambi-

---

54. *A Vindication of the Rights of Men*, p. 126. A similar point, almost a paraphrase, is made in *A Vindication of the Rights of Woman* (p. 449): "when any power but reason curbs the free spirit of man, dissimulation is practised." This is but one of a number of verbal and conceptual parallels that point up the necessity of considering the two *Vindications* together.

55. Throughout her works she vigorously attacks such irresponsibility. See, for example, *Original Stories* (p. vi): "reason, with difficulty, conquers settled habits, even when it is arrived at some degree of maturity: why then do we suffer children to be bound with fetters, which their half-formed faculties cannot break."

guity.[56] Almost as she was asserting the inalienable rights of all humanity the members of the French National Assembly were writing into their new constitution provisions which in practice assured the civil and political rights of adult males only. She must have learned soon of this action; she was to read an English translation of the French constitution and a defense of it in a book written by her friend and co-worker at Johnson's, Thomas Christie, for in 1791 Joseph Johnson published Christie's *Letters on the Revolution of France and on the New Constitution Established by the French Assembly.* Two classes of citizens were differentiated: "Active Citizens," i.e., native-born or naturalized men of twenty-five years or more, whose rights included exercise of the franchise, and "Passive Citizens," i.e., paupers, beggars, vagabonds, domestics, bankrupts and insolvent debtors, and children of bankrupts who had received any part of the fortune of their parents without paying their proportion of the debt. While women were not specifically mentioned as members of either class, it became clear that they had been assigned to the second. Defending the denial of full civil and political rights to women, Christie wrote:

[The French] have manifested superior wisdom, in shewing that they knew where to draw the line, and so to honour the sex as not to injure their *real* happiness, or endanger the welfare of society. They have rightly judged, in not raising them out of their natural sphere; in not involving them in the cares and anxieties of State affairs, to which neither their frame nor their minds are adapted.[57]

Mary was constrained to clear up the ambiguity. Her second *Vindication*, written during the latter part of 1791, is essentially a reaffirmation of the central thesis of her first but making explicit what had been implicit and thus too easily disregarded, that *woman* was co-inheritor of rights. Her dedication, to Talleyrand, reads like a direct reply to Christie's defense of the action of Talleyrand and his fellow legislators:

56. Mary Beard, *Woman as Force in History* (New York, 1946), p. 47. Mrs. Beard notes that "innumerable rights of person and property may turn upon the mere meaning of 'man' in laws, ordinances, and judicial opinions.... so many uncertainties appeared in the administration of the law in England ... that Parliament tried in 1850 to clear some of them away by legislation [in a] law ... [which] provided that 'words importing the masculine gender shall always include women, except where otherwise stated.' As a matter of fact, however, conflicts due to uncertainty of meaning did not end, even in England, respecting the use of the word *man* in statutes and judicial decisions" (pp. 49–50). 57. Christie, p. 218.

on what does your constitution rest? If the abstract rights of man will bear discussion and explanation, those of woman, by a parity of reasoning, will not shrink from the same test . . . .

Consider, I address you as a legislator, whether, when men contend for their freedom, and to be allowed to judge for themselves respecting their own happiness, it be not inconsistent and unjust to subjugate women, even though you firmly believe that you are acting in the manner best calculated to promote their happiness? Who made man the exclusive judge, if woman partake with him the gift of reason?

In this style, argue tyrants of every denomination, from the weak king to the weak father of a family; they are all eager to crush reason; yet always assert that they usurp its throne only to be useful. Do you not act a similar part, when you *force* all women, by denying them civil and political rights, to remain immured in their families groping in the dark? for surely, Sir, you will not assert, that a duty can be binding which is not founded on reason? . . . the more understanding women acquire, the more they will be attached to their duty — comprehending it — for unless they comprehend it, unless their morals be fixed on the same immutable principle as those of man, no authority can make them discharge it in a virtuous manner. They may be convenient slaves, but slavery will have its constant effect, degrading the master and the abject dependent.[58]

The philosophical radicals of the Johnson coterie who had done so much to shape and sharpen Mary's concepts of the necessary extension of civil and political power had not concerned themselves greatly with the possible subversions of that power by its new masters in the commercial and bureaucratic classes. The tyrannies they attacked arose largely from inequalities of class — inequalities of birth, of property, inequalities of opportunity for learning and advancement. Mary demanded removal also of inequalities based on sex, but although she castigated "tyrants of every denomination, from the weak king to the weak father of a family," her context, too, was social and political rather than economic until after she went to France in December 1792. In France, witnessing the dissolution of an old order and the shift of power to new groups, she became aware of other tyrannies — or the old ones in new forms — and wrote of her fears to her friends in England:

if the aristocracy of birth is levelled with the ground, only to make room for that of riches, I am afraid that the morals of the people will not be much im-

58. *A Vindication of the Rights of Woman*, pp. ix–xi.

MARY WOLLSTONECRAFT SHELLEY

(August 30, 1797–February 1, 1851)

PRINCIPAL WORKS

1817 History of a Six Weeks' Tour

1818 Frankenstein; or, The Modern Prometheus

1823 Valperga: or, the Life and Adventure of Castruccio, Prince of Lucca

1824 Posthumous Poems of Percy Bysshe Shelley (editor)

1826 The Last Man

1830 Perkin Warbeck

1835 Lodore

1835–1837 Lives of the Most Eminent Literary and Scientific Men of Italy, Spain, and Portugal

1837 Falkner

1838–1839 Lives of the Most Eminent Literary and Scientific Men of France

1839 The Poetical Works of Percy Bysshe Shelley (editor)

1840 Essays, Letters from Abroad, Translations and Fragments, by P. B. Shelley (editor)

1844 Rambles in Germany and Italy

1876 The Choice (*ca.* 1822)

1891 Tales and Stories (collected by Richard Garnett)

1922 Proserpine and Midas, Two Mythological Dramas (*ca.* 1820)

1959 Mathilda (1819)

LIFE

If hereditary influence could be trusted as a guide to character, the only offspring of the authors of *The Rights of Woman* and *Political Justice* would have been destined from birth to a strenuous advocacy of progress and emancipatory zeal. By an odd and perhaps significant irony, Mary's own prenatal influence on her parents was in the other direction. Mary Wollstonecraft, whose daughter by Gilbert Imlay was never legitimatized, and William Godwin, who had dismissed the state of wedlock with intellectual contempt, bowed to the expedient of giving their unborn child an even chance in the world as constituted. They had been married five months when Mary was born at the Polygon on August 30, 1797. Eleven days later she was motherless.[1]

So began that heightened father-daughter relationship that was to

---

1. "Sept. 10. Su. 20 minutes before 8 . . ." Godwin, Journal. See also "The Death of Mary Wollstonecraft," *Shelley and his Circle*, I, 196. For the Polygon see Somers Town, *ibid.*, p. 211.

be reflected in so much of the daughter's fiction.[2] There seems little doubt that Mary had a half-obsessive love for Godwin,[3] whose own immediate feeling for the abandoned infant bordered on panic. Like so many intellectuals who rejoice in theories, the philosopher jibbed away from the perplexing practical calls of daily life. He knew himself unfit to bring up children. When his far-flung efforts to provide a step-mother had closed in to his neighbor Mrs. Clairmont, the household economy was not simplified thereby but complicated. Mary at five years of age, instead of being cloistered like her fictional heroines with a wor-shiped father-figure had to take her chance with the defeatist Fanny Imlay, the boisterous Jane Clairmont, Jane's brother Charles, and the latest infant, William, son of Mrs. Clairmont and Mary's father. The bookshop had been opened in 1805, money was scarce, and it was nobody's business to ensure tranquillity and affection in the Skinner Street home.

Mary was driven inward, lonely and self-pitying, at odds with her companions and surroundings. The mood, experienced so early, was to clamp down recurrently on a nature that was otherwise gregarious and society-loving. Nor did Mrs. Clairmont's family excursions to Margate and Ramsgate rouse her to new pleasures. At home she read voraciously, imbibing an irregular education from her father's plenitude. Left so much to her own spiritual company she began to write romances, secretly.[4] Her first materially adequate friends were Isabella and Christy Baxter, the daughters of a Dundee merchant;[5] her first happy months were spent

2. For examples, see "The Elder Son," *Lodore* (where it occurs twice over), *Falkner* (an adopted daughter), and *Mathilda* (where it is sharpened toward incest).

3. After his death she was eager to collect his letters and write his life, but friends were uncooperative. (Crabb Robinson endorsed her request, "All the letters I was in possession of were applications for money.") The life remained unfinished.

4. "I did not make myself the heroine of my tales. Life appeared to me too common-place an affair as regarded myself. I could not figure to myself that romantic woes or wonderful events would ever be my lot; but I was not confined to my own identity, and I could people the hours with creations far more interesting to me at that age, than my own sensations." Introduction to *Frankenstein: or, The Modern Prometheus* (London, 1831), p. vi. (Introduction not in previous editions.)

5. William Thomas Baxter had met Godwin in 1809, on a visit to London, carrying an introduction from David Booth, a brewer of Newburg, Fifeshire. Although her senior by twenty-nine years, Booth was to marry Mary's closest friend, Isabella Baxter, and was responsible for a break in their relation-ship after Mary's elopement with Shelley. Baxter himself, however, was impressed by Shelley on visiting the two at Marlow in 1817. It was Booth, throughout, who insisted on a rupture.

in their Scottish home on two long visits in 1812 and 1813. She had here her earliest, perhaps her only, taste of quiet conventional life in a middle-class family. It is perhaps significant that she enjoyed it. Returning to the Godwin menage in March 1814 she again began her evasive tactics of taking books and meditations to her mother's grave in St. Pancras churchyard.

During her absence her father had made a new friend. Although it was Godwin's principles that had attracted Shelley, the needy philosopher had for two years encouraged his young admirer as a convenient source of financial aid. To Mary, inexperienced, intellectualized, on the brink of womanhood, still reverencing her father above all men, the impact of this kindred spirit in youthful shape was overwhelming. Shelley, to whom his Harriet was by now a "noble animal" but deficient in brain, had been gently dismissed by Cornelia Turner and her mother Mrs. Boinville. Elizabeth Hitchener, sister of his soul, had turned with Ovidean finality into a "Brown Demon." He was as lonely as Mary, who, at sixteen and a half, possessed blonde grace and beauty coupled with remarkable book-learning, and whose mother had been Mary Wollstonecraft.

Early in May, when he dined with Godwin, the two met. Thereafter, Shelley began to find his way to the grave in St. Pancras churchyard. Love was inevitable. According to Godwinian principles — as they thought — it was also permissible because Harriet no longer loved (or *was* loved — a mere extra word). If Shelley had a conscience, Mary had no need of one. All her frustrated, half-unrealized passions were unlocked. Two months went by in a fever of instability. When they planned to elope, an ironic note crept in for Mary: instead of a clean break with the Clairmont circus, it appeared that the swarthy-faced Jane — in time to be called Claire — was to accompany them. This impulsive, headstrong, naturally amoral "half-sister" (there was of course no blood relationship) was to be Mary's lifelong and inseverable fate. Through quarrels and irritations, dissembling affections, potent jealousies, the two would scratch alongside into middle age, not only on shared memories of dead poets but on each moment's trouble and alarm as life unfurled.[6]

6. In May of 1836 Mary was complaining of her to Trelawny: "We were never friends — Now, I would not go to Paradise, with her for a companion — she poisoned my life when young . . . . she has still the faculty of making me more uncomfortable than any human being — a faculty she, uncon-

For the present, Shelley more than doubled his shock to the pro-
prieties by sailing for the Continent on July 28 with, apparently, a lady-
love on each arm. The uncomfortable idyll, cut short when funds gave
out, was followed by those restless London months when Shelley,
embroiled with moneylenders, lawyers, and bailiffs, could meet Mary
only surreptitiously.[7] When they acquired lodgings, Claire was with
them. She would go out with Shelley while Mary, with some immature
notion of putting free love into plural practice, tried to console herself
with T. J. Hogg. In place of the hoped-for sympathy from Godwin there
was only censure. Her firstborn, a seven-month infant, died within a
fortnight.

The bleakness softened a little when they left town in the summer,
to live among the rural scenes at Bishopsgate,[8] but it was only in the
spring of 1816 that her fragmentary existence took on shape and color
from the gorgeous scenery of Lake Leman and the stimulating talk
of Shelley with their new, dynamic friend Lord Byron — for whose
acquaintance they could, for once, thank Claire. Quite suddenly, Mary's
mind seems to have expanded. She listened to discussions on mankind's
predicament and the source of life, felt a shudder of mystery at "Monk"
Lewis'[9] ghost stories, marveled at the peaks and glaciers of the Chamonix
valley, and — accepting a literary challenge — wrote *Frankenstein*.
Unaware, she had ensured herself a lasting, independent fame.

Meanwhile, the fall and winter, back in England, brought only
shadows. In October Fanny Imlay (Godwin), lonely and despairing,
fled from the impossible home and took her own life at a Swansea inn.
Two months later the drowned body of Harriet Shelley was dragged out

---

sciously perhaps, never fails to exert whenever I see her. . . ." (ALs quoted in Sotheby's Sale Catalogue, Dec. 16-17, 1963.)

7. Twenty years later Mary was to recall the circumstances eloquently in her novel *Lodore*.

8. In *The Last Man* (1826) Mary placed her abdicated royalties at Bishopsgate and Windsor, writing
with an evident love of the district and its memories.

9. Matthew Gregory Lewis, 1775-1818, author of *Ambrosio, or The Monk*, *The Castle Spectre*, and
other Gothic tales, translations, and dramas, spent some days with Byron at the Villa Diodati
in August 1816, between two trips to his West Indian estates. In her Journal, Shelley (not Mary)
summarized four ghost stories he told them on August 18, and a poem of the supernatural composed
by Lewis at the request of the Princess of Wales. Mary used the fourth of the prose tales in her essay
on "Ghosts" in *The London Magazine* for March 1824.

of the Serpentine. Mary's Journal is laconic over this event.[10] She had no cause to mourn her displaced rival, nor, it may be, wisdom to appreciate the intense shock it must bring to Shelley. On the credit side — since she was no lawbreaker by nature — it meant that her union could be legalized. To the great satisfaction of the Godwin parents, this was done on December 30 in their presence.

Quieter months were to follow during 1817 in Marlow, with excursions up the river in Peacock's company, with Shelley busy on his "summer's task," *Laon and Cythna,* while Mary corrected and transcribed her *Frankenstein.* On March 12, 1818, they crossed for the third time from Dover to Calais; and for the third time Claire was with them, now with her baby girl, Lord Byron's child. The years in Italy, restless, unsettled, bright with the joys of landscape and antiquities, dark with domestic dramas, rich with the masterworks Shelley was pouring out to an unheeding public, belong essentially to Shelley's biography. They have been studied, scrutinized, amplified as to detail, colored by new light from obtuse angles. When the Pisan circle found itself in being, Shelley was its center; and his movements, save for the smallest temporary divergencies, represent Mary's. In Rome, in Florence, enjoying a Neapolitan trip to "Baiae's Bay"; in Pisa, at the Bagni di Lucca, making a fearful dash to Venice from Este with a dying baby, sailing idyllically on the Serchio river . . . these activities were their dual life.

The real divergencies were in mind and temperament. It was becoming apparent that Mary, like her father, was developing conventionality. The vagabond life was by no means to her taste; still less was Shelley's never abandoned notion of a multiplicity of love and the objects of love without abating in warmth to any one of them:

> True love in this differs from gold and clay,
> That to divide is not to take away.[11]

For Mary there were too many in that division: Emilia Viviani, inspirer of the quoted lines; Jane Williams, who, with her unmarried mate Edward, had caught Shelley's fancy for a certain commonplace realism

---

10. Sunday, Dec. 15. "Draw. A letter from Hookham with the news of the death of Harriet Shelley. Walk out with Shelley. He goes to town after dinner. Read Chesterfield." *Mary Shelley's Journal,* p. 71.
11. *Epipsychidion,* lines 160-161.

behind her charm; the ubiquitous Claire Clairmont with her passionate neuroses. After the death of little William, Mary, childless again, withdrew in alienation, even though in 1819 her last-born, Percy Florence, should have provided a robust link. In Lerici, where the Williams couple shared the sea-fringed Casa Magni, Mary was moody, ill, and melancholy. Recovering from another miscarriage, she left Shelley and Edward to enjoy their "perfect plaything," the *Don Juan*, and in July to sail away high-spiritedly in her and welcome the Hunt family at Leghorn . . .

Looking back, when she could bear to, at the tragedy, Mary wrote on August 15 a long narrative letter to Mrs. Gisborne, setting the scene with omens and hallucinations. She told how she and Jane had posted in desperation to Pisa, thence to Leghorn, and back to Lerici; how couriers were sent searching along the coast, and how on July 19 Trelawny brought the news that quenched all further hope. Mary piled faith and gratitude on the Cornish adventurer who had made himself a sort of hero of the aftermath. "Your praises of my lost Shelley were the only balm I could endure."[12] She was not left friendless. In addition to Trelawny (who was to play off Mary and Claire against each other in those dragging later years) there were Leigh Hunt and his family; Maria Gisborne; Byron — fitfully; Peacock, working hard in England to secure her an essential allowance from Sir Timothy Shelley; and Jane Williams, her fellow sufferer. The circle was broken, but its remnants tossed and jostled against each other, while the immediate need of money jostled the advertised needs of her father. Living on in Genoa with the Hunts, Mary, guilt-ridden, poured sorrow and remorse for her spiritual withdrawal from Shelley into her longest poem, "The Choice":

> My heart was all thine own, — but yet a shell
> Closed in its core, which seemed impenetrable,
> Till sharp-toothed misery tore the husk in twain,
> Which gaping lies, nor may unite again.
> Forgive me! let thy love descend in dew
> Of soft repentance and regret most true —

The return to chilly England in 1823 seemed a second bereavement; yet the plaints that now began to fill her Journal gave only one face of

12. To Trelawny, November 1822, Mary Shelley, *Letters*, I, 203.

her character. She had met friends in Paris; in London a dramatized version of *Frankenstein* was being played. As the fair and talented widow of the poet she could hardly be unaware of her position among artists and intellectuals. The fashionable party-givers invited her, young men looked on her with a personal interest, she herself would gladly have given up the struggle against poverty to be married to some bright being with both talent and fortune. She was attracted by B. W. Procter, "whose voice, laden with sentiment, passed as Shelley's," and whose derivative verse, she might have added more critically, commanded the easy success and adulation that Shelley's poems had missed.[13] Procter and his dazzlement drifted by; he married Miss Skepper. Mary herself had a worshiper in John Howard Payne, the American dramatist and writer-of-all-work, whose finances were no healthier than her own. Much has been made of her wooing, through Payne, of the more "eligible" Washington Irving. No doubt she was magnetized by Irving's beauty and brilliance; but it was Payne himself who lent a spurious drama to the episode by staging a sacrificial act in passing her on to his hero. Nothing came of it. Irving was uninterested, and Mary, in London, was occupied with literature, with some homelier friends, the Hares and Robinsons, with the upbringing of young Percy Florence. The boy had little of Shelley in him, and might seem, in type, to have reverted to the grandfather at Field Place who grudged the funds for his schooling.

Glad enough that he should "think like others," Mary, whose association with a rebel had led to misjudgments in her outlook, insisted on exiling herself to Harrow so that Percy could be schooled there economically as a day pupil. Handicapped by Sir Timothy's ban on the name of Shelley, she was yet consolidating her position as "the Author of *Frankenstein*" with novels, stories, and journalistic essays. There were also Shelley's manuscripts to arrange and edit. This too she per-

13. *Mary Shelley's Journal*, p. 195. Bryan Waller Procter ("Barry Cornwall") 1787-1874, wrote imitative poems and "Dramatic Scenes" that deceived even Coleridge as to their merits, likewise Swinburne, who composed an elegy on his death. Browning wrote to his widow on receiving a memento, "You know very well that I would have gratefully treasured a glove or a shoe-string." (Quoted in Sotheby's Sale Catalogue, Dec. 16-17, 1963.) Shelley, on the contrary, wrote to Peacock who had denounced Procter's poetry, "I agree with you . . . decidedly . . . . The man whose critical gall is not stirred up by such *ottava rimas* as Barry Cornwall's, may safely be conjectured to possess no gall at all. The world is pale with the sickness of such stuff." (Feb. 15, 1821, Shelley, *Letters*, II, 261.) Evidently her husband's contempt for the poetry did not influence Mary's interest in the man.

formed, in 1839–1840, against obstacles, and with all her typical brooding and self-pity,[14] as she retraced a past that now seemed — as it never *had* been — paradise.

To some degree Mary came to terms with life as it must now be in those middle years, enjoying plays and operas when a theatrical friend would provide her with a box. She would attend the famous breakfast parties of Sam Rogers, or confide too naïvely in the egotistic little Irish bard, Tom Moore. Jane Williams' domestic slavery as Mrs. Hogg she recognized as a more restricted orbit than her own. And since the best years of her life with Shelley had been spent abroad, she still half-trusted that a continental round would be a journey back in time to the old memories, besides giving her material for a book. In 1840 and again in 1842–1843 she made long trips through Germany and Italy in the somewhat intermittent company of her son, who had now secured his B.A., and his college friends Knox and Ellis.[15] In July of the latter year she found herself in Paris, where the inescapable Claire Clairmont[16] had already made friends with a quintet of captivating young Italians. As Carbonari, the youths were penniless political exiles with ingratiating manners. They made a vivid appeal to the hearts and pockets of Claire and Mary, who even indulged some mutual jealousy over Gatteschi, the best-favored of the five. Claire gave him money, Mary engaged him to dig out political facts for her Italian travel book.

For two years the long, excited, argumentative letters the two

14. "In so arduous a task others might hope for encouragement and kindness from their friends — I know mine better." (Feb. 12, 1839, *Mary Shelley's Journal*, p. 207.) She had been attacked by Trelawny and Hogg for cutting *Queen Mab* and omitting the dedication to Harriet — "Poor Harriet, to whose sad fate I attribute so many of my own heavy sorrows, as the atonement claimed by fate for her death." (*Ibid.*)

15. Alexander Knox, a fellow undergraduate at Trinity College, Cambridge, was reading for the Bar. Later he became a journalist and worked for fourteen years on the staff of *The Times*. Robert Leslie Ellis, a mathematician of brilliant promise, had his career cut short by rheumatic fever and died in 1859. In Germany they visited another Trinity friend, Henry Hugh Pierson, composer of grand-scale oratorios on the German model. His musical settings of some of Shelley's poems pleased Mary.

16. Mary was finding Claire an insupportable drag on her freedom of movement, and had to be strict in imposing her own terms. "This uneasy sense you have, that you are illused if your friends act upon their own judgement, not upon yours — is natural — but it is a painful shackle to them." (October 13, 1843, Mary Shelley, *Letters*, II, 205.) On her own part Mary expected to dictate the times and places of Claire's travels, and was equally annoyed when not consulted.

women exchanged were filled with talk about Gatteschi. Having gradu-
ated from beggar to donor, Mary promised this alluring youth the profits
on her *Rambles*; from England she sent too many and too affectionate
letters. Then, in 1845, the bubble burst abruptly, and brought near-
prostration. Gatteschi had not only been enjoying an affair with Lady
Sussex Lennox for the better extraction of her worldly wealth, but was
blackmailing Mary over her hysterical correspondence. Now he was
writing "hideous," "vile" letters, "& would stab either of us willingly."[17]
"He insults & abuses me that he may preserve a good appearance of
being wronged,"[18] she complained to Claire in September. It was Percy's
friend Knox who came to the rescue, fixed him politically with the French
police, and got possession of Mary's letters. Barely relieved, she was in
the hands of another rogue, the forger, de Gibler who, calling himself
Major Byron, sold her a number of Shelley letters, real or spurious.[19]
These, too, involved intricate dealings and a Bow Street summons. With
such an embarrassment of villains Mary may be excused for seeing
another in Thomas Medwin when he published, in 1847, a life of his cousin
Shelley without her full approval.

Yet again she was to be a disappointed woman, economically and
emotionally. Although Sir Timothy's death in 1844 had at last freed the
Shelley estate for her and Percy, it was burdened with debts, legacies,
and other obligations. Percy, the son she had meant to idolize, proved
difficult; if faithful, true, and upright, he was also uncommonly indolent,
lacking in cultural interests and enthusiasms, though he followed his
father in a taste for sailing. Even there — Percy's "boat is quite a
failure," Mary reported to Claire; and a costly one at that. It was decided
(by whom remains uncertain) that he should stand for Parliament in the
1848 election as candidate for Horsham, being now in possession of
Field Place. Electoral scandals of the period, surviving the Reform Bill,
almost guaranteed him a safe seat.[20] They were living in the family

17. To Claire, Oct. 9, 1845, Mary Shelley, *Letters*, II, 256.

18. To Claire, Sept. 15, 1845, *ibid.*, p. 252.

19. Considering her naïve susceptibility to financial traps, it is odd to find Mary advising Claire,
like a wise aunt, on how to invest her money in the new and fashionable railway stock. "Buying &
selling in Railroads is an art & requires an apprenticeship." (To Claire, August 12, 1845, *ibid.*, p. 250.)

20. To Claire, Aug. 12, 1845, *ibid.*, p. 250. Bribery and corruption had so marked the previous election that the winning "Blue," Radical, candidate was unseated on petition by the rival party, and

mansion after nearly rejecting it as so dull, so damp, that if Percy lived there "he would either spend all his money going away from it — or be forced from sheer ennui to make love to the dairy maid."[21]

Before the election campaign was under way, Mary had met with a young widow, Jane St. John — a case of mutual regard and almost adoration. History hardly tells how Percy Florence was drawn into the conspiracy to provide him with a wife. His typical apathy no doubt had a hand in it. In June 1848, instead of winning a Parliamentary election by inactive methods he became the passive husband of that Jane who had, for Mary, all the virtues and attractions of her fictional heroines; and whose life-work was to venerate Percy Bysshe.

Possibly Mary felt her task was over. She no longer had a desperate need to write for money, and she had steered her unenterprising son into kindly hands. They arranged to leave the humidities of Field Place for Boscombe — a kind of Lerici by a grayer Hampshire sea. But on February 1, 1851, after an illness that was never clearly diagnosed, Mary died at her London residence, 24 Chester Square.[22] Both Claire Clairmont and Jane Hogg were to survive her by many a long year.

WORKS AND IDEAS

And Shelley, four-famed — for her parents, her lord,
And the poor lone impossible monster abhorred.[23]

It has long since been recognized that Mary Shelley does not survive solely as the poet's wife, nor even as his editor. Had Shelley lived on she

the "Pink" candidate, Fitzgerald, having used identical methods, could not claim the seat. In 1848 Sir Percy was adopted as Blue candidate, while the Pinks ran Fitzgerald again. The intention was for the Blues to allow Fitzgerald to be elected, get him unseated on a charge of bribery, so that Percy, having practiced restraint, sobriety, indolence, and economy, would be automatically elected. This is what actually occurred, in favor of Lord Edward Howard, who took Percy's place as Radical candidate. See William Albery, *A Parliamentary History of Horsham 1290–1885* (London, 1927), pp. 403–414.

21. To Claire, June 4, 1844, Mary Shelley, *Letters*, II, 222.

22. "Her illness puzzled the doctors so long, and presented so many different appearances that they could not make out what was the matter with her," Percy wrote to the friend of her girlhood, Isabella Booth. (*Ibid.*, p. 358, Appendix IV.)

23. Leigh Hunt, *Blue-stocking Revels, or, The Feast of the Violets*, Canto II, lines 209–210.

might never have schooled herself to turn from amateur to professional status in the writing of books and journalism. "The Author of *Frankenstein*" existed in her own right. She was not unsuspected to be Mrs. Shelley; yet the fiction-reading public, then as now, took note of novels and was largely unaware of contemporary poets who had not made the grade of popularity. *Frankenstein; or, The Modern Prometheus*, reprinted, translated, dramatized, and screened, has become a by-word with thousands who could never name its author, whereas *Prometheus Unbound* remains, on a general viewing, unread. More controversial is the question whether *Frankenstein* is really Mary's masterpiece, or how far it is a masterpiece at all.

Before attempting a decision we may take a glance at her personal and general matrix, at her inherent intellectual and emotional beliefs; that is, if any consistent ones can be established. One important gulf between the major and the minor writer is the presence or absence of a unifying motive, whether moral, political, or aesthetic — or indeed, as with the more abundant spirits, a blend of these and other aspects of man's multifarious life. Such a unity exists in Coleridge and Shelley. Admittedly it is rare in Leigh Hunt's "Blue-stockings," where literature and not life is the expression of it.

Mary was born of two most positive persons. Not that Mary Wollstonecraft was supreme in literature or confirmed in action; but her passionate views propelled her through despairs and follies, her perversities were reconciled, if irrationally, by a dynamic thrust. Godwin, daring and defiant intellectually, was tepid in practice; his failure to harmonize project and performance led increasingly to an obsession with life's expediencies, swamping the convictions that had made *Political Justice* a radical creed. These two, with parallel social aims, were so diverse in conduct that their daughter's want of a strong driving force is understandable. What she did inherit initially was an itch to write; while the spiritual loneliness of her childhood drove her, as we saw, to introspective daydreams. She is herself the most accurate chronicler of her condition:

As a child I scribbled; and my favourite pastime, during the hours given me for recreation, was to "write stories." Still I had a dearer pleasure than this, which was the formation of castles in the air — the indulging in waking dreams — the following up trains of thought, which had for their subject the formation of a succession of imaginary incidents. My dreams were at once more fantastic and agreeable than my writings.[24]

In a bookish household she had learned to read widely if unsystematically, and had no doubt absorbed the works of both her parents before she reread them with Shelley in the year of the elopement.[25] That year she also read *Queen Mab* with its impetuous notes reviling tyrants, marriage laws, and the encrusted totem-myths of Christianity. All this would be poured out too in Shelley's conversation, charged with the magnetism of his personality. She had been swept into appropriate action, willingly overturning the conventions, glad enough to back up her own emotional urge by his argument that a loveless fetter was obscene. Little wonder that her manifest rebeldom, joined with her heredity, led those who knew only her public image to expect a zealous reformer, marching in the van of socialistic schemes. Mary knew herself better. She could write sympathetically on the left-wing attitude, especially where Shelley, or a fictional Shelley-image, was in question;[26] but, for herself, she lacked the inner fire. Too much in the other camp attracted her: social living, gentle manners, the advantages of culture that in her day belonged far more exclusively to the hereditary titled class than they do today. The poor, in her novels, tend to be pitiable, untaught, and not very redeemable apart from possessing innocent ignorance and kind hearts. Except when some Shelleyan phantom drives her to expound his views she looks on the poverty of the masses as an established ordinance, a God-given scourge to be alleviated by charity, not abolished by egalitarian measures. (In defiance of Chartism and the industrial revolution many mid-Victorian worthies were to share this view.)

24. *Frankenstein* (1831), p. v.

25. During 1814 both of them read Mary Wollstonecraft's *Letters from Norway, Mary, Wrongs of Women, View of the French Revolution*: and Godwin's *Political Justice, Caleb Williams, Essay on Sepulchres.* (*Mary Shelley's Journal*, pp. 32–33.) The following year Mary read Godwin's *Fleetwood* and *St. Leon*, and his edition of her mother's *Posthumous Works*.

26. Her note on *Queen Mab* for the 1839 *Poetical Works* is one long plea for the tender socialistic spirit who wrote it. "His sympathy was excited by the misery with which the world is bursting. . . . He desired to induce every rich man to despoil himself of superfluity, and to create a brotherhood of property and service, and was ready to be the first to lay down the advantages of his birth." (Shelley, *Complete Works*, I, 166.)

The aristocracy was Mary's elite. No matter if Godwin pictured an elite of intellectuals, his daughter — like Tom Moore in Byron's estimate — "loved a lord." Among her acquaintances she was dazzled by Byron and Lord Dillon;[27] in her novels the protagonists were invariably titled, or heirs to an ancestral estate. At times she felt constrained, in her own life, to simulate the expected ardor for democracy. The effort of it is apparent in this letter of December 30, 1830, to Robert Dale Owen, colleague of the devoted reformer Fanny Wright:[28]

My enclosed letter to her [Fanny] speaks of the subject that must interest us all so highly. —the triumph of the *Cause* in Europe—I wonder if nations have *bumps* as well as individuals—*Progressiveness* is certainly finely developed just now in Europe—together with a degree of *tyrant quellingtiveness* which is highly laudable—it is a pity that in our country this should be mingled with an *sick destructiveness.*[29]

— and so on, ploddingly. What would Shelley have made of that ineptitude? Eight years later, tired of being "abused by pretended friends for my lukewarmness in 'the good cause,'" she wrote a long self-analytical statement in her Journal,[30] declaring her revulsion from violent extremes, from "the vulgar abuse of the inimical press," and from the selfish, ignorant, insolent Radicals. The apologia tails off, in feminine fashion, from the pretense of cool dissection to the plea of having "befriended women when oppressed," and a minor irrelevant rhapsody over Percy Florence (who planned to enter Parliament as a Radical in 1848).

27. Lord Dillon of Ditchley, author of an immensely long poem, *Eccelino*, attended Mary's evening receptions at her London home in Somerset Street, until his sudden death in 1832.

28. Frances (Fanny) Wright, 1795–1852, was, like Mary, the daughter of a man of liberal ideas. Visiting America in 1818, she returned there six years later eager to work for the civil rights of Negroes. Her settlement for Negro slaves on a tract of land near Memphis, Tennessee, proved disillusioning. In Europe she met Mary Shelley, to whom she confided (expecting to find a kindred spirit) her idea of an establishment where "affection shall form the only marriage." Later she became the pioneer of women lecturers in the United States, founding Fanny Wright Societies to urge social reforms. Robert Dale Owen (1801–1877), son of the Lanarkshire socialist Robert Owen, after joining his father's experimental colony at New Harmony, Indiana, collaborated with Fanny on a socialistic journal, the *Free Inquirer*. In 1843 he was elected to the House of Representatives, helping to pass Liberal bills and to secure property rights for women. He too, while attracted by Mary's personality, expected to find a replica of her mother's crusading feminism.

29. Mary Shelley, *Letters*, II, 37.

30. Oct. 21, 1838, *Mary Shelley's Journal*, p. 204.

A suspicion of persecution mania creeps into it; there was no need for Mary to be an ardent liberal in order to write popular fiction. What she was really evading in this "frank" confession was her fragmentation as a literary woman of many parts that failed to coalesce. Admittedly she had to write for money; but so did, and so do, many reputable authors, having reconciled the sordid need with an unwavering moral or artistic aim. Mary had neither; she was seeking all her life for subjects she could translate with no profound gestation into the required story. This she did with admirable industry and varying success.

Her fiction can be seen to emanate from three sources: (1) topics of discussion and speculation among inquiring minds (*Frankenstein, The Last Man*); (2) historical characters and incidents (*Valperga, Perkin Warbeck*); (3) the personalities of her early circle (*The Last Man, Lodore, Falkner*, and the novelette *Mathilda*). From the prevailing fiction fashions she imported into all of them a romantic flush that blended with her personal vein of sighs in solitude. (Under adversity her characters retire defeated from their fellow beings — to a wooded wilderness, like Mathilda, or an untamed American settlement, like Lord Lodore.)

One writes, at least when trying out a first novel, in the style of one's older contemporaries. In 1814–1815, besides the works of Godwin and her mother, Mary had read the Gothic-romantic confections of the moment. Her list includes *The Monk* and *Tales of Wonder* by M. G. Lewis, Mrs. Radcliffe's *Mysteries of Udolpho* and *The Italian*, and *Hermsprong; or Man as he is Not* by Robert Bage. Undoubtedly she had been through Shelley's raving blood-and-thunder thrillers, *Zastrozzi* and *St. Irvyne, or The Rosicrucian*. As a rule this gaudy product had a moral impaled on it but no space for sentiment; the Gothic had little appeal to an introspective writer,[31] who would prefer the novel of sensibility. Mary specialized in long self-communings; her approach was always a first-person one, unless prevented by a clear historical theme.

Here, then, in 1816, was this talented, melancholic but attentive spirit located for a spell among the mountainous Swiss glories while the thoughts of Byron and Shelley played like lightning flashes over the somber riddle of the universe, the origin, aim, and purpose of proud man

31. It was to appeal, rather, to the satirist — Peacock and Jane Austen.

"dressed in a little brief authority," and the weird, awe-fraught possibility of *producing life*. How should it be done? By present standards the debaters were not quite biochemists,[32] though Shelley kept up his lively regard for science, and the premises of "natural philosophy" intrigued them both. For clues to an origin of species they leaned on Erasmus Darwin, failing his future grandson Charles. This was the kind of speculation that came out of it:

Perhaps a corpse would be re-animated; galvanism had given token of such things: perhaps the component parts of a creature might be manufactured, brought together, and endued with vital warmth.[33]

Mary's Victor Frankenstein, having been deflected with scorn from the works of Paracelsus and Cornelius Aggrippa to a study of modern chemistry, seems to have combined the two suggestions. He spent sinister days and nights in charnel houses observing the corruption and decay of human bodies; and having discovered how to animate dead matter, set out "to prepare a frame . . with all its intricacies of fibres, muscles, and veins." We have here a discrepancy: the materials came from the dissecting-room and slaughter-house; yet —

As the minuteness of the parts formed a great hindrance to my speed, I resolved, contrary to my first intention, to make the being of a gigantic stature; that is to say, about eight feet in height, and proportionably large.[34]

This could hardly have been done with the collected bones, even if the oddments of muscle, vein, and ligament could be juggled to fit. True, the gigantic creature was, in some unspecified way, deformed, but not seriously enough to prevent his "scaling the overhanging side of Mount Salêve."

No matter how shuffling the creation, the broad fact remains that Mary Shelley has herself created Science Fiction. Natural phenomena have been pushed to the *un*natural; powers that contemporary humanity does not possess have been let loose; a creature unborn of woman walks the

32. Byron's doctor, John William Polidori, should as a medical man have led them; but as Polidori he was only a bad fourth.

33. *Frankenstein* (1831), p. x.

34. *Frankenstein: or, The Modern Prometheus* (London, 1823), I, 88. This edition was revised by Mary Shelley.

earth and leaps among the mountains. As in all later science fiction, the hypothesis is fantastic but permissible.[35] Once presented and accepted, the rest must follow like logic; the reader is prepared to swallow the camel, but will strain at gnats. There is a very large gnat in the synthetic monster. To the outward view this object made with trembling, half-revolted hands from scrap-material, and with an attempt at least of outward beauty, turned out, when animated by the life-spark, to be hideous.

His yellow skin scarcely covered the work of muscles and arteries beneath; his hair was of a lustrous black, and flowing; his teeth of a pearly whiteness; but these luxuriances only formed a more horrid contrast with his watery eyes, that seemed almost of the same colour as the dun white sockets in which they were set, his shrivelled complexion, and straight black lips.[36]

It was this abhorrent physical appearance that was to prejudice men and women against the monster and ruin his early efforts at benevolence. For such a legacy he blamed Frankenstein, as men, with less excuse, will rail at God. But it never occurred to Mary or the monster that he might have *thanked* his maker. For along with this giant parody of a human mammal went the brain of a university professor, or one of those French philosophers the young Shelley absorbed. The creature, launched with only primitive instincts, acquired speech in several languages, knowledge of world history, literature, geography, and ingenious power to turn them to his own designs. All this came through listening to the talk and reading of one small French family in a cottage, and through picking up three books to study for himself.[37] What magic helped the young experimenter? The body, watched anxiously in preparation, was poor prentice work. How came the brain to be so high among human averages?[38]

35. Midway between Mary and the moderns stand Jules Verne and H. G. Wells, whose scientific romances are models of their kind. Wells, having initially squared his circle, builds on it with a degree of plausibility and even character-drawing that establishes a perfect pseudo-realism.

36. *Frankenstein* (1823), I, 98.

37. These were *Paradise Lost*, a volume of Plutarch's *Lives*, and *The Sorrows of Werther*. Considering the style of his long narrative to Frankenstein, this last was obviously a plum.

38. Coleridge applied similar requirements of consistency to horror tales. Reviewing Lewis' *The Monk* in *The Critical Review* for February 1797 he wrote: "The romance writer possesses an unlimited power over situations; but he must scrupulously make his characters act in congruity with them.... we feel no great difficulty in yielding a temporary belief to any, the strangest of *things*. But that

The only answer is that here we leave SF for the other important aspect of this novel — its existence as an ethical romance. Whether romanticism and ethics *should* be mixed with science fiction cannot be decided by a general law; each example has to justify its method. In the case of *Frankenstein* its period, as noted, made the first inevitable; and the first invariably (even in the Gothic thriller) carried along the second. On the question of morality Mary is quite remarkably advanced. Instead of the black-and-white approach to good and evil she adopts a dual viewpoint. Frankenstein believes he has created something evil, refuses to increase and propagate it by producing — as implored — a female counterpart, and chases the monster-murderer with the one aim of destroying him. But the monster is eloquent in his own defense. Frankenstein made him in a form that renders every man his enemy and his own life hateful. From benevolent instincts he has been forced by his creator to turn fiend.[39] "Unfeeling, heartless creator! You had endowed me with perceptions and passions, and then cast me abroad, an object for the scorn and horror of mankind."[40] He has indeed so plausible an argument that one's sympathy with his maker is reduced.

Where she mars and minimizes her conception is in the management of story. Both the scientific and the ethical issue become submerged in tales of family origins and misfortunes that are all too plentiful in Mary's later works. The monster, flattened to the mere role of narrator, is lost in Mary's typical story of an exiled family, complete with that darling of the Christmas Annuals, a dazzling Oriental maid. These details are irrelevant and inimical to the strangeness, as apart from persecution, that should attend the progress of a man-made being. Dropping her chemical philosophy, Mary fails her theme and its implications; the romantic idiom intrudes too deeply, contracting the horizon long before the intended narrowing to a climax of pursuit on the Arctic ice.

It is only in *The Last Man* (1826) that any broad view of the social

situation once conceived, how beings like ourselves would feel and act in it, our own feelings sufficiently instruct us: and we instantly reject the clumsy fiction that does not harmonise with them." (Quoted by Kathleen Coburn, *Inquiring Spirit*, New York, 1951, p. 192.)

39. Shelley, like Blake, and like Milton himself to a degree, has the reformist's sympathy for the Arch-Fiend of *Paradise Lost*. There is little doubt, since the present monster had the text of it, that Mary intended the analogy.

40. *Frankenstein* (1823), II, 62.

economy of our planet is attempted. Her contemporaries took unkindly to this second essay in science fiction,[41] since the subject had not startled them by novelty. The literary air was heavy with last survivors, in both verse and prose. Here was the theme again, in three full volumes. Shelley and Byron, no longer living to supply the germ of it, were absorbed in phantom form into its narrative. Again there is an excess of domestic heart-throb, too much concern at first with personal sensibilities that have no flavor of the intended theme. But Mary, this time, grows to her commitments. After dwelling with an ex-king's family at Windsor, we find ourselves looking, as in Hardy's *Dynasts*, at the map of Europe. It is not Napoleon's army but the *plague* that rolls across it, making wars and victories hollow in the face of a common dread. By one of her too rare ironic appreciations she presents the English, smug in their island aloofness, confident that whatever disaster attacks foreign parts, "it could never happen here." The island is caught out, busy on home politics and disputed leadership, planning no measures to avert the peril, no organization to fight and counter it. Trade, however, is dislocated, refugees throng into England, the Irish fall foul of immigrant Americans . . . The unbounded view is all the time before us. Britain's self-made and ambitious Lord Protector crumples weakly, and it is ex-prince Adrian (the Shelley-figure) who takes charge.

The plague was in London! Fools that we were not long ago to have foreseen this. . . . But we are awake now. The plague is in London; the air of England is tainted, and her sons and daughters strew the unwholesome earth.[42]

In her *Rambles in Germany and Italy* (1844) Mary told how in 1837 a Papal procession of thanksgiving for preserving the city from cholera was caught in storms and rains that spread the disease among the crowd. In describing this outbreak she may well have felt her novel had been prophetic. In some ways it still reads prophetically — of the twentieth-century fear of nuclear destruction, of the bombing of London in the

---

41. Shelley had not been oversanguine about their reaction to the first; he advised against announcing *Valperga* as written by the author of *Frankenstein*; "it bears every indication of the greatest popularity, & many people might have been prejudiced by Frankenstein against a second attempt of the same author." (To Charles Ollier, July 27, 1821, Shelley, *Letters*, II, 312.)

42. *The Last Man* (London, 1826), II, 183–184.

1940's that left St. Paul's standing amid low ruin and willow-herb. As Mary puts it, "so much of what had in former days obscured this vast building was removed. Its ponderous mass, blackened stone, and high dome, made it look not like a temple, but a tomb."[43]

Such is the picture seen by the last band of British emigrants to the Continent (Mary had lived too much abroad to keep an insular outlook). They were heading for the suns of Italy, and nearly all of them — in an orgy of déspondent narrative — died and were buried on the way. Rome's ancient monuments being ruined already are only enhanced in eloquence by an absence of inhabitants. (Oddly enough, the plague attacked no animals. Doubtless the stray cats prowled in Trajan's Forum; and on all their travels, when the survivors sought a horse they went and found one, wandering but untainted.) These Roman pictures of untenanted streets and houses fascinate with the half-familiarity of a walk around Pompeii or the Palatine Hill; and Mary does not dodge the anti-Malthusian problem of a dwindling population when Death, having reaped in thousands, now stealthily attacks the precious few:

Man existed by twos and threes; man, the individual who might sleep, and wake, and perform the animal functions; but man, in himself weak, yet more powerful in congregated numbers than wind or ocean; man, the queller of the elements, the lord of created nature, the peer of demi-gods, existed no longer.[44]

In London, before the final exodus, some thousand were living; most of them up from the country (a good touch, this) taking their chance to see the famed metropolis. In France the emigrants, no heroic band, split into factions — the most aggressive led by an evangelical fanatic preaching his divine, exclusive mission as savior. Such mature felicities rise like bell-towers from the acres of turgid rhetorical sensibility that roll beneath them.

But again, as science fiction, *The Last Man* when reread today falls down. The events, since they embrace the entire world, must be laid in the future; they run from a republican England of 2073 to the final scenes in 2094. Mary was thinking, or should have been, some 240 years ahead. Yet she never tried to picture a world advanced in industry, transport,

43. *The Last Man*, III, 40.
44. *Ibid.*, p. 14.

architecture, or technology of any kind — with one exception that has been often overpraised: a sailing balloon that glides with feathered wings from Adriatic Italy over the Apennines and Alps, to land at Dieppe in the astonishing brevity of six days. Such an object was already being talked of, and is no invention of our novelist. Aside from that, and an occasional "steam packet," ships sail under full canvas — despite the project of Henry Reveley's steamboat in which Shelley so eagerly took part.

On land we find the hackney coach, the chariot, and the diligence (but the young bloods go on horseback); never a railway crosses England or the Continent,[45] never a petrol engine of the most primordial type. Towns have not grown, neither suburb nor factory has encroached on arable land. The scene, in its rurality, is almost retrogressive. When it came to imaging the future, Mary was not playing; her object was to trace out man's diminution, not his previous expansion. Nor would her immediate readers want it otherwise; how should the fate of an unrecognized world impress them? We, who are more than halfway to her future date, should curb our hindsight. As to the limited view of locomotion, let us spare our author; even the multiconscious Coleridge has been recorded as conversing of a time "when balloons, or these new roads upon which they say it will be possible to travel fifteen miles an hour, for a day together, shall become the common mode of travelling."[46]

Between the writing of these speculative novels Mary had reversed her tactics, burrowing among fourteenth-century records of Guelph and Ghibelline to write the historical *Valperga: or, the Life and Adventures of Castruccio, Prince of Lucca.*[47] *Valperga*, written between 1819 and 1821 under Shelley's approving eye, if far more densely packed (even after

45. Mary herself was to have a few trips by rail in Germany during her travels with Percy Florence and his friends. On July 22, 1842, she writes, "To-morrow we commit ourselves to a rail-road — blessings on the man who invented them." (*Rambles in Germany and Italy*, London, 1844, I, 215–216.) She did not anticipate him in imagination. Nor could she have guessed that in 1857 her novel *Perkin Warbeck* would be reissued in Routledge's *Railway Library* of books "suitable for railway and home reading." These suitable books included the works of Bulwer Lytton, Hawthorne, Maria Edgeworth, Jane Austen, Emerson, Fenimore Cooper, and Mary's one-time idol Washington Irving. On the Victorian railroads she was in good company.

46. Kathleen Coburn, *Inquiring Spirit*, p. 304.

47. "Raked out of fifty old books," Shelley wrote to Peacock, Nov. 8, 1820, Shelley, *Letters*, II, 245.

Godwin's pruning) than its successor, has no obvious quips of fancy to catch the attention. Yet it is refreshingly free of those debilitating troughs of plaintive monologue. The characters are objectified, and modeled with more substance and sophistication. Here, for example, is a pretty shrewd conception of the antihero:

Like many of his predecessors and successors in usurpation, Castruccio had a method in his tyranny; and he never proceeded to any act of violence, without first consulting with his council, and obtaining their sanction to his measures.[48]

The council — "this friendly assembly" — of course exists to back up the dictator; such autocracies are not exclusively medieval. One perceives a valid cause when Beatrice, the disillusioned prophetess (who has learned that her own miracle was effected by priestly fraud), passionately denounces wars, violation of treaties, and hard-hearted cruelty, citing the Tower of Famine, the Sicilian Vespers, and "the guilty policy of Popes." The examples are in period, the protest is Shelleyan, the evidence of man's inhumanity to man is not wiped out today. Castruccio has seduced the abandoned Beatrice; he has also declared his love for the highborn Euthanasia, whose castle he nonetheless attacks on his way to capture Florence.

All this is healthy, passionate romance. Like the later, and inferior, *Perkin Warbeck* it owes something to Scott, but more, one would say, had the dates been inverted, to George Eliot's *Romola*. Could she conceivably have read Mary Shelley?[49] *Valperga*, when we summon the strength and courage to read through it, is a solid achievement, more professionally conducted than those premature science fictions that will always be intriguing for their fanciful themes. That Shelley thought highly of it can be seen in the "preliminary puff" he sent to Ollier, recommending the book for publication.[50] Identifying the historical Castruccio, Shelley continued:

48. *Valperga: or, the Life and Adventures of Castruccio, Prince of Lucca* (London, 1823), II, 218.

49. The difference in status can be gauged by the recognition that *Romola*, as a deliberate historical task-work, is far inferior to *Middlemarch* and the other novels based on observation, while with Mary the attempt to picture her contemporaries is always weak.

50. Sept. 25, 1821, Shelley, *Letters*, II, 352–354. Ollier, however, refused to bite, and the novel, together with the copyright, was handed to Godwin.

He was a little Napoleon, and, with a dukedom instead of an empire for his theatre, brought upon the same all the passions and the errors of his antitype . . . The character of Beatrice, the prophetess, can only be done justice to in the very language of the author. I know nothing in Walter Scott's novels which at all approaches to the beauty and the sublimity of this — creation, I may almost say, for it is perfectly original.

To him it appeared "at least equal" to the *Tales of my Landlord* — that is to say, to the finest of Scott's work. The Italian historical setting makes such a comparison somewhat strained. But Scott was bestriding the fiction-world like a colossus, and every pretense at a period novel met his challenge. Later, while searching through early histories and documents for the preparation of *Perkin Warbeck*, Mary even wrote to Sir Walter (May 25, 1829) to ask, with the requisite flattery of the master, if he could supply "any document, anecdote or queer ballad" connected with her hero.[51] For her romantic purposes this hero was no imposter but the genuine Richard, Duke of York, legitimate heir to the throne. Thus, as in *The Last Man*, she was in comforting touch with princes bearing the distinguished manner of their house. History having already decreed Warbeck's failure, Mary's natural defeatism found congenial matter in a struggle that involved no perilous principles. Less bold than Shelley (who was judging better material) we can confidently give *Perkin Warbeck* precedence over some of Scott's excursions south of the border. Though hampered by outbreaks of archaic dialogue, Richard of York is doubly dynamic compared, for example, with the litter-borne hero of *Ivanhoe*.[52]

In Mary's third-source novels, the shadowy Byrons, Shelleys, and Trelawnys, embroiled with grotesques of Harriet, Claire, Emilia, or Miss Milbanke in a fluid interchange of identity, are something less than biographical clues. At times a circumstance will be fully reflected; more often the probability is that, taxing her tired mind for scenes and persons, Mary was forced back to the enchanted circle, and did her utmost to lay out new patterns by strenuous alteration and disguise. Good taste and camouflage failed her when it came to Trelawny-Falkner's burial of a

---

51. Mary Shelley, *Letters*, II, 15.

52. *Ivanhoe* had been unfairly cited as the model for Peacock's *Maid Marian*, written, though not published, before Scott's novel appeared in 1819.

beloved drowned body by a desolate sea. For this outrage we might "quarrel with her for ever," as Browning said of her more harmless *Rambles* when he found them dedicated by the widow of Shelley to the banker-poet Sam Rogers.

If the burial-narrative showed the lapses of a "second-rate sensitive mind," she had long since had one such aberration, during Shelley's lifetime, when she wrote the novelette *Mathilda*, and even dared to show it around to friends. Elizabeth Nitchie, who dug out the manuscript from deserved obscurity, and dated it 1819, calls the story "an important document"[53] for its light on Mary and her relationships. The light is dark enough. It reads like nothing so much as a burlesque of Mary's most lachrymose lucubrations. The self-blinded egoist Mathilda took her bleeding heart to live "on a dreary heath bestrewen with stones,"[54] and repulsed the youth who had likewise retired somewhere to "indulge his grief."[55] Mary herself, in one of her rare insights, evolved the fitting comment on this in later years: "All people who live in solitude become to a certain degree insane."[56] Meanwhile Mathilda assures us, "I never was really mad . . . [but] one who loved to be alone, and shrunk from observation; who never smiled; oh, no! I never smiled. . . ."[57]

Which brings us to Mary's leading handicap as a novelist (no doubt as a woman too): her appalling want of humor. That she wrote no comedies or witty satires is beside the issue. Humor implies a sense of the ridiculous, a healthy self-criticism that would recognize the swamps of sentiment and impose restraint. It is to some degree a negative quality that, like discipline, evokes a positive strength. It toughens and tautens the sinews of tragedy as they hang perilously over the trough of melodrama. It is, indeed, an absolute requisite of the unified artist and the balanced mind. Shelley himself has been accused of lacking it — truly enough in his floundering early years. But the mature Shelley curbed his young exuberance largely through the critical sense that comes through humor. Apart from the dramatic comedies and pointed satires, one has only to read some of his later letters, written as so many were

---

53. *Mathilda*, ed. Elizabeth Nitchie (University of North Carolina Press, 1959), p. vii.
54. *Ibid.*, p. 51. 55. *Ibid.*, p. 59.
56. *Lodore* (London, 1835), III, 263. 57. *Mathilda*, p. 50.

in haste and harassment, to note how gaiety would break in.[58] When he said that Mary did not understand him something of this cause was at the bottom of it.[59]

Without that organ, Mary was safest as a writer when the theme constrained her — either by historical claims or through responsibility to a challenging postulate. Left to her own "fields of fancy" (the title of her first draft of *Mathilda*) she could turn out tales of sentiment adequate for the Annuals which, designed and edited for the boudoir, were immune from the criticism of masculine minds. All such writing fell below her capabilities; and for boiling the pot she was more honorably employed in the fettered task — or chore, as we now label it — of summarizing lives of continental literati for *Lardner's Cabinet Cyclopaedia.*

By the 1830's Mary was a recognized literary bluestocking with a pride in her position countered by those outbreaks of humility and diffidence that served her, in default of humor, for humanity. Those who met this reputed "intellect" were pleasantly surprised at her social grace and modest bearing; the professional writer never swamped the woman. This too — since her manner was not artificially studied — can be reckoned an achievement. Her best work was behind her: three novels, each contending closely for first place. *Frankenstein* has the boldness of its subject but retreats from its responsibilities; *The Last Man* is a fine imaginative survey of the earth's predicament, marred only by diffuse irrelevance; *Valperga*, without thematic flights of fancy, has true character-drawing and a passion and harmony in its development that make it by far the most technically competent of the three. Out of curiosity, the modern will still pick *Frankenstein*, and not only for its theme but for its brevity; *Valperga* is too long by half.

By the Shelleyan, Mary's finest literary gesture must be seen as

58. Examples are his descriptions — both to Peacock — of the livestock sharing Byron's quarters at Ravenna, and of John Gisborne's prodigious, almost unforgivable nose. (Aug. [?10], 1821; Aug. [24, 1819], Shelley, *Letters*, II, 330, 114.)

59. To John Gisborne, June 18, 1822, Shelley, *Letters*, II, 435. It is typical of Mary that she omitted both *Peter Bell the Third* and *Swellfoot the Tyrant* from her first 1839 edition of the *Poetical Works*, fearing they might not "do honour to Shelley." In her second edition she called them "playthings," while discussing them with a solemnity that showed no true recognition of their humor. One detects her feeling for "the many, who will not see wit in those combinations of thought which were full of the ridiculous to the author." In such instances she has sympathy with Shelley, but not empathy.

the editing of his poetry and prose.[60] Scholarship, in textual minutiae, has gone far beyond her. Biographies, more biased than her narrative notes, were to succeed them. But the attempt now encouraged by our study of psychology to relate a poet's creative work to the relevant circumstances of both time and stress may be said to originate with Mary. Whatever her lacunae or shortcomings, any full edition of Shelley's works that should now appear without her annotations would seem truncated and outrage our sense of unity.

60. The first appearance of *A Defence of Poetry* in the 1840 *Essays and Letters from Abroad* gives the volume a particular value. Two periodical publications of the *Defence* had been frustrated by the demise of the organ: *Ollier's Literary Miscellany* in 1821 and John Hunt's *The Liberal* less than two years later.

MARY GODWIN TO T. J. HOGG:
THE 1815 LETTERS

THE FAMOUS collection of eleven letters which Mary Godwin wrote to T. J. Hogg in January–April 1815 has an interesting history.

After Hogg's death in 1862 these letters became the property of his daughter Prudentia (Mrs. Lonsdale). From her they passed to her cousin John Jefferson Hogg, and from him to his son Major R. J. Jefferson Hogg. In June 1948 they were sold at Sotheby's and thus came into The Carl H. Pforzheimer Library.[1]

In her *Life* of George S. Gordon, Mrs. Gordon has this illuminating paragraph about her husband, the late president of Magdalen College and vice-chancellor of Oxford University:

The latter part of Edmund Blunden's reminiscences [of Dr. Gordon, written for Mrs. Gordon] refer to a piece of work undertaken by G.S.G. in 1933. Some unpublished Shelley letters had just been discovered, tied up in a parcel, in an attic of Norton House, the home of Thomas Jefferson Hogg, the friend and biographer of the poet. His descendant, Captain R. J. J. Hogg, was willing to have them published, and the work was offered to G.S.G. As usual, busy though he was, he found the offer irresistible: it promised the kind of literary adventure that he loved. It proved however to be a much greater task than he had contemplated on account of the extreme illegibility of the letters [a matter of opinion] and the amount of annotation required. But the work fascinated him, and from the time of the discovery every vacation found him absorbed in it. He would lay it aside when term began, and pick up the loose-waving threads with a sigh in the next vacation. At the time of his death [in 1942] it was almost finished. A month or two of leisure would, he said, have completed it. It is hoped that it may yet be published.[2]

The Hogg manuscripts edited by Dr. Gordon included not only these eleven letters by Mary, but letters by Shelley, Hogg, Peacock, Leigh Hunt, and others — a total of ninety-odd letters. Dr. Gordon, a meticulous scholar, was notorious for his reluctance to commit his work to the press. By or before 1936 his edition of the new Shelley materials was not only near completion but was actually in proof. Also, arrangements with the publisher, Henry Holt and Company, had already been

1. "The Provenance of Shelley and his Circle Manuscripts," below, pp. 293–295.
2. Mary C. Gordon, *The Life of George S. Gordon* (London and New York, 1945), p. 92.

made for the American edition. In the meanwhile, Professor Newman I. White was writing his monumental *Shelley* (1940), with the confident expectation that Dr. Gordon's volume would be published years before his own work was finished. Henry Holt and Company had permitted him to have a proof copy of the Gordon book, and he had woven into his narrative the facts revealed by the letters and many quotations from them. White's book finally was in type and Gordon's book had not yet been published. An exchange of correspondence resulted in the necessity of White's excluding from his book, at great personal cost, all quotations from Gordon's book, though the use of the facts themselves was allowed.

In 1936 Frederick L. Jones began collecting and editing the letters of Mary Shelley. He also expected the Gordon volume to be published long before his edition was completed. When his *Letters of Mary W. Shelley* was published in 1944, Dr. Gordon had been dead two years and his book was still unpublished. Jones was able only to include a list of the Mary Shelley letters and a long note on their contents; he had copies of them through the courtesy of Newman I. White.

For some reason not yet made public, after Dr. Gordon's death in 1942 the manuscripts (which had been deposited in the Bodleian Library) and the privilege to publish them were withdrawn. They were then edited by Walter Sidney Scott (related to the Hogg family by marriage) and published by the Golden Cockerel Press in three thin volumes selling for three guineas each, as follows: *The Athenians* (1943), *Harriet and Mary* (1944), and *Shelley at Oxford* (1944). The arrangement and editing of these volumes are great handicaps to the usefulness of very valuable materials; many of the letters hitherto printed are given only in part. Mary's letters to Hogg are in *Harriet and Mary*. The contents of the three volumes of the Cockerel Press edition were combined and published in *New Shelley Letters* by the Bodley Head press in 1948 and Yale University Press in 1949.[3]

The interpretation of these letters is a matter of considerable importance, though it is easy to exaggerate this importance. Opinions will vary according to the temperament and competence of the writer. Fortunately, Newman I. White, with his unparalleled knowledge of Shelley scholar-

3. See "Shelley, Hogg, and Elizabeth Shelley," *Shelley and his Circle*, II, 668; Shelley, *Letters*, I, vii.

ship, was able to include a sound and sane view of the matter in his *Shelley*, and by the great prestige which attaches to his authoritative work to establish a view which is likely to prevail over many irresponsible interpretations. Any proper opinion must be based upon a thorough knowledge of preceding events in Shelley's life, a minute acquaintance with the facts during January–April 1815, and an exact use of the contents of the letters themselves. Since the opinions of the present writer are substantially those of White, except for emphasis on certain details, an analysis of White on the subject is superfluous. Some other views may be mentioned, but with the clear understanding that, though they may be interesting, they are not based on deep, extensive, and unquestionable scholarship.

In his *Harriet and Mary* the editor, Walter S. Scott, finds Mary making love to a wary and reluctant Hogg because Hogg is stable, reliable, and financially sound, in contrast with Shelley's instability and poverty. Mary's motive was therefore to make it easier for them to tap the financial resources of Hogg, who was at the time their chief financial support. The fallacy of this view is that Hogg was not their chief financial support at this or any other time. He did help occasionally on small and pressing occasions, but in nothing more. Shelley was in daily negotiations for loans far beyond Hogg's means, and his prospects of opulence were far greater than Hogg's, especially after the death of his grandfather, Sir Bysshe Shelley, on January 6, 1815, when Mary's relations with Hogg were in a flourishing state. The sordid view which Scott takes fits neither the idealism of the Shelleys nor the condition of their finances or prospects.

The authors of *The Shelley Legend*[4] are inclined to think that Mary and Hogg were guilty of sexual intimacy. In keeping with their sensationalism and their usual incompetency in scholarship, they proceed by inference and innuendo. Since this book has been thoroughly discredited, its hinted but unproved conclusions can be disregarded.

Though neither her *Child of Light*[5] nor her edition of Mary's selected

4. Robert Metcalf Smith and others, *The Shelley Legend* (New York, 1945).
5. Muriel Spark, *Child of Light: A Reassessment of Mary Wollstonecraft Shelley* (Hadleigh, Essex, 1951).

letters[6] carries much weight, Muriel Spark has tried honestly to fathom the meaning of these letters. She is inclined to waver from one view to another. Her most original, but untenable, suggestion is that "Shelley's rapture over his son [Charles, born November 30, 1814] seems to have decidedly set in motion some workings of Mary's feelings in Hogg's favour; he amused and consoled her."[7] Miss Spark's most sensible observation is the following:

> But people seldom act from one motive alone; if they do they are said to be obsessed. Mary had no obsession about Hogg as a potential lover; nor about money; nor for absolute principles. More probable it is, that a mixture of all the opinions outlined above, represent the true state of Mary's motives. She felt bitter about Claire; she was in love with Shelley; they needed money; and Hogg appeared at a favourable time to offer financial assistance and amorous consolation. Mary, with Shelley's frank approval, gladly accepted the more harmless of Hogg's attentions and his much-needed money, meanwhile delaying indefinitely the physical culmination of the flirtation.[8]

So uncertain is Miss Spark, however, that at the last moment she added a footnote suggesting "the faint possibility" that these letters represent "a private joke between Shelley, Mary and Hogg."[9]

Ivan Roe's *Shelley*[10] is a well-written and interesting book. The author has chosen to look at Shelley directly with his own eyes and has many acute and original observations to make. These are helpful and stimulating to the Shelley scholar, but the book as a whole is a dangerous guide to the neophyte, being a curious mixture of truth, common sense, and error of fact and interpretation.

Mr. Roe's fantastic explanation of the Mary-Hogg affair springs from his curious solution to the mystery of *Julian and Maddalo*, which he regards as significantly autobiographical. The "crisis of 1818" between Shelley and Mary, as revealed obscurely in the Madman's tale in the poem, is, he thinks, attributable to the "bare broad words" which Mary addressed to Shelley, thereby causing "a kind of earthquake in Shelley's

6. *My Best Mary: Selected Letters of Mary Wollstonecraft Shelley*, eds. Muriel Spark and Derek Stanford (London, 1953).
7. Spark, *Child of Light*, p. 38.
8. *Ibid.*, pp. 40–41.
9. *Ibid.*, p. 43.
10. Ivan Roe, *Shelley: The Last Phase* (London, 1953).

[87]

spirit ... Mary told Shelley, in a moment of intense grief following Clara's death, and when William Shelley was the only link, 'the association' between them, that she had once taken another lover."[11] In searching for this lover, Mr. Roe lights upon Hogg and uses Mary's letters of early 1815 to him as evidence. The central and absolutely necessary fact in this interpretation of Mary's letters is the total ignorance of Shelley that Mary and Hogg were having a love affair. Mr. Roe even attempts to show that Shelley's views on love in 1815 were abhorrent to a sharing of Mary with Hogg or anyone else. The argument is pursued with considerable ingenuity, but with a perverse blindness to the transparent fact that Shelley knew from the beginning what was going on, and that he encouraged it! Mr. Roe continues by suggesting that William, born at Bishopsgate on January 24, 1816, was Hogg's child, and that this was part of the revelation by Mary in 1818 which caused "a kind of earthquake in Shelley's spirit." This theory is nothing less than a startling example of how a theory can induce complete blindness to the plainest facts. It is quite true that Mary was still "in love" with Hogg when William was conceived. Newman White had clearly recognized this fact and had truthfully written: "From early September 1815 to early May 1816, while the Shelleys were living at Bishopsgate, Hogg was a frequent visitor. But William Shelley was born during this period on January 24 — and it is quite clear from numerous references by Shelley and Mary that they entertained no doubt that Shelley was the father."[12]

What the present writer considers essential is as follows. Since reading Godwin's *Political Justice* in 1810, Shelley had been fully convinced that formal marriage was an evil social institution. He appears to have alarmed his beloved Harriet Grove by the expression of such a view, as well as other radical views on religious and political matters. At the same time he attempted to promote a free-love union between his dear friend Hogg and his favorite sister Elizabeth, who were personally unacquainted with each other. Elizabeth proved to be unalterably orthodox on this point, and Hogg was by no means averse to marriage if Elizabeth insisted.

11. *Ibid.*, p. 141.   12. White, *Shelley*, I, 401.

When Shelley eloped with Harriet Westbrook in August 1811 and married her in Edinburgh, his opinion was in no way changed, except that he now considered the times unripe for the practical application of a theory; the suffering inflicted upon the woman by society was out of proportion to the ultimate benefit to society resulting from her example. Hogg's love-making to Harriet at York was unquestionably a great shock to Shelley and a severe test of his principles. Though there may have been some self-deception involved, Shelley's principles came through the ordeal undamaged. "Your crime has been *selfishness*," Shelley wrote to Hogg in November 1811.[13] There was no fault in his loving Harriet, but in making Harriet miserable by attentions and demands which were distasteful to her. Hogg was the victim of sensation; he had lost the high virtue of disinterestedness. Shelley wrote again: "Assert yourself be what you were. love! adore! it will exalt your nature, bid you a Man be a god. Combine it if you will with sensation perhaps they are inseperable. be it so. but do not love one who *cannot* return it . . ."[14] In another letter he is even more explicit: "If it merely relates to me my friend you were welcome to even this the dearest [i.e., Harriet] . . . but we must not sport with the feelings of others."[15] In another letter Shelley states with perfect clarity what seems to be not only his final position on the Hogg-Harriet affair, but his lifelong position on such matters:

I am not jealous, I perfectly understand the beauty of Rousseau's sentiment; yet Harriet is *not* an Heloisa, even were I a St Preux — but I am not jealous . . . Heaven knows that if the possession of Harriet's person, or the attainment of her love was all that intervened ~~against~~ between our meeting again tomorrow, willingly would I return to York, aye willingly & be happy thus to prove my friendship. Jealousy has no place in my bosom, I am indeed at times very much inclined to think that the Godwinian plan is best. particularly since the late events . . . But Harriet does not think so. She is prejudiced; ~~and~~ tho I hope she will not always be so —— And on her opinions of right & wrong alone does the morality of the present case depend; If *she* was convinced of its innocence would I be so sottish a slave to opinion as to endeavor to monopolize what if participated wd. give my friend pleasure without diminishing my own . . .[16]

13. *Shelley and his Circle*, III, 41. 14. *Ibid.*, p. 54.
15. *Ibid.*, p. 45. 16. *Ibid.*, p. 57.

Mary Godwin to T. J. Hogg

Shelley's amazing correspondence with Elizabeth Hitchener as the sister of his soul and her subsequent brief experience as a member of his household, which now also contained Harriet's sister Eliza — all of this is perfectly consistent with Shelley's views on the ideal association of people who love one another and share all things in common. Shelley did not then, nor at any time later, advocate promiscuous sex life. Sexual relationship could be sanctioned only when the spiritual relationship of any two concerned extended itself naturally to such a relationship. Obviously, with Eliza and Miss Hitchener this was not the case.

Shelley's opinions with reference to free love remained substantially the same throughout the remainder of his life. *Epipsychidion* (1821) is in itself sufficient evidence of this; witness especially the famous passage:

> I never was attached to that great sect,
> Whose doctrine is, that each one should select
> Out of the crowd a mistress or a friend,
> And all the rest, though fair and wise, commend
> To cold oblivion, though it is in the code
> Of modern morals, and the beaten road
> Which those poor slaves with weary footsteps tread,
> Who travel to their home among the dead
> By the broad highway of the world, and so
> With one chained friend, perhaps a jealous foe,
> The dreariest and longest journey go.

The final lines of *Epipsychidion* bid his verses to haste

> Over the hearts of men, until ye meet
> Marina, Vanna, Primus, and the rest,
> And bid them love each other and be blessed:
> And leave the troop which errs, and which reproves,
> And come and be my guest, — for I am Love's.

It is impossible to lay too much emphasis upon Shelley's views on love and the relationship of the sexes, for it is in these firmly held and long-fixed views, and in these alone, that the Mary-Hogg affair of early 1815 can be satisfactorily explained. What Shelley ardently believed in 1811 and 1821, he believed and was willing to practice in 1815.

For reasons too well known to be repeated here, Shelley and Harriet became estranged. While in a highly disturbed state of mind, Shelley met Mary Godwin, who both physically and intellectually overwhelmed him: she was his ideal mate. A separation from Harriet by mutual agreement proving impossible, Shelley, in complete harmony with his principles, eloped with Mary on July 28, 1814. The famous letter of August 13 from Troyes, France, inviting Harriet to join them and to live happily in a household in which Mary would be his soul and physical mate and Harriet only a soul mate, is perfectly consistent with Shelley's opinions since 1810. Shelley's own words are:

I write to urge you to come to Switzerland, where you will at least find one firm & constant friend, to whom your interests will be always dear, by whom your feelings will never wilfully be injured . . . . You shall know our adventures more detailed, if I do not hear at Neufchatel, that I am soon to have the pleasure of communicating to you in person, & of welcoming you to some sweet retreat I will procure for you among the mountains.[17]

The months in London which followed Mary's and Shelley's return in September 1814 from the famous six weeks' tour to Switzerland were in some respects the most difficult of their lives. Abandoned by an angry Godwin, who nevertheless kept hounding Shelley for money, penniless themselves and actually separated for about two weeks in October because of the necessity of Shelley's avoiding arrest by pursuing bailiffs, shifting their lodgings frequently while Shelley haunted the moneylenders, they (usually with Claire) lived precariously.

But it would be a mistake to think that they were unhappy. Mary's Journal, occasionally written by Shelley, and the letters exchanged by Shelley and Mary while Shelley was hiding from the bailiffs, prove conclusively that their love was strong and their youthful spirits high. They continued to read voraciously (as they always did), especially Mary, who was pregnant and had to stay at home while Shelley and Claire were out most of the day either trying to raise money or looking for new lodgings. Moreover, Fanny Godwin visited them surreptitiously and Charles Clairmont more openly and kept them posted on the Skinner Street news.

More important is the fact that they formed a small social group of their own with the addition of Thomas Hookham, Peacock, and (later)

17. Shelley, *Letters*, I, 391–392.

Hogg. The conversations, reading, and chess games in the evenings were exciting occasions. Highly significant for our immediate purpose is a scheme which they devised and discussed enthusiastically for four days, September 30–October 3, as both Mary's and Claire's journals reveal to us. They talked of "converting and liberalizing two heiresses,"[18] Shelley's sisters Elizabeth and Hellen, who were near at hand at Mrs. Hugford's school. With Shelley's financial help Peacock was to marry his beloved Marianne de St. Croix, and the whole party — Shelley, Mary, Claire, Peacock and Marianne, Elizabeth and Hellen — would go (Mary called it a "running away scheme") to the west of Ireland and, obviously, set up a sort of ideal society of liberalized individuals. Hogg was not in on this plan, for he did not call on Shelley and Mary until November 14; but he was thought of at the time in that Shelley wrote him on October 4. At this time Shelley was by no means sure that Hogg would fit into his ideal group. Though the scheme quickly fell through, it is very important in proving conclusively that Shelley was still dreaming of illustrating by example that a group of liberalized people could live ideally.

Since Shelley and Harriet had left York suddenly in November 1811, and had exchanged letters with Hogg in November and December from Keswick, they had ceased all correspondence with him for a full year. In the spring of 1812 Hogg went to London to continue his law studies, entering the Middle Temple and serving a three-year apprenticeship under a "pleader," all of which he professed to dislike. His account of Shelley's sudden invasion of his quarters at ten o'clock one evening early in November 1812[19] is justly famous, though probably as inaccurate as his *Life of Shelley* usually is. This resumption of their friendship was limited mainly to an infrequent exchange of letters until the Shelleys took up residence in London in April 1813 for several months, and then at Bracknell. Again Hogg became a frequent and welcome visitor in the Shelleys' household; this time, however, there seems to have been between Harriet and Hogg nothing more than a cordial friendship. Though the evidence is not conclusive, it would appear that Shelley did not at this time give Hogg his unreserved friendship, though Hogg would

18. Mary Shelley, Journal, Sept. 30, 1814.   19. Hogg, *Shelley*, I, 364.

lead us to believe that he did. Certain it now is that Hogg was by no means well acquainted with the growing rift between Harriet and Shelley in the latter part of 1813 and first part of 1814 and of his love for and elopement with Mary Godwin in the summer. Shelley's long and extremely important letter to Hogg, written on October 4, 1814, and printed for the first time in 1944 in *Harriet and Mary*,[20] in which he gives a full account of his love for Mary and their illegal association, is ample proof that when these significant matters were in progress, Hogg knew nothing about them, that he was by no means Shelley's confidant. What view Hogg would take concerning Harriet or Mary, Shelley did not know. Convinced as he was of the rightness of his own conduct, Shelley was very naturally suspicious of his friend's views. Godwin, the Boinvilles, his family, and virtually every other friend had either renounced or neglected Shelley and Mary, and where Hogg stood now was still a question.

Because of his suspicions about Hogg's possible attitude, and because his finances and connection with Harriet and Godwin were more pressing matters, Shelley did not approach Hogg either in person or by letter after his elopement with Mary on July 28, 1814, until October, when he wrote him the important letter referred to above, in which he gives him an account of the situation which led to their elopement. Hogg's reply was received on October 17, the long interval being occasioned by Hogg's being on vacation at his father's estate at Norton.[21] Shelley first saw Hogg again on November 7, when they both "drank tea at Peacock's . . . very witty but Shelley says very cold" — so wrote Mary in her Journal.[22]

Under the circumstances of mutual suspicion and uncertainty it was natural that Shelley should decide that his intimacy with Hogg would depend upon whether Hogg liked Mary (and, in consequence, would take a tolerant view of Shelley's relationship with her). When Hogg called on November 14, as Shelley records in Mary's Journal, "He was pleased with Mary."[23] Mary was also pleased with Hogg, whom

---

20. See *New Shelley Letters*, pp. 75–79; Shelley, *Letters*, I, 401–403.
21. Mary Shelley, Journal, Oct. 17, 1814.
22. *Ibid.*, Nov. 8, 1814.   23. *Ibid.*, Nov. 14, 1814.

she saw for the first time, and her "illness disappears for a time."[24] Shelley was pleased, too, because "this was the test by which I had previously determined to judge his character."[25] Suspicions on both sides quickly disappeared, and from this time on Hogg was a constant visitor. He sometimes stayed overnight with the Shelleys, and when his vacation came on he was their inmate until it was concluded. He read with Mary, was often present while Shelley was away, and in fact seemed to be again a liberalized individual.

Since Shelley was so often from home, and Hogg was attentive, amusing, and useful, Mary apparently "fell in love" with him in the Shelleyan sense. Did not Shelley's principles not only tolerate such an affection but actually advocate its cultivation? It is beyond all question that Mary made known to Shelley her affection for Hogg, and that he approved it. Perfectly clear, too, is Mary's great love for Shelley at the same time. Indeed, it is Mary's belief that Shelley will be made happy by her ability to live ideally, free from all prejudice and false custom — it is this which seems to be her main purpose. It is possible, too, that Shelley recalled the Harriet-Hogg affair and had a suspicion that he had then not quite lived up to his own philosophy. He was, he had said, willing to share Harriet with Hogg if Harriet were willing, as she was not. Now that Mary was willing, how could he fail to live up to his principles?

Though unquestionably Mary and Hogg had "an affair," and though Mary evidently contemplated sexual connection with Hogg after her recovery from her approaching childbirth, a sound interpretation seems to be that the idea which was uppermost in Mary's mind all the while was a belief in Shelley's doctrine of free love and a willingness to demonstrate its validity as a practical mode of life.

The illusion did not last long. Just when it terminated is impossible to say because Mary's Journal for May 14, 1815, through July 20, 1816, is missing. But we can be fairly sure that it ended soon after Mary's last love letter to Hogg of April 26, 1815.[26] It is most unlikely that Hogg would have failed to preserve later letters in the series. Moreover, the Shelleys left London in June 1815 and never lived there again except for a few

24. *Ibid.* 25. *Ibid.*
26. Below, page 118.

brief periods and numerous visits, and these were mainly by Shelley without Mary. Hogg continued to see them at Bishopsgate and Marlow, but the early 1815 daily intimacy was never resumed. There seems to have been no definite break with Hogg, merely a gradual cooling. It is well known that Mary came fairly soon to dislike Hogg. On March 18, 1817, she wrote the Hunts from Marlow: "Hogg is at present a visitor of Peacock [who was living in Marlow]. I do not like him and I think he is more disagreeable than ever. I would not have him come every week to disturb our peace by his ill humour and noise for all the w[orld]."[27] This shows clearly that Mary's ill opinion of Hogg was already of long standing. Her attack upon Hogg in a letter to Leigh Hunt from Rome, April 6, 1819, is longer and more violent. She speaks of "his manners which when unrelieved by the presence of half a dozen people, always disgust me [and] make him as a constant daily – hourly visitor, which he insists upon being with us, absolutely intolerable —"[28] Nevertheless, throughout her life Mary felt a strong attachment for Hogg as Shelley's oldest and once dearest friend.

Finally, too much emphasis cannot be placed upon the youthfulness of everyone concerned: Mary was seventeen years of age, Claire sixteen, Shelley and Hogg twenty-two. Shelley never gave up his belief that people ought to live naturally and rationally together, but he did come to recognize the great practical difficulties involved.

27. Mary Shelley, *Letters*, I, 24.
28. *Ibid.*, p. 66.

SC 270 MARY GODWIN TO T. J. HOGG, JANUARY 1, 1815

AL signed *Mary*, 2½ pages. Double sheet, 4to (8.8 x 7.2 inches).
Laid paper. Watermark: [posthorn in crowned shield].
Seal: wafer, red.
Postmarks: 1. (receiving house stamp, London): Two Py Post| Unpaid| West Lambth|; 2. (delivery stamp, London): 7 o'clock| 1 JA| 1815 NT|.

PROVENANCE: Thomas Jefferson Hogg; Major R. J. Jefferson Hogg (Sotheby, June 30, 1948, lot 77).

January 1——1815

Dearest Hogg

             both
    As they have~~all~~ left me and I am here all alone I have nothing better to
5 *do than take up my pen and say a few words to you — as I do not expect you*
this morning.

    You love me you say — I wish I could return it with the passion you
deserve—but you are very good to me and tell me that you are quite happy
with the affection which from the bottom of my heart I feel for you—— you
10 *are so generous so disinterested that no one can help loving you But you know*
Hogg that we have ~~kw~~ known each other for so short a time and I did not think
about love——so that I think that <u>that</u> also will come in time & then we shall
be happier I do think than the angels who sing for ever or even the lovers of
Janes world of perfection. There is a bright prospect before us my dear
15 *friend — lovely — and — which renders it certain—wholly dependant on*
our selves —— for Shelley & myself I need promise nothing——~~to~~ nor to you
either for I know that ~~t~~ you are persuaded that I will use every effort to
promote your happiness & such is my affection for you that it will be no
hard task——

20   *But this is prattle—I tell you what you know so well already — besides*
you will be here this evening —— The sun shines it would be a fine day to
visit the divine Theoclea but I am not well enough—I was in great pain all
night & this morning & am but just getting better

                              Affectionately yours
25   *Mary*

You need not answer this scrall

[Address, page 4]

Thomas Jefferson Hogg Esq.
Arundel Street
34 Strand

line 1. *January 1:* the letters are progressively faint and the figure *1* which follows is barely legible; *——1815* is written with pen freshly dipped, the dash crowding the *1*.

line 5. *than:* *n* written through *t*.
line 7. *passion:* the first *s* written through *?j*.
line 15. *dependant* (sic)
line 26. *scrall* (sic)

THIS FIRST letter in the Mary-Hogg series written on Sunday, January 1, 1815, needs to be studied with great care. It clearly reveals several things: (1) that Hogg's declaration of love was very recent; (2) that Mary, though very fond of Hogg, was not yet sure that she really loved him, but found nothing objectionable in doing so if she could; (3) that Shelley was *already* acquainted with Hogg's declaration ("for Shelley & myself I need promise nothing"); and (4) that their happiness in love would have no disrupting influence of any kind in Mary's relationship with Shelley.

The situation is probably reflected in the cryptic entries of January 1–2 of Mary's Journal, which are as follows: "January 1st Sunday [*Shelley writing*] S & M. talk in the morning. A note & present from Hogg to the own Maie [Mary's pet name at this time] Charles [Clairmont] comes. Clara & S. walk to Hookham's Westminster Abbey & Mrs. Peacock's. Hogg comes in the evening. S goes to sleep. Monday 2nd [*Mary writing*] Write an answer —"[1]

In the light of Mary's letter to Hogg, these entries probably mean that Hogg declared his love for Mary in the note (accompanied by a present) received by Mary Sunday morning. She immediately communicated the situation to Shelley ("Shelley and Mary talk in the morning"), who expressed no opposition and possibly enthusiasm. When Claire and Shelley left for Hookham's, Mary began to "Write an answer" to Hogg, which must be this first letter of the series.

A difficulty arises here in that Mary's Journal entry for "Write an answer" is dated January 2, whereas the postmark on the letter proves that it was posted before seven p.m. on January 1. The answer to this dilemma is that Shelley wrote the entry for January 1, and when Mary wrote the entry for January 2 she wished to note having replied to Hogg's declaration of love, but did not take the trouble to indicate that she had written it the day before.

For the "divine Theoclea," see the next letter.

1. Mary Shelley, Journal. The word "Sunday" in the entry for January 1 was inserted by Mary; with the exception of this word, the entire entry for that day is in Shelley's hand.

SC 271   MARY GODWIN TO T. J. HOGG, JANUARY 4, 1815

AL signed *Mary*, 2 pages. Double sheet, 4to (8.7 x 7.1 inches).
Wove paper (coarse, light green).
Seal: wafer.

PROVENANCE: Thomas Jefferson Hogg; Major R. J. Jefferson Hogg (Sotheby,
June 30, 1948, lot 78).

> *January —1815*
> *Nelson Square*

My dearest Hogg

  I have been trifling away my time thinking it early when to my infinite
5 *astonishment I learn that it is past two —— It is useless to think of going*
to Theoclea today — but tomorrow will do as well ——

  Shelley & Jane are both gone out & from the number & distance of
the places that they are going to I do not expect them till very late — perhaps
you can come and console a solitary a lady in the mean time —— but I do
10 *not wish to make you a truant so do not come against your conscience.*

  You are so good & disinterrested a creature that I love you more &
more ——

  By the bye when Shelley is ł in the country we shall never be alone so
perhaps this is the last opportunity for a long time but still I do not wish
15 *to persuade you to do that which you ought not.*

  With one kiss Goodbye
>   *Affectionately yours —— Mary*
If you cannot come now perhaps you can come earlier this evening than usual

[Address, page 4]
T. J. Hogg Esq.
20 *——Hobroyd Esq—*
Gray's Inn

line 10. *conscience: s* appears to be written through *c*.

T HE DATE of this letter must be January 4 because Mary had not
yet seen Theoclea (mentioned on January 1) but expected to do
so on the morrow. Her Journal reads as follows for January 5: "Thursday

5th Go to breakfast at Hogg's — S. leaves us there, and goes to Humes —
When he returns ~~beg~~ we go to Newman Street—see the statue of Theoclea;
it is a divinity that raises your mind to ~~He~~ all virtue & excellence."

This letter shows that the affair was moving rapidly. Mary sends
her note by hand to Hogg's office, dares even to suggest (though cautiously) that Hogg might leave the office before the usual time, intimates
the pleasure of their being alone, and sends a kiss. Mary's insistence here
and elsewhere that Hogg is "disinter~~r~~ested" shows her very high opinion
of Hogg's liberal principles at this time. This quality Shelley had long
regarded as the most important; its possessor was guided solely by
rational principle, without the slightest intrusion of purely personal or
selfish interest.

SC 272 MARY GODWIN TO T. J. HOGG, JANUARY 7, 1815

AL signed *Mary*, 1 page. Single sheet, 4to (8.7 x 7 inches).
Wove paper (coarse, light green).
Seal: wafer, green.
Postmarks: 1. (receiving house stamp, London): Two Py Post| Unpaid| Gt
[?George] S^{t}|; 2. (delivery stamp, London): [   ] Clock| JA 7| 1815| N^{T}|.
Additions: 1. outer enclosure sheet: single sheet, 4to (8.6 x 7.1 inches), wove paper
(coarse, light green), wafer seal (green); 2. inner enclosure sheet: single sheet,
8vo (7.2 x 4.4), laid paper, posthorn in crowned shield (upper quarter) water-
mark; 3. lock of hair bound in three ringlets (in inner enclosure sheet).
PROVENANCE: Thomas Jefferson Hogg; Major R. J. Jefferson Hogg (Sotheby,
June 30, 1948, lot 80).

Dearest Hogg
    *I send you what you asked me for — I sincerely believe that we shall all
be so happy. My affection for you athough it is not now exactly as you would
wish will I think dayly become more so — then what can you have to add*
5 *to your happiness — I ask but for time — time which for other causes
beside this – phisical causes – that must be given — Shelley will be subject
to these also — & this dear Hogg will give time ~~to~~ for that love to spring up
which you ~~desever~~ deserve and will one day have*

[99]

All this – you know is sweet hope but we need not be prudent now –
10 *for I will try to make you happy & you say it is in my power*

Most affectionately yours

Mary

[Address, page 4]
T. Jefferson Hogg Esq-
Arundel Street–
15 *34 Strand*
[Inner enclosure sheet]
To Alexy from his
affectionate Mary

line 3. *happy: py* written through *py.*   line 9. *now: w* written through *t.*
  athough (sic)   line 11. *Most:* seal tear. *Mos* is visible on scrap
line 4. *dayly* (sic)   still attached to seal.
line 6. *phisical* (sic)
line 9. *need not: need* added (in left margin)
before *not.*

As MARY'S Journal shows, on the morning of January 6 she walked with Claire to Mrs. Peacock's house. From that place she sent Hogg the following note:[1]

43 Southampton Buildings

Dear Alexy

Will you come with me to Theoclea — I wait here at Mrs. Peacock's for your answer. By an advertisement in the paper we learn that this & tomorrow are the last days — will you not see that lovely creature again?

Yours very truly Mary.

I only ask you for the pleasure of your company, not because I want someone to go with me, so you refuse if you are busy.
[Address]
  Mr. Hogg Mr. Holroid Gray's Inn.

Hogg responded favorably, and Mary's Journal continues: "walk with Hogg to Theoclea — she is ten thousand times more beautiful

1. *New Shelley Letters*, pp. 81–82.

today than ever — tear ourselves away —." Hogg accompanied Mary to Nelson Square and returned again in the evening.

Since Shelley and Claire were attending one of Garnerin's scientific lectures and did not return until ten o'clock, Mary and Hogg had a goodly session alone. What time Hogg left is not stated, but there is some significance in Mary's January 6 notation in her Journal: "Talk with Shelley afterwards for some time — at length go to sleep S goes and sits in the other room till 5 [he was probably reading] — then call him — talk — S goes to ~~steep~~ sleep." There is some meaning to these periods of "talk," and in the extremely unusual fact that Shelley sat up until five a.m. and had finally to be called to bed.

Whatever these things may mean, it is certain that Hogg had on Friday, January 6, requested a lock of Mary's hair. On Saturday, January 7, Mary wrote the letter above and enclosed the lock — "what you asked me for" (line 2) — which still accompanies the manuscript and is a beautiful light gold.

The most significant thing about this letter, however, is Mary's intimation (the pronouns are very confusing) that Hogg may expect sexual intimacy if her love develops as she hopes it will. She needs time for further consideration; moreover, there are physical causes (her pregnancy) which will force abstinence, and which also apply to Shelley; luckily these two causes of delay are concurrent instead of existing separately. This is the only letter in the eleven which offers any clear proof that Mary contemplated sexual intimacy with Hogg.

SC 275   MARY GODWIN TO T. J. HOGG, JANUARY 23, 1815

AL signed *Mary*, 3 pages. Double sheet, 4to (8.8 x 7.2 inches).
Laid paper. Watermark: [posthorn in crowned shield].
Seal: wafer, red.
Postmarks: 1. (receiving house stamp, London): Two Py Po| Unpaid| Exet[er] S^t S[ ]|; 2. (delivery stamp, London): 7 o'Clock| 24 JA| 1815 N^T|.

PROVENANCE: Thomas Jefferson Hogg; Major R. J. Jefferson Hogg (Sotheby, June 30, 1948, lot 81).

Monday morning —
When you return to your lodgeings this evening dearest Alexy I hopes it will cheer your solitude to find this letter from me that you may read & kiss before you go to sleep ——.

My own *Alexy* I know how much & how tenderly you love me and I
rejoice to think that I am capable of constituting you happiness — We look
forward to joy & delight —— in the summer when the trees are green when the
suns brightly & joyfully when dearest Hogg I have my little baby with what
exquisite pleasure shall we pass the time — you are to teach me Italian you
10   know & how many books we will read together but our still greater happiness
will be in Shelley —— I who love him so tenderly & entirely whose life
hangs ~~of~~ on the beam of his eye and whose whole soul is entirely ~~wha~~ wrapt
up in him —— you ~~p~~ who have so sincere a friendship for him to ~~h~~ make
him happy —— no we need not try to do that for every thing we do will
15   make him that without exertion but to see him so — to see his love his tenderness dear dearest *Alexy* these are joys that fill your heart almost to bursting
& draw tears more delicious than the smiles of love from your eyes.
        When I think of all that we three in ea——————————
        Here have been called away for a couple of hours from finishing your
20   letter so I can not finish the sentence I began or say much more —— for when
the course of ~~ome~~ ones feelings ~~they will~~ is interrupted they will not run
rightl< > again besides now Shelley & Clar< > are talking beside me
which is not a very good accompaniment when one is writing a letter to one,
one loves
25   Goodnight then —— Good dreams to my *Alexy* —— *Mary*
[Address, page 4]
Thomas Jefferson Hogg Esq
34 Arundel Street
Strand

line 6. *you* (sic)
line 8. *suns brightly* (sic)
line 22. *rightl*<*y*>: tops of *t* and *l* visible above
seal tear.

line 22. *Clar*<*e*>: top of *a* and first stroke of
r visible on paper adhering to seal.

I F MARY's "Monday" (line 1) is not an error for "Tuesday," Hogg did
not receive this letter "this evening," for it is postmarked seven p.m.
January 24 (a Tuesday). The delay of a couple of hours referred to near
the end of the letter could not account for a twenty-four-hour delay.

This letter was written from 41 Hans Place, to which the Shelleys
and Claire had moved from Nelson Square, Lambeth, shortly after
January 7, a place further removed from Hogg's Arundel Street address
and requiring a three-instead of a two-penny postal fee. The exact
address we know from Shelley's letter of January 17 to Hayward.[1]
The change of lodging is explained by Mary's Journal entry for January
2: "Harriet sends her creditors here. nasty woman. now we must change
our lodgeings." On January 7, the Journal notes that Shelley and Claire
"take a long walk in search of a house." Two pages are missing from
Mary's Journal, leaving January 8–11, 15–27, and parts of the adjacent
days unaccounted for, so that it is impossible to determine the exact
day on which the move to 41 Hans Place occurred.

The eloquent second paragraph is unassailable proof that Mary's
chief purpose in loving Hogg was to please Shelley: "I who love him so
tenderly & entirely whose life hangs of on the beam of his eye and
whose whole soul is entirely wha wrapt up in him —— you p who have
so sincere a friendship for him to h make him happy . . ." What could be
clearer than this? They were both to make Shelley happy by proving how
people can live purely and rationally when they are free from false ideas
and social conventions.

1. Shelley, *Letters*, I, 423–424.

SC 278   MARY GODWIN TO T. J. HOGG, MARCH 2, 1815

AL signed *the Maïe*, 2 pages. Double sheet, 4to (8.9 x 7.2 inches).
Wove paper.
Embossed stamp: [?crown].
Seal: wafer, green.

PROVENANCE: Thomas Jefferson Hogg; Major R. J. Jefferson Hogg (Sotheby,
June 30, 1948, lot 82).

My own dear Hogg — you must come to us today in our new lodgeings —
for it is such a fine day that we have determined remove — for this is a very
horrid place and we are in great danger of arriving without any money for
the old woman is determined to fleece us —

5   *What a horrid man that Peacock is talking of nothing but greek letters*
and type —

I write in hurry for the sun is hastening away and I ought to journey
by its light

We shall see you tonight and soon always — which is a very happy
10   *thing*

Your most affectionately
the Maïe

Mal il soit qui mal il pense
bring my garters

[Address, page 4]

T. J. Hogg Esq
——Hobroyd Esq
Holborn Court
4
Grays Inn

line 1. *lodgeings* (sic)   line 2. *determined remove* (sic)

THIS letter was sent by hand to Hogg's office at Gray's Inn. It was written from 1 Hans Place on the very day the Shelleys moved to new lodgings at 13 Arabella Road, Pimlico. On Wednesday, February 8, Mary wrote in her Journal: "We are to move today, so Shelley and Clary go out to look for lodgeings. . . . S & C do not return till three— tha they do no have not succeeded & go out again—— they get apartments at 1 Hans Place —— move." This is, therefore, a second address in Hans Place, the move being from 41 Hans Place. Mary describes the removal to 13 Arabella Road on March 2 in her Journal: "A bustle of moving. . . . I and my baby go about 3— S & C do not come till six— Hogg comes in the evening."

The move on March 2 seems to have been instigated by a grasping landlady rather than the usual debt collectors. Moving was a rash action, for Mary's child was born prematurely on February 22 and was therefore only eight days old. Though Mary's labor was relatively easy, neither mother nor child should have been subjected to housemoving at this time, the more so in that, as Shelley wrote in Mary's Journal for February 22, "The child is not quite 7 months– The child not expected to live." The landlady probably made trouble for them because of the addition of a child to her house.

Mary's displeasure with Peacock's conversation arose from her boredom of the preceding evening. In her Journal for March 1 she wrote: "In the evening Peacock comes talk about types— editions greek letters all the evening— H comes they go away at ½11."

Mary's signature, "the Maië," is one of three pet names which Shelley and Hogg used for her at this time, Pecksie and Dormouse being the other two. "Maië" appears in Mary's Journal for the first time in the entry for January 1, 1815 (by Shelley). Hogg's pet name became "Alexy," derived from his recently published novel, *Memoirs of Prince Alexy Haimatoff* by "John Brown" (1813). This name first appears in the Journal entry for February 7, 1815 (again by Shelley). These pet names are in themselves indicative of the joint happiness of Mary, Shelley, and Hogg.

"Bring my garters" is both cryptic and provocative, as Mary herself knew. It is more likely that Mary had commissioned Hogg to buy her a pair of garters than that she had left a pair in his apartment.

SC 279 MARY GODWIN TO T. J. HOGG, MARCH 6, 1815

AL signed *Mary*, 1 page. Single sheet, 4to (8.9 x 7.3 inches).
Laid paper. Watermark: 1811.
Seal: wafer, brown.

PROVENANCE: Thomas Jefferson Hogg; Major R. J. Jefferson Hogg (Sotheby, June 30, 1948, lot 83).

*My dearest Hogg my baby is dead — will you come to me as soon as you
can — I wish to see you —— It was perfectly well when I went to bed ——
I awoke in the night to give it suck it appeared to < >e sleeping so quietly
that I would not awake it —— it was dead then but we did not find that out*
5 *till morning —— from its appearance it evidently died of convulsions ——*
   *Will you come — you are so calm a creature & Shelley is afraid of a
fever from the milk —— for I am no longer a mother now*

                                                          Mary

[Address, page 2]
T. J. Hogg Esq.
10 *——Hobroyd Esq.*
   Holborn Cout
   4 Grays Inn

line 3. <*b*>*e*: seal tear. The top of *b* and begin-   line 11. *Cout* (sic)
ning stroke of *e* are visible on paper adhering to
seal.

THIS is one of the most touching letters Mary ever wrote. Its utter simplicity and directness in a deeply pathetic situation are the finest qualities for true tragedy. Her Journal entry for March 6 is also very brief and brave: "Find my baby dead —————— Send for Hogg — talk—— a miserable day . . . H. sleeps here." The baby probably died, as so many infants have, of suffocation from phlegm in the throat.

There is no indication that this child ever had a name, nor as to its place of burial. When Mary notes in her Journal next day that "Shelley & Clary go after breakfast to town," she probably meant that they were attending to the burial. Mary felt the loss keenly. For some time she was greatly depressed. Though very little sentiment is permitted to enter her Journal, she gives way to her feelings occasionally. The most extended of her lamentations she wrote down a week later, on Monday, March 13: "Stay at ho< > home — net & think of my little dead baby this is foolish I suppose yet, when ever I am left alone to my own thoughts & do not read to divert them they always come back to the same point that I was a mother & am so no longer."

Mary summoned Fanny for comfort, but she apparently was not able to come for a week. When she did arrive on March 13, she was "wett through."[1]

In her state of nervous depression Mary began to insist that Claire should reside elsewhere. On Saturday, March 11, she wrote in her Journal: "Talk about Clary's going away nothing settled I fear it is hopeless she will not go to Skinner St. then our house is the only remaining place I see plainly — What is to be done?"[2] Claire was especially in the way since Hogg's holidays had begun on March 10 and he was residing with the Shelleys during their duration. Claire must certainly have been an alien factor which interfered with the ideal relationship of Shelley, Mary, and Hogg, which Mary was making such a valiant effort to realize. Claire was not got rid of until May 13, on which day Mary wrote in her Journal: "I begin a new journal with our regeneration."

1. Mary Shelley, Journal, March 13, 1815.

2. William Godwin lived at 41 Skinner Street; Claire had lived there until she went on the elopement trip with Shelley and Mary in late July 1814.

SC 280   P. B. SHELLEY TO T. J. HOGG, MARCH 7–MAY 12, 1815

AL (in pencil) signed *PBS.*, 1 page. Double sheet, 8vo (7.4 x 4.5 inches).
Laid paper. Watermark: PICKFORD

PROVENANCE: Thomas Jefferson Hogg; Major R. J. Jefferson Hogg (Sotheby,
June 30, 1948, lot 53).

My dear friend
        Mary wished to speak with you alone, for which purpose I have gone
out & removed ~~her~~ Clare.
        If you should return, before this evening & are at leisure I need not
5 *direct your steps —*

                                        Affectionately Yours
                                              PBS.

[Address, page 4]
T. Jefferson Hogg Esqr

line 3. ~~her~~ *Clare:* one loop of the *C* of *Clare*
runs completely through *her* and is apparently
intended to cancel it.

T HAT the above letter belongs to the period of the Mary Godwin–
        T. J. Hogg correspondence of 1815 is indicated by its content. As
it is written in pencil, is unsealed, and bears neither address nor postmark, it was probably written at a time when Hogg was living in the
household with Shelley, Claire, and Mary, and was left for him there.
And this is indicated by the contents also: it was apparently written
early in the day; it says nothing about Hogg's coming to visit them
but only about his returning; Shelley and Claire have "gone out."

The indication is that the note was left for Hogg to see when he got up in the morning; he would find Shelley and Claire gone; Mary wanted to speak to him alone (perhaps as part of a scheme to get rid of Claire).

If this hypothesis holds we can narrow the date range to March 7–May 12, 1815. On March 6 Mary sent for Hogg; her Journal records that he stayed overnight; from March 9 to April 17 (as the Journal also tells us), Hogg lived in the household. From April 17 to May 12 he appears to have stayed overnight from time to time. Early in the day on May 13 Claire left for Devon.[1]

Why, however, did Shelley need to write a note at all? If Hogg and Mary were left alone in the house one might expect that Mary would simply have told Hogg that she wished to talk to him. The answer may be that Mary was not well and was staying in bed and so could not herself summon Hogg. The note then was perhaps written on the morning of a day when (a) Mary was not feeling well, (b) Claire and Shelley had left in the morning, and (c) Hogg was in the house. As some pages are torn out of the Journal it is not possible to pick out a specific date with any certainty, but we might note that March 7 (the day following the death of Mary's baby) fits these conditions:

Tuesday 7 Write to Fanny Shelley & Clary go after breakfast to town —— Hogg stays all day with us — talk with him & read the fall of the Jesuits & Rinaldo Rinaldini — not in good spirits — H. goes at 11. ———— a fuss. ·—— to bed at 3[2]

---

1. Mary Shelley, Journal, March 6; March 9 through April 17; April 18; May 6; May 13. Some leaves are missing between March 29 and April 6, April 11 and 14, April 24 and May 4.

2. F. L. Jones (Shelley, *Letters*, I, 423) dates the letter "[Nelson Square, ?1 January 1815]" but gives no reason for doing so.

                                                                    K.N.C.

SC 285   P. B. SHELLEY TO T. J. HOGG, APRIL 24, 1815

AL (fragment) unsigned, ¼ page. Single sheet, 4ᵗᵒ (9 x 7.2 inches), also contain-
ing SC 286.
Laid paper. Watermark: [posthorn in crowned shield, upper part].
PROVENANCE: Thomas Jefferson Hogg; Major R. J. Jefferson Hogg (Sotheby,
June 30, 1948, lot 84).

My dear friend
        We shall be absent from London one day & one

MARY Shelley's Journal entry for April 23, 1815, gives no hint of
leaving London, and the entries from April 24 into May 4 are
torn out. SC 287 is dated April 25 from the village of Salt Hill (later
named Slough); it records receiving "letters" from Hogg (probably one
to Mary and one to Shelley). Mary and Shelley, then, must have left
London suddenly on April 24 for Salt Hill.

As the above fragmentary letter was written on the same manuscript
as Mary's letter informing Hogg that they were leaving London and as
it was intended to convey the same message, it can be safely dated
April 24, 1815. That it was written earlier than Mary's letter is shown
by the fact that Mary writes around it. Apparently what happened was
that Shelley began to write a letter informing Hogg that they would be
gone for one day and one night, then broke off and Mary took over.

Shelley began to write on a single (unfolded) quarto sheet. That he
intended to write only a short note is shown by the fact that he began
about one quarter of the way down the page. Then Mary took the sheet
and folded it so that Shelley's writing came on the inside (page 2). She
began on page 1 and then continued on page 3, ended the letter on page 3,

addressed it, made a notation, then had some afterthoughts and put them on page 2. The last two words of her first sentence were "Salt Hill." "Salt" came at the end of line three; line four was occupied by Shelley's "My dear friend," so Mary placed "Hill" after "friend."[1]

1. This placement has resulted in a curious error. In Frederick L. Jones's edition of Shelley's letters, letter number 286 is headed to "Mr. Hill, London," and the complete letter is given as follows:

> My dear friend Hill —
> We shall be absent from London one day & our.

There is, of course, no such "Mr. Hill" (and *our* should read *one*). Professor Jones failed to note that the word *Hill* was in Mary's hand and referred to Salt Hill, an error which is all the more strange as he gives the reading of Mary's letter correctly in editing it for the present text (first published in *Shelley and his Circle*), and this editing was done several years prior to the publication of his edition of Shelley's letters. When we turn to the index of Professor Jones's edition of Shelley's letters we find: "Hill, Mr.: S's letter to, i. 425; tells Godwin Harriet was unfaithful to S., i. 528n." The Hill who was supposed to have told the story about Harriet was Thomas Hill, part owner of *The Monthly Mirror*. Professor Jones' error must have arisen from a misreading of the above manuscript, of which he had a photostat.

K.N.C.

SC 286 MARY GODWIN TO T. J. HOGG, APRIL 24, 1815

AL signed *The Pecksey Dor to answer for*, 3¼ pages. Double sheet, 8vo (7.2 x 4.5 inches), also containing SC 285.
Laid paper. Watermark: [posthorn in crowned shield, upper part].

PROVENANCE: Thomas Jefferson Hogg; Major R. J. Jefferson Hogg (Sotheby, June 30, 1948, lot 84).

Dear Jefferson
I am not hardhearted but Clary will explain to you how we are obliged
to go away — you will perceive that it was indispensable
We shall return tomorrow night or the next morning so dear Jefferson
5 *do not think very hard of the p<   > Pecksey who would not for all the world*
make you uncomfortable for a moment if she could help it. ——
Clary says that she will not ge get lodgings so will you —— but she will
of course alter her mind — dear Jefferson love me all the time as I do you
Affectionately yours
The Pecksey Dor to answer for
10

*We shall be very very glad to see you tomorrow evening if you can spare time
at Salt Hill —*

    *I will write however & you must go to A. Row for the letter as I shall
send it by coach you must not tell Clare of the invitation*

15 ~~*you can*~~ *write directly as C. shall direct*

[Address, page 4]

Jefferson ————

line 5. *p* < *?oor* > : seal adhesion

      would: the bottom of *ld* visible below seal
adhesion.

line 11. Lines 11–14 are written vertical to the
text; line 15 is written on the address page,
upside down to the text.

M ARY's Journal shows how she kept herself busy studying Latin and
reading books, and how her activities abroad increased con-
siderably. Thus she gradually recovered from the sorrow of losing her
first baby. By the time of the sudden and brief trip (April 24–26) to Salt
Hill, she was happier and more playful than she had been since her
pregnancy began.

    The Salt Hill expedition was doubtless occasioned by the necessity
to change lodgings again in order to escape creditors. Since going into
the country was not absolutely required, the decision to ruralize for a day
(their original intention) must have been a whim to have a short holiday.
Certainly Mary's delight in green fields and fresh air is very sincere and
infectious. Their lingering through two more days beyond the one
initially planned shows how deep was Mary's need to get away from
narrow rooms and streets and crowded buildings and people.

    It is obvious that Claire delivered this letter by hand, and obvious
too that, though Hogg was welcome to follow them to Salt Hill, the
vacation from Claire was as desirable as rural beauties.

    (For the uncanceled beginning of a letter by Shelley on page 2,
see above, page 110. "A. Row" refers to Hogg's lodgings at 34 Arundel
Street.)

SC 287 MARY GODWIN TO T. J. HOGG, APRIL 25, 1815

AL signed *Your affectionate Dormouse* ————, 3¼ pages. Double sheet, 4to
(8.9 x 7.2 inches).

[112]

Laid paper. Watermark: J WHATMAN| 1811|. Gilt edges.
Seal: wafer.

PROVENANCE: Thomas Jefferson Hogg; Major R. J. Jefferson Hogg (Sotheby, June 30, 1948, lot 85).

> *Windmill Inn — Salt Hill*
> *April 25 – 1815 ——*

Dear Jefferson

It would have required more than mortal fortitude (and such the Pecksie
5　*does not boast of) to have resisted the sight of Green fields and yew trees &*
have jogged up to London again — When your letters arrived Shelley's
distitch ~~would~~ was truly applicable

> *On her hind paws the Dormouse stood*
> *In a wild & mingled mood*
10　> *Of Maïeishness & Pecksietude*

Would it be treating you ill & would it be too much expence Shelley said that
it would not be too much expence I said that you would not be angry with a
dormouse who had escaped from her London Cage to green fields & acorns —
dear Jefferson I am sure that you are not so selfish (pardon the word) as to be
15　*very very ~~sory~~ sorry.*

Well here am I sitting in a parlour of the Windmill Inn seeing the little
~~pails~~ white pales of the garden before where the yew & Cypress flourishes in
great abundance after I have written to you & Clary I mean to construe
some Ovid & to be very industrious.

20　*What a shocking place London is how truly I hate it Would that I were*
never to enter ~~t~~ it again – dear Jefferson do give up the Law and come down
& pass your days here — ay at the Windmill Inn if you please I am sure
that it's a better place than the Inns of Court.

Now notwithstanding your ill humour which would not allow you to
25　*write to me yesterday night — I expect a very long letter tomorrow & a very*
kind forgiving one ~~two~~ₐor I never will speak to you again.

Well Jefferson take care of yourself and be good —— the Pecksie will
soon be back all the better for her dormouseish jaunt & remember nothing
30　*take away from my Maïeishness*

[113]

> For Maië girls are Maië girls
>   Wherever they're found
> In air or in water
>   Or In the ground

35   *Now think of me very kindly while I am away & receive me kindly*
when I come back or I will be no more
    Your affectionate Dormouse ———

———

I will write again in the evening or early tomorrow & tell you all the sights
that I have seen
[Address, page 4]
40 *Jefferson Hogg Esq.*
34   arrundel Street
Strand

line 4. *than: n* written through *t*.
line 7. *distitch* (sic)
line 10. *Maiëishness: n* written through *?u*.
line 12. *expence* is the last word on the line, and

Mary, like Shelley, uses this placement as a kind of punctuation.
line 23. *place: l* written through *?a*.
line 41. *arrundel* (sic): *Arundel*.

THIS letter was written on the morning of April 25. Besides its extraordinary playfulness and delight in the rural scene, it contains a passage (lines 11–15) which, though by no means clear, lends some support to the (certainly exaggerated) opinion of W. S. Scott that the Shelleys were at this time finding Hogg financially useful. Mary does seem to mean that the prolongation of their stay at Salt Hill involves an expense to which Hogg may object, and how could Hogg object if his funds were unaffected? In her letter of April 26 (sc 290) Mary very frankly asked Hogg for money: "I wish if there is time that you would send us some money as I do not think we shall have quite enough."

There can be no doubt that during these very trying months when Shelley spent day after day among the moneylenders and solicitors and had to move often to keep from being arrested for debt, Hogg must have saved them more than once from some small financial embarrassment. But it is ridiculous to suppose that the Shelleys sponged on him for any

considerable portion of their needs. That he should be permitted to
assume some obligations where Mary was concerned was a natural thing
with Shelley, who believed that friends should have everything in
common. This would be especially so now that Mary and Hogg were
recognized as "lovers." Shelley's grandfather Sir Bysshe Shelley had
died on January 6, and it was now only a matter of time until Shelley's
finances would be in a prosperous state.

SC 288   MARY GODWIN TO T. J. HOGG, APRIL 25, 1815

AL signed *Runaway Dormouse*, 3 pages. Double sheet, 4to (8.9 x 7.2 inches).
Laid paper. Watermark: J WHATMAN| 1811|.
Seal: wafer, green.
Postmarks: 1. (local Penny Post stamp, Colnbrook): COLNBROOK| Penn[y Post]|;
2. (evening duty stamp, London): B| 26 AP 26| 1815|.

PROVENANCE: Thomas Jefferson Hogg; Major R. J. Jefferson Hogg (Sotheby,
June 30, 1948, lot 86).

My dear Jefferson
I am no doubt a very naughty dormouse ⤳ *but indeed you must*
forgive me — Shelley is now returned — he went to Longdills — did his
business & returned he heard from Harriets attorney that she meant (if
5 *he did not make a handsome settlement on her) to prosecute him for athe-*
ism.——
How are you amusing yourself with the Pecksie away very doleful
no doubt but my poor Jefferson I̶ ̶d̶ shall soon be up again & you may
remember that even if we had staid you would not have seen much of me as
10 *you must have been with me ———*
Do you mean to come down to us — I suppose not Prince Prudent well
as you please but remember I should be very happy to see you. If you had
not been a lawyer you might have come with us ———
Rain has come after a mild beautiful day but Shelley & I are going to
15 *walk as it is only showery*
How delightful it is to read Poetry among green shades Tintern Abbey
thrilled me with delight ———
But Shelley calls me to come for

>   *The sun it is set*
20   *And night is coming*
> *I will write perhaps by a night coach or at least early tomorrow* ——
> *I shall return soon & remain till then an affectionate but*
>   *Runaway Dormouse*

[Address, page 4]

~~Mr~~ *Jefferson Hogg Esq*

25 *Arrundel Street*

34

Strand

line 2. *dormouse:* drawing in manuscript.   line 18. *calls: s* written through *?es.*
line 7. *the: t* written through *?C.*   line 25. *Arrundel* (sic): *Arundel*

THIS letter was written late on April 25. It enclosed the preceding letter (sc 287) written on the morning of the same day, and was posted on the morning of the 26th.

Mary had been alone most of the day, Shelley having gone to London early and returned late. But Mary had been very happy wandering "among green shades" and reading, most appropriately, Wordsworth's "Lines Written a Few Miles Above Tintern Abbey." Her letter shows a trifling irritation with Hogg for not writing and not following her to Salt Hill. In her morning letter she had hinted lightly that Hogg might be "selfish"; now she impudently calls him "Prince Prudent," a name which probably was not intended to carry any moral implications but to apply only to business. It is evident, however, that Mary was beginning to suspect those qualities in Hogg which later were glaring.

P. W. Longdill was Shelley's solicitor; he was busy negotiating with Sir Timothy's solicitor, William Whitton, in an attempt to settle various matters involving the Shelley estates incident to the death of Sir Bysshe Shelley.

Enclosed with Mary's morning and evening letters was a brief and highly significant note from Shelley to Hogg, written on the morning of April 26, though not dated by Shelley. This note is also in The Carl H. Pforzheimer Library and is printed below (sc 289). Anticipating their return to London the next day, Shelley begins: "I shall be very happy to see you again, & to give you your share of our common treasure of which you have been cheated for several days." His next sentence is not at all clear or grammatical, but its humorously intended meaning is apparently this: Hogg loves Mary so much that Shelley has to take her into the country occasionally in order to get his share of her. Shelley goes on to say: "Do not fear. ~~A few months~~ We will not again be deprived of this participated pleasure." There is nothing here to prove that Shelley meant to include sexual relationship between Mary and Hogg, or that this had already occurred. Quite certain it is, however, that Shelley's principles allowed this, Mary being willing, and that since the birth of her child on February 22 Mary's "phisical reasons" had vanished.

(The local Penny Post stamp on the above letter is interesting. At first the Penny Post was restricted to London; then it opened to larger towns such as Manchester and Liverpool; after 1808 it was extended to villages, but no village Penny Post stamps have been found earlier than 1812. Prior to this extension of the Penny Post system, the above letter would have gone only through the Inland Mail system and had only a mileage stamp from Colnbrook, plus the regular London evening duty stamp, indicating that it had arrived in London. Colnbrook was a village four miles on the road to London from Salt Hill, itself twenty-one miles from London. The letter was mailed at Colnbrook and one penny paid to the local post office; then it was put in with the regular Inland Mail and delivered to London — where Hogg paid 1s.7d. for it as the postal fee shows. K.N.C.)

SC 289   P. B. SHELLEY TO T. J. HOGG, APRIL 26, 1815

AL signed *P B Shelley.*, 1 page. Single sheet, 4to (8.9 x 7.3 inches). Laid paper. Watermark: J WHATMAN|.

PROVENANCE: Thomas Jefferson Hogg; Major R. J. Jefferson Hogg (Sotheby, June 30, 1948, lot 61).

My dear friend

         I shall be very happy to see you again, & to give you your share of our common treasure of which you have been cheated for several

days. The Maie knows how highly you prize this exquisite possession,
5 *& takes occasion to quiz you in saying that it is necessary for me to absent*
from London, from your sensibility to its value. Do not fear. A few months
We will not again be deprived of this participated pleasure.——

    I did all the requisite acts at Longdill's yesterday at one o'Clock &
returned immediately to the Pecksie. I could not persuade her to come to
10 *London.*

                                       Very affectionately yours
                                           P B Shelley.

[Address, in Mary Godwin's hand, page 2]
Mr Tom. Hogg.

line 5. *to absent* (sic)

SC 290 MARY GODWIN TO T. J. HOGG, APRIL 26, 1815

AL signed *A Runaway Dormouse*, 3½ pages. Double sheet, 4to (8.9 x 7.2 inches). Laid paper. Watermark: J WHATMAN| 1814|.
Seal: wafer, green.

PROVENANCE: Thomas Jefferson Hogg; Major R. J. Jefferson Hogg (Sotheby, June 30, 1948, lot 87).

                                 Windmill Inn
                                 Salt Hill
                                 April 26th 1815

Dear Jefferson
5   *You must not go to courts very early tomorrow as it is most likely we*
shall be with you about nine — We shall try to get a place in the mail which
comes into London about seven so you must rise early to receive the Dormouse
           from
all fresh grubbing under the oaks.

10   *But you must know that I think it very dangerous for Shelley to remain*
in London — the Bailiffs know Longdill to be his attorney and of course will
place spies there and indeed what part of London can he walk about free
in — none I fear. — Have you not thought of this & what do you think of
it now — but more of this when we meet.

The Dormouse is going to take a long ramble to day among green fields
& solitary lanes as happy as any little animal could be in finding herself
in her native nests again — I shudder to think of breathing the air of London
again —— Jefferson Jefferson it is your duty not keep any creature away
from its home so come — I shall expect you tonight and if you do not come
20 *I am off — not for London I promise you ——*

But dear Jefferson all things considered the danger of Shelley remaining
in London and my hatred of it do you not think that you ought to come to
Salt Hill <u>incontinently</u> —— Remember I shall believe that your love is
all a farce if you do not — so I expect you Adieu—— though he is but
25 *a bad sort of a personage yet he is good enough for you <u>adieu</u> therefore*

Yours — as we shall see when we know how you behave

A Runaway Dormouse

you have not chosen to write to me very well I know by this what you are
good for

30 *I wish if there is time that you would send us some money as I do not think*
we shall have quite enough

[Address, page 4]

Jefferson Hogg Esq.

Arrundel Street

34

35 *Strand*

---

line 3. *1815: 5* written through *4.*

line 18. *not keep* (sic)

line 22. *and:* seal tear; *a* on paper adhering to seal.

line 28. *write:* seal tear; *w* on paper adhering to seal.

       you are: seal tear; *ou* on paper adhering

to seal. Lines 28–29 are written along the right-hand edge of page 4.

line 30. Lines 30–31 are also written on page 4, upside down to the general direction of the page; they were perhaps written after the letter was folded but before it was sealed.

THIS letter, the last of the famous Mary-Hogg "love" letters, shows that the delightful excursion to Salt Hill, Mary's first fling in the country for many months, came to an end when she and Shelley took a seven o'clock morning coach back to London on April 27, 1815.

Where they took lodgings in London does not appear, Mary's Journal entries being missing at this point. The remaining entries for May 4–6 and 8–13 show clearly, however, that the same daily intimacy with Hogg continued for some time, and that when Claire finally left them on May 13, Mary was greatly pleased. It can hardly be doubted that part of her satisfaction arose from the thought that then she, Shelley, and Hogg could live ideally. The volume of Mary's Journal for May 14, 1815, through July 20, 1816, is lost, as is all other exact evidence as to the duration of the affair with Hogg. It probably ended normally through a gradual and mutual decline of interest in the arrangement, and could hardly have survived the long separation which began in June 1815. Shelley's affairs with his father had finally been settled on May 13, and the first quarter of his newly established £1,000 annuity was paid on June 24. In June Shelley and Mary toured the southern coast of Devon. In August they took a house at Bishopsgate (the eastern entrance to Windsor Great Park).

Rightly interpreted, the Mary-Hogg affair tells us much that is important about Shelley. It occurred with his full knowledge and consent, and all the evidence available indicates that he viewed the whole situation with great satisfaction. That in this respect Shelley differed fundamentally from the average man is very evident. Certain it is that he was following principles which he had long ago adopted and which he never afterwards relinquished.

THOMAS LOVE PEACOCK

(October 18, 1785–January 23, 1866)

PRINCIPAL WORKS

LIFE

THOMAS LOVE PEACOCK, only child of a London glass merchant and the daughter of a Master of the Royal Navy, was born at Weymouth in Dorsetshire of parents no longer very young. Of his father, Samuel Peacock, very little is known; from a daybook which came down in the family it is clear that he was in business as early as 1768, and by 1778 he was listed in *Kent's Directory* as operator of a glass warehouse at Holborn Bridge, a listing continued in *Kent's Directory* for 1781, which included a number of other glass merchants and manufacturers of the same name.[1] *Bailey's British Directory* for 1784 listed Samuel Peacock in partnership with one Thomas Peacock at "No. 46 Holborn-bridge" but by 1790 this firm was in the hands of Thomas and George Peacock and there was no listing at all for Samuel Peacock.[2] Family tradition as reported by Thomas Love Peacock's granddaughter in her "Biographical Notice" of 1875 had it that Samuel Peacock died before 1788, when his

1. Van Doren, *Peacock*, pp. 1–2. Peacock's mother, Sarah Love Peacock, was born in Devonshire on November 10, 1754 (Peacock, *Works*, I, xviii, and VIII, 439). On the daybook see *Works*, VII, 527–528.

2. *The Universal British Directory of Trade and Commerce* for 1790 lists George Peacock as partner of Thomas and locates their firm of glass manufacturers at 46 Fleet Market, a number at the head of the street next, or very near, to the site of Holborn Bridge. This partnership appears in *Andrews London Directory* for 1793 and *Lowndes London Directory* for 1794. H. F. B. Brett-Smith and C. E. Jones report a listing for Samuel as late as 1794 (Peacock, *Works*, I, xiv) which we have been unable to confirm. (The directories cited above were consulted at The Guildhall Library, London.)

wife and child left London for the Thames-side village of Chertsey.[3]
We know from a reference to his father in Peacock's first letter to his
mother, in August 1792, that Samuel Peacock was then still alive, but
we have no further information about him nor any clue as to why his
wife moved away from London with her little boy; both Sarah Love
Peacock and her son were extremely reticent about personal and family
matters.[4] The child was later to have direct experience of the world of
London merchants in which his father had lived — and to write of it
satirically — but his traditional loyalties and his interests stemmed from
the seafaring men of his mother's family.

From 1788 until past the turn of the century the dominant male
influence in Peacock's life was his grandfather, Thomas Love, a Devonshire man who had been a Master in the Royal Navy until he was
wounded in action and retired. With his wife he had settled at Chertsey
in Surrey where his eldest daughter, Mrs. Peacock, joined him with her
young son of three years. The boy delighted in his grandfather's stories
of battles in the West Indies during the 1770's and 1780's and learned to
share his grandfather's excitement over the victories of the English forces
in the later wars against the French, at the turn of the century. His
enthusiasm is illustrated by the elegiac lines he turned out in the summer of 1801 "On the Death of Sir Ralph Abercromby" and in the verse
letter he wrote to his grandfather from London after the victory of the
English off Algeciras against the combined French and Spanish fleets.
One of Peacock's uncles, Thomas Love, Jr., was also a Master; a younger
uncle and a cousin became commissioned officers.[5] It has not been empha-

3. Edith Nicolls, "A Biographical Notice of Thomas Love Peacock," Peacock, *Works* (1875), I, xxv.

4. Peacock wrote very few private letters and seldom talked with his own family about his personal
affairs, having — his granddaughter recalled — "the greatest aversion" to this activity. Consequently Edith Nicolls (later Mrs. Clarke) had often to rely on family traditions for her "Biographical
Notice." (Peacock, *Works*, 1875, I, li; and H. F. B. Brett-Smith, "The L'Estrange-Peacock Correspondence," *Essays and Studies by Members of the English Association*, 1932, XVIII, 122–148.)
While she was sometimes led into minor errors, there is almost always a core of truth in her accounts.
Thus, even though Samuel Peacock did not die in 1788, this date marks his separation from his wife
and child. When Peacock's friends became the object of reminiscence he protested vigorously to his
cousin Harriet Love "against this system of biographical gossip," and in his *Memoirs of Shelley*
against "the old village scandal on a larger scale. . . . No man is bound . . . to tell the public all
he knows." (Peacock, *Works*, VIII, 249 and 39–40.)

5. See obituary notice of Thomas Love in *The Gentleman's Magazine*, LXXV (December 1805),
ii, 1239. This was first mentioned by Van Doren (see *Peacock*, p. 32, fn. 2).

sized sufficiently that as a boy growing up in this atmosphere of ships and sailing, Peacock listened to technical discussions as well as rollicking songs and salty talk.[6] That the seafaring Loves influenced some of the characterizations in Peacock's novels has long been known (for example, Captain Hawltaught of *Melincourt* was modeled on old Thomas Love). But the Loves had as deep and lasting an effect on Peacock's other career, at the East India House, where he became deeply concerned with ship design.

In the latter part of 1791, near his sixth birthday, Thomas Love Peacock went to school. His earliest memories were of the countryside around Chertsey, and his sojourn at Englefield House School simply extended the area of his acquaintance westward to the edge of Windsor Great Park, Englefield Green lying between Egham and Windsor. Here, by his own account, he remained six and a half years.[7] One of his school friends, Charles Barwell, also lived at Chertsey, in an old mansion built on the site of the Chertsey Priory and called the Abbey House. In his middle years, when he turned back, in a series of brief sketches based on memories of his childhood, Peacock recalled this first close friendship:

> Charles was fond of romances. The *Mysteries of Udolpho*, and all the ghost and goblin stories of the day, were his familiar reading. I cared little about them at that time; but he amused me by narrating their grimmest passages. He was very anxious that the Abbey House should be haunted; but it had no strange sights or sounds, and no plausible tradition to hang a ghost on. [Seeing, one summer evening, what he thought might serve for a ghost, the younger boy alerted the Barwell household.] . . . At last, the master of the house leading the way, we marched in a body to the spot, and unravelled the mystery. It was a large bunch of flowers on the top of a tall lily, waving in the wind at the edge of the grove, and disappearing at intervals behind the stem of a tree. My ghost, and the compact phalanx in which we sallied against it, were long the subject

6. G. A. R. Callender, *The Story of H. M. S. "Victory"* (London, 1929), noted that "the master was primarily responsible, under the captain, for the sailing of the ship. All that is comprehended in the word navigation was his province. . . . The master's technical knowledge was amazing, even to the sailor-men" (pp. 53–54).

7. T. L. Peacock to Thomas L'Estrange, June 23, 1862, Peacock, *Works*, VIII, 259; see also Peacock to L'Estrange, *ibid.*, pp. 254–255, and "The Last Day of Windsor Forest," pp. 145–154, for Peacock's reminiscences of the area he roamed in during his Englefield days. (The manuscript of "Windsor Forest" is in The Carl H. Pforzheimer Library.)

of merriment. It was a cruel disappointment to Charles, who was obliged to abandon all hopes of having the house haunted.[8]

In this we sense the beginning of that amused skepticism which was characteristic of the older Peacock; "One thinks," commented Carl Van Doren, "of a later friendship of Peacock's, when the unearthly spirit of Shelley found so congenial this caustic analyst of mystery."[9]

Young Charles Barwell was a descendant of William Barwell (1705–1769), a former East India Governor and a member of a family long intimately connected with the East India Company;[10] this association is thus the first of a series pointing toward Peacock's later employment at East India House, and it may well have been the direct link with Peter Auber (through whom, in 1818, Peacock got his position).[11]

Before his thirteenth birthday, which fell in October 1798, Peacock left school. About a year later he was at work in London as a clerk for Ludlow, Fraser & Co., merchants, on whose premises at 4 Angel Court, Throgmorton Street, he lived with his mother for some five or six years.[12]

8. "Recollections of Childhood: The Abbey House," *ibid.*, pp. 33–35. This essay was first published in *Bentley's Miscellany* (February 1837) and is one of several articles of reminiscence Peacock wrote in his middle years.

9. Van Doren, *Peacock*, p. 9.

10. William Barwell's second son, Richard (1741–1804), became a member of the Council-General under Warren Hastings; his fourth son, Roger, was a Writer on the Bengal Establishment. Peacock did not fully identify his friend Charles, and it was Van Doren who first connected him with the prominent Anglo-Indian family, evidently on the basis of property records, calling him the son of "a Roger Barwell, son to a former official of the India Company" (*Peacock*, p. 8). William Barwell, the former governor, had bought the Abbey House in 1751 and had left it on his death to his son Roger. But Roger died in 1772 and was buried with his parents in old St. Peter's parish church at Chertsey. Peacock's friend Charles was not born before 1781 (probably in 1782 or 1783; he was "two or three years" older than Peacock). The Abbey House, however, remained in Barwell hands until 1809, and there were grandsons of William Barwell with the Bengal Civil Service well into the 1830's. (Owen Manning and William Bray, *History and Antiquities of Surrey*, London, 1814, III, 219–220 and 237; *Victoria County History of Surrey*, Westminster, 1902–1912, III, 408; H. E. Busteed, *Echoes from Old Calcutta*, London, 1908, p. 160; *DNB*.)

11. If so, this would account for the tradition which dated Peacock's friendship with Auber from the Englefield House school days. On Peter Auber (1770–1866), see also Van Doren, *Peacock*, pp. 12, 137–138, and Peacock, *Works*, I, xci–xcii.

12. H. F. B. Brett-Smith and C. E. Jones (editors of the Halliford Edition of Peacock's *Works*) report the first entry showing Ludlow, Fraser & Co. at 4 Angel Court in *Kent's Directory* for 1797 (printed, most likely, near the end of the previous year). They report an entry giving Mrs. Peacock's residence as 4 Angel Court in Holden's *Triennial Directory* for 1805–1807 and in Holden's *Directory* for 1808. (Peacock, *Works*, I, xxv–xxvi.) As they suggest, there is probably some "unchecked repeti-

Here he wrote a verse "Answer to the Question 'Is History or Biography the more improving Study?'" which won an extra-prize — "not," said the editorial statement, "as a specimen of poetry particularly excellent, but as an extraordinary effort of genius in a boy of this age." The verse essay was published in *The Monthly Preceptor, or, Juvenile Library* for February 1800; Leigh Hunt won fourth prize in the same contest.[13]

John Wicks, the master of the private school at Englefield which Peacock attended, had the gift of inspiring his students with a love of learning, and he also had good classical assistants. Although Peacock left school in his thirteenth year, he kept up his reading — maintaining the serious interest in the classics which later permeated so much of his writing, both serious and comic. When he was about sixteen or seventeen years old (some two or three years after *The Juvenile Library* prize), he seems to have found time for systematic study, and he seems also to have had access to a collection (or collections) in London which contained sculpture and ancient artifacts as well as books. The clues to this period of study can be found in the family tradition:[14] at "about sixteen years of age," his granddaughter wrote, he "removed with his mother from Chertsey to London" and "commenced a line of study at the British Museum, where he devoted his whole time to reading the authors of ancient Greece and Rome, studying at the same time the architectural remains — the statues, bas reliefs, &c."[15] Although it raises a number of questions, that part of the tradition which has Peacock at the British Museum Reading Room cannot be disregarded — he may have been given time to go there occasionally at sixteen or seventeen, more fre-

tion" here, but Mrs. Peacock may well have remained in London until late 1805, her son until some time in 1806, when entries for the following year were being collected.

13. The quotation is from the copy of *The Juvenile Library* in The Carl H. Pforzheimer Library. This was Peacock's sole appearance in the periodical. See below, "Leigh Hunt," p. 147 fn. 4.

14. On the sifting of clues from the mixture of fact and distortion in Peacock family tradition, see above, fns. 4 and 11.

15. Peacock, *Works* (1875), p. xxvii. Edith Nicolls wrote the passage which mentions the British Museum; however, Peacock's friend Henry Cole, of the Record Office, added a long footnote in which he emphasized the classical treasures available at the British Museum, and it may well have been he who made a vague tradition specific. Neither Peacock's granddaughter nor his friend Cole knew of the *Juvenile Library* publication and its information about Peacock's employment, at fourteen, with the London mercantile firm.

quently as he reached twenty; he may have spent his last months in London entirely at the Reading Room.[16]

Another possibility, however, should not be overlooked, the "Oriental Repository" at the East India House. Peacock turned sixteen in October of 1801, the year in which the library at the India House (the "Oriental Repository") got under way. Charles (later Sir Charles) Wilkins was appointed librarian in February and in December the first sizable gift, the Orme bequest, was received; in this month, also, all printed books previously dispersed about the India House and the warehouses were gathered together.[17] We do not know what relations Peacock had had with the "Oriental Repository" before 1810, when he wrote Peter Auber at the India House asking him "to enquire of the E.I.H. librarian the title of the best History of Persia,"[18] but it seems reasonable to assume that he had had some contact with it — through Auber or the Barwells — quite possibly during his early London years.[19]

We know little more of the pattern of his life during these years than what can be derived from the occasional verse he wrote. The verse letter to his grandmother on July 16, 1801, about Peter Bohea, the ambitious apprentice, gives something of Peacock's attitude to the problems of young men with their way to make in the City. The verse letter to his grandfather shows his continued interest in the war at sea against the forces of Napoleon. The poems he wrote to Lucretia

16. All biographers of Peacock have found his place of study in these years a problem. As H. F. B. Brett-Smith and C. E. Jones note, "It is unlikely that clerical duties would allow him time for the Reading Room even if, at that age, his presence there would have been permitted." (Peacock, *Works*, I, xxvi–xxvii.) The rules for the Reading Room may not have been so rigidly enforced in the early years of the century; the extensive reorganization of the British Museum belongs to the 1820's.

17. A. J. Arberry, *The Library of the India Office: a Historical Sketch* (London, 1938), pp. 10–11, 24–28. The Library of the East India Company (styled "the Oriental Repository" in the Public Letter of the Court of Directors of May 1798 and in the resolution of appointment of Charles Wilkins in February 1801) became the India Office Library in 1858, on the transfer of the Company's powers and material possessions to the Crown. Following the Indian Independence Act in 1947, the library came under the control of the Secretary of State for Commonwealth Relations. (S. C. Sutton, *A Guide to the India Office Library*, London, 1952, p. 1.) Miss Jane Cock, librarian of the Commonwealth Relations Office, and Mr. S. C. Sutton, Librarian of the India Office Library, very kindly made available materials on Peacock in the India Office Library.

18. Reported in letter from Peacock to Hookham, Feb. 26, 1810, Peacock, *Works*, VIII, 178–180.

19. The library was open on Mondays, Thursdays, and Saturdays from 10 until 3. (See Arberry, *Library of the India Office*, p. 43; William Foster, *The East India House*, London, 1924, pp. 148–150.)

Oldham of Shacklewell Green and Mrs. St. Croix of Homerton (two of the villages just north of London)[20] tell us something of his early flirtations and friendships.[21] To this first London period belongs also his first publication. In 1804 his pamphlet poem, *The Monks of St. Mark*, was printed by T. Bensley, Bolt Court, Fleet Street (and probably paid for by Peacock himself), and in the following year his first full-length book appeared (issued in December 1805, with the title page dated 1806, as was the custom with year-end books[22]).

Mrs. Peacock probably returned to Chertsey before the end of 1805, for in December of that year her father died, leaving a seventy-nine-year-old widow much in need of care. Peacock spent the holiday season with his mother and grandmother, sending a letter from Chertsey on December 26, 1805.[23] His first letter to the bookseller and publisher Edward Hookham, written in August 1807 from Chertsey, acknowledged "numerous favors" and a "generous offer" evidently to become Peacock's publisher; a later letter to Hookham recalled a solitary walking tour in Scotland in the autumn of 1806.[24]

We can pick up the story again in May 1808, when Peacock began a year's service on board H.M.S. *Venerable*. Little more has been known previously about this experience than has been gleaned from those letters which survive of Peacock's correspondence with Edward Hookham, and the letters exhibit a discernible bias against shipboard life — in part, no doubt, in accommodation of Hookham's viewpoint. But the enthusiasm for military valor expressed in the four pieces written for amateur theatricals on board (two of them in The Carl H. Pforzheimer Library[25]) would suggest that Peacock found much of his naval service agreeable;

20. See *Shelley and his Circle*, I, 47, map.

21. See *ibid.*, pp. 314–317, for further discussion of the Lucretia episode and reasons for believing it part of Peacock's London experience. Mrs. St. Croix was the mother of Peacock's friend William de St. Croix (called "St. Croix" in Peacock's letters and brief diary).

22. Peacock, *Works*, VI, 335–336.

23. *Works*, VII, 194, fn. 476.

24. For the text of Peacock's letters to Hookham see *Works*, VIII, 160–191; for notes and discussion on this correspondence, *ibid.*, pp. 507–509.

25. sc 96 (January 1809) and sc 97 (January–March 1809).

the first part of *The Genius of the Thames* (which Shelley found too commercial and chauvinistic: "Mr. Peacock concieves that commerce is prosperity; that the glory of the British Flag, is the happiness of the British people . . . ."[26]) was written during this year.

It is necessary to go to other sources to determine the nature of Peacock's naval duties and environment and to attempt to assess their influence. The Muster Books of H.M.S. *Venerable* show that he was a volunteer and did not hold Navy rank, that he served as Captain's clerk, with his term of service from May 14, 1808 (he was twenty-two), until April 2, 1809, and that from May 10 to December 18, 1808, Sir Home Riggs Popham was Captain of the *Venerable*.[27] The Captain's influence on Peacock must have been considerable. He was an effective teacher, insisting that his juniors become proficient in the scientific branches of their profession, and in Peacock, whose youth had been spent among navigators, he may well have found a ready student.

But Peacock's determination to be a poet prevailed. His year of service over at the beginning of April 1809, he left the *Venerable* at Deal and walked home to Chertsey by way of London where he saw the Hookhams and discussed publication of his new poem, *The Genius of the Thames*, of which Part I was virtually completed. During June he took a walking tour from Chertsey to the source of the Thames to get material for Part II, to which his letters to Edward Hookham, playful and mocking, furnish an interesting parallel since they are essentially a prose treatment of the same material.[28]

When *The Genius of the Thames* was published in the spring of 1810 he was in Wales. There he met the Reverend Dr. John Gryffydh of

26. P. B. Shelley to T. Hookham, Aug. 18, 1812, Shelley, *Letters*, I, 325.

27. Public Record Office, London: ADM. 37/1234-1236 (Muster Books of H.M.S. *Venerable*, 1808-1809). We are indebted to Professor J. G. Bullocke of the Royal Naval College, Greenwich, for the suggestion that the Muster Books — not previously used by students of Peacock — be searched. Sir Home was reappointed to the *Venerable* on July 4, 1809, just before the ill-fated expedition to Walcheren which brought Shelley to Popham's defense. (See MacCarthy, *Shelley*, pp. 78-85; and Cameron, *The Young Shelley*, pp. 49-51.) Peacock had left the ship before preparations for the campaign were under way. His last months had been in the service of Captain Andrew King, appointed December 17, 1808. (Public Record Office: Commission and Warrant Books [IND]. 9246 and 9236].)

28. Peacock, *Works*, VIII, 168-176.

Maentwrog and his daughter Jane, whom he was to marry some ten years later. Old Mrs. Love died in December 1810, but Peacock did not return to Chertsey until the following spring. At home the easy pattern of his life continued — walking or boating in the summer, studying and writing when the weather or the season held him indoors.

Late in 1812 he met Shelley, an encounter evidently planned by the Hookhams; in August, Thomas Hookham had sent Shelley two volumes by Peacock, both bearing his firm's imprint, *The Philosophy of Melancholy* and the second (combined) edition of *The Genius of the Thames, Palmyra and Other Poems*, and when Shelley came up to London with Harriet in October he met Peacock at the Hookhams' shop in Old Bond Street.[29] Their discussion of Peacock's work and the books used as background is reflected in Shelley's long book orders of December 17th and 24th from Tanyrallt, which include a number of the more recondite classical authors and several such established Peacockian favorites as Gillies' *Ancient Greece*, Drummond's *Academical Questions*, Horne Tooke's *Diversions of Purley*, and Monboddo's *Origin and Progress of Language*.[30] Shelley and Harriet were in London again in April 1813, seeing Peacock once or twice before he set off for his second trip into Wales. His way leading through Tanyrallt, he inquired into the famed "assault" on Shelley, concluding that it was a "semi-delusion," of a type he was to observe again in his friend.[31]

Acquaintance became friendship only after Peacock's return from Wales in July, when he found Harriet and Shelley established within walking distance, at Bracknell, near Windsor Great Park. He spent most of his time with them and their friends the Boinvilles and Newtons; "a numerous society," each with "some predominant crotchet of his or her own, which left a number of open questions for earnest and not always temperate discussion." Peacock no doubt aired crotchets of his own, for he enjoyed lively discussions. But he had also a keen sense of the ridiculous and "was sometimes irreverent enough to laugh at the fervour with

29. Van Doren, *Peacock*, p. 56.

30. See Shelley to Hookham, Dec. 17, 1812, and to Clio Rickman, Dec. 24, 1812, Shelley, *Letters*, I, 343. For an analysis of Shelley's book orders, see Notopoulos, *Platonism*, pp. 40–41; other influences, namely Godwin and John Frank Newton, are reflected also.

31. Peacock, *Memoirs*, pp. 66–69; see also pp. 74, 101–103.

which opinions utterly unconducive to any practical result were battled for as matters of the highest importance to the well-being of mankind; Harriet Shelley was always ready to laugh with me, and we thereby both lost caste with some of the more hot-headed of the party."[32]

Under Peacock's tutelage Shelley began intensively to study Greek, beginning at Bracknell and continuing through the trip into Scotland in October and November of 1813. Harriet's "new carriage" being crowded with their numerous party, Peacock had shipped separately "his small trunk . . . containing books."[33] Near the end of the sojourn in Edinburgh Shelley wrote Hogg that he had read Homer, Tacitus, Cicero's philosophical works, Laplace, and Hume and had translated Greek with his guest Peacock, "a very mild agreable man, & a good scholar."[34]

In the spring of 1814 came the estrangement between Harriet and Shelley (which was not confided to Peacock),[35] and in the early summer Shelley's elopement to France with Mary Godwin. While Peacock admired Mary's greater intellectual abilities, he could not forget Harriet's agreeable qualities nor disregard the painful results for her of Shelley's inevitable growth beyond her capacities. In the acrimonious exchanges of the memorialists many years after the deaths of the three protagonists, Peacock spoke out for Harriet.[36]

From 1814 to 1818 we know of Peacock largely through the Shelleys — from Shelley's letters and later from Mary Shelley's Journals. Only from her record of the winter of 1814–15 do we have any knowledge of Peacock's activities during that period, and they make up a strange chapter, indeed.

In July 1814 Shelley and Mary Godwin had eloped. After their return

---

32. *Ibid.*, pp. 70–71.

33. Shelley to Hookham [endorsed Oct. 6, 1813], Shelley, *Complete Works*, IX, 77.

34. Quoted from the original letter [postmark Nov. 26, 1813] in The Carl H. Pforzheimer Library.

35. Peacock could not reconcile Shelley's remarriage to Harriet in 1814 with any prior (or contemporaneous) estrangement. (See Peacock, *Memoirs*, pp. 89–90.) In this we can only conclude that he was unseeing and/or uninformed. He was proved correct, however, in his assertion that the separation was not by mutual consent (*ibid.*).

36. On certain aspects of the lives of the Shelleys — Percy, Harriet, and Mary — Peacock remains the soundest authority; in any matter which he has chosen to discuss, his point of view must be considered, if only as counterweight.

to London in mid-September, Peacock, who had moved up to London
with his mother, became a frequent caller and Shelley's confidant on
money matters. During the first nine days of November, Shelley hid
out from the bailiffs at the rooms Peacock and his mother had taken in
the Southampton Buildings. Mrs. Sarah Peacock, too, helped the fugitive,
calling for his letters at the London Coffee House.[37]

During the autumn there was considerable discussion of Peacock's
contemplated marriage with a member of the St. Croix family of Homerton, whom he had known during his years as a clerk in the City. In her
Journal for September 30th, Mary noted: "Peacock calls. talk with him
concerning . . . Mariann. Arrange his marriage."[38] On October 14th
Shelley and Peacock talked "of Marian," and Peacock's name recurs
frequently until November 15th, when it is dropped abruptly. Then on
January 1st Shelley called on Mrs. Sarah Peacock, evidently living alone.
There is a suggestion in the Journal that her son was off on some adventure, but Shelley heard few details from her. On January 3rd, from Marianne, he got the story, which Mary recorded in her Journal: "a rich
heiress has fallen in love with Peacock and lives with him — she [the
heiress] is very miserable — God knows why — P. is on her account &
that of M. St. C. & M. is miserable on her own account." Less than a
fortnight later (probably January 12th; the dated beginning of the entry
is torn out) Mary recorded: "Letter from Peacock to say that he is in
prison — the foolish man lived up to Charlottes expectancies who turns
out to have nothing — her behaviour is inexplicable — there is a terrible
mystery in the affair — his debt is £40 — a letter also from Gray who
knows nothing about her — this is a funny man also — write to Peacock
& send him £2 —"[39] It is a tale worthy of *Nightmare Abbey*. We know
nothing more of the "heiress." But Peacock was free by March 1st, for
he called that day on the Shelleys. By mid-April he seems to have been
reinstated in Marianne de St. Croix's favor, for he discussed with Shelley
"his plan of going to Canada & taking Marrianne [*sic*]." Instead, in the

37. The "Mrs. P." of Shelley's letter to Mary [Friday, Nov. 4, 1814] is Peacock's mother. Shelley, *Letters*, I, 419.

38. Mary Shelley, Journal. (Abinger Manuscripts, Pforzheimer Microfilm, reel I.) Marianne's name is variously spelled in the earlier entries, but "Marianne de St. Croix" on December 1st and later.

39. *Ibid.*

early summer, Peacock left London for Marlow, where one of his mother's brothers lived.

The purpose of Peacock's winter in London can only be guessed. Nearing his thirtieth year and contemplating marriage, he must have given serious thought to his economic future. Although three volumes of poetry had been published over his signature and two without it (*Sir Hornbook* and *Sir Proteus*), he was scarcely able to maintain even himself with his writing (Shelley had given him some financial help). Peacock may well have tried to establish himself, once more, in business or a profession. Whatever the plans, the year seems to have been a loss.

Back in the Windsor area, at Marlow, Peacock began to write again, turning now to prose and beginning *Headlong Hall*, the first of the novels on which his fame was to rest. In August the Shelleys moved to Bishopsgate, at the eastern entrance to Windsor Great Park, and Hogg often came down from London. It was a period of intense intellectual activity: Shelley's *Alastor* was written; Peacock finished *Headlong Hall* and began *Melincourt*, which was published in the spring of 1817.

The Shelleys moved to Marlow where they were visited by Godwin and the Leigh Hunts.[40] There were walks up to London, where Shelley was introduced to two of Peacock's enthusiasms, the theater and opera. In 1818 Shelley and Mary prepared to leave England. On their last night they went with Peacock to hear Rossini's *Barber of Seville*. Then Peacock returned to Marlow. He wrote to Hogg that he felt "lonely as a cloud, and as melancholy as a gib cat. . . . I have filled my shelves with a portion of Shelley's books [and] intend to pass the interval between Easter & Christmas . . . in writing a novel of which the scene will be in London [and] . . . another Pagan poem."[41]

Nothing came of these projects. After a summer-long interlude Peacock began a course of study preparatory to competing for one of the positions newly opened in the Examiner's Office at the East India House. In January 1819 he began probationary work there, and in May four provisional appointments were made to the Examiner's Office, Edward Strachey, James Mill, J. J. Harcourt, and Peacock — the youngest and

40. Peacock, *Memoirs*, p. 106.

41. Peacock to Hogg, Marlow, Mar. 20, 1818. (Original in The Carl H. Pforzheimer Library.)

lowest paid of the group.[42] Three and a half decades of his life were to be spent in the Examiner's Office — from 1819 to 1856, when he retired on pension. Peacock's duties at the India House were varied, his career a quietly distinguished one. He was Chief Examiner from 1836 on, succeeding James Mill.

His prospects on being firmly employed allowed him to think of marrying. Shelley and Mary expected that the bride would be Marianne de St. Croix of Homerton, but for some reason she refused him, and on November 20th, after a silence of eight years, he wrote to Jane Gryffydh of Maentwrog. Within the month she replied and they were married in Wales in March 1820.[43]

Peacock brought Jane to 18 Stamford Street, Blackfriars. Here, in July 1821, their first child, Mary Ellen, was born. After the birth two years later of Margaret Love, their second child, he moved his mother and his family to Lower Halliford, across the Thames from Chertsey. Two children were born to Peacock and Jane at Halliford, Edward Gryffydh, his only son, and Rosa Jane. Between the two births came the sudden death, in 1826, of little Margaret Love Peacock. Jane Peacock, sadly affected, was a "nervous invalid" for the rest of her life.[44] Sarah Peacock, then in her seventy-second year, took over the housekeeping and cared for the children until her death in 1833. Through the 1830's Peacock's writing gradually decreased and then for two decades was suspended; he continued his classical studies, however, in the early morning hours.

Although Shelley was drowned in July 1822, his will was not proved until Sir Timothy's death in 1844, by which time Peacock was left sole executor. When Mary Shelley needed assistance in negotiating

---

42. Strachey's salary was to be £1000 annually, Mill's and Harcourt's each £800, Peacock's £600 "To commence from Xmas last" (Minutes of May 12, 1819, Court Book no. 127, consulted at the India Office Library). Harcourt had long been a clerk in the Examiner's Office; of the three new men, two (Strachey and Mill) were in their mid-forties while Peacock was thirty-four.

43. Peacock to Jane Gryffydh, Nov. 20, 1819, Peacock, *Works*, VIII, 217–218; Jane Gryffydh to Peacock, Nov. 30, 1819, *ibid.*, p. 477.

44. Van Doren, *Peacock*, pp. 151, 224. A neighbor's child, Mary Rosewell, who bore a striking resemblance to the dead child, was brought into the family and lived with them until after Peacock's death. To Mary Rosewell, Peacock willed all his property and insurance and she was, in effect, his executrix. (Peacock, *Works*, I, clxxxvii.)

with Sir Timothy or his solicitor, Whitton, it was Peacock who helped her.[45]

The old friends whom Peacock saw regularly in these years were Thomas Jefferson Hogg, Walter Coulson, a lawyer and the amanuensis to Jeremy Bentham, and Horace Smith, the author. Henry (later Sir Henry) Cole of the Record Office was a much younger man, but there developed a warm friendship through the years of walking to work together, from Stamford Street by Bankside and over Old London Bridge. Although Peacock did not make a practice of intimacy with fellow workers, he had some close friends in the Examiner's Office: Edward Strachey and his son (later Sir Edward), Horace Grant and Francis Prideaux. With the Mills, father and son, he was not particularly friendly, but through James Mill he met Jeremy Bentham, with whom he dined weekly until Bentham's death in 1832.

The only close friend he made in his later years was Sir John Cam Hobhouse, who was Byron's executor. In 1830 there had been a brief exchange of correspondence when Peacock, reviewing Moore's *Letters and Journals of Lord Byron*, had submitted some questions to Hobhouse, but the two men evidently did not meet until April 1839, after Hobhouse had become President of the Board of Control (the "India Board").[46] The friendship developed rapidly — there being great mutuality of taste, temperament, and interests — and in October of the following year Peacock made his first visit of many to Hobhouse's country seat in Wiltshire. He was there in December 1851 when he received the news of his wife's death.

In the years following his mother's death in 1833, Peacock had given a good deal of attention to the education of his eldest daughter, Mary Ellen. She was a brilliant, gifted young woman and had evidently been encouraged to write. Widowed in 1844 a few months after her marriage to Lieutenant Edward Nicolls of the Royal Navy, she became one of a

---

45. Peacock's letter of August 6, 1822, to Sir Timothy, notifying him of his son's death, is in The Carl H. Pforzheimer Library as are also letters to Whitton about money for Mary Shelley, a receipt for money received for her, and a letter of June 24, 1824, on the question of her purchasing an annuity.

46. A number of manuscripts in The Carl H. Pforzheimer Library derive from Peacock's association with the East India House.

literary group which included her brother Edward, Peter Austin Daniel and Hilaire de St. Croix (two of Edward's fellow clerks at the East India House), George Meredith, and Henry Wallis.[47] Through 1848 and 1849 five of this group, all but Wallis, issued *The Monthly Observer*, a manuscript periodical containing their work. In August 1849 Mary Ellen Nicolls and Meredith were married — an event which brought an abrupt end to the periodical. Thomas Love Peacock approved to the extent of attending the wedding; and during the few years the marriage lasted gave the young couple what help he could within the limitations of his temperament.[48] The ill-starred marriage came to an end in the summer of 1857 when Mary Ellen left for a trip to Wales, her companion the painter Henry Wallis.[49] The rest of her life was a tragedy of abandonment and illness, but not, as some of Thomas Love Peacock's biographers have thought, of estrangement from her father, who was with her almost constantly in her last illness, although he spared himself the pain of attending her funeral.[50]

After his retirement in 1856 from the East India House, Peacock wrote his seventh, and last, novel, *Gryll Grange*, and, in a series of answers to Hogg and other biographers of Shelley, his own *Memoirs* of his friend. He wrote little in the last year or two before his death in 1866 but continued to read, in his library or in his sunny garden by the river. Two new friends entered the narrowing circle, both as admirers of his work. The Belfast solicitor, Thomas L'Estrange, inquired about Peacock's early years and elicited a series of informative letters, thus earning the gratitude of all biographers of this most reticent of writers. Robert Buchanan, then a student in Scotland, wrote and later visited, leaving in his "Personal Reminiscence" our best account of Peacock in his years of retire-

47. Lionel Stevenson, *The Ordeal of George Meredith* (New York, 1953), pp. 23–38.

48. Meredith caught much of the essential quality of that temperament — and of Mary Ellen's — in the characters of Dr. Middleton and Clara in his novel *The Egoist*.

49. Stevenson, pp. 44–47, 58–59. Henry Wallis is thought to have used Meredith as the model for his "Death of Chatterton" which now hangs in the Tate Gallery, London. The picture was painted in the chambers of P. A. Daniel, who became one of the executors — with Wallis' son by Mary Meredith — of Henry Wallis' will (now at Somerset House). Wallis painted a portrait of Peacock in January 1858 which now hangs in the National Portrait Gallery.

50. Compare Van Doren, *Peacock*, pp. 229–231, 250; Peacock, *Works*, I, cxc–cxci; and Stevenson, *Meredith*, pp. 95–98.

ment, "a stately old gentleman with hair as white as snow, a keen merry eye," sitting in his garden by the river. "Age had mellowed and subdued the 'cameo-leopard [*sic*],' but the 'fine wit,' as I very speedily discovered, was as keen as ever."[51]

WORKS AND IDEAS

Thomas Love Peacock is remembered today chiefly for his witty, ironic novels of talk; he began, however, as a poet.[52] As a young man he wrote some light, satiric verse, but during his first period (that is, before his meeting with Percy Bysshe Shelley late in 1812) he expended his major energies on poetry of more serious intent: *Palmyra and Other Poems, The Genius of the Thames*, and *The Philosophy of Melancholy*.

The poems by Peacock printed in the first two volumes of *Shelley and his Circle* give a fair idea of his early development in prosodic skill. For example, there is evidence in the reworking of such an early bit of occasional verse as "Sir Peter Bohea" of his striving for greater precision in the choice of words and a more effective play of accentual pattern (qualities which carried over later to the prose style of his novels). His craftsmanship in the short lyric can be seen developing from the stanzas "To a young lady netting" of 1803 to the poignant "Remember Me" four years later.[53]

Despite his skill, and his obvious delight, in humorous verse, the prevailing tone of Peacock's early poetry is romantic, and there is evidence in his letters to Edward Hookham, who was to be his publisher for *The Genius of the Thames*, that this choice of attitude toward his

---

51. Robert Buchanan, "Thomas Love Peacock: A Personal Reminiscence," *The New Quarterly* (April 1875), pp. 240–241. "Cameleopard" and "fine wit" are from Shelley's description of Peacock in his *Letter to Maria Gisborne*, lines 232–247.

52. Perhaps because of Peacock's reputation as a novelist, we tend to think of his novels as having found a much larger contemporary audience than his volumes of poetry; but although the first two long poems, *Palmyra* and *The Genius of the Thames*, had a second, joint, edition in 1812 (when *The Philosophy of Melancholy* also appeared), only *Headlong Hall* went into a second edition before the 1837 Bentley reprint (in one volume) of *Headlong Hall, Nightmare Abbey, Maid Marian*, and *Crotchet Castle. Melincourt* did not have a second edition until 1856, and *The Misfortunes of Elphin* was not reprinted in Peacock's lifetime. It is unlikely that large editions of any of the novels were ever printed; the discovery in 1870 of stocks of unbound sheets of *The Misfortunes of Elphin* and *Crotchet Castle* tells its own story. (Peacock, *Works*, IV, 154–155.)

53. For these poems see *Shelley and his Circle*, I, 277–280, 314, 421–423.

material was deliberate. "The Thames is almost as good a subject for a satire as a panegyric," he wrote from Oxford,[54] with no doubt in his mind, however, that he was correct in preferring the more serious, "panegyrical" mode. And although he intended to make some use of his own experience and observation in the second part of *The Genius of the Thames* and had journeyed up the river to gather impressions, there was also no doubt in his mind that the proper themes for a serious poet were to be found in books. When he was back at his home in Chertsey he wrote again to Hookham: "I have thought of various subjects for an episode, but cannot hit on any thing to suit my fancy, unless, in my reflections on the mutability of empire, I were to introduce one on the fall of Carthage. I think this subject highly susceptible of poetical ornament." And later in the same month he wrote again to ask for a number of books on travel and history: "I want several of these for the purpose of manufacturing notes."[55]

Peacock passed through this romantic and rhetorical period, notes Oliver Elton, "as through a kind of measles." And his novels, which belong to his mature years, became — perhaps because of this early exposure — "part of the comment of the 'romantic period' upon itself; we cannot fully understand it without them."[56]

Peacock's transition from romanticist to satirist followed on his friendship and close association with Percy Bysshe Shelley, who is generally felt to have significantly influenced the transition.[57] Until the advent of the younger poet and his friends (who were of all ages and kinds of opinion) Peacock had been largely a solitary worker. The two men evidently had many discussions about their own writing and that of other writers of their age. Out of his association with Shelley and the circles who gathered at Bracknell and, later, at Marlow, came a great deal of self-knowledge and also, inevitably for a mind as objectively

---

54. Peacock to Hookham, June 6, 1809, Peacock, *Works*, VIII, 172.

55. Peacock to Hookham, Sept. 5, 1809; Peacock to Hookham, Sept. 19, 1809. (*Ibid.*, 175, 176.)

56. Oliver Elton, *A Survey of English Literature: 1780-1830* (London, 1948), I, 379.

57. Carl Van Doren saw this as a friendship between opposites which resulted in "a mental repulsion which brings out strongly the genuine character of each." His analysis remains one of the most perceptive. (Van Doren, *Peacock*, p. 74; see also Notopoulos, *Platonism*, pp. 38-41, especially fn. 44.)

critical as Peacock's, a growing awareness of Shelley's greater poetic talent.

The change in Peacock's tone and his attitude toward his subject matter first became obvious in *Sir Proteus: A Satirical Ballad: by P. M. O'Donovan, Esq.*, which was published in March 1814. In this verse satire appeared Peacock's first published criticism of contemporary poets (including both their poetry and their politics, subjects he was to return to in his novels). Robert Southey, newly-made Poet Laureate, was the primary target, but the other Lake poets, Wordsworth and Coleridge, were brought in, and the whole was dedicated, tongue-in-cheek, to Lord Byron: "For versification undecorated with the meretricious fascinations of harmony, For sentiments unsophisticated by the delusive ardor of philanthropy, For narrative enveloped in all the Cimmerian sublimity of the impenetrable obscure."[58] ("Are we alive after all this censure?" commented Byron.[59])

It was not until he turned to the novel, however, that Peacock found a literary genre to which his gifts were truly suited. With the first of these, *Headlong Hall*, it was clear that he had perfected his tone and widened the range of his subject matter to take in a great "array of false pretensions, moral, political, and literary."[60] He had, moreover, worked out his form — the virtually plotless novel of talk, in which characters who are addicted to some single viewpoint or "crotchet" are brought together at a country house party, or in an isolated neighborhood given to visits, or sent on a journey. It was to serve, with but minor modifications, for his seven works of prose fiction[61] and was to be,

58. The last eight lines of the dedication.

59. Byron to Samuel Rogers [June 1814], *Letters and Journals*, III, 90.

60. Peacock, "Preface" to the volume of Bentley's Standard Novels, *Headlong Hall* [etc.] (London, 1837), pp. vi-vii.

61. While two of the novels, *Maid Marian* and *The Misfortunes of Elphin*, are laid in the past and draw on legendary sources, closer examination reveals more resemblance than difference between these "romances" and the five "novels of talk." (See J. B. Priestley, *Thomas Love Peacock*, London, 1927.) For example, the journeys through Sherwood Forest made by Brother Michael and the little friar in *Maid Marian* parallel the trip in the mail coach to Headlong Hall or the journey up the Thames in *Crotchet Castle*. The journey in the mail coach probably reflects in part that of Shelley, Harriet, and Peacock to the Lake District and Scotland in the late autumn of 1813; the journey up the Thames is a close approximation of the trip made by Shelley and Mary, the Clairmonts (Charles and Claire), and Peacock in 1815.

indeed, Peacock's original contribution to the form of the English novel.[62]

Peacock's novels are all in some measure *romans à clef*, the leading characters of successive books often repeating a portrait: aspects of Shelley, for example, appear in Mr. Foster of *Headlong Hall*, in Mr. Forester of *Melincourt*, and in Scythrop Glowry of *Nightmare Abbey*; Peacock's grandfather, Thomas Love, recurs in such tippling eccentrics as Captain Hawltaught of *Melincourt*, Prince Seithenyn and the Abbot of Avalon of *The Misfortunes of Elphin*, Friar Michael of *Maid Marian*, and such hosts as Squire Headlong and Ebenezer MacCrotchet. Occasionally a character in one of the novels combines qualities represented in more than one of the people Peacock knew; thus, the Reverend Dr. Gaster of *Headlong Hall* propounds some of the views of John Frank Newton as does Mr. Escot, a character generally felt to be modeled on Peacock himself (the Peacock of the period of *Ahrimanes*, a long and serious work embodying many of Newton's deteriorationist theories[63]). Newton appears again as Mr. Toobad of *Nightmare Abbey*, father of the brilliant Stella, who was drawn primarily from Mary Godwin but who reflected some elements of that other disciple of the younger Shelley, Elizabeth Hitchener. Emily Girouette, Scythrop's first love, reflects Harriet Grove, and Emily's refusal of Scythrop's suit provokes his father, Mr. Glowry, to compare marriage with a lottery — a parody of Godwin's views on marriage as expressed in *Political Justice*. (Godwin's *Mandeville* appears as "Devilman, a novel.") Harriet Westbrook serves in part as the model for the pretty, lighthearted Marionetta, but one of the elements making up her name came from that of Marianne de St. Croix, one of

---

62. The followers of Peacock who come most readily to mind are Norman Douglas (especially in *South Wind*, with its contrast between ironic talk and romantic setting); Aldous Huxley (especially in the visit of the house party guests to the piggery in *Crome Yellow*, the Soho restaurant scene in *Antic Hay*, and the character sketches from members of Huxley's own circle which enliven *Point Counter Point*); Ronald Firbank (in particular, Mrs. Henedge's party to celebrate the discovery of a new fragment by Sappho which opens *Vainglory*, and *Inclinations*, a novel consisting almost entirely of Peacockian talk at house parties and on excursions).

63. On the relationship of Peacock's unfinished *Ahrimanes* to Newton's zodiacal philosophy and deteriorationist theories, see Peacock, *Works*, VII, 263, 420-421, and 513; see also I, lvii. Peacock was much more a disciple of Newton during this early period than he was later willing to admit. Two manuscript versions of *Ahrimanes* are in The Carl H. Pforzheimer Library.

two young women whom Peacock (like Scythrop) found he could love at the same time.[64] Skillful paraphrase occurs in *The Misfortunes of Elphin* when old Seithenyn defends his laissez-faire policy toward upkeep of the Welsh embankment with sentiments which echo Canning's speeches on reform, just as Mr. Fax's dinner talk at Melincourt Castle echoes Malthus' essay in the *Edinburgh Review*.[65]

In all the novels there are dinners, trimmed to their dramatic essentials and presented virtually as plays[66] — for example, Chapter V of *Headlong Hall* (called "The Dinner" in the third and subsequent editions) or Chapter XVI of *Melincourt*, called "The Symposium" (a frequent chapter title in subsequent novels). With his third novel, *Nightmare Abbey*, he had become highly skillful in the timing and cadence of the dinner scenes, as in the farewell banquet for Mr. Cypress (modeled on Byron):

MR. GLOWRY.
You are leaving England, Mr. Cypress. There is a delightful melancholy in saying farewell to an old acquaintance, when the chances are twenty to one against ever meeting again. A smiling bumper to a sad parting, and let us all be unhappy together.
MR. CYPRESS (*filling a bumper*).
This is the only social habit that the disappointed spirit never unlearns.
THE REVEREND MR. LARYNX (*filling*).
It is the only piece of academical learning that the finished educatee retains.
MR. FLOSKY (*filling*).
It is the only objective fact which the sceptic can realize.
SCYTHROP (*filling*).
It is the only styptic for a bleeding heart.[67]

64. On Marianne de St. Croix and the "heiress" Charlotte (because of whom Peacock spent some time in prison) see above, pages 133–135 and fn. 38.

65. But care must be exercised in fixing any Peacockian identifications too firmly. As Carl Van Doren (*Peacock*, p. 90) pointed out in his analysis of the characteristics assigned to Mr. Escot and Mr. Foster in *Headlong Hall*: "What Peacock took was merely the original situation, the intellectual contention of two men. . . . This scheme once hit upon, it was natural enough that each disputant of the novel should be made to assume opinions appropriate to his character and business in the story, or even to take on characteristics opposed to those of his prototype." That Shelley understood this technique is clear from his amused acceptance of his own portrait as Scythrop. (Shelley, *Complete Works*, X, 58–59, 65; White, *Shelley*, I, 705, fn. 47.)

66. Peacock had experimented with this pattern in some light farces written about 1811–1813 (see *Works*, VII, 289–412, 523–530, and I, li–lii).

67. Quoted from the first edition of *Nightmare Abbey*, pp. 149–150.

At the farewell dinner Mr. Cypress is made to talk in paraphrases of stanzas of the third and fourth cantos of *Childe Harold*, the precise reference obligingly cited each time in a footnote. The use of footnotes to underline or support a point or to add a bit of the curious lore which Peacock delighted in accumulating is a characteristic of all his novels though most frequently used in *Melincourt* and *Gryll Grange*. For Sir Oran Haut-Ton of *Melincourt*, the silent simian who played the flute and was elected as one of the two representatives of the Borough of One-vote, Peacock drew heavily on Lord Monboddo's *Ancient Metaphysics* and *Origin and Progress of Language* and he ironically quotes long passages of this and other authorities on the "natural man" in his footnotes.

He does not cite his authority for the theory of education held by the father of one of his most delightful learned heroines, Anthelia Melincourt, who was "at the age of twenty-one, . . . mistress of herself and of ten thousand a year."[68] She had been taught by her widowed father, "one of those who maintained the heretical notion that women are, or at least may be, rational beings."[69] Her trained mind and studious habits had earned the approval of Mr. Forester, who noted that the general conduct of men

in this respect, is much like that of a gardener who should plant a plot of ground with merely ornamental flowers, and then pass sentence on the soil for not bearing substantial fruit. If women are treated only as pretty dolls, and dressed in all the fripperies of irrational education; if the vanity of personal adornment and superficial accomplishments be made from their very earliest years to suppress all mental aspirations, and to supersede all thoughts of intellectual beauty, is it to be inferred that they are incapable of better things? But such is the usual logic of tyranny, which first places its extinguisher upon the flame, and then argues that it cannot burn.[70]

Peacock was reflecting here his own knowledge of the works of Mary Wollstonecraft and his awareness of their effect on his friend at the time of Shelley's meeting with Mary Wollstonecraft's daughter. These passages from *Melincourt* should be compared with the passages in the Introduction to *A Vindication of the Rights of Woman* on reason in women and on their education, and with Mary Wollstonecraft's many

68. Quoted from *Melincourt*, first edition, the opening sentence.
69. *Ibid.*, I, 7.   70. *Ibid.*, II, 7.

discussions of the "logic of tyranny" in her earlier *Vindication of the Rights of Men*.[71] But Peacock is not only indebted for these ideas to Mary Wollstonecraft, he has caught — in his half-joking paraphrase — her trick of the vivid juxtaposition of extremes in metaphors drawn from homely tasks. He went elsewhere for the phrase "intellectual beauty," however, combining it with Mary's views on woman's potentialities for education. "Intellectual beauty" came from the same source as the prototype for Peacock's "natural man," Sir Oran Haut-Ton ("ouran-outang"); that is, from Monboddo's *Origin and Progress of Language*.[72]

It is clear from his novels that in evolving his form, Peacock drew freely on his own experience as well as on his vast reading. He found the model for his country house parties of eccentrics partly in the Bracknell circle, that "numerous society" of men and women, each with "some predominant crotchet."[73] He found in Plato the device of the dinner enlivened with opinion; Dr. Gryll of *Gryll Grange* is only the last of a series of Peacockian characters aware of "how much instruction has been conveyed to us in the form of conversations at banquets, by Plato and Xenophon and Plutarch. I read nothing with more pleasure than their *Symposia*: to say nothing of Athenæus, whose work is one long banquet."[74] It is perhaps of interest to note that Peacock attempted to

71. See *A Vindication of the Rights of Woman* (1792), pp. 69–70 and Chapter IX; *A Vindication of the Rights of Men* (1790), *passim*; and *An Historical and Moral View of . . . the French Revolution* (1794), *passim*.

72. Peacock also has Anthelia Melincourt use "intellectual beauty" in her description of Forester (*Melincourt*, II, 14), who was modeled on Shelley. Shelley's "Hymn to Intellectual Beauty" was written in Switzerland, in the summer of 1816, but was not published until January 1817 (White, *Shelley*, I, 446–451, 475, 713). Peacock could have seen the manuscript while he was working on the latter part of *Melincourt*, but it is important to remember that a goodly portion of this novel had been finished before Shelley returned to England (it was advertised as "in the press" in August 1816 although not published until early 1817; see Peacock, *Works*, I, lxix). What is clear is that the term came to both men from the same source (see Notopoulos, *Platonism*, pp. 129, 197 for Shelley's source; Notopoulos does not mention Peacock's use of the term) and that they were putting it to use about the same time; they had probably discussed it before Shelley left for Switzerland. Mary Wollstonecraft, too, knew Monboddo, whom she quoted in *A Vindication of the Rights of Woman*, page 111 (see Notopoulos, *Platonism*, p. 88, fn. 34). From the standpoint of technique, the interesting thing here is Peacock's clever combination — in a half-serious, half-mocking tone — of ideas and stylistic devices drawn from Monboddo, Mary Wollstonecraft, and Shelley in a speech by the Shelleyan Mr. Forester to the Wollstonecraftian Anthelia.

73. Peacock, *Memoirs*, p. 70.

74. Quoted from the first edition of *Gryll Grange*, p. 168.

reproduce the conversational banquet in his first year in London, inviting to his dinners some members of the old Bracknell circle. In the spring of 1819 Shelley wrote of Mrs. Boinville and "the amiable circle once assembled round her . . . . I hear they dined at your lodgings,"[75] and in August: "You don't tell me if you see the Boinvilles, nor are they included in the list of the *conviti* at the monthly symposium. I will attend it in imagination."[76]

After Shelley left England, in March 1818, Peacock felt keenly the loss of intellectual companionship. But Shelley's going had a deeper effect: without his moral and financial encouragement, Peacock could not justify giving himself over to the life of the poet-scholar (his books simply had not found a paying audience).[77] Several months after Shelley's departure, Peacock qualified for work at the East India House; after he received his appointment to the Examiner's Office, in May 1819, the course of his life, both as man and writer, changed radically. It was not only that literature became, as a result of his business commitments, an avocation, but also that he was thrown into a very different intellectual milieu, that of Jeremy Bentham, James Mill, and the English Utilitarians. Eventually Peacock was to write a series of reviews and essays for the periodicals they dominated, although — characteristically — he was too amused by some aspects of their philosophy and practice to fully identify himself with them. For *The Westminster Review* he wrote scathing reviews of Thomas Moore's *The Epicurean* (1827) and Moore's edition of *The Letters and Journals of Lord Byron* (1830) and a warmly informative review of T. J. Randolph's *Memoirs . . . of Thomas Jefferson* (1830); he was associated with *The Westminster*'s successor, *The London Review*, only during its first two years, his last articles, on Bellini and Paul de Kock ("The Épicier"), appearing in January 1836.[78]

75. Shelley to Peacock, Apr. 6, 1819, Shelley, *Complete Works*, X, 45–46.

76. Shelley to Peacock, Aug. ?22, 1819, *ibid.*, p. 73.

77. Three times, at least, Peacock had yielded to family pressures to establish himself in a business or service career: when he went with the firm of city merchants, Ludlow, Fraser & Co. (from about 1799 to 1805); when he became a Captain's clerk in the Navy (1808–1809); and when he took on some unknown work in London in the winter of 1814–1815.

78. See George L. Nesbitt, *Benthamite Reviewing: The First Twelve Years of the Westminster Review: 1824–1836* (New York, 1934), pp. 27, 34, 109, 111–112, 137. See also Michael St. John Packe, *The*

But before this he had written his most notable essay, *The Four Ages of Poetry*, which appeared in *Ollier's Miscellany* (1820). It was, in one sense, his protest against the world which made necessary his change of vocation.[79] Much of the material of *The Four Ages of Poetry* is foreshadowed in the correspondence between Peacock and Shelley after the Shelleys reached Italy in the summer of 1818, in Peacock's *Nightmare Abbey* (published later in 1818), and in Shelley's *Letter to Maria Gisborne* (written in the summer of 1820).[80] But only in his correspondence does any of Peacock's bitterness manifest itself, most particularly in his letter of December 4, 1820, which accompanied *The Four Ages* to Italy.[81] Shelley received the essay and the letter in February 1821 and soon began his own *Defence of Poetry*, which has — with an irony Peacock could have appreciated — quite overshadowed the work to which it is an answer. H. F. B. Brett-Smith's edition for The Percy Reprint Series, a century later, was the first joint publication of this culmination of Peacock's and Shelley's conversations, letters, and works on poetry, the poet, and his audience.

In his fourth and fifth novels, *The Misfortunes of Elphin* (1829) and *Crotchet Castle* (1831), he made "the progress of useful art and science" the object of his satire, causing his friends among the Utilitarians no

Life of John Stuart Mill (London, 1954), pp. 61–64 (on *The Westminster Review*), and pp. 191–217 (on *The London Review* during Peacock's association). Peacock did not write for the journal after it came under the sole management of John Stuart Mill, and the two men were not on cordial terms in their later years; thus Mill's early letter to Albany Fonblanque (Dec. 25, 1834) is important: "We have promises of support (as writers) from my father, . . . Peacock, . . . everybody in short whom we thought worth asking" (Packe, pp. 196–197).

79. See Van Doren, *Peacock*, p. 152, and H. F. B. Brett-Smith, "Introduction," *Peacock's Four Ages of Poetry, Shelley's Defence of Poetry, Browning's Essay on Shelley* (Percy Reprints, no. 3) (Boston, 1921), p. xii.

80. See the letters of Shelley to Peacock from Apr. 20, 1818, through to Feb. 15, 1821 (when he acknowledged receipt of *The Four Ages* and Peacock's letter of Dec. 4, 1820) and see Peacock to Shelley from May 30, 1818, through to Dec. 4, 1820, in Peacock, *Works*, VIII, 192–220.

81. H. F. B. Brett-Smith published the letter of December 4, 1820, with *The Four Ages* in The Percy Reprint Series edition cited above.

Lytton Strachey, reading Brett-Smith's edition, wrote to Virginia Woolf that he found Peacock's essay brilliant. "That man knew how to write prose — vide the last enormous sentence." (*Virginia Woolf & Lytton Strachey: Letters*, ed. Leonard Woolf and James Strachey, New York, 1956, p. 137.)

little embarrassment by putting some of their prominent members into his novels.[82] It tended to create a distance between Peacock and the supporters of the Mills. It was his family concerns and an increase of professional responsibility, however, rather than any marked coolness in his professional relationships which got in the way of his writing during the late 1830's and the 1840's.

His talent proved remarkably durable, and after his retirement from the East India House at sixty-seven, he wrote his *Memoirs of Shelley* (in a series of reviews for *Fraser's Magazine*) and his last novel, *Gryll Grange*, in which he held up to scorn, in the familiar mocking way, the "world of misnomers" where "a gang of swindling bankers is a respectable old firm; that men who sell their votes to the highest bidder, and want only 'the protection of the ballot' to sell the promise of them to both parties, are a free and independent constituency; that a man who successively betrays everybody that trusts him, and abandons every principle he ever professed, is a great statesman, and a Conservative, forsooth, *à nil conservando*; that schemes for breeding pestilence are sanitary improvements; that the test of intellectual capacity is in swallow, and not in digestion; that the art of teaching everything, except what will be of use to the recipient, is national education; and that a change for the worse is reform."[83]

---

82. The Benthamite reviews "provoked their own colleague, Peacock, to write into *Crotchet Castle* the absurd Mr. MacQueedy, for whom they had to chide him a few years later" (Nesbitt, *Benthamite Reviewing*, p. 58). In the same novel was the Steam Intellect Society, which burlesqued the Society for the Diffusion of Useful Knowledge. There developed a serious shortage "of literary men with Utilitarian bias [after 1831]. . . . Their best candidate, Peacock, had gone and written *Crotchet Castle*, and what could one do with a man like that?" (*ibid.*, pp. 158–159).

83. Quoted from *Gryll Grange*, first edition, p. 2.

LEIGH HUNT

(October 19, 1784–August 28, 1859)

PRINCIPAL WORKS

1808–1822 The Examiner (editor)

1816 The Story of Rimini

1819–1821 The Indicator (editor)

1822 The Liberal (editor)

1828 Lord Byron and Some of His Contemporaries

1832 Christianism (The Religion of the Heart)

1844 Imagination and Fancy

1846 Wit and Humour

1847 Men, Women, and Books

1850 Autobiography

1859 Selections from the English Poets (editor)

1860 Poetical Works

LIFE

LEIGH HUNT, like William Godwin, came from a family of ministers, not liberal ministers, however, but Tories, and not in England but in the West Indies, where the family had moved in the seventeenth century to escape the wrath of Puritan ascendency. In the next century a second revolution moved them back to England. Leigh Hunt's father, Isaac Hunt, who had gone to Philadelphia to college, attempted to forward his Tory creed in pamphlets, "drew on him the popular odium" — writes his son in his *Autobiography* — and "had a narrow escape from tarring and feathering."[1]

Returning to England and there encountering financial difficulties, Isaac moved in the opposite direction; and his wife, mother of Leigh Hunt, who came from a Philadelphia family and who had in her youth been offered guitar lessons by Benjamin Franklin, moved with him:

I have spoken of my mother during my father's troubles in England. She stood by him through them all; and in everything did more honour to marriage, than marriage did good to either of them: for it brought little happiness to her, and too many children to both. Of his changes of opinion, as well as of fortune, she partook also. She became a Unitarian, a Universalist, perhaps a Republican; and in her new opinions, as in her old, was apt, I suspect, to be a little too peremptory, and to wonder at those who could be of the other side.[2]

It was on these new opinions that the Hunt children were nourished; and when a West Indian aunt visited them they were shocked beyond

1. Hunt, *Autobiography*, I, 8–9.   2. *Ibid.*, p. 28.

words: "It was frightful to hear her small mouth and little mincing tones assert the necessity not only of slaves, but of robust corporal punishment to keep them to their duty."[3]

Leigh Hunt's first direction, however, was not, as was his brother John's, into politics but literature:

> For some time after I left school, I did nothing but visit my schoolfellows, haunt the book-stalls, and write verses. My father collected the verses, and published them, with a large list of subscribers, numbers of whom belonged to his old congregations. I was as proud, perhaps, of the book at that time as I am ashamed of it now. The French Revolution, though the worst portion of it was over, had not yet shaken up and reinvigorated the sources of thought all over Europe.[4]

It was not, as Hunt here states, that the French Revolution had failed to move English opinion. It had moved it, as *Political Justice* alone can testify; but the opinion had been suppressed. By 1801 the leading English intellectual radicals had either, like Godwin, fallen silent, or, like Coleridge and Southey, moved into the Tory camp. But within a few years came a revival:

> At the beginning of the year 1808, my brother John and myself set up the weekly paper of the *Examiner* in joint partnership. . . . The main objects of the *Examiner* newspaper were to assist in producing Reform in Parliament, liberality of opinion in general (especially freedom from superstition), and a fusion of literary taste into all subjects whatsoever. It began with being of no party; but Reform soon gave it one.[5]

Shortly after the founding of *The Examiner*, Leigh Hunt married: ". . . I had never ceased to be ready to fall in love with the first tender-hearted damsel that should encourage me. Now it was a fair charmer, and now a brunette; now a girl who sang, or a girl who danced; now one that was merry, or was melancholy, or seemed to care for nothing, or for everything, or was a good friend, or good sister, or good daughter.

3. Hunt, *Autobiography*, p. 104.

4. *Ibid.*, p. 119. The book of verses, *Juvenilia*, collected by Leigh Hunt's father, appeared in 1801. In the same year Hunt published a poem in *The Monthly Mirror*. He had first appeared in print the preceding year in the *Juvenile Library*, a monthly which featured the "Prize Productions of Young Students." See also "Thomas Love Peacock," above, p. 125, and Landré, *Hunt*, I, 29.

5. Hunt, *Autobiography*, I, 192, 194.

With this last . . . I ultimately became wedded for life." The name of the versatile and many-mooded bride was Marianne Kent, daughter of a court milliner.

The founding of *The Examiner* was to have effects that Hunt and his brother did not anticipate. As a result of the new reform movement, led first by Sir Francis Burdett (and observed by the youthful bards of Field Place, "Victor" and "Cazire"), *The Examiner* was, indeed, "given" a policy and a party. But, more than that, it became the organ of the independent intellectuals who were rising to take the place of the older generation that had fallen by the wayside, the organ of Byron, Keats, Shelley, Hazlitt, and a host of now forgotten others. *The Examiner* became not so much a weekly paper as an institution and Leigh Hunt was transformed from an obscure poet and essayist into an influential editor, a man whose opinions were read and admired by thousands of readers week by week for some thirteen years.

It was as such that he was addressed on March 2, 1811, by an undergraduate of University College, Oxford, who had a scheme for the furtherance of the cause of reform:

> Permit me, although a stranger, to offer my sincerest congratulations on the occasion of that triumph so highly to be prized by men of liberality; permit me also to submit to your consideration, as to one of the most fearless enlighteners of the public mind at the present time, a scheme of mutual safety and mutual indemnification for men of public spirit and principle, which if carried into effect would evidently be productive of incalculable advantages; of the scheme the enclosed is an address to the public, the proposal for a meeting, and shall be modified according to your judgment, if you will do me the honour to consider the point.[6]

A few months later he was visited in London by his young admirer but had no clear recollection of the occasion:

> I first saw Shelley during the early period of the *Examiner*, before its indictment on account of the Regent; but it was only for a few short visits, which did not produce intimacy. He was then a youth, not come to his full growth; very gentlemanly, earnestly gazing at every object that interested him, and quoting the Greek dramatists.[7]

6. Shelley to Leigh Hunt, Mar. 2, 1811, Shelley, *Letters*, I, 54.

7. Hunt, *Autobiography*, II, 27–28.

Shelley had a more vivid memory of the occasion, and wrote to his friend T. J. Hogg, on May 8, 1811, of Hunt's anti-clerical views and his "triumph," which was "to be prized by men of liberality." The path of *The Examiner* on the course of reform had not been smooth. Three times had it been prosecuted by the government and three times had the verdict been "not guilty." The third of these occasions — arising from an article protesting military flogging — was the "triumph" referred to by Shelley.

The fourth time, however, the government did not fail. An article assailing the Prince Regent as "a libertine over head and ears in disgrace . . . the companion of gamblers and demireps" caught the eye of the attorney general; "the result to the proprietors was two years' imprisonment, with a fine, to each, of five hundred pounds."[8]

Although Hunt romanticized his imprisonment in his *Autobiography*, it still remains one of the strangest imprisonments on record, and his account of it something of a classic:

The doctor then proposed that I should be removed into the prison infirmary; and this proposal was granted. Infirmary had, I confess, an awkward sound, even to my ears. I fancied a room shared with other sick persons, not the best fitted for companions; but the good-natured doctor (his name was Dixon) undeceived me. The infirmary was divided into four wards, with as many small rooms attached to them. The two upper wards were occupied, but the two on the floor had never been used: and one of these, not very providently (for I had not yet learned to think of money), I turned into a noble room. I papered the walls with a trellis of roses; I had the ceiling coloured with clouds and sky; the barred windows I screened with Venetian blinds; and when my bookcases were set up with their busts, and flowers and a pianoforte made their appearance, perhaps there was not a handsomer room on that side the water. I took a pleasure, when a stranger knocked at the door, to see him come in and stare about him. The surprise on issuing from the Borough, and passing through the avenues of a gaol, was dramatic. Charles Lamb declared there was no other such room, except in a fairy tale.

But I possessed another surprise; which was a garden. There was a little yard outside the room, railed off from another belonging to the neighbouring ward. This yard I shut in with green palings, adorned it with a trellis, bordered it with a thick bed of earth from a nursery, and even contrived to have a grass-plot. The earth I filled with flowers and young trees. There was an apple-

8. Hunt, *Autobiography*, I, 255–256.

tree, from which we managed to get a pudding the second year. As to my flowers, they were allowed to be perfect. Thomas Moore, who came to see me with Lord Byron, told me he had seen no such heart's-ease.[9]

Hunt was particularly touched by the attentions of Byron, who had already "awakened" to find his fame as the author of *Childe Harold*:

Lord Byron, as the reader has seen, subsequently called on me in the prison several times. He used to bring books for the *Story of Rimini*, which I was then writing. He would not let the footman bring them in. He would enter with a couple of quartos under his arm; and give you to understand that he was prouder of being a friend and a man of letters, than a lord.[10]

Hunt's erstwhile breakfast guest, then in Wales with "my Harriet," learned of the trial:

I am boiling with indignation at the horrible injustice and tyranny of the sentence pronounced on Hunt and his brother, and it is on this subject that I write to you. Surely the seal of abjectness and slavery is indelibly stamped upon the character of England.

Although I do not retract in the slightest degree my wish for a subscription for the widows and children of those poor men hung at York, yet this £1,000 which the Hunts are sentenced to pay is an affair of more consequence. Hunt is a brave, a good, and an enlightened man. . . . Well, I am rather poor at present but I have £20 which is not immediately wanted. Pray begin a subscription for the Hunts; put [down] my name for that sum, and when I hear that you have complied with my request I will send it you. Now if there are any difficulties in the way of this scheme of ours, for the love of liberty and virtue overcome them. Oh that I might wallow for one night in the Bank of England! . . . . If no other way can be devised for this subscription, will you take the trouble on yourself of writing an appropriate advertisement for the paper, inserting by way of stimulant, my subscription. On second thoughts, I enclose the £20.[11]

On his emergence from prison (in 1815), Hunt was greeted by a sonnet by another "young poet," John Keats; and the following year his real friendship with Shelley began. He announced Shelley (along with Keats) to the world as a new, promising poet in *The Examiner*, December 1, 1816, stuck with him, day by day, through the crisis of the death of Harriet, and never failed to lend the powerful voice of *The*

9. *Ibid.*, II, 8–9.   10. *Ibid.*, p. 86.

11. Shelley to Thomas Hookham, Feb. 15, 1813, Shelley, *Letters*, I, 353–354.

Examiner to his support against the attacks of the Tory *Quarterly* and other journals:

> The article in the *Quarterly* alluded to in my last letter, is a pretended review of Mr. Shelley's poem, entitled *Prometheus Unbound*. It does not enter into any discussion of the doctrines contained in that poem. It does not pretend to refute them. It knows very well that it does not dare to enter into the merit of Mr. Shelley's propositions, and answer them as it would answer a treatise by a theological sectarian. And the reason is obvious. I do not mean to say that all those propositions are unanswerable; but I say the Quarterly Reviewers, by the very nature of their office, as civil and religious State-hirelings, are not the men to answer them fairly; and accordingly their criticism has all the malice of conscious inability to reply, and eagerness to put down.[12]

In time it was felt that *The Examiner* needed to be supplemented in its battle with the *Quarterly* by a more literary and less directly political journal; and it was for the purpose of establishing such a journal in conjunction with Byron and Shelley that Hunt and his family went to Italy in the summer of 1822. The meeting (after four years' absence) between the two friends was noted by the observant eye of little Thornton Hunt, aged twelve:

> Some years elapsed between the night when I saw Shelley pack up his pistols — which he allowed me to examine — for his departure for the South, and the moment when, after our own arrival in Italy, my attention was again called to his presence by the shrill sound of his voice, as he rushed into my father's arms, which he did with an impetuousness and a fervour scarcely to be imagined by any who did not know the intensity of his feelings and the deep nature of his affection for that friend. I remember his crying out that he was "so *inexpressibly* delighted! — you cannot think how *inexpressibly* happy it makes me!"[13]

Within a few days Shelley was dead; within a few weeks Hunt was one of the few spectators at the cremation of his body.

The ceremony of the burning was alike beautiful and distressing. Trelawny, who had been the chief person concerned in ascertaining the fate of his friends, completed his kindness by taking the most active part on this last mournful occasion. He and his friend Captain Shenley were first upon the ground, attended

12. *The Examiner*, June 16, 1822, quoted in *Shelley-Leigh Hunt*, pp. 64–65.

13. Quoted in *Shelley and Keats as They Struck Their Contemporaries*, ed. Edmund Blunden (London, 1925), p. 22.

by proper assistants. Lord Byron and myself arrived shortly afterwards. His lordship got out of his carriage, but wandered away from the spectacle, and did not see it. I remained inside the carriage, now looking on, now drawing back with feelings that were not to be witnessed. . . . The beauty of the flame arising from the funeral pile was extraordinary. The weather was beautifully fine. The Mediterranean, now soft and lucid, kissed the shore as if to make peace with it. The yellow sand and blue sky were intensely contrasted with one another: marble mountains touched the air with coolness; and the flame of the fire bore away towards heaven in vigorous amplitude, waving and quivering with a brightness of inconceivable beauty. It seemed as though it contained the glassy essence of vitality.[14]

With the death of Shelley, Hunt and *The Liberal* — as the new journal was called — were left alone with Byron; and Byron's interest in the enterprise was not equal to Shelley's. Moreover, Byron was subjected to pressures from England for his association with two such radicals as Hunt and Shelley, and not — as Hazlitt testifies — by the Tories only:

Who would have supposed that Mr Thomas Moore and Mr Hobhouse, those staunch friends and partisans of the people, should also be thrown into almost hysterical agonies of well-bred horror at the coalition between their noble and ignoble acquaintance — between the patrician and 'the newspaper-man'? Mr Moore darted backwards and forwards from Cold-Bath-Fields Prison to the *Examiner* office, from Mr Longman's to Mr Murray's shop in a state of ridiculous trepidation, to see what was to be done to prevent this degradation of the aristocracy of letters, this indecent encroachment of plebeian pretensions, this undue extension of patronage and compromise of privilege. The Tories were shocked that Lord Byron should grace the popular side by his direct countenance and assistance; the Whigs were shocked that he should share his confidence and counsels with any one who did not unite the double recommendations of birth and genius — but themselves! Mr Moore had lived so long among the great, that he fancied himself one of them, and regarded the indignity as done to himself. Mr Hobhouse had lately been black-balled by the Clubs, and must feel particularly sore and tenacious on the score of public opinion.[15]

The result was that Byron, after contributing his brilliant *The Vision of Judgement* and other pieces, gradually withdrew his support and *The Liberal* folded after four numbers. With his departure for Greece, one

14. Hunt, *Autobiography*, II, 101.

15. William Hazlitt, quoted in Blunden, *Leigh Hunt*, pp. 178-179.

year after the death of Shelley, Hunt was left in Italy in difficult circumstances. In the fall of 1825 he returned to England to find himself hailed —
along with Godwin — as one of the elect in Hazlitt's *The Spirit of the Age*
and to become one of the most prolific essayists and general writers and
editors of a new era. His comments on moving, in 1833, to Chelsea give
a good picture of his literary activities:

> In this house we remained seven years; in the course of which, besides
> contributing some articles to the *Edinburgh* and *Westminster Reviews*, and
> producing a good deal of the book since called *The Town*, I set up [in 1834] the
> *London Journal*, endeavoured to continue the *Monthly Repository*, and wrote
> the poem entitled *Captain Sword and Captain Pen*, the *Legend of Florence*, and
> three other plays which are yet unpublished.[16]

Among Hunt's neighbors in Chelsea was Thomas Carlyle, and in his
friendship with Carlyle Hunt links the "Romantic" period with the
Victorians. It is from Carlyle that we get one of the most vivid sketches
of Hunt during these years:

> Dark complexion . . . copious clean strong black hair, beautifully shaped head,
> fine beaming serious hazel eyes; seriousness and intellect the main expression
> of the face (to our surprise at first); he would lean on his elbow against the
> mantelpiece (fine clean elastic figure, too — he had five feet ten or more) and
> look round him nearly in silence, before taking leave for the night, "as if I
> were a Lar," said he once, "or permanent household god here" (such his polite
> ariel-like way). Another time, arising from this Lar attitude, he repeated (voice
> very fine), as if in sport of parody, yet of something very sad perceptible,
> "While I to sulphurous and penal fire" . . . as the last thing before vanishing.[17]

In his later years Hunt's literary activities and reputation changed.
He was no longer the vigorous reformer of *The Examiner* but the gentle
essayist, poet, and critic. The change was noted also by the government,
which acknowledged past injustices and made some provision for the
future. In June 1847 Hunt received a letter from Lord John Russell,
Prime Minister and first Lord of the Treasury:

> Sir,–I have much pleasure in informing you that the Queen has been
> pleased to direct that, in consideration of your distinguished literary talents,
> a pension of Two Hundred Pounds yearly should be settled upon you from

16. Hunt, *Autobiography*, II, 208-209.   17. Quoted, *ibid.*, II, 209-210 fn.

the funds of the Civil List. Allow me to add, that the severe treatment you formerly received, in time of unjust persecution of liberal writers, enhances the satisfaction with which I make this announcement.[18]

The radical causes of 1810–1813, for which the Hunts had been prosecuted, had, by 1847, become part of the general social fabric and were no longer radical. The cause of reform had triumphed; and Hunt (like Godwin) reaped some of the benefits of his courageous pioneering.

In 1850 he achieved a new triumph with the publication of his *Autobiography*. "An excellent good book," declared Carlyle, "by far the best of the autobiographic kind I remember to have seen in the English language."[19] And his opinion was generally shared by the reviewers and the reading public. The *Autobiography* became one of the classics of its kind; and has held its own in spite of all competition.

In his later years Hunt himself also became something of a classic, one of the literary great to whom visitors in London came to do honor. It was as such that he was visited by Emerson and Hawthorne. "A beautiful and venerable old man," wrote Hawthorne, "buttoned to the chin in a black dress-coat, tall and slender, with a countenance quietly alive all over, and the gentlest and most naturally courteous manner."[20] Time had not dealt too harshly with the friend of Shelley:

> You will see Hunt — one of those happy souls
> Which are the salt of the earth, and without whom
> This world would smell like what it is — a tomb;
> Who is, what others seem; his room no doubt
> Is still adorned with many a cast from Shout,
> With graceful flowers tastefully placed about;
> And coronals of bay from ribbons hung,
> And brighter wreaths in neat disorder flung;
> The gifts of the most learn'd among some dozens
> Of female friends, sisters-in-law and cousins.
> And there is he with his eternal puns,
> Which beat the dullest brain for smiles, like duns
> Thundering for money at a poet's door;
> Alas! it is no use to say, 'I'm poor!'

18. Quoted in Blunden, *Leigh Hunt*, p. 297.

19. Quoted, *ibid.*, p. 303.   20. Quoted, *ibid.*, p. 324.

Or oft in graver mood, when he will look
Things wiser than were ever read in book,
Except in Shakspeare's wisest tenderness.[21]

Hunt died nine years after the publication of his *Autobiography*. His last piece of writing was, characteristically, a defense of Shelley against what he considered the distortions of Hogg's biography.[22]

WORKS AND OPINIONS

The versatility of Hunt's talents has long been recognized: his contribution to dramatic criticism — "the first English dramatic critic" (according to William Archer);[23] his remarkable insights in literary criticism — "Time," wrote Ernest Bernbaum, "has shown him nearly always right in his opinions about poetry from Chaucer to Browning";[24] his championing of Shelley and Keats; his talents for verse drama; his writing of the first major literary autobiography; his development of the literary periodical and the English essay — "To no single man," wrote George Saintsbury, "is the praise of having transformed the eighteenth century magazine, or collection of light miscellaneous essays, into its subsequent form due so much as to Hunt";[25] his democratization of English journalism; his widening of English literary taste by revealing the qualities of Continental — particularly Italian — literature. All this is true; yet in the telling something of the essence of Hunt seems to get left out. Beneath the versatility there lies a common factor. Hunt was not, as was Godwin, a social philosopher, or, as was Shelley, a great poet. He developed no new school of thought; he created no work of genius, no *Prometheus Unbound* or *Don Juan*. But his heart was endlessly alight

21. Shelley, *Letter to Maria Gisborne*, lines 209–225. "Shout" was Robert Shout, maker of plaster casts. The "sisters-in-law" included Elizabeth Kent, sister of Hunt's wife Marianne.

22. *Leigh Hunt's Letter on Hogg's Life of Shelley*, Privately Printed (Cedar Rapids, Iowa, 1927).

23. *Dramatic Essays, Leigh Hunt*, ed. William Archer (London, 1894), p. vii. See also *Leigh Hunt's Dramatic Criticism, 1808–1831*, eds. Lawrence Huston Houtchens and Carolyn Washburn Houtchens (New York, 1949).

24. *Guide through the Romantic Movement* (New York, 1949), p. 271. The range and quality of Hunt as a literary critic can now be sampled in one compact volume: *Leigh Hunt's Literary Criticism*, eds. Lawrence Huston Houtchens and Carolyn Washburn Houtchens (New York, 1956).

25. *The Cambridge History of English Literature*, XII, 245.

with the flame of human compassion. He had no reasoned belief in Necessity producing an ultimate egalitarian order. But where he saw injustice he attacked it; and he continued to attack it no matter what the consequences.

Hunt has been praised for the languid grace of his writings; he has been, correlatively, criticized for a certain lack of vigor. And, so far as his later writings are concerned, there is some truth to the criticism. But Hunt has been judged too much by his later writings. *The Examiner* has tended to be forgotten. There is no lack of vigor in *The Examiner*, but power and indignation and scorn linked with controlled skill of sentence and sharp turn of phrase. Let us note, for instance, his protest against child labor (which we might compare with Godwin's in *Fleetwood*):

instead of ruddy and sparkling faces, they have pale and careful ones; instead of the fresh air, they breathe the deadly fumes of fires and metals; instead of the birds, they hear nothing but the click of combs or the grinding of engines, or oaths and ribaldry; instead of genial exercise, they are moved like mill-horses, or use only their arms or their fingers, the rest of their bodies being imprisoned by inactivity; and all this lingering torture is called *habits of industry!*[26]

The "famous victory" of Waterloo might rouse Wordsworth or Southey to paeans of vengeful joy; but Hunt saw also the human picture:

What is the happiness that is struck dead, to the misery that is left alive? — What is it all to the fatherless, the childless, the husbandless? — to the mind's eye haunted with faces it shall never see again, — to voices missed in the circle, — to vacant seats at table, — to widowed wakings in the morning, with the loved one never more to be in that bed?[27]

In the later Hunt, when liberalism had triumphed, there was a certain mellow generosity toward the causes and persons of the opposite side but when he was in the fight there was no such feeling and some of his finest passages were struck off in a mood of acid indignation, for instance, on Southey's acceptance of the laureateship:

To see the changes in this mortal life! Formerly Mr. SOUTHEY was all ardent aspiration after principle and public virtue; now he is content to fall in

26. *The Examiner*, Apr. 5, 1818, quoted in *Shelley-Leigh Hunt*, pp. 251–252.
27. *The Examiner*, July 2, 1815, p. 417.

with expediencies, and muster up arguments for apostacy: — formerly he was
for founding romantic colonies in America, where all should be equal and happy,
and the very sound of a corrupt world be kept at a distance; — now he has
plunged into the very thick of the corruption, and begins to suspect that even
romance may be wickedness: — formerly, you would have roused all the lofty
impulses of his fancy, all the severities of his youthful beauty of virtue, by
suggesting the bare possibility of his ever consenting to countenance royalty,
— much less a royalty of an ordinary or coxcombical species, — and still less
one that set no good example on the score of a wife; — now virtue, in his mind,
is not justified in objecting to vice; royalty, no matter how foolish or vicious,
had better be left as it is, and even flattered in it's [*sic*] vices by the countenance
and service of the respectable; — and in fine, our primitive, high-minded, and
pure-minded colonist is to go to Court in a sword and bag-wig, and to kiss
with a smirking gratitude the hand of the Prince of WALES!"[28]

His pen covered the whole range of English public life, social and
intellectual, and beyond into international affairs. He attacked the slave
trade and advocated the emancipation and education of the Negroes;
of a Negro ship captain from New Bedford he wrote: "Let us welcome
then our negro visitor as one of the forerunners of an equal race of
beings."[29] He opposed the military's scheme of covering England with
a network of barracks; and he exposed the horrors of Army floggings
(with a cat-o'-nine-tails): "punishments that mangle and convulse, that
tear away the flesh with knotted cords saturated with blood."[30] He
assailed those who turned their backs on poverty and restricted their
perambulations to "glittering shops and trim quiet streets, with lazy
footmen at the doors."[31] On Lord Ellenborough, a great pronouncer of
sentences — and object also of Shelley's wrath — Hunt in turn pronounced sentence: "he was a flatterer of those above him, and a dogmatist
to those beneath."[32] For some thirteen years there was no major topic,
domestic or international, on which Hunt failed to speak and on all he
spoke with complete fearlessness. When he was imprisoned he continued
to edit *The Examiner* from prison and to edit it as before:

28. *The Examiner*, Sept. 26, 1813, p. 609.

29. *The Examiner*, Aug. 4, 1811, quoted in *Shelley-Leigh Hunt*, p. 191.

30. *The Examiner*, July 3, 1814, quoted, *ibid.*, p. 231.

31. *The Examiner*, Aug. 10, 1817, quoted, *ibid.*, p. 245.

32. *The Examiner*, Jan. 10, 1819, quoted, *ibid.*, pp. 283–284.

We took leave of our Readers last year, to go to prison; — we now address them in prison; and thank Heaven, that in every thing which fortune has left in our controul, we can still say that we are the same men. Independence was always one of our greatest enjoyments; the companionship of adversity has rendered it one of our dearest friends; and if to forfeit it then would have been foolish, to abandon it now would be insane.

In the mean time, our Paper has been conducted as well perhaps as could be expected under the circumstances, and in some respects better.[33]

In view of the times, it is no wonder that, as Hunt states, in his *Autobiography*, "in the course of its warfare with the Tories, the *Examiner* was charged with Bonapartism, with republicism, with disaffection to Church and State."[34] But Hunt was no republican, as were Shelley and Godwin; he wished not to abolish but to reform the aristocracy and monarchy. He was not, as was Hazlitt, a hero-worshipper of Napoleon. And he had no other designs on "Church" than to hope that it would return to the humanitarian principles of its founder. "We are not Christians ourselves; we believe in nothing but GOD and the beauty of virtue; and as we make reason and conscience our guides, we make the good of our fellow-creatures our object."[35] Here is the creed that was transmuted into poetry in "Abou Ben Adhem":

'What writest thou?' — The vision raised its head,
And with a look made of all sweet accord,
Answered, 'The names of those who love the Lord.'
'And is mine one?' said Abou. 'Nay, not so,'
Replied the angel. Abou spoke more low,
But cheerly still; and said, 'I pray thee then,
Write me as one that loves his fellow-men.'

"I do not," writes the editor of the Oxford edition of Hunt's poems, "claim greatness for Leigh Hunt, but it seems to me clear that he has been unduly neglected, and his genuine qualities obscured by adventitious criticism of his personality, and even more by concentration on his weak points, of which he has many." The main "weak point" of Hunt's verse is that in breaking with the aristocratic formalism of the heroic couplet he

33. *The Examiner*, 1813, p. i, "Postscript."

34. Hunt, *Autobiography*, I, 195.

35. *The Examiner*, May 3, 1812, quoted in *Shelley-Leigh Hunt*, p. 207.

fell into a sometimes slipshod informality. But this weakness has too often been ridiculed without recognition of the important service Hunt rendered to English poetry by his innovations even though he went too far. With *The Story of Rimini*, for all its faults, a new fluid quality entered English poetic narrative, and stylistic foundations were laid not for *Endymion* alone but for *Julian and Maddalo* and even, on a new plane, *Epipsychidion*. This fluidity is apparent also in the short dramatic narratives, in *Mahmoud*, or, as the above-quoted lines suffice to show, in "Abou Ben Adhem." Hunt was attempting to create a new poetry for the new middle class.

Nor was the importance of his attempt limited only to its pioneering quality or its influence on greater poets. Hunt was not a great poet but he was nevertheless a poet, and a poet of rather remarkable range, from the light delicacy of "Jenny kissed me" to the dramatic verse of *A Legend of Florence*, from the rollicking satire of *The Feast of the Poets* to the somber, bitter power of *Captain Sword and Captain Pen:*

> Through fair and through foul went Captain Sword,
> Pacer of highway and piercer of ford,
> Steady of face in rain or sun,
> He and his merry men, all as one;
> Till they came to a place, where in battle-array
> Stood thousands of faces firm as they,
> Waiting to see which best could maintain
> Bloody argument, lords of pain;
> And down the throats of their fellow-men
> Thrust the draught never drunk again.

Although Hunt as an essayist is not as original as Lamb or Hazlitt, nevertheless, it is Hunt's essay style and not theirs that has prevailed. The ancestry of the magazine article of today can be traced more readily to Hunt than to any other English writer; and the intellectual periodical of today stems from *The Examiner*. Hunt may lack the brilliance of Lamb or the power of Hazlitt, but he lacks their idiosyncrasies also. He created — beyond Addison — a style of informal ease and clarity that provided a general model. And at times, as in the delightful little sketch of Izaak Walton, he concedes the crown to no one: "A friend of ours, who is an admirer of Walton, was struck, just as we were, with the likeness of the old angler's face to a fish. It is hard, angular, and of no expression. It seems to have been 'subdued to what it worked in;' to have become native to the watery element. One might have said to Walton, 'Oh flesh how art thou fishified!' He looks like a pike, dressed in broadcloth instead of butter. . . . Now, fancy a Genius fishing for us. Fancy him baiting a great hook with pickled salmon, and twitching up old Isaac Walton from the banks of the river Lee, with the hook through his ear. How he would go up, roaring and screaming, and thinking the devil had got him!"

LORD BYRON

(January 22, 1788–April 19, 1824)

PRINCIPAL WORKS

1807 Hours of Idleness

1809 English Bards and Scotch Reviewers

1812 Childe Harold, I and II

1813 The Giaour; The Bride of Abydos

1814 The Corsair; Lara

1815 Hebrew Melodies

1816 The Siege of Corinth (written 1815); Parisina (written 1814); Poems of the Separation; The Prisoner of Chillon; Childe Harold, III

1817 Manfred

1818 Beppo; Childe Harold, IV

1819 Don Juan, I and II

1821 Marino Faliero; Don Juan, III–V; Sardanapalus; The Two Foscari; Cain

1822 The Vision of Judgment; Heaven and Earth

1823 The Age of Bronze; The Island; Don Juan, VI–XIV

1824 Don Juan, XV–XVI

LIFE AND WORKS

GEORGE GORDON BYRON was born on January 22, 1788, at 16 Holles Street, London, where Mrs. Byron had taken temporary lodgings during flight from the creditors of her profligate husband. By 1789 the parents and child were settled in her native Scotland, in Aberdeen, though Captain John Byron soon fled from her scolding. By the time the boy was three — a beautiful child but clubfooted and with a temper as fierce as his mother's — his father ceased even occasional visits, unable to reach the remnant of the Gordon fortune, now settled in trust. Half a year later "Mad Jack" Byron died in France at thirty-five and Catherine Gordon Byron was wildly grief-stricken at the loss of her darling if impossible Johnny. "I was not so young," Byron later observed, "but that I perfectly remember him; and had very early a horror of matrimony, from the sight of domestic broils. . . ."[1]

In Aberdeen, living in respectable lower-middle class poverty and introduced to the Bible and the tenets of a severe Calvinism by his nurse but with little other education until enrolled at seven in the Grammar School, Byron was nevertheless proudly and frequently

---

1. Medwin, *Byron*, p. 58.

reminded that "I was born of the aristocracy . . . and am sprung, by
my mother, from . . . kings. . . ."[2] When he was six and one-half, the
death of a young man in the battle of Calvi in Corsica made George
Gordon the heir presumptive to the title and estates of the fifth Lord
Byron. When he was ten that "Wicked Lord" expired and Byron "was
sent for by the master of the school who gave him some cake & wine &
told him that his paternal great uncle was dead and he was now a
lord — Byron added that the little treat and the respectful manner of
the master gave him at once high notions of his new dignity."[3]

The first chapter of any biography of Byron quickly fills with the
colorful legends and traits of his wild ancestors. Byron would later make
good use of these in his own legend, though in realistic moments he
would take little stock in physical inheritance — one had heard "nothing
remarkable" of the sires of a Caesar or a Bonaparte — and would
attribute "the true breeding of a gentleman" to the pirate Lambro.[4]
The more important framework within which he had to construct his
life was given by the economic and social and especially the political
conditions of his heritage: estates in Nottingham and Lancashire supposedly rich in lumber (though the best oaks had been stripped by the
fifth lord) and coal (though the Rochdale mines illegally sold by the
same lord would have to be recovered by litigation) and farms and
cottage industry (though inflation was ruining the stocking weavers);
rights and duties as liege lord of manors in Rochdale and Nottingham;
a mouldering Gothic pile, Newstead Abbey, almost stripped of furniture
and scarcely habitable without repairs; a feud with neighboring cousins,
the Chaworths, with one of whom the youthful poet fell in love; and,
when he was twenty-one, a seat in the House of Lords, not recently
occupied and, figuratively, as mouldering as the walls of the abbey.
Chiefly lacking was money, but also legal control, overseers, and plans
for improved farming and mining. Gradually Byron was to find out the
realities of all these matters, but the need for "floating capital" was
immediately obvious — and only less urgent to the young baron than

2. Byron, *Letters and Journals*, IV, 483; reply to *Blackwood's Edinburgh Magazine*.
3. Hobhouse, in a marginal note in his copy of Moore's *Life of Byron* (Marchand, *Byron*, I, 44).
4. *Don Juan*, III, xli, 3.

the need to display his true nobility by lavish outlay.[5] The larger problem might be solved in due time by marriage: theoretically Captain Jack's precedent of marrying one heiress after another and squandering their fortunes need not be followed in toto. When Byron came to "marry for love" it was incumbent on him to choose within the circle of the well dowered; when, twice, he proposed to Annabella Milbanke he believed he was doing so: it was a bitter irony that their year of marriage was as plagued with duns and bailiffs as his infancy had been.

He never made any direct effort to be a gentleman farmer — a race he observed to be "worn out quite" — and ultimately he had to sell Newstead to get clear of debt. Without the peerage his life would unquestionably have been simpler, in this era of careers opening to talents. Even while fortune was declaring to George Gordon his feudal rights, the French Revolution and ensuing wars were offering the world stage to blackguards, cutthroats, leaders of the people. Mrs. Byron, intelligent but semiliterate, could offer her son almost nothing in the way of "the true breeding of a gentleman" but she held the door wide open to the winds of change: "I am very much interested about the French," she wrote to a friend in November 1792, when debate was raging over the fate of the imprisoned Bourbons; ". . . I am quite a Democrat and I do not think the King, after his treachery and perjury, deserves to be restored."[6] Bonaparte was inevitably the star of Byron's boyhood. Nurtured pride and his social isolation obliged Lord Byron to maintain the whole heritage and paraphernalia of nobility; yet in the world of action the downright "blackguard" seemed to have the fairest prospects. "All history and experience," as Byron read them, were in favor of a republic, and the best "model of force, and freedom, and moderation" appeared to be America; yet consider "all the coarseness and rudeness of its people."[7] Having to resuscitate his legal heritage almost wholly by his own efforts, even as he took in with every breath the revolutionary spirit of an age of self-made heroes, he grew up with such puzzling inner tensions between radical aristocrat and aristocratic radical that he came

5. See Byron to Lady Melbourne, Sept. 28, 1812, Byron, *Correspondence*, I, 88; for a larger survey, see David V. Erdman, "Lord Byron and the Genteel Reformers," *PMLA*, LVI (1941), 1072.

6. J. D. Symon, *Byron in Perspective* (London, 1924), p. 63.

7. Byron to Hobhouse, Oct. 12, 1821, Byron, *Correspondence*, II, 204.

to feel guided, for good or ill, by a fate as imperious as Napoleon's: a destiny in his own hands yet out of his control.

His looking forward, from an early age and with an extravagant notion of what was possible, to taking an active part in the conduct of affairs of state gave a direction and a practical intensity to his youthful reading in history and historical or at least heroic novels and plays — an intensity imperfectly comprehended by his more frivolous companions and by the more purely literary historians or biographers ever since.[8] At twenty he felt he could "aver, without hyperbole, . . . that few nations exist, or have existed, with whose records I am not in some degree acquainted, from Herodotus down to Gibbon." Directly preparatory for the House of Lords were his readings in oratory, "Demosthenes, Cicero, Quintilian, Sheridan, . . . and Parliamentary Debates from the Revolution to the year 1742."[9]

Nevertheless he was forced almost at once to a philosophical position of detached but defiant fatalism. Despite a rich assortment of traits of personality traceable to various courtly, enterprising, violent, morose, and hangdog ancestors, Byron was left by fortune almost entirely to improvise the right behavior of a peer of the realm. "Byron, on entering life, found himself out of the pale of this *sanctum* [aristocratic society], to which, by birth, he had so good a title."[10] His lameness — and his striking beauty of face and voice — his insecurity as only child under the alternating tyranny and fond indulgence of a mother who became, in his adolescence at least, an insufferable "Mrs. Byron *furiosa*" — his acuteness and his relative social isolation — combined to equip him with a defensive pride and an insatiable hunger for demonstrative affection: the literary consequence of which was the poetry of proud misanthropy that took society, within and outside the *sanctum*, by an increasingly sensational series of storms.

8. Exceptions are Viscount Morley, who recognized Byron as "among the most essentially political" of English poets (John Morley, *The Collected Works*, London, 1921, VI, 107), and G. Wilson Knight, who considers him to have "possessed, from the start, the *will* towards a comprehensive historical understanding" (Knight, *Lord Byron: Christian Virtues*, New York, 1953, p. 19). It would be wrong to think of the young Byron's reading as systematic, however, or his aim in life as sharply focused.

9. Notebook of 1807 quoted in Thomas Moore, *Letters and Journals of Lord Byron: with Notices of his Life* (London, 1830), I, 97.

10. Sir Egerton Brydges, *An Impartial Portrait of Lord Byron* (Paris, 1825), p. 53.

In his social behavior he combined indifference to applause or ridicule with an incessant courtship of attention, the reverse of chameleon-like. Playing every encouraged role, he watched keenly the responses that might authenticate or explode it. If the responses were too severely controlled — as were Annabella Milbanke's when he began trying what it would be like to be her husband — his experimental histrionics knew no bounds. "Unless the countenance is flexible," he bewailed during their engagement, "it is difficult to steer by mere looks."[11] But he usually managed to break through other people's reserve and his own, with his candor and his highly developed sense of the absurd — a sense which peeps out from some of his earliest verses, pervades his letters, and ultimately supplies the ground tone of his greatest poetry.

When he was sent to Harrow at thirteen, Byron was still very much an untamed bear cub. He and his mother had tried living in the ancestral Newstead Abbey, long enough for its ruined Gothic grandeur to fix itself in his imagination as the proper setting for the heroic self-portrait he was shaping with the aid of a hundred novels. The sister of his earlier nurse had come along from Aberdeen and given him lessons in sexual liberty and Calvinist piety; he had fallen passionately in love with a beautiful cousin, during a brief intimacy which inspired his "first dash into poetry";[12] and painful attempts had been made by a quack surgeon to "cure" his lameness. It was not until his second year at Harrow that friendships with other boys developed, some very intense. In his third year, still reading voraciously, he began versifying, and he displayed an increasing "propensity to make others laugh and disregard their Employments," as the headmaster, Drury, explained in a letter to Mrs. Byron after a traumatic episode which had threatened his developing aristocratic personality. Byron's tutor, in irritation at his distracting another boy during services, used a weapon that offended the young baron's class-consciousness, the epithet "blackguard" denoting servile or proletarian. He thus expostulated to his mother:

11. Byron to Lady Melbourne, Nov. 4, 1814, Byron, *Correspondence*, I, 287.

12. Marchand, *Byron*, I, 61–62, emphasizes the two contrasting but "parallel developments in Byron's relations with women, both awakening his sensibilities at an abnormally precocious age, and both with tremendous implications to his later life."

. . . I was talking . . . *that* perhaps was not right, but . . . after Church he spoke not a word to me, but he took this Boy to his pupil room, where he abused me in a most violent manner, called me *blackguard*, said he *would* and *could* have me expelled from the School, and bade me thank his *Charity* that *prevented* him; this was the Message he sent me. . . . Is this fit usage for any body? . . . Better take away my life than ruin my *Character*. . . . I fear him not; but let him explain his meaning; 'tis all I ask. . . .[13]

Here is the cry, in first draft, of the outraged Byronic hero.

The appeal to reason and justice was effective: Byron was shortly placed in a higher form. During his last year or so he was extremely happy. His physical and moral courage and his passionate intensity — he did not let his lameness keep him out of cricket, and developed habits that made him later an expert boxer, fencer, horseman, and long-distance swimmer — earned him the respect of the older boys and the devotion of the younger ones.

There seems to have been a perfect coincidence of self-dramatization and popularity in his successful recital, during his final Speech Days (June and July 1805), of Lear's address to the storm and the apologia of Zanga from Young's *The Revenge*. This "acting" was the triumphant climax of his school days, according to his valedictory account ("On a Distant View . . . of Harrow on the Hill," 1806). The applause for his Zanga made him fancy "that Mossop himself was outshone," and his Lear received such "loud plaudits and self-adulation" (note the double look at himself) that he felt "a Garrick revived."[14]

Three years later *The Revenge* was his choice for private theatricals at Newstead. The role of Zanga offers a delineation of nobility shining through outlawry — and vice versa: a gentleman driven by his code of honor to a deed of savage cruelty against another gentleman whose manifestation of comradely equality has not effaced an earlier act of condescension which insulted Zanga's manhood and his black nation, defeated in war. Zanga is a passionately articulate if not very convincing blend of Iago and Othello: a Moor with noble motives using ignoble

13. To Mrs. Byron, May 1, 1803, Byron, *Letters and Journals*, I, 13.
14. See Byron, *Letters and Journals*, I, 29 fn.; David V. Erdman, "Byron's Stage Fright: The History of his Ambition and Fear of Writing for the Stage," *ELH, A Journal of English Literary History*, VI (September 1939), 224; Marchand, *Byron*, I, 96, fn. 5.

means; a scourge to the vanity of a ruling oligarchy.[15] His defiance of the rack with "fix'd and noble mind" foreshadows Manfred's defiance of apparently absolute power. His final discovery that vengeance is empty dust prefigures the portrait of Lara and other Byronic selves.

Lear invoking the "oak-cleaving thunderbolts" and Zanga defiant gave way to gentler drama when Byron joined in private theatricals in Southwell, his mother's residence while Newstead was being rented (to Lord Grey de Ruthvyn) until Byron's coming of age. During the Harrow period he had begun a brisk correspondence with his half-sister Augusta, whom he had not known earlier and who idolized her "Baby Byron" from their first meeting. She was marrying her shiftless cousin George Leigh but was able to give her younger brother the kind of receptive attention his stormy Mama was now particularly short of, and he confided the saucier portions of his feelings in a merry, affectionate outpouring of letters from Trinity College, Cambridge, where he entered spacious rooms in late October 1805. By the end of December he was asking Augusta for a loan; at term's end he went to London, frequented the rooms of Angelo, the fencing-master, borrowed at steep interest from moneylenders, and further pursued his "gradations in the vices" initiated at Cambridge, remaining away from college until the spring months and then retiring to Southwell until June 1807, a year later. "Improvement at an English University to a Man of Rank is," he had told his mother, ". . . impossible, and the very Idea *ridiculous*."[16]

Approaching his "dawn of life," he saw it overcast with debt, the collapse of his education, the departure of Love. Mrs. Byron vetoed a proposal to go to a serious university on the Continent, and Byron busied himself writing verses. In November 1806, his first collection of *Fugitive Pieces* was privately printed — only to be quickly withdrawn when Southwell friends protested against the erotic frankness of his "effusions ,that spring from the heart." A "correct and miraculously chaste" revision was published, still anonymously, by January 1807 when the newspapers began quoting excerpts. In the summer a further and still more cautiously selected edition, with a title suggested by the printer,

15. Years later, in Pisa, when *Othello* was the play chosen for private theatricals, the part Byron chose for himself was Iago. (Medwin, *Byron*, I, 160.)

16. To Mrs. Byron, Feb. 26, 1806, Byron, *Letters and Journals*, I, 95.

Hours of Idleness, was published over the slightly provocative subscription of "George Gordon, Lord Byron, a Minor."

There were some encouraging reviews, and then, half a year later, the *Edinburgh Review* for January 1808 issued a sneering but not otherwise unmerited critique, addressed particularly to the braggadocio:

. . . His effusions are spread over a dead flat [like] so much stagnant water. As an extenuation of this offence, the noble author is peculiarly forward in pleading minority. We have it in the title-page, and on the very back of the volume; it follows his name like a favourite part of his *style*. Much stress is laid upon it in the preface; and the poems are connected . . . by particular dates, substantiating the age at which each was written. . . .

His other plea of privilege our author rather brings forward in order to waive it. He certainly, however, does allude frequently to his family and ancestors — sometimes in poetry, sometimes in notes; and, while giving up his claim on the score of rank, he takes care to remember us of Dr. Johnson's saying, that when a nobleman appears as an author, his merit should be handsomely acknowledged. . . .

This reviewer (Henry Brougham,[17] though Byron suspected Francis Jeffrey, the editor) was too busy taking up the gantlet of Lord Byron's self-advertisement to pay much attention to the verse. Yet it was a misfortune that the livelier occasional lyrics of the first edition had been replaced by too many ancestral ruminations and tedious imitations and translations. What remained in the edition that reached reviewers was indeed "imitative, sentimental, and mawkish enough" to invite their ridicule.[18]

There was a political surprise, as well as a shock to his *amour propre*, in the attack of the *Edinburgh*. Byron took it as a direct insult from the Holland House center of Whigdom, without considering that his own politics might not have been self-evident to the reviewer, and his first thought was to order his name scratched from the Cambridge Whig

17. " 'Fare Thee Well' — Byron's Last Days in England," below, pp. 208 ff.

18. Marchand, *Byron*, I, 129. Only in recent years, with publication of some verses omitted even from the first issue — "To Miss H. an ancient virgin . . ." and "[Prim Mary Ann]" (Willis Pratt, *Byron at Southwell*, Austin, Texas, 1948, pp. 51–59) — and with critical attention to the contents of that issue, has it come to be recognized that the youthful Byron wrote realistic and satiric poetry, including lines that "seem almost like trial verses for such a sophisticated poem as *Beppo*" (Marchand, *Byron*, I, 118–119, referring to "To a Lady, Who Presented the Author a Lock of Hair, Braided with his Own, and Appointed a Night in December to Meet Him in the Garden").

Club. When more sober he revoked the order, however, "as I could not abandon my principles," and took up the first weapon that lay on his desk. This was an exercise in neoclassical satire on "British Bards" which he had been writing; in his fury he transformed it into a slashing attack on most of the "English Bards and Scotch Reviewers" he could think of, "right and left" as his boxing-master had taught.[19]

Standing beside him for moral support and also accountable for some of the self-assurance of this outburst were the new Cambridge friends he had found when he finally returned, bearing his printed *Hours*, in the summer of 1807. These included John Cam Hobhouse, son of a Bristol M.P. with political and literary ambitions, who would become Byron's steadiest if perhaps also stuffiest friend; Charles Skinner Matthews, a man of witty intellect expended in practical and verbal jokes; Scrope Berdmore Davies, a fashionable gambler who would introduce Byron to the London dandies; and Francis Hodgson, a cleric and classicist with wenching proclivities. It was Hobhouse and Byron, with about seven others, including the Marquis of Tavistock, who formed the Cambridge Whig Club, grounded on the proposition that a "Revolution Whig" loyal to the establishment of 1689 was distinct from a "Whig *party* man."[20]

Nevertheless Byron almost failed to survive the last year of his minority, what with bouts of serious illness and fits of depression and a good deal of reckless, Prince Hal-like behavior: gambling, boxing, orgies of fornication and drinking. At times his mood was that of his lyric, "I would I were a careless child." In 1808 he stayed away from Cambridge, except to take his M.A. (as a nobleman's perquisite) in June. With Hobhouse and Davies he went to the seaside resort of Brighton, where he sailed and swam (and almost drowned) and talked desperately of marriage — as we may deduce from his wagering with several drinking companions, at fantastic odds, that he would never wed.[21] In the autumn he returned to Newstead Abbey and renewed his vision of manorial splendor. Since he was now over £12,000 in debt, if he would not sell Newstead he must listen to the advice of his mother: "He must marry

19. Byron to Hobhouse, Feb. 27, 1808, Byron, *Correspondence*, I, 2; Journal of Nov. 22, 1813, Byron, *Letters and Journals*, II, 330.
20. Hobhouse to John Murray, November 1820, *ibid.*, IV, 500.
21. See *Shelley and his Circle*, III, 384–392.

a Woman of *fortune* this spring; love matches is all nonsense" — or as he put it himself, "I suppose it will end in my marrying a *Golden Dolly* or blowing my brains out." Even getting clear title to those mines in Rochdale would not immediately help (said Mrs. Byron) "unless, indeed, Coal Mines turn to Gold Mines."[22]

In January 1809 he celebrated his coming of age and prepared to enter the House of Lords, announcing that he meant to "stand aloof, speak what I think, but not often, nor too soon."[23] But he had to produce documents to attest his legitimacy and was humiliated — and delayed — by the refusal of his cousin, the Earl of Carlisle, to help out. Finally in March he was able to take his seat, and the attendance records show that he went down to the House of Lords seven times in March, April, and May. It was not his fault that the issues on which he felt "tempted to say something"[24] never reached the upper house. It was, perhaps, that he was ignored by the Whig leaders, who had evidently not yet heard of the Cambridge Club. Also in March his satire had come out, lashing not only at reviewers including "blundering Brougham" but at Holland House and Melbourne House as responsible for these "hirelings." This was, in effect, Byron's proud way of knocking on their doors. Three years later he would find within them friends, mistresses, and a wife, but in 1809 nobody answered. His prepared escape, when the session ended, was a modern Grand Tour.

In July, having to skirt the continental empire of Napoleon, Byron and Hobhouse sailed for Lisbon. Journeying through Portugal and Spain they reached Malta in September and Albania in October. There Byron, having at his friend's insistence destroyed an intimate journal of his early life, began "a long poem in the Spenserian stanza"[25] which grew into *Childe Harold's Pilgrimage*, Cantos I and II, with a hero at first named Childe Burun. At the end of the year they settled in Athens, and during the next year and a half Byron, with and without Hobhouse, made various excursions through Greece and Turkey. He stood on the

22. Mrs. Byron to J. Hanson, March 4, 1809, Byron, *Letters and Journals*, I, 206 fn.; Byron to Hanson, Dec. 17, 1808, *ibid.*, p. 205; Mrs. Byron to Hanson, Jan. 30, 1809, *ibid.*, p. 205 fn.
23. Byron to John Hanson, Jan. 15, 1809, *ibid.*, p. 210.
24. To William Harness, March 18, 1809, *ibid.*, p. 218.
25. Hobhouse diary, Oct. 31, 1809, quoted in Marchand, *Byron*, I, 212.

plains of Troy, swam the Hellespont, learned Albanian, attended an audience with the Sultan Mahmoud II but was piqued by the Turks' refusal to recognize his rank in official processions, and acquired a strong sympathy for the cause of Greek independence despite the deplorable servility of most Greeks. And despite bouts of misanthropy, abstention, debauch, and fever, he got along famously with a great variety of people in several languages. He returned to England in July 1811 on a boat carrying some of the statuary being removed from Athens by Lord Elgin, bringing with him besides *Childe Harold* two satires in heroic couplets — a sequel to *English Bards* and a bitter *Curse of Minerva* condemning Elgin as a despoiler of Greece.

His travels, as he had assured his mother they would, increased his knowledge of mankind and matured his political judgment.[26] His *Childe Harold* was a "pilgrimage" for English readers, all but the hardiest of whom were island-bound throughout the war. Byron took them directly to the Tagus (which he swam), to the beautiful "image" and the "unwash'd" reality of Lisbon, the "ruin'd splendour" of Vathek's wealth-formed Paradise (what Newstead could have been with money), and the Edenic hall of Cintra, newly haunted by the "fiend" of a Convention signed there and loathsome to the British as giving Bonaparte a new lease. Then to Spain, almost on the heels of Wellesley (Wellington) who was pushing the French toward Madrid.

With his gift for participating in each social group and to an extent tolerating its mores, he obtained a close view not merely of the scenes of war but of the people's feelings. His disapproval of blood sports (including war) does not prevent his writing a vivid account of a bull-fight in Cadiz, but it leads him to frame it within a satiric contrast of London and Spanish tastes in holiday "fooleries" and a philosophic speculation on the interconnection of blood sports and demonic states of mind. If "the demon Thought" of Harold, who has "known the worst," that is, the Hell that lies in the heart of man, owes too much to shoddy Gothicism, it must yet be noted that the Hell he refers to is in "Man's heart" and not just his own, in short that the source of the poet's melancholy is the human condition *circa* 1811. Furthermore, his analysis

26. Byron to Mrs. Byron, Nov. 2, 1808, Byron, *Letters and Journals*, I, 195.

of the war in Spain and of the range of spirit within Ottoman Europe, from philanthropy and warlike virtue on the fringes of Albania to the resignation of "hereditary bondsmen" in Athens, presents a dynamic picture of history in the making, however bloody it may be in one sector or protracted in another. The sons of Spain who "were never free" naturally fight for Freedom with the cry, "War even to the knife!" The Greeks, though they may obtain French or Russian — or British — help to overthrow their "proud despoilers," will win their own free state only by their own efforts, perhaps of "a thousand years."

Today these early cantos are famous only for the fame they brought to Byron. Yet they share with *Don Juan* a quality much valued in the later poem, an evasive medley spirit deriving from a tradition which permits variations of tone from grave to gay, including antiromantic mockery. Byron when he began the poem misled Hobhouse by letting him see that he was reading some stanzas of the *Faerie Queene* in a book of *Elegant Extracts*. Actually he could see nothing in Spenser and owed him little but his stanza ("this old structure of versification") and a few quaint terms (whilome, ne, losel, ween, certes, etc.) which had become the stock in trade of the mock-Spenserians of the eighteenth century. The sentimental excesses of Byron's "vagrant Childe" are a great joke — yet authentic. Both seriously and reductively, in his opening stanzas and again in his 1813 "Addition" to his Preface, Byron insists that his hero's "name and lineage long" are not worth mentioning, that "monstrous mummeries" is the right term for the "chivalry" of the "good old times" — or any times — and that it is not the author's fault but truth which prevents him from showing the hero as more agreeable and less immoral or more active and less talkative. Beneath the specious archaism on the one hand and the Childe's secret sin on the other, what the reader is permitted to see is an Englishman too sensitive to what monarchs are doing to rustics, citizens to bulls, Turkish chains to Greek helots, to be able for long to enjoy the "sweetness in the mountain air" or the "voluptuous ways" of exotic cities. We are confronted by a potentially humane, amorous, joyous young man, frustrated by his very inability as a mortal to accept illusions. Influences from *Tom Jones* as well as Rousseau's *Confessions* are not far to seek.

The "modern Timon," returning for his second siege of London, was better armed this time for offense and defense. His cantos would advertise the vast experience in "successful Passion" that lay within his "seeming marble heart."[27] His satiric *Hints from Horace*, which he might choose to publish first, were calculated to "bring all Grub street" about his ears. And this time, in his *Curse of Minerva* and sprinkled among his stanzas and couplets and notes, there was no mistaking the volcanic sentiments of an up-to-date "Revolution Whig" flaring up at the "perfidious" foreign and colonial policies of his native "Albion" and threatening to shake their "red shadow o'er the startled Thames." But before any of these manuscripts were given to be printed, indeed only two weeks after his return to London and before he had gone home to Newstead, his mother died and then, in succession, news reached him of the deaths of the witty, independent Matthews and of John Edelston, the choirboy whose "guiltless" kiss had warmed his Cambridge days. The shock and grief inevitably slackened his sense of purpose and seemed to supply "fresh cause to roam." To advice from Hodgson "to banish care" he replied with an "Epistle to a Friend" warning that England was to have him only on sufferance.

In harsh truth the greatest problem confronting Byron was the mountainous debt he had temporarily escaped. And behind that was the desperate plight of his weaver tenants, resorting to the illicit strike action called Luddism against the merchants who owned the stocking frames in their houses. Learning of the tangled insolvency of his estates, he feared he would "always be an embarrassed man" and imagined himself joining the queue of "broken shopkeepers" for whom rebellion might prove the only recourse.[28]

There would now be income from the coal mines — when he could find capital. But he knew no heiress who might be pleased to allow him "to ennoble the dirty puddle of her mercantile blood."[29] Immediately,

27. *Childe Harold*, II, xxxv, xxxiii.

28. Byron to Hobhouse, Nov. 3, 1811, Byron, *Correspondence*, I, 57. On the Luddites as "An Army of Redressers," see E. P. Thompson, *The Making of the English Working Class* (New York, 1964), pp. 547–602. Byron seems to have been more alert to the revolutionary overtones of Luddism than most of its historians.

29. Byron to Augusta, Aug. 30, 1811, Byron, *Letters and Journals*, II, 12.

however, if he could bring himself to turn out his "old bad tenants, and take monied men, they say Newstead would bear a few hundreds more from its great extent."[30] During his Christmas visit, although "not twelve hours elapsed without some fresh act of violence"[31] by the desperate weavers, "meagre with famine, sullen with despair," he ended by letting his agents double the rents.[32] The embarrassment of his position kindled an angry fire behind his Opposition principles. "All my affairs are going on very badly, and I must rebel too," he fumed, "if they don't mend."[33]

In this mood he returned to London for the session of Parliament that was to bring his oratorical ambition to the test, with a maiden speech opposing legislation against frame-breaking and a second speech supporting Catholic Emancipation, and to lead him rapidly to the discovery that indifference was the order of the day. At an earlier — or later — period, Byron's mixture of humanitarian realism and satiric eloquence might have found a Parliamentary channel and a national response. But the session of 1812 was like an isolating fog. Half expecting such weather, he came forward prepared to find the voice of wise counsel unheeded "in the senate of the sinking state" while the "idle merchant" watched his wares "rot piecemeal" and

> The starved mechanic breaks his rusting loom,
> And desperate mans him 'gainst the coming doom.

Byron evidently added such lines to *The Curse of Minerva* while composing his vigorous February 27 speech making the same points against the ministers' bill which offered capital punishment as cure for the weavers' despair. Both Holland and Grenville, of the moderate and conservative Whig factions, and some courteous Tories welcomed the newcomer's oration with high compliments. But privately they considered

---

30. To Hobhouse, Oct. 14, 1811, Byron, *Correspondence*, II, 50.
31. Byron's speech of Feb. 27, 1812, Byron, *Letters and Journals*, II, 424.
32. To Hobhouse, Jan. 16, 1812, Byron, *Correspondence*, I, 69. Knight, *Lord Byron: Christian Virtues*, p. 75, neglects this point when he quotes, out of context, Byron's statement that he "cannot think of raising the rents." Byron was generous and charitable, but within limits; he would rather feel guilt for his tenants' famine than sink with them into their despair.
33. To Hobhouse, Dec. 15, 1811, Byron, *Correspondence*, I, 67.

it, like the speeches of the radical Burdett, "a sarcastic discourse, adapted rather to the taste of a popular meeting than to the business of a legislative assembly."[34] Only a handful of the opposition shared Byron's radical disapproval of such legislation; even *The Examiner* thought that Luddism had created a situation in which it was "but humanity to repress [the workers] by violence."[35]

Holland and Byron had been prodded by the liberal burgesses of Nottingham, including Major John Cartwright, who had served under Byron's grandfather, Foulweather Jack, the admiral, and was now fair and foulweather organizer of the movement for Parliamentary Reform. Only Byron responded enthusiastically and used the argument in Cartwright's "requisition" protesting the importation of troops: that the workers were the victims of heartless industrial speculators and a repressive government. In delayed response to Holland's persistently friendly overtures, Byron had sought and received his help, but he placed only secondary emphasis on the main argument of the Whigs, the "certain inefficacy" of repression. "I am a little apprehensive," he told Holland, "that your Lordship will think me too lenient towards these men, and *half a frame-breaker myself*."[36] Anxious though he was to please the Whig leader, offering even to "take some other line . . . or be silent altogether," he could not refrain from making a thoroughly radical speech, addressed more to the nation out of doors than to the "hirelings" within. He was flattered by public compliments in the ensuing speeches of Lords Holland and Grenville and by formal replies from Lords Eldon and Harrowby, but he received the most sympathetic praise from Sir Francis Burdett, who had stepped in from the Commons to hear him: "*He* says it is the best speech by a *lord* since the '*Lord* knows when'. . . ."[37] He sat on the committee which managed to replace the death penalty with "fine or imprisonment," only to see the death clause restored when the bill went back to Commons. In a vitriolic "Ode" in *The Morning Chronicle* he anonymously threatened broken

34. Horace Twiss, *Life of Lord Eldon* (London, 1844), II, 73, 190; see David V. Erdman, "Lord Byron as Rinaldo," *PMLA*, LVII (1942), 196, 212.

35. *The Examiner*, May 10, 1812.

36. Byron to Lord Holland, Feb. 25, 1812, Byron, *Letters and Journals*, II, 104.

37. To Hodgson, March 5, 1812, *ibid.*, p. 105.

frames to the "Framers of the Frame Bill" who "when asked for a *remedy*, sent down a *rope*."[38]

Meanwhile *Childe Harold*, published by John Murray two days after Byron's speech, was taking the world by storm, and by March 10 he was aware that the renown he desired had come, not from oratory but from poetry. It was the Childe and not the frame-breaker that soon made Holland House and Melbourne House "his most flattering resorts." Yet for some time, even while "all London were in raptures about his *Childe Harold*," he talked earnestly to fellow peers of his poems "as mere amusements, and seemed full of the idea of distinguishing himself in Parliament as a politician and an orator."[39] He had expunged certain passages from *Childe Harold* to avoid offending Lord Holland, and for the same reason he suppressed *The Curse of Minerva* and let *English Bards* go out of print. He joined the Whigs in a vote censuring the Prince Regent in their call for a new administration, and in April he prepared a lengthy and documented speech on the perennial Catholic question and joined the Whig lords in signing a petition for the record.

Yet this second speech proved more fiery and radical than his first in its contempt for the "petty cavils" and "Lilliputian sophistries" of his legislative colleagues and its sympathy for the "fierceness of despair" of the starving peasants of Ireland and manufacturers of Nottingham. It expressed more acutely the feeling that he was an outsider, one of the angry "people" desperately indicting "you, my Lords" and "his Majesty's ministers." And this time Byron was made rather painfully to feel, by a continual roar of laughter, that oratory of this sort "would not answer." There was no flagging of encouragement from Holland House, but one understood that radical "sentiments" were not relished there.[40]

In May in the House of Commons there was a momentary sign of cooperation between Whigs and independents when Byron heard his Cambridge friend Lord Tavistock second a motion supported by Burdettites and moderate and radical Whigs for "a Reform radical, as far as it went to the root of all corrupt influence, and moderate as far as

38. Published in *The Morning Chronicle*, March 2, 1812. See Byron, *Letters and Journals*, II, 97 fn.
39. *The Diaries of Sylvester Douglas (Lord Glenbervie)* (London, 1928), II, 190.
40. For details see Erdman, "Lord Byron as Rinaldo," pp. 196–197, 212, 216–217.

it restrained itself within the limits of practical good sense." But the vote of 88 to 215 was the lowest Reform vote in years. Three days later Prime Minister Perceval was shot by a bankrupt merchant.[41] And the conservative and moderate Opposition groups began to calculate their chances of entering a coalition ministry and to "renounce a community of political conduct" with even such mildly radical Whigs as Tavistock, Whitbread, and Brougham.[42] Byron, who attended an opposition caucus at Lord Grenville's on June 3, must have recognized that he had no credit to lose when he allowed a radical friend, probably Burdett, to enroll his name a few days later in a new caucus of Whig and independent Reformers called the Hampden Club.

Historically this junction of Whig reform and popular reform was of great importance. "It gave hope that the Whig party might one day be educated. It brought the Whigs into touch with the people — at any rate vicariously. It ultimately made it possible for Brougham to remain a Whig, and for Grey to take command in 1830."[43] Drafting its program, Major Cartwright looked to Byron and other aristocratic leaders "for the same glorious results produced to our ancestors by the Barons assembled on the fields of Runnymede," and he elaborated his appeal in *Six Letters to Lord Tavistock* after the club's first semiannual dinner — which Byron missed. But Tavistock did not respond, Whigs and "people" were still many fields apart, and no further motion for reform would be made in Parliament for five years. At the Whig caucus Byron had asked "what was to be done" and received the answer, nothing. Most of the Reformers, at least among "the genteel part" with whom he was willing to associate, could have given him no better answer.[44]

41. The deranged assassin was believed to have no political motive or connections; multitudes in London, Nottingham, and elsewhere, nevertheless, greeted Perceval's death "with joy and exultation" — to the alarm of Wordsworth (who blamed an inciting speech of Burdett's and might have added Byron's if he had read it), Southey (who decided it was time "to write upon the French Revolution for the *Quarterly*," feeling that "At this moment the army is the single plank between us and destruction") and Romilly (who feared the English character had "undergone some unaccountable and portentous change"). (Southey to J. Rickman, May 18, *Southey's Life and Correspondence*, ed. C. C. Southey, London, 1849–1850, III, 283–284; *Memoirs of the Life of Sir Samuel Romilly . . . Edited by his Sons*, London, 1841, II, 256.)

42. *Report on the MSS of J. B. Fortesque* (London, 1927), X, 246; *The Creevey Papers* (New York, 1904), I, 157.

43. Michael Roberts, *The Whig Party 1807–12* (London, 1939), p. 293.

44. For details, see Erdman, "Lord Byron as Rinaldo," p. 218.

Meanwhile it was a relief for disappointed Whigs and dispirited Reformers, and especially their wives and daughters, to have for the center "of conversation, of curiosity, of enthusiasm . . . not Spain or Portugal, Warriors or Patriots, but Lord Byron!"[45] And Byron, at long last among lords and ladies, overacted his hero like a shy performer driven to a hundred encores by applause. Nor was he given time to get his balance. Just as in politics he ripened too soon for his slower Cambridge friends, Radicals of the future, so in the suddenly easy game of adultery he permitted a sufficiently madcap affair with Lady Caroline Lamb to escalate into "amorous passion in its most virulent form."[46]

Caroline, "red-hot headed," sensitive, more than his match in ability to play a part and in volcanic egotism, was a woman of patrician sophistication, and an indifference to scandal which scandalized *him*. Violent quarrels and scenes and, finally, an impulsive effort at elopement only just prevented by the firmness of Hobhouse checkered the affair, and an element of Zanga-like revenge showed itself in his compulsion to destroy her freshness and naïveté, specifically her fondness for her husband.

Byron came to realize that to attend to the "perplexities" Caroline Lamb stirred up he would be forced to "sacrifice his senatorial duties" not to mention the quieter social pleasures.[47] In an attempt to disentangle himself from Caroline, he grew conspiratorially intimate with her mother-in-law Lady Melbourne, and from Cheltenham spa, whither he had retreated in August with a "very pleasant set" of Whig families including the Jerseys and Hollands,[48] he began a correspondence that affords a most sincerely comic version of the rest of his days in England. Remembering now her virtuous and well-dowered niece, Annabella Milbanke, and expecting from the sale of Newstead to be in an honorable solvency soon, he suggested that Lady Melbourne save him from her daughter-in-law by conveying a proposal of marriage to her niece:

---

45. Duchess of Devonshire to her son, n.d., quoted in Marchand, *Byron*, I, 335.
46. *Ibid.*, p. 340.
47. To Lady Melbourne, Nov. 6, 1812, Byron, *Correspondence*, I, 102.
48. To W. Bankes, Sept. 28, 1812, Byron, *Letters and Journals*, II, 163–164.

Miss M[ilbanke] I admire because she is a clever woman, an amiable woman, and of high blood, for I have still a few Norman and Scotch inherited prejudices on the last score, were I to marry. As to *love*, that is done in a week. . . .[49]

She had been the most reserved of his springtime worshipers, had indeed been less conscious of her worship than he had, yet had read the message of *Childe Harold* astutely, both in the poem and in his performance of the role. "His poem sufficiently proves that he *can* feel nobly," she had written privately, and, "I continued my acquaintance with Lord Byron, and was additionally convinced that he is sincerely repentant for the evil he has done, though he has not resolution (without aid) to adopt a new course of conduct & feeling."[50] It had been for him deceptively easy to read these hints in her earnest observation of him on his pedestal among shriller admirers; or perhaps he sensed a sexual intensity in her reserve. Reasoning upon his indirect and unromantic proposal, however, she was now able to reject him. It was a sensible conclusion for both, and he expressed no chagrin; yet the rejection was an offense he would not forget, and unfortunately she grew henceforth increasingly attracted to him.[51]

Byron meanwhile found a way, "infinitely more to my taste," of rendering "a renewal with C next to impossible"[52] by going off from Cheltenham with Lady Oxford, and her obliging Potiphar, to their country home in Herefordshire. There he could relax in the fascination of her soothing "autumnal charms" (she was all of forty to his twenty-four) and imagine himself the seduced pilgrim, or crusader, embowered by "the Enchantress," a Rinaldo to her Armida.[53]

Actually, as he well knew, Lady Oxford was the tutelary genius of the radicals, one who "always urged a man to usefulness or glory," and a retreat to her Circean palace could be a prelude to action. She it may have been who drew Byron into the Hampden Club, for Hobhouse records his own resistance to her recruiting efforts. She was an abettor

49. To Lady Melbourne, Sept. 18, 1812, Byron, *Correspondence*, I, 79.
50. Annabella Milbanke to her mother, March 26, 1812, Malcolm Elwin, *Lord Byron's Wife* (London, 1962), p. 106; journal of April 15, 1812, *ibid.*, p. 109.
51. On the engagement, see *Shelley and his Circle*, III, 387.
52. Byron to Lady Melbourne, Nov. 6, 1812, Byron, *Correspondence*, I, 101.
53. For the matter of this and the next three paragraphs, see Erdman, "Lord Byron as Rinaldo," pp. 189–231.

of the career of Sir Francis Burdett, long her lover, and had bestowed her favors on a series of handsome men who seemed ready to share her interest in radical causes. Soon urging Byron upon his "senatorial duties," she doubtless wished him to play a part in the upper house similar to Sir Francis' in the lower. But in the winter of 1812–13 the cause occupying the attention of the Oxford and Burdett circles was, as Byron's instinct told him when he resisted bringing it up in the new Parliament, an "immaculate riddle" which no act of Parliament could solve. For some time Lady Oxford had been a close confidante of Princess Caroline, whose successive disappointments with her Tory, conservative Whig, and moderate Whig friends, and her inability "to storm Holland House," had brought her to rely on Burdett and on Brougham, her official legal counsel. In the grievances of Caroline and her daughter Charlotte against their husband and father the Prince Regent, there lay a cause attractive to the discontent of all classes and a hope that a monarch who had turned Tory might be exchanged for a monarch who was "most decidedly" in Opposition. At the death of the king, in 1820, she would precipitate a crisis that would fill the streets and seem to threaten monarchy itself. In the first months of 1813 Byron frequented Princess Caroline's "very merry parties" and some of her councils of war, and on a small scale he saw a rehearsal of the crisis of 1820.

The Burdettites hung back, but on Brougham's advice the princess took her cause — in February — to the newspapers. She received addresses from craft guilds and city councils and mass assemblies organized by such "democratical" radicals as "Orator" Hunt and William Cobbett. She filled the streets with petitioners — too few to impress Parliament, hence quite enough to cool the "genteel part of the Reformers" and embarrass Brougham. A year later she left England. In June the Oxfords sailed for Italy; Byron had gone down to Portsmouth with them, half intending to follow his *amie* abroad. But he did not, and when he returned to London his sister was there, as pat as in a picaresque novel.

On the first of June, during Lady Oxford's last days in London, Byron had made his third and last speech, this time not only radical in tone but under wholly radical auspices and without Whig support or protection. Despite Hampden Club inertia, Major Cartwright had collected 199,000 signatures on Reform petitions and had prepared an introductory petition for the right to petition, censuring the magistrates' attack on that right in regions where Luddite strikes had resumed and Reformers were being arrested. Unable to get the Reform Whig leader Samuel Whitbread to present this in the lower house, he called on Byron to read it in the upper. No longer harboring any illusions, Byron enjoyed the defiant occasion though he was supported only by Cartwright's onetime "comrade," Earl Stanhope, and was attacked not only by Sidmouth but by the Whig Lords Lauderdale and Norfolk. "Stanhope and I stood against the whole House, and mouthed it valiantly — and had some fun and a little abuse for our opposition."[54] This was the swan song of Byron's senatorial ambition. During his last three years in England he would occasionally attend public debate, and vote, but no longer speak or sign the Whigs' protests.

In July and August (1813) Byron grew more familiar with Augusta, taking her to the theater and balls and assemblies and finding "a great comfort" in her combination of social sophistication and perfectly sympathetic affection; "never having been much together, we are naturally more attached to each other."[55] That the attachment soon developed into an incestuous affair may be laid to her amorality, his fascination for the forbidden, and his tendency to yield to present temptation despite a consciousness of dangerous social consequences. But to understand the state of mind in which he was almost heedless of consequences at this point, we must take cognizance of his increasing boredom in a bored society.

With many humane and radical causes in eclipse, with the wind being taken out of opposition sails by the government's increasingly momentous military and diplomatic victories over Napoleon, Byron took a very chilly view of the stranded patrician society which was to have been his milieu of prowess and renown:

---

54. Byron's Journal, Dec. 1, 1813, Byron, *Letters and Journals*, II, 359.

55. To Thomas Moore, July 8, 1813, *ibid.*, pp. 229–230. Neither Augusta nor Byron is done justice in the traditional portrayal of Augusta as "soft and voluptuous" but "amoral as a rabbit and silly as a goose" (Marchand, *Byron*, I, 395, 404). Her letters in Elwin reveal a mind of considerable social and psychological subtlety, though sometimes lacking in judgment. To accept her silliness as extreme is to accept Byron's defensive deprecation at face value.

. . . all the refuse of the Regent and the Red Book — Bedfords, Jerseys, Ossul-
stones, Greys, and the like; . . . the women . . . tied back to back upon half
a dozen woolsacks . . . hating each other and talking, and the men . . . sprinkled
round the corners in dull duets.[56]

It distressed him "to see Scott and Moore, and Campbell and Rogers,
who might have all been agents and leaders, now mere spectators" —
like himself. He was inclined to "go on with" the Whigs, but only from
a sense of honor and on a basis of "indifference on the subject altogether." What the country needed, he had maintained to Lady Oxford,
was "a little 'civil buffeting' to bring some of us to our senses." And
this would become his fixed view of English politics: that "Parliamentary
mummeries" were futile, that "certain issues strokes should arbitrate,"
"that revolution | Alone can save this earth from hell's pollution."[57]

Saying this was a dramatic way of postponing his hope to "take a
decided part in politics, with pen and person; and . . . in the house. . . ."[58]
It was also a response to the larger historical frame of those politics.
Byron never forgot that the war with Napoleon had grown out of
Britain's attempt to subvert the French Revolution. He had hoped
that Napoleon's fall would clear the stage for a French republic ("What
right have we to prescribe sovereigns to France?") and perhaps a series
of republican revolutions throughout Europe; "that all this was not a
mere *jeu* of the gods, but a prelude to greater changes and mightier
events."[59] Instead, the European situation turned out to be only a
sorry replica of the English, leaving a man like Byron with nothing to
do but "make life an amusement, and look on while others play":

. . . here we are, retrograding, to the dull, stupid old system, — balance of
Europe — poising straws upon kings' noses, instead of wringing them off! Give
me a republic, or a despotism of one, rather than the mixed government of one,
two, three. A republic! — look in the history of the Earth — Rome, Greece,

56. To Lady Melbourne, July 1, 1813, Byron, *Correspondence*, I, 162. In February 1811, the Prince
of Wales on becoming Regent had chosen to continue the Tories in office instead of bringing in his
ancient Whig friends, though he still accepted their dinner invitations.
57. Journal, Jan. 16, 1814, Byron, *Letters and Journals*, II, 381; Byron to Lady Melbourne, Dec. 27,
1812, Byron, *Correspondence*, I, 122; Byron quoting Macbeth to John Murray, July 24, 1814, Byron,
Letters and Journals, III, 112; Journal, Nov. 14, 1813, *ibid.*, II, 318; *Don Juan*, VIII, li.
58. To Hobhouse, Oct. 12, 1821, Byron, *Correspondence*, II, 204.
59. Journal, Feb. 18, 1814, and Nov. 24, 1813, Byron, *Letters and Journals*, II, 384 and 339.

Venice, France, Holland, America, our short (*eheu!*) Commonwealth, and compare it with what they did under masters. . . . To be the first man — not the Dictator — not the Sylla, but the Washington or the Aristides — the leader in talent and truth — is next to the Divinity! . . .

And now such leadership seemed impossible. "I shall never be any thing, or rather always be nothing. The most I can hope is, that some will say, 'He might, perhaps, if he would.'"[60]

Little wonder that, with a sense of yielding to his fate, Byron managed to drift into behavior that seemed to court his own destruction and that brought his affairs at length into so parlous a state that he too had to abdicate, to find his Elba — not, he might hope, his St. Helena — in Italy. His explanation of what amounted to a decision, in January 1814, to give open offense to the Prince Regent reveals his mood: "The 'lines to a Lady Weeping' must go with *The Corsair*," he wrote to his publisher. "I care nothing for consequences, on this point. My politics are to me like a young mistress to an old man — the worse they grow, the fonder I become of them." The consequences, a fierce and protracted assault from all the government papers — "I am an *atheist*, a *rebel*, and, at last, the *devil* (*boiteux*, I presume)" — were a foretaste of the attack that would drive him into exile two years later.[61]

A much deeper challenge to the world and a solace to his growing misanthropy was his continuing affair with Augusta. As his corsair, Conrad, says to his affectionate Medora in their private tower: "My very love to thee is hate to them." Yet Byron was not a corsair. Though he thought very seriously of eloping with his sister, the alarmed responses of Lady Melbourne stopped him short. His comment at the birth of Augusta's child in April 1814, "Oh! . . . it is *not* an '*Ape*,'"[62] was probably meant to reassure Lady Melbourne that the child was no imp of incest. Yet to agree to its being named Elizabeth Medora was, if innocent, provocative.

He continued to assume that at some point short of public scandal he would domesticate into "a quiet, mercantile politician, or a lord in waiting." Five months after Napoleon's abdication, Byron wrote to

60. Journal, Nov. 24, 1813, Byron, *Letters and Journals*, II, 339–340.
61. To Murray, Jan. 22, 1814; to Moore, Feb. 10, 1814, *ibid.*, III, 17, 33.
62. April 18, 1814, Byron, *Correspondence*, I, 251. See Marchand, *Byron*, I, 446.

Miss Milbanke inquiring if there was a remote chance that "any line or change of conduct" on his part could possibly remove her previous "objections" to marriage. (If nothing could, he was ready to sail with Hobhouse to Italy and Lady Oxford.) "At all events," he urged, perhaps without intentional irony, "I would willingly know the worst." She immediately let him know.[63]

Biographers dwell on the folly of Annabella's "false hope that she could reform him."[64] But Byron in offering to change his conduct was not simply humoring her pious rationalizations. He was indicating the only terms on which he could accept the yoke at all: that his wife should exert some magic power to tame him to conventional goodness. Marriage to the niece of Lady Melbourne was to be one last chance for English society to try if it could chain the lightning of his mind.[65]

Even before the wedding, January 2, 1815, there were serious moments of misgiving on both sides. Long before its thirteen months were out the marriage was a plain failure. The uxorious part of their life together was apparently satisfactory, almost up to the moment when Annabella returned to her parents, in February 1816, with "little Miss Legitimacy," their daughter Augusta Ada. Their intellectual and emotional life never attained any symmetry or coherence. He began with half-jesting warnings that she had married him two years too late, and rapidly convinced himself that this was so. His behavior was sometimes cruel and his language often wild in his efforts to perturb her somehow; in the end he was surprised that he had succeeded vastly. Her most curiously unsympathetic remark was her parting advice against "versifying."[66] But to understand what mental cruelty Byron was capable of — at bottom the most painful reality in the final months of the marriage — we have only to observe the evolution of the Byronic hero into a creature loathsome to the author himself in the sixth of those Turkish Tales which Byron wrote during his last three years in England "to wring my thoughts from" an increasingly painful "reality." Shocked and

63. Sept. 9, 1814, Elwin, *Lord Byron's Wife*, p. 207.

64. Marchand, *Byron*, I, 476.

65. On Byron's serious effort, see Marchand, *Byron*, II, 483.

66. For a fuller account of the separation, see "'Fare Thee Well' — Byron's Last Days in England," below, p. 203.

delighted readers — including Annabella — read the portraits in *The Giaour* (first version, May–June 1813), *The Bride of Abydos* (November 1813), *The Corsair* (December 1813), *Parisina* (spring 1814, published 1816), *Lara* (May–June 1814), and *The Siege of Corinth* (January–June 1815) as more or less literal revelations of the true Byron: mad, dangerous, an invader of harems, a pirate; perhaps guilty of murder, extensive manslaughter, adulterous incest (but only, in *Parisina*, by technical definition); yet implicated in such crimes only because of a passionate heart unable to forget a woman's glance, an infraction of the code of honor, or an insult to his pride.

Doubtless the author, supped full of Gothic horrors, spent hours before his mirror in the nice practice of a curling lip, and dredged his memories for authentic decor of the mysterious East. It is usual to dwell on his heroes' similarities to himself and to each other and to take them as a composite self-portrait, "an indulgence of the poet's imagination."[67] To do so is to overlook the element of self-criticism in these portraits and in their progression from 1813 to 1815. We may, however, view them as a sort of outlaw's progress, a series of pictures of Dorian Gray, advancing from the mysterious and remorseful Giaour of the first two Tales, to the organized pirate of *The Corsair* who develops into the seditious baron of *Lara*, to the horrible but contrasting sequels: Hugo, in *Parisina*, who is immensely sympathetic yet, for embracing his father's bride, justly sentenced to the headsman's axe and "meekly" dies "as erring man should die, Without display, without parade" — and at the other extreme, Alp, in *The Siege of Corinth*, the "Mr. Hyde" of the type, almost utterly unsympathetic, whose dishonorable and bloody deeds are not at all mysterious but are heaped before the reader in nightmare verisimilitude, and whose "promised bride" is an apparition he cannot even recognize as such (the living Francesca having given up her ghost at news of his approach, to escape defilement).

Psychologically, *The Siege*, written during the first months of Byron's marriage, combines a horrified view of his bride's inaccessibility and his own cruelty and "interminable pride" with a warning of the total destruction which his utter rejection by "Corinth" might unleash.

67. William J. Calvert, *Byron: Romantic Paradox* (University of North Carolina Press, 1935), pp. 118–119.

Francesca's noble father, after a Thermopylae-like defense of the Christian garrison, finally lights the powder-magazine to blow into cinders every living or dead friend or foe including himself and Alp: and "Thus was Corinth lost and won!"[68]

Each of the heroic figures in the Tales is at least potentially a commanding genius. And in a general way these imaginings seem to be a warning to the oligarchic English government of "one, two, three" as to the strength of their potential modern Cromwell — or King Ludd. The various actions of Conrad, Lara, and Alp suggest imaginary alternatives to the author's rudderless drifting, deeds he might do if driven to brandish his saber and become (as he had threatened in 1811) one of the worst anarchs of the age.

At the same time the author is turning the light of political-moral criticism upon each hero and finding fatal inadequacies. Every one of the military actions fails or is rendered worthless because skill and bravery alone are not enough. The most sympathetic flaw of the hero is his susceptibility to passion, combined with unswerving commitment to the code of chivalry. The more sinister flaw is misanthropy, in political terms an insufficient dedication to the good of mankind. Although Lara shows toward the wretched about as much compassion as Byron showed his tenants, the poet reveals Lara's courtesy and bounty, and even the mildness of his rule and his freeing of the serfs, as mere "policy" motivated by revenge. Byron's candor, influenced by La Rochefoucauld and Rousseau and reinforced by his consciousness of divided feelings as aristocrat and revolutionary, would always qualify even his belief in "freedom's wars," though he would define these as the only "holy" wars. Napoleon in his abdication had shrunk to pettiness just before Byron began writing *Lara*, and this hero exhibits the same fatal flaw

---

68. An attempt to melt all these and still other Byronic heroes into one is Carl Lefevre's "Lord Byron's Fiery Convert of Revenge," *Studies in Philology*, XLIX (1952), 468–487. Unhappily the least typical, Alp, is taken as the archetype or prototype, and the critic fails to note that Alp is the only actual "renegade" and the only one in the Tales who merits his epithet "convert of revenge." The others are more or less motivated by revenge but they do not turn their coats or their religion. Lefevre blurs the distinction between Alp and Lara, between aristocrat turned Tory or worse (betraying his country to a foreign foe) and aristocrat turned radical.

A very different hero, Hugo, has been transformed into a Freudian Messiah in a more recent study — William Marshall, *The Structure of Byron's Poetry* (Philadelphia, 1962) — but the interpretation is based on a misreading of pronouns in the text.

as Napoleon, thus apostrophized by "the unflattering Muse" of *Don Juan* in later years:

> You *did great* things, but not being *great* in mind,
> Have left *undone* the *greatest* — and mankind.[69]

Byron saw the same faults in the "blackguard Reformers" who, if they could "throttle their way to power," would make Robespierre "a Child, and Marat a Quaker in comparison. . . ."[70] And at the same time he was ready to extend the same cynicism to himself as a potential champion of the people:

> Without *me*, there are demagogues enough.
> . . . I wish men to be free
> As much from mobs as kings — from you as me.
>
> The consequence is, being of no party,
> I shall offend all parties: — never mind![71]

Another source of self-mistrust is shown in the havoc wrought on others. The Byronic hero's ability to inspire passion is even more fatal to the women: only Gulnare does not drop dead, go mad, or get flung into the Bosphorus in a sack. Gulnare, however, called Kaled in *Lara*, is a sort of Caro Lamb figure, the aggressor and chiefly a nuisance — more easily tolerated in imaginary than real life. Biographically, again, there is a revealing contrast between Medora's dying from grief at her hero's departure, in the Tale written in the fifth month of Augusta's pregnancy, and Francesca's dying from terror at her hero's approach, in the Tale written during the first months of Byron's marriage.

And yet even in these Tales Byron points to the particular historical conditions under which he would, ultimately, commit himself to a battle command. The men of action in his Tales are heroes insofar as they, for whatever motives of romantic revenge or self-defense, attack the power of "tyrant" Turkish rulers. In his 1813 meditations upon government, Byron wrote: "The Asiatics are not qualified to be republicans, but they have the liberty of demolishing despots, which is the next thing to it."[72]

69. *Don Juan*, IX, x.

70. To Hobhouse, June 26, 1819, Byron, *Correspondence*, II, 115; to Murray, Feb. 21, 1820, Byron, *Letters and Journals*, IV, 411.

71. *Don Juan*, IX, xxv, xxvi.

72. Journal, Nov. 24, 1813, Byron, *Letters and Journals*, II, 340.

In each Tale the hero is more or less estranged from his Christian and European origins yet avails himself of the liberty of demolishing a Turkish "tyrant." The exception, Alp, in *The Siege of Corinth*, is a "convert of revenge" and "renegade" who has sold himself wholly to the Turks and is therefore pure villain rather than hero. But here the poet takes pains to dissociate himself from the action of his leading figure by defining Greece as precisely the legitimate place to fight for "freedom":

> When man would do a deed of worth
> He points to Greece, and turns to tread,
> So sanctioned, on the tyrant's head.

While writing thus of the unhappy warrior, Byron was busy gathering the impressions of London society that would fill and authenticate his later satires. Mere "fashionable society" gradually palled, but he was fascinated by talk of more active times of political struggle, such as the treason trials of 1794 and the Irish insurrection of 1798 in which, if old enough, Byron told himself, "I would have made an English Lord Edward Fitzgerald."[73]

By January 1816, Byron and Annabella had exceeded the limits of mutual tolerance, and they agreed to break up the Piccadilly establishment they could not afford. He apparently thought that she and the child would stay for a time with her parents, leaving him to live his own life in London or on the Continent. She backed cautiously away from the husband she considered "diabolical" (whether from insanity or malevolence) and once safely home had no intention of rejoining him. "Don't be taken in by hearing of his tender speeches about me," she warned her mother. "We have had too much of them. . . ."[74] And soon she was intent on the battle for public opinion.[75] Byron at first began involving himself in political schemes, abetted at last by his close friends Hobhouse and the Kinnairds as well as Burdett, and responsive to a new spirit abroad in postwar England. Parliament opened February 1. The

73. Journal, March 10, 1814, *ibid.*, p. 396.

74. Undated letter quoted in Elwin, *Lord Byron's Wife*, p. 363.

75. "My only fear of coming off *second best*," she says in the same letter, "arises from the extreme policy with which he has conducted himself towards me," yet wonders whether, through his very concern for "his character in the World" he may not "be brought to terms?" (*Ibid.*, pp. 362–363.)

next day Byron's Corinth was exploded by a letter from his wife's father proposing a legal separation.

Until terms were agreed upon six weeks later, he was "a prey to the alternate passions of pity, regret, love, and indignation," according to Hobhouse.[76] "He was at least no longer bored."[77] On April 25 he sailed from Dover, never to return. There was relief as well as pain in the feeling that "the day of my destiny's over, | And the star of my fate hath declined."[78]

Even during the agonized weeks of litigation a new strength came into his poetry. The tact of "Fare Thee Well" and "A Sketch from Private Life" may be questioned, but not their power. And Byron's ringing "Ode from the French," though imperfect in execution, speaks for "the voice of mankind" with an apocalyptic vigor that anticipates Shelley's political songs of 1819.

Napoleon's Hundred Days in early 1815 had erased Byron's low opinion of the hero who abdicated; Waterloo supplied a more impressive image — if only in its massive futility. Wellington talked of the "moral lesson" of Waterloo,[79] but Byron, speaking in his "Ode" as a French revolutionary, defines the dearly bought lesson of that holocaust as the indispensability of freedom from *any* monarch, whether "Capet or Napoleon." Millions of mankind, the poet announces, are ready to assemble in Freedom's name "once more"; tyrants who think this an "idle threat" will yet weep crimson tears. "Freedom ne'er shall want an heir."

Napoleon's having "sunk into" a tyrant proves that the day of tyrants is passing — and that Byron is no longer fated to "remain nothing." Superficially the "moral lesson" of the separation, like that of Waterloo, was that legitimacy should triumph. Byron's complaint that he never learned the charges against him was, technically, disingenuous. But philosophically his aim was to bring into the open the

76. Lord Broughton [John Cam Hobhouse], *Recollections of a Long Life*, ed. by his daughter, Lady Dorchester (London, 1909–1911), II, 259.

77. Calvert, *Byron: Romantic Paradox*, pp. 124 ff.

78. "Stanzas to Augusta" (July 1816), lines 1–2.

79. Byron probably echoed the phrase from Walter Scott's *Field of Waterloo* (October 1815), stanza vi, line 3.

creed which compelled his wife — and the world — to see evil in him rather than good, to give him up as beyond tolerance.[80] And since no litigation could formulate the arraignment of Love as Sin, of Sincerity as Vice, it remained for the poet to formulate it again and again in his works, especially *Manfred* and *Cain* — and to insist upon its injustice. For the completeness of the break we may thank the rigor of Annabella's virtue. Byron now dropped his amateur status and accepted money for his poems. They reached the world, but he wrote them for England and kept alive the hope to resume his destiny in an England transformed somehow into a "country *fairly free.*"[81] And he managed to settle down, in a series of makeshift domestic arrangements, to a fairly steady routine of composition.

His first objective on the Continent was of course the field of Waterloo, which satisfied him as the equal of Marathon. He galloped across it as though trying out his boyhood dream of leading a troop of "Byron's Blacks" in the new war for freedom. And he began writing a new *Childe Harold*, minus the spurious Gothicism and mock-Spenserian clowning of Cantos I and II. Also, while still at Waterloo, he was given a copy of Abate Giambattista Casti's mocking *Novelle Galanti*, satiric tales which pointed the way to the true Byronic burlesque of *Beppo* and *Don Juan*, now less than a swift year and a half away. But his immediate need was for romantic, not burlesque, sincerity; he must discharge the "lightning" of his reaction to the world's moral lessons and transform the Byronic outlaw into a hero of "chainless mind."

He began his sober third canto in the first days of May, with stanzas defining the romantic melancholy of such "unquiet things" as Napoleon and himself. Then going quickly up the Rhine he met Shelley at Geneva, a most fortunate conjunction brought about by Mary Godwin's stepsister, Claire Clairmont, who had become Byron's mistress in April and who bore him a daughter, Allegra, in January 1817. Out of their midnight sessions, their visits to the shrines of Rousseau and Gibbon,[82] their talk and poetizing against a backdrop of Heaven-piercing Alpine "palaces

---

80. For Annabella's private formulation of her creed's application, see her "Statement H," quoted in Elwin, *Lord Byron's Wife*, pp. 345–346.

81. To Hobhouse, Oct. 12, 1821, Byron, *Correspondence*, II, 203.

82. See Shelley to Peacock, July 12, 1816, Shelley, *Letters*, II, 486–488.

of Nature" perfectly styled for one who wished "To fly from" but "not . . . to hate, mankind,"[83] Byron derived such reinforcement of his faith in the "for ever bounding spirit"[84] of Freedom that he was able to inform the third canto with a genuine, if temporary, metaphysical idealism and to produce a series of Promethean poems from which in turn Shelley drew sustenance. For Shelley and Byron it was a season as vital as the famous *annus mirabilis* of Wordsworth and Coleridge.

The first fruits were Byron's "Prometheus," further "Stanzas to Augusta," "The Dream," a "Monody on the Death of Sheridan," and a "Fragment" expressing acceptance of the flow of "the river of my years." Despite his sympathy with Napoleon in his fall, Byron under Shelley's encouragement not only chose to read that "mighty lesson" negatively but went on to derive a positive lesson from Prometheus, whose "Godlike crime was to be kind," and a strategy, from Christ, of forgiveness. In these poems of July in Diodati, the tortures of Prometheus by Zeus, of Napoleon by fate, of Sheridan by slander and poverty, and of Byron himself by Zeus, fate, slander, poverty, and Lady Byron, are not sharply differentiated; but the conquest of torture is achieved by founding one's perseverance on a higher ethic. Prometheus could act to lessen human wretchedness because he did not *despise* it. Sheridan shook the nations with pity for the oppressed. The Byronic "Wanderer" of "The Dream" would find even in poisons "a kind of nutriment" and hold converse with mountains and stars and "voices from the deep abyss" — but keep the "secret" they reveal to him.

Manfred, begun still under Shelley's influence in September but completed the following May in Rome, presents a more frankly self-focused "Promethean." Manfred depreciates his own "noble aspirations" to be an "enlightener of nations" as but youthful and mistaken visions. Nevertheless his refusal to yield the sovereignty of his mind either to the priests of compromise or to the "Destinies" who serve the god Arimanes, "the spirit of whatever is," his rebellion against the creed of guilt, and his transformation of his own *despair* into a rock of endurance combine to make the poem a manifesto of European romanticism. The

---

83. *Childe Harold*, III, lxii, lxix.
84. "Ode from the French," stanza v, line 10.

postwar era of reimposed legitimacy and tyranny, which must be resisted if mankind is not to perish, is represented in the actions of Nemesis and other spirits serving Arimanes: repairing shattered thrones, restoring dynasties, goading the wise to madness, stifling the minds that dare "To weigh kings in the balance, and to speak Of freedom, the forbidden fruit."

Victorian critics insisting on a purely personal interpretation of the poem could regard the words "put into the mouth of the Destinies" as comprising a scene "most strangely disfigured by some political allusions, and . . . altogether misplaced and gratuitous."[85] And *Manfred* is still too often discussed within the narrow compass of biographical and literary sources. One of its literary progeny, however, is Shelley's *Prometheus Unbound;* and the spirit that united Shelley and Byron, in 1816 and again in 1818 and even later, despite disagreement about many things, including the proper education of Allegra, was the spirit of Promethean resistance to the Holy Alliance and all the tyrannies which it typified.[86]

From the point of view of Byron's developing critique of the hero, however, it is notable that in *Manfred* and other incarnations of the Byronic hero in this period, including the "Prisoner of Chillon," we are confronted with men of action whose only action is to endure and to adjust their minds to inaction without loss of integrity. Thanks to Shelley and the Alps and Wordsworth's poetry of Nature read through Shelley's eyes, the hero's heart which had been "wean'd . . . from all worldlings" by disgust and self-torturing sophistry was able for a time to find comfort in "Maternal Nature," and "High mountains," and the stars, "which are the poetry of heaven," and (this is the running theme of *Childe Harold*, Canto III) his will taught itself "to steel The heart against itself." Yet this involved a concealment or suppression not only of hate and grief, but also of love and zeal (III, cxi). In the "metaphysical" canto of *Childe Harold* he could express the *wish* to discharge all his grief and

85. L. F. Tasistro, in *The New Monthly Magazine*, X (1842), 230.

86. "The great task of Byron's life was to subdue, or rather raise, the Napoleonic to the Promethean," according to G. Wilson Knight (*Byron: Christian Virtues*, p. 243), who regards Shelley's attraction to the titanic in Byron as ambivalent — but who himself approaches the adoration of Byron as a demigod. See the latter portion of his chapter, "The New Prometheus." (Knight is certainly mistaken, however, in equating the maniac in *Julian and Maddalo* with Byron rather than Shelley.)

guilt and wrath in one burst of "Lightning," "sheathing it as a sword" (III, xcvii). But this was an inevitably transient state of mind.

As soon as Byron began to regain his balance, including his sense of the absurd, as soon as he got down from the mountains to Venice and established himself in a comfortable animalistic social life incomprehensible to Shelley,[87] he began to look upon what his English friends praised as the "magnificence" of Canto III with some misgivings. "I am glad you like it," he wrote to Moore in January 1817, "it is a fine indistinct piece of poetical desolation, and my favourite."[88] But indistinctness was not his own ideal. "I was half mad during the time of its composition, between metaphysics, mountains, lakes, love unextinguishable, thoughts unutterable, and the nightmare of my own delinquencies." Now that he was less likely to blow his brains out, he could put aside the "immortal" but unreal "beings of the Mind . . . not of clay." The temporary idealism of 1816 and of Canto III had been a necessary "refuge" but he opted now for the "strong reality" of truth and reason.

One thing he obviously had to do was discharge the lightning of his curse, which he had sheathed in Canto III. The curse must, of course, be directed toward good. There are trial curses in *Manfred*, thought to have been written originally for the benefit of Lady Byron but now turned inward upon the hero, who is like the Spartan boy holding the fox which destroys only himself. But the climactic Byronic curse was meditated in the Roman Coliseum in May 1817, and given to the world in stanza cxxxv of Canto IV of *Childe Harold*. Here Nemesis, who served Arimanes in *Manfred*, is called upon to serve the poet himself, and the mountainous curse he is to "pile on human heads" in Byron's name (the accumulated revenge of all his heroes from the Giaour to Alp):

> That curse shall be Forgiveness. — Have I not —
> Hear me, my mother Earth! behold it, Heaven! —
> Have I not had to wrestle with my lot?
> Have I not suffered things to be forgiven?
> Have I not had my brain seared, my heart riven,
> Hopes sapped, name blighted, Life's life lied away?
> And only not to desperation driven,

87. See Shelley's letter to Peacock (postmarked Dec. 22, 1818), Shelley, *Letters*, II, 57–58.
88. Byron, *Letters and Journals*, IV, 49.

Because not altogether of such clay
As rots into the souls of those whom I survey.

In the next stanza the poet explains that he has learned that he bears something within him which shall ultimately move "hearts all rocky now" to love. But he is hardly displaying it at the moment, and the curse sounds stronger than the forgiveness. Even as a stratagem it is less like an appeal than a declaration of power.[89] Shelley was understandably upset by Canto IV. The rejection of idealism generally, and the "tone of mind" exhibited in the curse particularly, made him feel that he had "remonstrated with [Byron] in vain."[90] That he was "a great poet" Shelley could recognize from "the address to Ocean" in the closing stanzas, but that he seriously and not perversely meant that he drew sustenance from poison was hard to grasp. Shelley began a sonnet "To Byron":

O mighty mind, in whose deep stream this age
Shakes like a reed in the unheeding storm,
Why dost thou curb not thine own sacred rage?

The answer of course was that such rage is not to be curbed but is to be expended — or transformed. And Shelley himself, able to define it as sacred, took over the work of transformation in his own *Prometheus Unbound*. But Byron in Canto IV makes a "complete break," as Calvert observes, with "all that marks him as the romantic and visionary poet." He discards the fictitious Harold as a "phantasm" and speaks in his own person. "He is from now on committed to truth and reason," relentlessly "pulling his imagination down to earth."[91] In his historical

89. Byron's reaction to the news, a year and a half later, that Romilly had "cut his throat for the loss of his wife," is the gloating note to Lady Byron: "It was not in vain that I invoked Nemesis in the midnight of Rome from the awfullest of her ruins. Fare you well." Nov. 18, 1818, *ibid.*, pp. 268–269; cf. p. 263. For Byron's blaming Romilly, for the loss of Lady Byron, see *Shelley and his Circle*, III, 248–251.

90. Shelley to Peacock (postmarked Dec. 22, 1818), Shelley, *Letters*, II, 57–58. Shelley was too emotional about the matter to realize that the "true source of these expressions of contempt and desperation" could hardly be Byron's present associates but was his undying wrath at the English detractors who had, in effect, called him blackguard. See Byron, *Letters and Journals*, IV, 262–263, where Byron tells Moore that his desire to be revenged on those who piled desolation "upon me, when I stood alone upon my hearth . . . has comparatively swallowed up in me every other feeling. . . ." (Venice, Sept. 19, 1818).

91. Calvert, *Byron: Romantic Paradox*, p. 149.

tragedies of 1820–1821 he resumes his series of aristocratic rebels, fatally flawed heroes who are, once more, driven to shedding blood; but whereas he thought of the Turkish Tales as an escape from "reality," he intends the tragedies "to be as near truth as the drama can be."[92]

Actually Byron *had* quite satisfactorily uttered his Promethean defiance in the rewritten third act of *Manfred* and discharged his lightning in the last canto of *Childe Harold*. Even while at work on the latter he had written the satiric, mock-idyllic *Beppo*, with "half a mind to tumble down to prose,"[93] and shortly he began *Don Juan*, a work in which no Titans are to be found (except of a most human sort in some of the author's moods) and in which the sacred rage is only rarely in evidence and then directed against such appropriate villains as "butchers in big business," "renegade" journalists, and "all who war with Thought," in short, against all cant as well as tyranny. Now that Byron was psychologically ready to make use of the conversational medley informality of the ottava rima tradition, he found it conveniently available from his Italian reading and he employed it at once with artful ease. In writing the nine-line Spenserians of *Childe Harold* he had learned the weaving of rhymed stanzas, which forced upon him a necessary combination of regularity and variety, but the tighter frame of the octave stanza permitted more nimble acrobatics. Its concluding couplet enabled him to draw upon the wit-processes learned in the school of English heroic satire, and the "planlessness" of its burlesque tradition, which he believed to be "old as the hills in Italy,"[94] supplied a venerable precedent for breaking all the rules, which delighted his aristocratic radicalism. The poet of *Don Juan* and *The Vision of Judgment* is both democratic and Olympian in an impregnable combination.

Shelley had encouraged Byron to "feel that you are chosen out from all other men to some greater enterprise of thought" perhaps on the theme of "the Revolution of France."[95] And when he had read enough of *Don Juan* (Cantos I–V) "to do it justice," he was able to see that it was fulfilling, "in a certain degree," what he had "long preached of pro-

92. To Murray, Sept. 11, 1820, Byron, *Letters and Journals*, V, 75.
93. Stanza lii.
94. To Moore, Oct. 1, 1821, Byron, *Letters and Journals*, V, 385.
95. Shelley to Byron, Sept. 29, 1816, sc 342.

ducing." Shelley's comment is still pertinent to critical discussions of *Don Juan:*

It is a poem totally of its own species, & my wonder and delight at the grace of the composition no less than the free & grand vigour of the conception of it perpetually increase. . . . This poem carries with it at once the stamp of originality and a defiance of imitation.[96]

You unveil & present in its true deformity what is worst in human nature, & this is what the witlings of the age murmur at, conscious of their want of power to endure the scrutiny of such a light.[97]

Shelley and Byron lived by extremely different moral and intellectual principles, but Shelley could appreciate within the antiromanticism of *Don Juan* a humanitarianism which gives positive direction to the burlesque assault upon sentiment and solemnity and cruelty. What he approved of as "wholly new" was what we should call a new kind of romanticism, freed of anticlassical excesses, returning from the mountains and lakes to the "stove of society" and reducing all the rituals of civilization and the postures of individuals to risible absurdity, and yet quietly asserting an immense hope for individuals and nations. The modern criticism which reads *Don Juan* as completely reductive, as "spoiling" everything with its facetiousness, is the expression of a much later and more thoroughgoing cynicism, not romantic but existential.[98]

In these comic cantos Byron has outgrown the Byronic hero; instead of looking at his faces in a mirror he looks out upon the contemporary world which is yet the world of his origin, the world that cannot and yet

96. Shelley to Byron, Oct. 21, 1821, Shelley, *Letters*, II, 357. This meant that Shelley's epic dramas and *Don Juan* were not competitive, for one thing. "I despair of rivalling Lord Byron, as well I may: and there is no other with whom it is worth contending." Shelley found fault with parts of the first two cantos (1819) but of the fifth (1821) there was "not a word which the most rigid assertor of the dignity of human nature [i.e., Shelley himself] could desire to be cancelled." Shelley to Mary Shelley, (postmarked Aug. 15, 1821), *ibid.*, p. 321.

97. Shelley to Byron, Oct. 21, 1821, *ibid.*, pp. 357–358.

98. For a brilliant but un-Byronic reading of *Don Juan* as "a poem of intelligent despair — an inspired gibbering in the lazarhouse of the human condition," see Paul West, *Byron and the Spoiler's Art* (London, 1960), p. 127. West employs his title phrase to describe an art of elimination and spoiling, in the sense of rendering worthless, with a shade perhaps of the sense of plundering — a shift of values which distorts Byron's original meaning. Childe Harold, in Canto II, stanza xxxiii, has a heart "not unskilful in the spoiler's art" which involves spreading "snares"; the apparent ingenuousness masks a calculated design upon the hearts of others, to despoil them in the sense of "seduce." This should mean that the author of *Don Juan* has a purpose beneath his facetiousness; W. J. Calvert's analysis (*Byron: Romantic Paradox*) makes precisely that point.

still does survive, in order to observe how one does, in reality, live in such a world; the "need of fatality" turns into a recognition of (improbable) necessity. What Byron intended to do with the nominal hero, the youthful Juan, was something of a joke, but a true historical one. After a rake's progress through the Mediterranean, continental, and English centers of the prerevolutionary world of Byron's infancy Juan was to make his gesture of allegiance to the new world in revolutionary Paris, only to end at the guillotine. It would be a comic variant of the destiny of every one of Byron's radical aristocrats. Freedom ne'er should want an heir — but was notoriously profligate of her sons.

An art thus based on historical reality suited a poet who valued "actions" above rhymes and considered poetry only a "next best" occupation for times when "we cannot contribute to make mankind more free and wise" by participation in "more serious affairs."[99] From 1818 to the end of his life he kept *Don Juan* going for entertainment, for his comment on freedom and wisdom and all the magnanimous humor of his conversation and correspondence. More earnestly he could still write a "Prophecy of Dante" (1819) defining poetry in Promethean terms. But he kept a bid in for participation in more serious affairs as they might develop in Italy, in England and in Greece.

The ardently patriotic admirer of Dante and Petrarch who commissioned him to write the "Dante" poem was his new mistress, Teresa Guiccioli, the young wife of an elderly count; "a sort of an Italian Caroline Lamb, except . . . much prettier, and not so savage."[100] The attachment to Teresa, though Byron grumbled at the severities of the convention of the *cavalier servente*, lasted for the rest of his domestic life and afforded about as comfortable a mode of living as his penchant for irregularity could tolerate. Through Counts Ruggero and Pietro Gamba, her father and brother, Byron joined the *Carboneria*, a northern Italian insurrectionary society formed to throw off the Austrian rule

99. To Moore, April 28, 1821, Byron, *Letters and Journals*, V, 272; Pietro Gamba, *A Narrative of Lord Byron's Last Journey to Greece* (London, 1825), I, 48. But most striking is Byron's explosive (and early) disapproval of the active statesman William Windham's *regret* "that 'he had not entirely devoted himself to literature and science!!!' . . . What! would he have been a plodder? . . . a rhymer?" Journal, Nov. 24, 1813, Byron, *Letters and Journals*, II, 343.

100. To Kinnaird, April 24, 1819, *Byron, A Self-Portrait: Letters and Diaries, 1798 to 1825*, ed. Peter Quennell (London, 1950), II, 444.

imposed by the Congress of Vienna. Though there were some workmen in his section, the *Turba* (Mob) or *Mericani* (Americans), Byron discovered that the nobility who comprised most of the society were disinclined to persistent concerted action.[101] With the peasantry fatally indifferent, little could be done by leaders without followers.

At times his "Coal-heavers" were on the brink of insurrection; when those with arms were being arrested, he let his house serve as a depot; when a thousand in Ravenna were imprisoned or banished, he lingered to serve the "poor proscribed exiles." But the day of Italian freedom was far off. The chief practical result of these complottings was that the Gambas and Guicciolis, with Byron following, were forced to move to Pisa in November 1821 — where Byron rejoined Shelley in a circle that included the Greek nationalist leader Prince Mavrocordatos — and a year later to Genoa.

Shelley in his thinly disguised portrait of Byron as "Maddalo" had called him "capable, if he would direct his energies to such an end, of becoming the redeemer of his degraded country," and the country might be translated as Italy or England, or both. Byron's determination to keep in touch with an English audience gives a double point to his writing in exile when the ostensible subject is Venice, or Florence, or Rome. And he kept alive in all his correspondence a legend that he might one day return from his Elba — perhaps to challenge his maligners to a round of duels, perhaps to make these a mere by-blow of a civil war. The unlikelihood of any dramatic canceling of old scores kept him away; yet waves of hope passing through his correspondence and his poetry reveal an important source for the energy in both.

Even before the end of 1816, during the first surge of postwar discontent, Shelley and Claire Clairmont back in England wrote to Byron of an uprising of "his" Nottingham weavers, of Radical meetings in London, and of the sullen and "tumultuous state of England," and he wrote merrily of joining any revolution of "the weavers — the breakers of frames — the Lutherans of politics — the reformers":

> As the Liberty Lads o'er the sea
> Bought their freedom, and cheaply, with blood,
>   So we, boys, we

101. See Marchand, *Byron*, II, 867; Knight, *Lord Byron: Christian Virtues*, p. 169.

> Will *die* fighting, or *live* free,
> And down with all kings but King Ludd![102]

Three years later during nationwide protests over the Peterloo Massacre, letters from Byron inspired a rumor that he believed England to be "upon the brink of revolution" and was offering "to put himself at the head of a squadron of cavalry" and wield his broadsword for "the *New Government*."[103] Published at this anxious time, the first two cantos of *Don Juan* struck alarmed countrymen as anything but quietly facetious.

Characteristically he contemplated the redemptive role such emergencies might thrust upon him with great distrust of his own motives:

... I will make one amongst them, if we are to come to civil buffeting; and perhaps not the mildest. I would wish to finish my days in quiet; but should the time arrive, when it becomes the necessity of every man to act however reluctantly upon the circumstances of the country, I won't be roused up for nothing, and if I do take a part, it will be such a one as my opinion of mankind, a temper not softened by what it has seen and undergone, a mind grown indifferent to pursuits and results, but capable of effort and of strength under oppression or stimulus, but without ambition, because it looks upon all human attempts as conducting to no rational or practicable advantage [the proviso that always disturbed Shelley], would induce me to adopt. And perhaps such a man, forced to act from necessity, would, with the temper I have described, be about as dangerous an animal as ever joined in ravage.

There is nothing which I should dread more than to trust to my own temper, or to have to act in such scenes as I think must soon ensue in England.[104]

The revolutionary junta would include his friends Hobhouse, Kinnaird, and Burdett but also inevitably Cobbett and Orator Hunt and other "blackguards."

In March 1820 the arrest of Thistlewood and other Cato Street conspirators who (at urging of a government spy) had planned to assassinate the cabinet ministers while at dinner at Lord Harrowby's brought out his baronial scorn but also his evaluation of the conspirators' tactics as those of fellow *Carboneria:*

102. To Thomas Moore, Dec. 24, 1816, Byron, *Letters and Journals*, IV, 30.

103. *Diary and Correspondence of Charles Abbot, Lord Colchester* (London, 1861), III, 101. See David V. Erdman, "Byron and Revolt in England," *Science & Society*, XI (1947), 240–248.

104. To Augusta Leigh, Jan. 2, 1820, Byron, *Letters and Journals*, IV, 397.

What a set of desperate fools these Utican conspirators seem to have been. As if in London, after the disarming acts, or indeed at any time, a secret could have been kept among thirty or forty. And if they had killed poor Harrowby — in whose house I have been five hundred times, at dinners and parties; his wife is one of "the Exquisites" — and t'other fellows, what end would it have answered? . . . but really, if these sort of awkward butchers are to get the upper hand, *I* for one will declare *off*.[105]

When an English revolution was "inevitable," he would be ready to fight for the republic — even though the final result might be that worst government of all, democracy, i.e., "an Aristocracy of Blackguards."[106]

The immediate literary consequence of Cato Street was Byron's first regular tragedy, *Marino Faliero*, begun in the next few days, the story of a Venetian conspiracy led by (but not noticeably purified by) a Byronic nobleman, "a prince *with* the Commons against the aristocracy, and losing his life therefor."[107] The Byronic Marino is superficially like the Byronic Lara, but the difference is immense. No longer is the hero's guilt a private or mysterious sin but the public fact that he is a member of a ruling oligarchy which is so corrupt that human integrity requires him to act against it. The focus of interest is in the long monologues explaining the stand he *must* take by the code of nobility itself. Yet Marino is allying himself with as desperate a set of fools as the Cato Street conspirators, and his failure is inevitable. Humanely speaking, to succeed would be catastrophic.

Byron was proud to document his poem from Venetian history and insist it had no English politics; yet it was written for the English public. There are indications that despite great protestations he approved in his heart of Murray's arrangement to have the play performed on the stage as well as published; he wrote two more tragedies "to make a *regular* English drama," *Sardanapalus* and *The Two Foscari*, while under the impression that *Marino*, which actually played only seven nights, was having a successful run.[108] But in the mirror of *Marino Faliero* what

105. To Hobhouse, March 29, 1820, Byron, *Correspondence*, II, 137–138. And see David V. Erdman, "Byron and 'the New Force of the People,'" *Keats-Shelley Journal*, XI (1962), 62.

106. To Hobhouse, Oct. 12, 1821, Byron, *Correspondence*, II, 203; Byron's Journal, May 1, 1821, Byron, *Letters and Journals*, V, 404–406.

107. To Murray, July 17, 1820, *ibid.*, p. 54.

108. See Erdman, "Byron's Stage Fright," pp. 240–243.

would the English be shown? If Byron were right about the impending crisis, his tragedy should educate them, it should direct them to seek less desperate alternatives. His instinct for performance was correct; the stage is where a society can confront its largest conflicts. But what this drama and its sequels reveal is the unbridged gap between Byron and "the people," a gap which for one thing shows why there was not a revolutionary crisis in England. Byron's friends among the "Genteel part" of the Reformers were not in association with the stocking-weavers; on the other hand Cartwright, Cobbett, and Orator Hunt were not preparing an insurrectionary movement but the finally *popular* phase of the movement for Parliamentary Reform.[109] There was no white horse for Byron to mount should he land at Dover.

This he recognized clearly enough in quieter times. And the political remarks in his quieter writings — *Don Juan, The Vision of Judgment,* and even *The Age of Bronze* — served a general reforming, humanitarian purpose and appealed to the more liberal spirits of all parties. The *Vision* magnanimously laughs King George the Third into celestial retirement by way of showing where a democratic nation can afford to establish a no longer functioning "constitutional monarch." Yet the quieter course was also the more boring, and Byron quickly lost interest in *The Liberal,* the new journal he and Shelley had invited Leigh Hunt to edit from Pisa: not only because Shelley died shortly after Hunt's arrival and because Hunt and his family proved difficult at close quarters, but because the crisis in England passed and the purpose of a Byronic English journal would have been to announce his descent upon the fold, a "Tenda Rosa" in reminder of Tamberlane's gesture of pitching a red tent the day before opening siege.[110]

Ultimately, having "no Freedom to fight for at home," Byron organized an expedition to assist the Greeks, who were at last showing signs of resolute struggle. Here he faced no conflicts about his own role

---

109. The "revolutionary Cap of Liberty," observes E. P. Thompson, was "lost, somewhere on the way between Peterloo and Cato Street. Indeed, the prominence in the agitation [in 1820 in defense of Queen Caroline] of Brougham, Wood and Hobhouse was a portent of the shape of the new movement of the 1820's, under the guidance of the middle-class Utilitarians and younger Whigs." Thompson, *The Making of the English Working Class,* p. 709.

110. See Byron to Moore, Dec. 25, 1820, Byron, *Letters and Journals,* V, 144–145.

except those engendered by the almost chaotic conditions among the
Greek factions and their various "friends." Here too he qualified his
hopes with skepticism about human nature; yet from a military-political
point of view he continued to believe, as he had long done, that however
long and difficult the preliminaries might be a revolution itself was "'but
a word and a blow,'" despotisms being notoriously "timid" about trying
to put down a successful revolt.[111] It is fashionable to say, in the words
of Harold Nicolson, that Byron "accomplished nothing at Missolonghi
except his own suicide; but by that single act of heroism he secured the
liberation of Greece."[112] But this is nonsense if it is taken to mean that
he sought death and that his continued living presence would have
accomplished nothing. Until overwhelmed by illness Byron exhibited
"great practical grasp and power of leadership amid an incredible
confusion of factionalism, intrigue, and military ineptitude"[113] — a
confusion not incapable of yielding to the leadership he had begun to
assert. Said Moore: "He but looked upon himself — to use a favourite
illustration of his own — as one of the many waves that must break and
die upon the shore before the tide they help to advance can reach its
full mark."[114]

111. *Ibid.*, pp. 451–452.
112. Harold Nicolson, *Byron: The Last Journey: 1823–1824* (London, 1924), quoted in the Introduction to Byron's work by M. H. Abrams, in *The Norton Anthology of English Literature* (New York, 1962), p. 257.
113. Abrams, *ibid.*
114. Quoted in Knight, *Lord Byron: Christian Virtues*, p. 182.

"FARE THEE WELL" — BYRON'S LAST DAYS IN ENGLAND

Byron's "Fare Thee Well" to Lady Byron marked the termination of their ill-starred marriage. Yet the message of the poem — and his sending her a copy, with a brief letter of apologetic despair ("I send you the first thing I ever attempted to compose upon you — and, it may be, the last I shall compose at all") —[1] indicated a strong reluctance to concede failure. Annabella's going home to her parents, on January 15, 1816, had been a welcome development, but just as Byron had begun to enjoy the comforts of absentee husbandship her request for a formal separation had reached him, on February 2, to deliver a "cureless wound" from the arm which had "once embraced" him (as he added in self-pity when he revised the poem for printing).[2] On March 17 Byron signed the preliminary separation agreement; on the 18th he wrote "Fare Thee Well"; two days later he posted it to Annabella; and soon afterward Hobhouse found him "in great spirits at prospect of going abroad directly."[3] But there was to be another month of vexations and contest before the final signing, April 21, and his departure from London to Dover the next day.

What the poet declared that his heart would never do it had been doing all along: rebelling and seeking to inflict wound for wound. "Fare Thee Well" and its bitter sequel "A Sketch" reveal not only the frustration of the separation but the fantastic unreality of the marriage. His verses depict a goddess-wife of pure Beauty and Genius, untouched by Deceit, Indulgence, or Envy, immune to the lures of Flattery, Fortune, Pride, Passion, and even unspoiled by any infirmities accompanying her Virtue — which is so pure that it does not include forgiveness.[4] But to call this "wanting one sweet weakness" was to admit that he had found her essentially inaccessible. Annabella, on the other hand, having fallen in love with the Childe Harold image, secret crime and all, never attained true insight into the nature of the man she married.

1. Letter of March 20, 1816, quoted in Malcolm Elwin, *Lord Byron's Wife* (London, 1962), p. 448, from a transcript of a copy of the lost original.
2. Her uncompromising response to his poem fixed his need to realize there was no cure.
3. Hobhouse diary, March 22, Ms. book 12, The Berg Collection, The New York Public Library.
4. "A Sketch," lines 18–32, Byron, *Poetry*, III, 541–542.

She had led too sheltered an existence to understand his "excessive horrors" at having bailiffs camped in their too-costly Piccadilly apartment.[5] The seriousness quite escaped her — let alone the irony — of the fact that her parents in this time of need were unable to supply any immediate assistance from the fortune that Byron knew was hers even though he had *not* married her for it. She understood Byron and his friendships so little that she developed a theory that Hobhouse was an accomplice — or blackmailer — in some crime committed on their Eastern travels, probably murder.[6] As for Byron's heavily emphasized intimacy with Augusta, Annabella retrospectively came to view her role in the ménage à trois with Byron and his sister as an "experiment" that would have involved her connivance in a whole web of sexual, criminal, and political immoralities.[7] Her parting advice, on January 15, had been: "Don't give yourself up to the abominable trade of versifying — nor to brandy — nor to any thing or any body that is not *lawful & right*."[8] Had she really meant that Childe Harold should cease writing poetry? Possibly; she may well have shuddered to think what sort of Turkish Tale the versifying of their marriage year might produce. And perhaps his tentative "the last I shall compose at all" was meant to reassure her. At the moment she more probably had in mind his practice of sending tendentious and even treasonous verses to *The Examiner* and *The Morning Chronicle* — though if this advice had any effect on Byron it was evidently that of countersuggestion. His last newspaper verse, in *The Examiner* of July 30, 1815, had been "Napoleon's Farewell." His reaction to the separation was to prepare a farewell of his own.

5. See Marchand, *Byron*, II, 546.

6. See Elwin, *Lord Byron's Wife*, pp. 288, 341.

7. In "Statement H," quoted, *ibid.*, p. 346, Annabella explained that "it was not the positive evidence of any one crime of which he had been guilty— nor the malignity of his conduct towards me that formed my motives at the time— but the conviction derived from an experience persevered in to the utmost extent of duty [i.e., from the experience of trying to put up with him?], that his mind was thoroughly depraved, and that his object was as he so often told me before I would believe it— to execute all the wickedness his Imagination could devise. I could not have remained with him except on the terms of becoming his accomplice, and the attempt to make me so, if carried any further, would only have added to his guilt & future remorse."

8. Her letter is quoted in Elwin, p. 351, from the original manuscript. For attempts to explain the reference to "versifying," see Marchand, *Byron*, II, 563 (notes, p. 57). For Byron's own puzzled response, see Elwin, p. 354.

At first, Annabella's departure meant freedom for Byron to participate in the new surge of Opposition politics inspired by the postwar
discontent. On January 17, Byron and Hobhouse dined with James
Perry of the Whig *Morning Chronicle*, and two days later Byron entertained his sister with "reading a very *nau[ghty]* paper about a business
which is to come on before the H. of Lords."[9] Leigh Hunt in *The Examiner* of January 28, lamenting the dearth of talent in both houses and
taking a "glance at the persons who appear most likely to take prominent
part" against "the present facetious Ministers," began his list with
Lord Byron, "of acknowledged genius" and "a keen sight... for
human nature. How is it that he does not speak oftener, and make the
country sensible of his parliamentary as well as poetical existence?"
With alacrity Byron replied that, despite the dullness and corruption
within Parliament, as soon as "a proper spirit is manifested 'without
doors,' I will endeavour not to be idle within. Do you think such a time
is coming? Methinks there are gleams of it."[10] Parliament opened on
February 1 but Lady Byron's request for a separation came on the 2nd,
with the predictable immediate effect of turning his thoughts to the
Continent. Even in replying to Hunt, Byron had expressed more interest
in revolution than in parliamentary business; now he cast his eye on
the prospect of a European revolution against restored legitimacy. On
March 15 *The Morning Chronicle* published his "Ode from the French,"
predicting a reversal of the defeat of Freedom at Waterloo when at last
the "millions" would unite against the "tyrants." Ostensibly a translation of the sentiments of a French Jacobin, the ode is lurid and out-
rageous — and fascinating as a prediction of both Byron's and Shelley's
Promethean poems to come, including Shelley's *The Masque of Anarchy*,
to which its images and rhymes would contribute (some having, in turn,
been suggested by "The Ancient Mariner"). At Waterloo, says the poet,
the blood of Freedom was shed on the plain like dew. But instead of
sinking, the blood is

> Rising from each gory trunk,
> Like the water-spout from ocean,

9. Augusta's letters, quoted in Elwin, pp. 354, 357.
10. Byron to Hunt, Jan. 29, 1816, Byron, *Letters and Journals*, III, 259.

With a strong and growing motion—
It soars, and mingles in the air

. . . .

A crimson cloud it spreads and glows,
But shall return to whence it rose;
When 'tis full 'twill burst asunder—
Never yet was heard such thunder
As then shall shake the world with wonder—
Never yet was seen such lightning
As o'er heaven shall then be bright'ning![11]

On April 7, in *The Examiner,* another Jacobin manifesto appeared, "On the Star of 'The Legion of Honour'," presented cautiously by Leigh Hunt "rather as by a Frenchman than an Englishman." Although "darkness must again prevail" after Waterloo, only the "bright promise" of Freedom keeps life from becoming "but a load of clay."[12]

Byron had meanwhile begun to circulate in manuscript his verses of farewell to his wife. And finding her adamant and the gossip against him increasing, he versified a second outcry. Still determined to put the blame on others than Annabella (or himself), he singled out as the Iago among her advisers — not inappropriately, as the record shows — her former governess and present ramrod Mrs. Clermont. This "hag of hatred" he accused of "soul-hardened scheming" in a vitriolic "Sketch from Private Life" which he wrote on March 29 or 30 and sent at once to his publisher, John Murray, requesting "*50* copies (for *private distribution*) struck off— and a proof tomorrow— if possible."[13] On April 2 when he was revising the proof Byron decided to "print the 'Fare thee well' with these— as a relief to the shade."[14] Murray's senate of wits, Rogers, Canning, and Frere, judged "A Sketch" an admirable

11. Byron, *Poetry,* III, 431. This would be one of the first poems Byron was likely to show Shelley when they joined forces in Switzerland.

12. Both poems were published anonymously but both were recognized at once as Byron's, probably from the style and themes, and with the aid perhaps of the grapevine of conversation.

13. Byron, *Letters and Journals,* III, 277–278; Byron, *Poetry,* III, 540, fn. 1. On March 30 Byron wrote "I send you my last night's dream"; this could mean that he began the poem on the 29th, but the "original MS." is inscribed as "written . . . 30th March." For a beginning in prose, see the letter of March 26, quoted in Elwin, *Lord Byron's Wife,* p. 452.

14. Byron, *Letters and Journals,* III, 279.

satire and one of Byron's best things, without apparently giving thought to the consequences of its use as defamation.[15] Both "Fare Thee Well" and "A Sketch" were printed by April 8 and put into circulation among friends and foes. "There is no evidence that Byron at this time meant to publish," observes Prothero,[16] but the threat to do so was implied by the printed circulation. Lady Byron was treating the separation as a battle for public opinion, hoping to bring Byron "to terms" (for the mischief had been compounded by a groundless supposition that Byron would seek to deny her custody of their child, Augusta Ada) by threatening "his character in the World," and she spoke of her "only fear" as that of "coming off *second best*."[17] She had recognized the tone of "Fare Thee Well" as "very tender" and judged the poem as a cunningly effective Byronic plea. She feared that its circulation was turning "The Tide of feeling" against her, and decided that the charge that she was "unforgiving" (line 5) ought to be countered by newspaper publication of her "Declaration."[18] This was an equivocal document in which she denied responsibility for spreading injurious rumors against Byron yet refrained from denying their truth. She was dissuaded from the indiscretion of publishing it.

The indiscretion which Byron ought to have been dissuaded from was the writing and circulation not of "Fare Thee Well" but of "A Sketch." To many the farewell poem seemed "an *amende* honourable" which did Byron "infinite credit."[19] But the assassination of Mrs. Clermont's character in "A Sketch," however clever it may have seemed

---

15. Murray wrote to Byron that they had "all seen and admired the lines; they agree that you have produced nothing better; that satire is your forte." (Quoted in Byron, *Letters and Journals*, III, 278, fn. 1.) Murray was understandably reluctant to follow Byron's command to send a copy to Lady Byron, however, and gave Mrs. George Lamb (through whom he transmitted one) the impression that he had printed the poem "with pain & reluctance" (unless she was fibbing). See her undated letter to Lady Byron quoted in Elwin, *Lord Byron's Wife*, p. 462.

16. Byron, *Letters and Journals*, III, 278, fn. 1. But Mrs. Lamb (see preceding note) assumed that Byron's next step would be to publish—and she pointed out the advantage to Annabella: "I think I never read any thing so artful & abominable . . . If *he* publishes it releases you from all obligations of silence." (Elwin, *Lord Byron's Wife*, p. 462.)

17. *Ibid.*, pp. 362–363, 375, 389, 409, *et passim*.

18. Doris Langley Moore, *The Late Lord Byron* (Philadelphia and New York, 1961), pp. 163, 164, 246; Elwin, *Lord Byron's Wife*, pp. 448, 461.

19. Thus Sir Francis Burdett, in Byron, *Letters and Journals*, VI, 18–19, fn. 2.

to the wits, and however gratifying to Byron's sense of revenge, was an offense against the code of honor, being the attack of a nobleman upon a servant and a female, "Born in the garret, in the kitchen bred, . . . Even worms shall perish on thy poisonous clay." Annabella was not alone in considering it "*blackguard* beyond belief."[20] And the man who arranged for its publication, while he happened to be one of her legal advisers, need not have been prompted by her to recognize the deadly effect this weapon would have against the poet who had forged it.

On Sunday, April 14, the scandal of the separation was brought into the public domain by the publication in John Scott's *Champion* of "Fare Thee Well" and "A Sketch from Private Life" under the heading, "Lord Byron's Poems On His Own Domestic Circumstances," which were preceded and followed by two skillful pieces of moral and political criticism alluding to the scandalous rumors — and to Byron's recent verses more French than English. As Scott was able somewhat disingenuously to observe, when resuming the subject two weeks later, "the appearance of such verses as those *on the Star of the Legion of Honour* . . . just as Lord Byron's Poems to his wife, and his wife's governess, came out, did tempt one to allude to the connection between such politics and such conduct."[21] Scott did his righteous task effectively; he may even have felt sincerely that "it would not be doing justice to the merits of such political tenets, if they were not coupled with their corresponding practice in regard to moral and domestic obligations";[22] yet Scott had been an older schoolfellow of Byron's at Aberdeen and was an admirer of his poetry: he would not have gone to such lengths if he had not been influenced by what he later described to Byron as "rather extraordinary means."[23]

The one responsible for bringing those means to bear proves to have been Henry Brougham, a person supposedly on Byron's side in

20. Elwin, *Lord Byron's Wife*, p. 463. While "Fare Thee Well" was included in Byron's *Poems*, 1816, "A Sketch" was omitted from authentic editions until 1819. There were numerous immediate piracies.

21. *The Champion*, April 14, 1816, pp. 113–114, 117–118; April 28, 1816, p. 134.

22. *Ibid.*, April 14, 1816, p. 118.

23. According to Byron in 1821, Scott told him "that he and others had been greatly misled; and that some pains, and rather extraordinary means, had been taken to excite them." (Byron, *Letters and Journals*, V, 576.)

politics, if not morality,[24] and sufficiently "personally acquainted with Lord B.," according to Lady Byron, for her to consider him acceptable as a "Mediator" while knowing him to be safely on *her* side. An associate of Romilly, who remained largely behind the scenes in this case, Henry Brougham was nevertheless described by Annabella — with a perhaps intentional pun while writing about *The Champion* — as one "who has been my warmest champion throughout." (Byron's "incessant persecutor" would be Murray's phrase.)[25] At a party at Lady Jersey's on April 6 (as somebody informed Annabella, perhaps Brougham himself) "Mrs. G. Lamb cut both him [Byron] & Mrs. Leigh [his sister]— Brougham & some other Gentlemen, *him*."[26] The separation verses soon reached Brougham,[27] and he lost no time in putting the match of Byron's indiscreet "versifying" to the prepared fuse of rumors of adultery, incest, and homosexuality or something else which gossip regarded as too horrible to mention. Within the next few days Romilly, as Brougham told Lady Byron, interrupted a legal conference to express his "indignation" at the Clermont satire,[28] and Brougham persuaded John Scott to publish both poems in the next Sunday's *Champion*, quite

24. Brougham was no doubt sincerely outraged by Byron's excesses in both departments. Yet, for example, both men regarded Sir Francis Burdett as the limit of *respectable* radicalism; while Byron's "independent principles" seemed held within that limit, Brougham could assure Douglas Kinnaird that they lent "a great additional charm" to his agreeable manner. (See Byron, *Letters and Journals*, II, 397, fn. 1, quoting a letter of Dec. 9, 1814.) As for morality, when Byron tried to guess what had offended Brougham he thought it might have been his failure to recognize the liaison between Brougham and Mrs. George Lamb, which became public knowledge only when they joined each other on the Continent that summer. (For Annabella's efforts to save "Caro George" from being ruined by her righteous adviser, see Moore, *The Late Lord Byron*, pp. 248–249.)

25. Elwin, *Lord Byron's Wife*, pp. 410, 465; Byron, *Letters and Journals*, IV, 69, fn. 3.

26. Lady Byron to her mother, April 12, quoted in Elwin, *Lord Byron's Wife*, p. 463. The closeness of "Caro George" and Brougham in this report is only one of many indications of their working as a team. The tone of Caroline's gossip may be gathered from a letter of March 22 from the Duchess of Devonshire to her son: ". . . he [Byron] must be mad or a Caligula. Caro will have told you some of the stories. It is too shocking." (Vere Foster, *The Two Duchesses*, London, 1898, p. 413, quoted in Marchand, *Byron*, II, 585, fn. 9.)

27. *The Champion* of April 21 (p. 125) claims that "the two Poems were sent under cover to Members of Parliament, directly from Mr. Murray. Mr. Murray gave numerous copies of them, in his shop, to applicants; they were read at Parties: we had half a dozen copies sent to our office, from various quarters; and we have scarcely a single acquaintance that had not seen them." If we divide it by six, this reckoning is credible. Brougham was probably on Byron's select list of M.P.'s. See also Elwin, *Lord Byron's Wife*, p. 462.

28. Annabella to her mother, April 15, *ibid.*, p. 466. Mrs. Lamb's hint — "If *he* publishes it releases you . . ." — was a step toward the idea of getting them published first.

possibly making some suggestions for the carefully prepared editorial commentary. On Saturday, April 13, Brougham dined with Lady Byron, obtaining her approval of the publication only when it was rather too late for her to interfere if she had wished to.[29] She had written an imitative reply, entitled in her notebook "By thee Forsaken — March 1816," but apparently with no intention of entering it in the lists against "Fare Thee Well."[30]

The well-kept secret of Brougham's connection with *The Champion* has only recently been discovered by biographers of Byron, and it has not been perfectly assimilated, since it conflicts with the traditional attribution of *The Champion*'s attack to Tory politics. Journalistic necessity led to the swift and extensive reprinting of both poems in the rest of the London papers, and it is true that (except for fair treatment from the Tory *Courier*[31]) vituperation accompanied them in the Tory

29. Brougham may have done this in the form of letting her know of the pending publication, or she may have been more directly implicated than her letter to her mother, our source of the information, acknowledges. Written on Monday, April 15, this letter (*ibid.*, pp. 465–466) conflates details from Brougham's conversation of Saturday ("after dinner . . . in private") with details supplied by an emissary of Mrs. Lamb (and Brougham?) on Monday morning:

> He . . . gave me his opinion on several points. The public feeling has been still more turned against Lord B. by the publication of his verses in the Champion of yesterday — and some comments were added to expose the duplicity of their author — by which a wonderful effect has been produced. So Lady Granville . . . has told me — She came this morning, having been particularly requested, by Mrs. G. Lamb. . . .

According to Benjamin Haydon's *Diary*, in an entry made May 15, 1824, at news of Byron's death, John Scott of *The Champion* "called on Brougham by chance" and was given a copy of Byron's "Farewell"; Scott then called on Haydon "on his return from Brougham & shewed me the 'Farewell' & told me his intention of printing it, which I disapproved." Scott was evidently offhand about his tie with Brougham, though "by chance" admits a custom of calling without specific appointment. Haydon's recollection was that "Scott attacked him [Byron] from mere spite, because he met Byron at Hunt's table when he was in Prison, & Byron took no notice of him" — but also because "Scott's paper lagged in circulation" (a cliché which Haydon perhaps picked up from the April 21 *Examiner*; *The Champion* of April 28 reminded Hunt that he used to be contemptuous of such nonsense when it was leveled at himself). (*The Diary of Benjamin Robert Haydon*, ed. Willard Bissell Pope, Harvard University Press, 1960, II, 482; quoted in Moore, *The Late Lord Byron*, pp. 162–163, but with mistaken characterization of Scott and with no warning that the entry was not made in 1816.)

30. See Elwin, *Lord Byron's Wife*, p. 470 (where the two concluding stanzas are given), and p. 531, note. But manuscript copies were circulated in later years.

31. To draw on Leigh Hunt's summary (*The Examiner*, April 21, p. 248):

> Even a Writer in the *Courier* [April 18], who has not escaped altogether from the influence of these poisonous suggestions, says that 'if Ladies be the best judges upon such points, their opinion will be very different as to the first poem ["Fare Thee Well"]: — at least,' he

papers and defensive comment in the Whig *Morning Chronicle* and *Sunday News* and in the independent *Examiner* and *The Independent*

continues, 'one fair correspondent says that if her husband had bade her such a farewell, she could not have avoided running into his arms, and being reconciled immediately.' . . . But hear what is said of ["A Sketch"] also by the writer in the *Courier*, — who by the way has behaved with a manliness on the occasion, that would shame any calumniator unhabituated to a resolute want of delicacy. 'Let it deserve,' says he, 'all the censure that has been bestowed upon it, still the fierce vengeance, the spirit of libellous invective, if you will, the deep, unmeasured, rancorous hatred, however culpable, that dictated it, may afford some proof of affection for the object whom his Lordship, whether erroneously or not, we do not say, conceives to have been alienated from him by the person against whom the Sketch is directed.'
I believe that this unexpected manliness of the venal *Courier* can be accounted for if we recall that an occasional contributor and adviser to that newspaper was S. T. Coleridge and notice that precisely at this moment in history he happened to be "bewitched" in Byron's favor, finding a sun-god where others suspected a demon. Normally some of the gossip accompanying the separation might have shaken Coleridge, but in the spring of 1816 he was under very strong obligations to Byron: for encouragement as a playwright, for a donation of £100 in February, and for a contract with Murray to publish the *Christabel* volume (in May). On April 10 Coleridge sent his "literary Counsellor and Amanuensis" J. J. Morgan to Byron with the Ms. of *Zapolya*. On April 12 he had a visit from Murray, with "flashes of praise, which Lord Byron had coruscated respecting . . . Christabel." And some time before, or on the morning of, April 15 — and thus at least three days before *The Courier* review — he called on Byron at 13 Piccadilly Terrace, enjoying "half an hour" of "the sweetest Countenance that I ever beheld — his eyes are really Portals of the Sun, things for Light to go in and out of. — I mean to read all his works together: & shall then form my opinion. — " (Fragment of a letter of "5 [May 1816?]," Coleridge, *Letters*, IV, 636.) The open mind and manly words of the "writer in the *Courier*" are too close in spirit for pure coincidence. The style is not strikingly Coleridgean, but the idea and the psychological argument seem to be Coleridge's.
Whether or not Coleridge had seen *The Champion* before he met Byron, those eyes, as he later put it, "bewitched me in his favour." In another room at the same moment was Byron's frequent visitor Leigh Hunt, who remembered hearing Coleridge recite *Kubla Khan* "one morning, to Lord Byron," who was "highly struck with his poem, and [with] how wonderfully he talked." And the morning must have been that of April 15, on the evening of which Coleridge arrived at Gillman's. Hobhouse, coming in that day, "found Sam Rogers & Leigh Hunt up in arms at the publication of Fare thee well and the Sketch in Scott's Champion of yesterday with violent abuse of Lord Byron." The only undocumented link is a visit to *The Courier* office by Coleridge or Morgan — or a letter. In May, Daniel Stuart, owner of *The Courier*, visited Coleridge and received a long letter from him tracing the paper's gradual decline into a partisan servant of the government — but offering to supply new life with a series of essays. In June *The Courier* printed a splendid review of *Christabel* (borrowed, however, from *The Times*).
The manliness of *The Courier* had been, however, but a momentary aberration. The sympathetic comment of April 18 ends about half-way down a full column headed "LORD BYRON." It is followed by a quite unsympathetic excursus beginning "We have already said that we are totally unacquainted with the circumstances . . ." and putting "the severest blame upon Lord Byron, for permitting" publication. The active editor, T. G. Street, here had seized the pen, asserting: "With none of the parties have we the honour to be personally acquainted. Lord Byron we know but by his talents, which too often have been miserably applied." In following issues *The Courier* joined the hue and cry. (For details used in this reconstruction see Coleridge, *Letters*, IV, 622, 626–628, 630, 634 n., 636, 638, 641; Marchand, *Byron*, II, 597 and fn. 8; 601.)

Whig.[32] Yet the actual alignment was more complicated and more damaging than any simple battle of Tory against Opposition. Scott's *Champion* and Hunt's *Examiner* were both independent Opposition papers, largely in agreement about postwar politics though they had differed over the recent war with Napoleon. Both were pleased to receive advice and contributions from Brougham, who was an energetic organizer of press support for his political campaigns. Leigh Hunt's ideal grouping of political talent would have been led by Brougham in the Commons and Byron in the Lords. Brougham was on trial with the party Whigs, whose leadership in Commons he had begun to assume, but he was not one of the aristocracy and he was mistrusted by many of them; he was at the same time attempting "to build up a new political connection of his own out of advanced Whigs and moderate Radicals," including Francis Place and James Mill, the friend of Bentham.[33] Byron, Brougham, Hunt, and Scott were of one accord in their censure of the Prince Regent and of the reactionary foreign and domestic policies of the Liverpool-Castlereagh government. Byron should have figured in Brougham's political schemes, and evidently he did — as a marked man.[34]

32. Only the Tory *Morning Post* resisted printing "A Sketch" (though Hunt quoted only the virtuous portion). For details of the newspaper reprintings, see Byron, *Poetry*, III, 532–535, where, however, *The Champion* is called "a Tory paper."

33. See Arthur Aspinall, *Lord Brougham and the Whig Party* (Manchester, 1927), chapter IV, esp. pp. 52–53.

34. Teresa Guiccioli's story, in *My Recollections of Lord Byron* (London, 1869), I, 40 fn., that when
    the persecution . . . had attained its greatest height an influential person — not belonging to
    the peerage — came to visit him [Byron], and told him that, if he wished to see how far the
    folly of men went, he had only to give orders for having it shown that nothing said against
    him was true, but that he must change politics and come over to the Tory party,
has only fixed the legend that Byron's attackers were Tories and his defenders Whigs. But the story itself makes sense, if its ambiguities are cleared up. Suppose the "influential person" were George Canning, for instance, a Tory whom Byron respected and who admired "A Sketch" as satire. He had just accepted an invitation to join the shaky Liverpool-Castlereagh government a few days before March 19, when the Whigs led by Brougham voted down its tax bill. The Tories were fighting for dear life (they would have resigned, "had later constitutional practice been in vogue" — Aspinall, *Lord Brougham and the Whig Party*, p. 60); Canning might well have proposed something to Byron when the Whigs began to desert him; as for changing the tune of the government papers, Canning was accustomed to use such tactics. Or, the suggestion about "the folly of men" may have been made more in philosophical amusement than in earnest. The rest of Teresa's account, after Byron rejects the proposal nobly, must be understood to refer to Whigs, not Tories: "Hereupon the person in question said that he must suffer the consequences, which would be heavy, since his [i.e., Byron's] colleagues were determined on his ruin, out of party spirit and political hatred." The account goes on to illustrate those colleagues' behavior:

The demolition of Byron in *The Champion* of April 14 begins with a letter to the editor signed "A. S.," which alleges to be a belated exposure of Byron's *Morning Chronicle* poem of March 15, here called his "Ode on the battle of Waterloo." The critic deplores this eulogy of "the worst enemies of liberty that the world ever knew," written by an Englishman who has "great powers of poetry" and "to whom all his countrymen would wish to look with unmingled feelings of approbation and admiration." Unhappily the poem is a "melancholy instance of the prevalence of . . . that utter indifference to . . . principle, that French mania . . ." — and so forth. This letter takes up parts of the first and second pages of the issue. On the fifth and sixth pages appear the two poems, followed by a long unsigned critique agreeing with what we know were Lady Byron's and her lawyers' sentiments: that the poems were written "to attempt to turn the whole current of public reproach and displeasure against his wife."[35] The critique is probably by Scott, with some help

> It was at this time that, going one day to the House, he was insulted by the populace, and even treated in it like an outlaw. No one spoke to him . . . except Lord Holland. . . . Others — such as the Duke of Sussex, Lord Minto [but Minto had died in 1814], Lord Lansdowne and Lord Grey — would fain have acted in a like manner; but they suffered themselves to be influenced by his enemies, amongst whom more than one was animated by personal rancour because the young lord had laughed at them and shown up their incapacity.

The lords named are the Whig phalanx; if "party spirit" kept them from greeting Byron, it was fear of tainting the party with his infamy. Brougham, who worked closely with Grey, may have had the latter's support in keeping them in line. Enemies among Tories (the usual reading) would hardly have influenced them, but Whigs animated by personal rancour included those Byron had laughed at in *English Bards:* "blundering Brougham," "drivelling" Carlisle (the cousin with whom Byron may never have "made it up," as he talked of doing in 1815), and perhaps some of Holland's "hirelings" who had not, like Holland, forgiven the attack.

Except for the proposal to join the Tories, Teresa's account seems influenced by a passage in Medwin (*Byron,* pp. 49–50), which is a distortion of Byron's own narrative written in 1821 (Byron, *Letters and Journals,* IV, 479). Instead of "insulted by the populace," Medwin has Byron say "hissed as I went to the House of Lords, insulted in the streets, afraid to go to the theatre." Byron himself wrote: "I was advised not to go to the theatres, lest I should be hissed, nor to do my duty in parliament, lest I should be insulted by the way"; he went on to say that he was "not deterred . . . from seeing Kean . . . nor from voting according to my principles." It does not follow that since he did go he was hissed. (Marchand, *Byron,* II, 602 fn. 4, quotes Hobhouse's flat contradiction of Medwin but gives only a reference to Byron's account and ignores Teresa's.) The visit to Parliament occurred on April 2, too early for the public furor in any event. We cannot suppose a later, unrecorded, visit, for although Teresa says he quitted the House "after a few moments," Byron says he stayed to vote. (There was a vote on April 2 but no division; the House met only six more days that season. See *Journal of the House of Lords.*)

35. The serial pagination is given in fn. 21. Cf. Moore, *The Late Lord Byron,* pp. 163–164.

from Brougham. Its justification is the argument that the greater the genius the greater the offense. In all Byron's satires there is found to have been a "looseness of aspersion" and a lack of "gentlemanly" restraint in attacking individuals. Yet occasion is taken to recollect some of Byron's shafts of poison that were applauded because "so fairly aimed" — that is, aimed at the person called "Charles to his People, *Henry to his Wife!*"[36] The italics aim the second phrase at Byron himself, though his original was directed at the Regent. *The Champion* by this device, without naming either name, could proceed to heap the strongest terms of disapproval on both persons as "savage and profligate." This may be Scott's cleverness, but the violence smacks of Brougham. At least Brougham would relish it, for he had just recently, March 21, in the House of Commons indulged in an intemperate and untimely castigation of the Regent, with an eye to the Radicals (and Leigh Hunt) out of doors, but with the effect of dismaying the Whigs. On March 19 Brougham had led the Opposition in a resounding defeat of the government's bill to renew the income tax, and for a day or so he and his Whig associates were expecting to be invited to form a new administration — under this same Regent. Brougham's attack was a characteristic access of hubris, due to miscalculation or madness; it lost him the party leadership, just as his expression of contempt for some of the Radicals (and for Bonaparte) would shortly cost him the bid to represent Westminster. And the ironic thing about his maneuvering against Byron is that, however effective in securing Byron's exile, it probably contributed to the continuing Whig mistrust of Brougham himself. Insofar as it remained secret, his use of the press did him no harm, but his brashness overreached itself in the cutting of Byron at Lady Jersey's party, where Byron was among his Whig friends, as it did again shortly afterward when he attempted to blacken Byron's reputation by purveying to his staunch defender Perry some gossip about nonpayment of rent, which Hobhouse could immediately brand a lie.[37]

36. Byron's "Windsor Poetics," written April 1813, thought not to have been published until 1818. But Scott says, "We all well remember his famous" poem.
37. Hobhouse, dining with Perry on April 26, found that "Brougham has been with him telling him that B cheated the Duchess of Devonshire [his landlady at Piccadilly Terrace] of 500£ — I said it was a lie out loud." (Diary entry quoted in Marchand, *Byron,* II, 614.) The cutting at Lady

Hunt's attempt to defend his friend Byron in the next *Examiner*[38] was inept, but it did make the point, nowadays overlooked, that *The Champion*'s publication of the separation poems had not been the beginning of its defamation of Byron. As we look back over earlier issues of *The Champion*, we can find not only the pervasive influence of Brougham and some severe yet judicious criticism of Byron's poetic career, but also some invidious allusions to his private life and some political and personal fulminations against his friends Kinnaird and Hobhouse. (Lady Byron called these friends "the Piccadilly crew of blackguards," on April 12,[39] but may have done so earlier as well; it is a nice question whether she or Brougham or Scott first thought of the men of Piccadilly Terrace as infected by a coarse mania more French than English.) *The Champion* of February 11, reviewing *The Siege of Corinth* and *Parisina*, quite sagely warned Byron of the impasse in his poetic career: "the moment has arrived when Lord Byron must either lose part of his popularity, or it must continue at the expence of public discernment." The Tales were getting worse. "The Ode to Napoleon Buonaparte" (of 1814, currently in its twelfth edition) "was a piece of stormy precipitation . . . and the *Hebrew Melodies* were——bad." And now Byron was perverting his political talent and destroying "the healthy tone of the public's sensibility." Then a moment's flash of steel: *The Champion* would not *now* "lay any accusation against his Lordship's morality."[40] Two Sundays later it *would*, picking up from *The Morning Chronicle* a denial of "scandalous and malicious reports" about Byron and taking a very dark look at the connection between his morals and his politics:

Our public sentiment must be preserved, if possible, from those seductions that are zealously practised by the *Anglo-gallic* school that now exists among us; and we must be excused if, for this purpose, we refer to the conduct of its most notorious professors. If they are the introducers of French morals among us, it will at least be easy to account for the tone of their publications.[41]

Jersey's on the 8th may have been a sequel to that in the House of Lords (not, of course, directly involving Brougham) on the 2nd.
38. April 21, 1816, p. 249.
39. Letter to her mother, quoted in Elwin, *Lord Byron's Wife*, p. 463.
40. *The Champion*, Feb. 11, 1816, p. 46.
41. *Ibid.*, Feb. 25, 1816, p. 62.

The reference in the plural is explained in the next *Champion*, when the leaders of the *"Anglo-gallic* school" are named:

Lord Kinnaird, and his friend Mr. Hobhouse, are commonly reported to be the writers of various letters which appeared in the *Morning Chronicle*, &c. when Buonaparte was last in France, containing . . . very indisguised tributes of good-will towards his cause.[42]

This was year-old news. But at the head of the Piccadilly crew stood Byron, and if at first we wonder how John Scott could know that Byron was going to write his provocative verses "From the French," we come to realize that Byron's writing and publishing them in *The Morning Chronicle* and *Examiner* in the following weeks can be considered in part his defiance of *The Champion*'s menaces. For after identifying the "school," Scott in the same issue (March 3) pointedly threatens to publicize the separation scandal, alluding again to "certain gross violations of domestic decencies and duties, the news of which has startled the town, and called up a general sense of indignation,——nay, we may say of horror."[43] (Lady Byron writes the same way on April 15, after she has dined with Brougham.) Scott goes on to warn that French laxness of moral propriety will not find impunity in England, "thank God," and that

the Prince or the Poet who plays the ruffian with his wife [note the equation of Regent and Byron which takes fuller shape April 14], or the rogue with his neighbours [Kinnaird and Hobhouse again?], finds his vices estimated according to what would be the influence of his virtues, and the consequent interest which society has in their example.

"It was but the other day," *The Champion* continues, "that we saw an attempt made to place side by side, in a general division as to mental discrimination and political principle, such very dissimilar persons as

42. March 3, 1816, p. 65. Lord Kinnaird and his brother Douglas Kinnaird were both in close association with Byron and Hobhouse this season: e.g., both were with Byron at the signing of the separation agreement.

43. *The Champion*'s insinuations are very cautiously placed. When the names are given, March 3, the only charge is political. But when the names are not given, February 25, sinister immoral practices are attributed to the "notorious professors" who *may* be "the introducers of French morals." Applied to Byron's friends and scandals, the comments on the *"Anglo-gallic* school" are hints at (1) the rumored seduction of the actress Mrs. Mardyn and (2) a licentious company of males at Piccadilly Terrace.

Lords Byron and Kinnaird and Messrs. Wordsworth and Bentham."
The reference is to Hunt's essays in *The Examiner* of January 28 and
February 4, 1816, describing Wordsworth as independent, Coleridge as
"with the Whigs at present," and acclaiming Brougham, Moore, Byron,
Cobbett, and Bentham (among others) as leaders of a new era.[44]

It would seem that Brougham and Scott lay in wait for many weeks
until Byron supplied them, first with his own Anglo-gallic prophecies,
then with "Fare Thee Well" and the highly explosive "Sketch," at
which they could discharge punishing fire from their prepared positions.

Byron, when safely on the Continent, was informed by Murray and
Hobhouse of some part of Brougham's activity against him; ultimately
he discovered that it had been Brougham who wrote the *Edinburgh
Review* disparagement of his *Hours of Idleness* in 1808: "that blackguard
Brougham"![45] Against John Scott he held no grudge, nor indeed, after
the main attack, did Scott carry the vendetta much further. On April 21
The Champion reported "The Remarks of the Daily Press" — quoting
both the hostile *Times* and the defensive *Morning Chronicle* — and on
the 28th it gave heavy attention once more to Hobhouse and Byron in
a long essay upon "French Principles and Modes of Thinking," with
some nostalgia for the time when *The Champion* and *The Examiner* had
been in the lists together "on the side of sound politics, and the best
English sentiments." Thereafter, however, Scott returned to ranking
Byron among the poets of true genius along with Wordsworth, Moore,
and Coleridge.[46] And his correspondents wrote innocently of some of

44. Both Leigh Hunt and John Scott were hoping for some liberal postwar guidance from Wordsworth. His poems on Waterloo, printed in *The Champion* February 4, must have been painful to
Hunt; just possibly Byron's "French" poems were meant to right the balance. Scott incorporated
some of Wordsworth's thoughts on the duty of an English Opposition (in Wordsworth's letter to
him of February 22), in his editorial of March 31, distinguishing what had justly been the soul of
policy in war from what ought to be the soul of policy in peace. On March 21 Wordsworth protested
that Scott's friend Brougham was a bit too sympathetic to Napoleon for his taste; on June 11,
irked at Scott's granting Byron genius, Wordsworth argued that "All men of *first* rate genius have
been as distinguished for dignity, beauty, and propriety of moral conduct." (*The Letters of William
and Dorothy Wordsworth: The Middle Years* [1806–20], ed. Ernest De Selincourt (Oxford, 1937), II,
720, 746–747.)

45. Marchand, *Byron*, II, 614, fn. 3, on Hobhouse's reports. John Murray, writing to Byron February 18, 1817, described Brougham as "your incessant persecutor B., who was the source of all
affected public opinion respecting you." (Byron, *Letters and Journals*, IV, 69 fn.)

46. *The Champion*, June 9, 1816, p. 181.

Byron's lyrics as "the favourites of all his Lordship's poems, because they appear to be records of his private feelings" and of "Shakespeare, Milton, Fletcher, and Lord Byron" as having "best understood the loveliness of female ˙character" — as if no savage and profligate abuse of an injured wife and a defenseless governess had ever existed.[47] When in 1819 Scott looked him up in Venice, whatever curse Byron may have intended for his ancient schoolmate was lifted. Scott hesitated to enter Byron's gondola. "'Oh!' said Byron . . . 'you need not be afraid of anything happening to you while you are with me, *for we are friends now.'*"[48]

47. *Ibid.*, June 2, 1816, p. 174 (signed "J. H. R[eynolds]."); June 23, p. 198, in a series ultimately signed "C.B."

48. P. G. Patmore, *My Friends and Acquaintance* (London, 1854), II, 285, quoting Scott. In literary history it has been the misfortune of John Scott (1784–1821) to fall into disparate fragments, one in the biographies of Hazlitt, Lamb, and Reynolds (who wrote at times for his *Champion* and later his *London Magazine*); one in the life of Coleridge (in defense of whose literary privacy, invaded, as he was given to believe, by highway journalism, he died fighting a duel); and a villain and sensation-monger in the biography of Byron (see Elwin, *Lord Byron's Wife*, p. 466, and Moore, *The Late Lord Byron*, pp. 162–163). To periodical historians, however, his *Champion* was "one of the ablest weekly papers in the kingdom," committed to gradual reform yet "at times so incensed at the Tory organs, 'slavish, venial and crafty,' that he felt it 'safer to join the small but lively system of thoughtless dissent and ingenious captiousness . . . than to run the risk of fostering a proneness to receive the yoke.'" (Josephine Bauer, *The London Magazine 1820–29*, Copenhagen, 1953, pp. 223, 38, quoting *The Champion* of January 14, 1816.) Said Byron: "He did not behave to me quite handsomely in his capacity of editor. . . . The moment was too tempting. But he died like a brave man, and he lived an able one." (Byron, *Letters and Journals*, V, 576.)

SC 320   LORD BYRON, *FARE THEE WELL*, MARCH 18, 1816

HOLOGRAPH MANUSCRIPT, 3 pages. Double sheet, 4to (8.9 x 7.2 inches). Laid paper. Watermark: J WHATMAN| 1814|. Gilt edges.

PROVENANCE: Alfred Morrison*; John A. Spoor (Parke-Bernet, April 26, 1939, lot 121).

*THE COLLECTION of AUTOGRAPH LETTERS and HISTORICAL DOCUMENTS formed by ALFRED MORRISON (Second Series, 1882–1893). London: Strangeways and Sons. Printed for Private Circulation. 1893.

March 18ᵗʰ 1816.——

Fare thee well —— and if forever —

   ~~*Still*~~
  ~~Fare thee~~ Still for ever —fare <u>thee</u> well ——
    ^

Even though unforgiving never
            shall my heart rebel —
'Gainst thee ~~not can my~~
      ^

Would that   were
~~Were my~~ breast ~~laid~~ bared before thee!
 ^   ^   ^

10   *Where thy head so oft hath lain*
~~Not a thought is pondering oer thee~~
   While that placid sleep came oer thee ——
     Which thou neer can'st ~~thus~~ know again —

       by   glanced
15 *Would that breast ~~before~~ thee ~~read~~ over*
         ^   ^

   Every inmost thought could show!
Then thou would'st at last discover
     ~~How it bled beneath the blow.~~ ——
   ~~'Twas not just to spurn it so.~~ ——
20   *'Twas not well — to spurn it so.* ——
Yet — oh yet — thyself deceive not —

       sink by slow
Love may ~~wither to~~ decay ——
     ^^ ^^ ^

      wrench
25 *But by sudden ~~blow~~ believe not* ——
       ^ ^

     thus
Hearts can ~~eer~~ be torn away ——
      ^

Still thine own its life
~~If thine own a spark~~ retaineth
   ^   ^   ^   ^   ^

30   must
Still ~~in~~ mine – though bleeding – beat
    ^

     torment   thought which
    lasting
And the ~~moment most that~~ paineth
35   undying /   ^
        ^

   Is that we no more may meet ——
     deeper
These are words of ~~deadlier~~ sorrow —
          ^

   Than ~~the~~ bewail above the dead ——

> Both   yet
> ~~Still will live — but &~~ every
> ~~Every future Night &~~ Morrow
>   ^   ^ ^   ^   ^
> *Wake us from a widowed bed* ——
> *And when thou would'st solace gather*

45
>   When our
> ~~From thy~~ *child's first accents flow*
>   ^   ^
> *Wilt thou teach her to say "Father"?*
> Though his care she must forego?
> ~~With unaltered eye and brow?~~ —

50
> *All my faults perchance thou knowest* ——
>   madness
> *All my* ~~follies~~ *none can know* ——
>   ^
> *All my hopes — whereer thou goest —*
>   Wither ——

55
> ~~Blighted~~ — *yet with thee they go.* ——
> *Every feeling hath been shaken* ——
>   not   could bow
> ~~Even that~~ *Pride which* ~~could~~ *a world* ~~defy~~ ——
>   ^   ^ ^
> Faints   Bows to thee: —

60
> ~~Fades Falls at once:~~ – *by thee forsaken* —
>   ^
>
>   soul
> ~~Humbled to the soul~~ am   ~~I~~ —
> ~~Exiled loveless myself~~
> ~~Few have humbler thoughts than I.~~ ——
>   ^ ^ ^   ^   ^

65
> *Even my soul forsakes me now.*——
>   all
> *But tis done* —— ~~and~~ *words are idle*
>   ^
>   Words from me   vainer
> ~~Tears and sighs~~ *are* ~~idler~~ *still*
>   ^   ^ ^   ^

70
> *But the thoughts we cannot bridle*
> *Force their way without the will* —— —
> *Fare thee well: — thus* ~~lone and blighted~~
>   disunited —
> *Torn from every nearer tie*

75
> *Seared in heart — and lone — and blighted* ——
> *More than this I scarce can die.* —

When her little hands shall press thee
  When her lip to thine is prest
Think of him whose prayer shall bless thee

80

                 him   *love*   *hath*
                                    had
    Think of ~~one~~ thy ~~once~~ oft ~~heaven~~ blessed. —
           ^   ^

Should her ~~features~~ lineaments resemble
  Those thou never more may'st see

85   *Then*
  ~~Still~~ thy heart will softly tremble
    ^
    With a pulse yet true to me.

line 5. *unforgiving: ing* written through *en*.

line 9. *bared:* first written *bare*, the *d* added in revision.

line 12. *came: am* written through *?am*.

line 23. *may: y* written through *y*.

  ~~wither~~: perhaps followed by a dash.

line 27. *away:* heavy ink smudge above the second *a* trailing a long smear; this could be attributable to one of the tears that Byron is reported to have shed while composing, but closer inspection shows that the smear is a shadow of a word heavily blotted out on the reverse side of the page.

line 39. *bewail: be* is an addition, to change the reading from *the wail*; in later drafts Byron returned to his first reading.

line 42. *Morrow: M* written through *m*.

line 47. *Wilt: t* written through *l*.

  her: er written through *er*. Did Byron start to write *him*?

line 50. *All: Al* written through *M*.

line 52. *know: k* and *w* written through *k* and *w*.

line 58. *Pride: P* written through *p*.

line 63. *~~loveless~~:* probable reading; cramped and lined through, and in the fold of the paper.

line 64. This line and its revisions (lines 61, 62, 63, 65), and the rest of the Ms. were written with a sharpened pen and closer spacing, suggesting the possibility of a lapse of time after the penultimate line of the seventh stanza.

line 65. *Even: en* written through *en*.

  now.——: the dash deleted by loops.

line 70. *bridle:* line under *le* perhaps meant for dash at end of line.

line 71. *way: y* written through *y*.

line 77. Lines 77–87 are written sideways between pages 2 and 3; in subsequent versions they follow line 48.

line 82. *thy: y* written through *ou*.

  ~~heaven~~: probable reading.

COLLATION.

The following table of variants will show the revisions in text and punctuation subsequent to the final text of sc 320. Only readings different from sc 320 are given. The Murray manuscripts and proofs are used by the kind permission of the late Sir John Murray. For convenience, the versions have been assigned letter designations A through F:

A. Byron manuscript (sc 320), dated March 18, 1816, final readings.
B. Fair copy by Augusta Leigh, also dated March 18, 1816. (Murray Manuscripts.)
C. Corrections made in B. Some of these are clearly in Byron's hand; all probably are so.
D. Fair copy by Byron, dated March 18, 1816. (Murray Manuscripts.)

E. Printed proof of 52 lines, 3 pages, dated March 18, 1816 in type at the end. With corrections and additions in Byron's hand. Additions bring total to 60 lines. (Murray Collection.)

F. Printed proof of 60 lines, 3 pages, undated. Corrections in the hand of William Gifford collated. (Murray Collection.)

	A	B	C	D	E	F
line 2.	well—			well! —	well!	
	forever —	for ever			for ever—	
line 4.	ever —	.		ever	ever,	
	well ——			*well* —	*well* —	
line 5.	unforgiving	unforgiving,		unforgiving,	unforgiving,	
line 6.	rebel —				rebel. —	
line 9.	breast	heart				
line 10.	head				own	~~own~~ head
	lain			lain,	lain,	
line 12.	oer thee ——	o'er thee—		oer thee	o'er thee	
line 13.	neer	ne'er			ne'er	ne'er
	again —			again:	again:	
line 14.	glanced over				glanc'd over,	
line 17.	Then				Then,	
	discover	discover —				
line 20.	well —	well			well	
	so. ——	so —			so—*	
line 21.	oh yet				oh, yet	
line 23.	decay —			decay,	decay,	
line 24.	wrench				wrench,	
line 25.	not —	not			not,	
line 27.	away ——			away;	away;	
line 28.	its			it's		
line 29.	retaineth			retaineth –	retaineth —	
line 31.	mine –		mine, –			
	– beat	– beat,	, –beat,	–beat,	–beat,	
line 36.	Is		Is –	Is —		
	meet ——			meet. —	meet. —	
line 39.	bewail		the Wail	the Wail	the wail	
	dead ——	dead		dead,	dead,	
line 40.	yet		but	but	but	
line 41.	will live—			shall live—	shall live —	
line 42.	Morrow	morrow			morrow	
line 43.	bed —			bed. —	bed. ——	
line 44.	gather		gather—	gather,—	gather—	
line 46.	flow			flow –	flow—	
line 47.	"Father"?	"Father"		"Father!"	,— "Father!"	
line 50.	faults	faults —		faults—	faults—	
	knowest ——	knowest				
line 51.	madness	madness —		madness —	madness —	
line 52.	know —				know ;	
line 53.	whereer	where'er		~~where~~ whereer	where'er	
	goest —	goest				

	A	B	C	D	E	F
line 55.	thee			*thee*	*thee*	
	go.——	go —			go—	
line 56.	shaken ——	shaken		shaken,	shaken,	
line 57.	bow			bow—	bow—	
line 58.	a world		the world	the world	the world	
line 59.	thee: —	thee—		thee—	thee—	
line 60.	forsaken —	forsakes	forsaken	forsaken	forsaken	
line 65.	now.——	now —				
line 67.	tis	'tis		'tis	'tis	
	idle	idle—		idle—	idle—	
line 69.	still	still,			still;	
line 70.	bri<u>dle</u>	bridle		bridle	bridle	
line 71.	will —— —	will —		will. —	will. —	
line 72.	well:—	well —		well ! ——	well ! —	
line 73.	disunited —			disunited		
line 74.	tie	tie,		tie,	tie—	
line 75.	and lone			~~alone~~ & lone	and love (corrected to "lone" in ink)	
	die.—	die—				
line 76.	scarce			~~can~~ scarce		
line 77.	thee			thee ——	thee—	
line 78.	prest			prest —	prest——	
line 79.	thee			thee ——	thee—	
line 80.	had	*had*		~~hath~~ had		
line 82.	blessed. —	blessed —		bless<u>éd</u>. ——	blessed. —	bless d.
line 84.	see			see —	see —	
line 87.	me.	me —		me. ——	me. —	

* Two additional stanzas are written in the right margin of E (the early proof) and guided to go in after line 20 (end of third stanza):

> Though the world for this commend thee —
>   Though it smile upon the blow
> Even it's praises must offend thee
>   Founded on another's woe——

> Though ~~to thee my~~ ^{my many} faults defaced me
>   ∧   ∧
> Could no other arm be found
> Than the one which once embraced me
>   ~~Thus~~ To ~~plant~~ ^{inflict} a cureless wound?
>   ∧

In the last line, *To* is written through *to*. To the left of these stanzas is written, in Murray's hand (date change in pencil and perhaps not by Murray): 181<del>7</del>|⁶ April 4| Thursday|.

These two stanzas are printed in F with the following changes: "blow," "its" "thee," "defaced me;". The fourth line was printed "Founded upon" and the "up" was deleted by pen. In the upper right-hand corner of the first page of this proof is an inscription by John Murray "Correct &| 50 Copies as early| as you can| tomorrow" and (perhaps added later) "Sunday| Ap¹ 7. 1816".

T HE MANUSCRIPT transcribed above is manifestly the first draft of "Fare Thee Well": many of the lines are constructed before our eyes by the rapid trial and rejection of words, phrases, and even rhymes. We may look in vain for "the marks of tears," but external proof that Byron wrote with "real feeling" is no longer called for.[1]

The fair copy (B) made by his sister Augusta contains only one substantive change from the original.[2] In line 9 she wrote "heart" instead of "breast." But Byron, revising her copy, replaced "breast." He also restored the capital in "Morrow" (line 42) and corrected "forsaken" which she had misread "forsakes" (line 60); he turned a "yet" to "but" (line 40) and "a world" to "the world" (line 58); and he brought line 39 into focus by changing "bewail" to "the Wail."

The copy which Byron sent to his wife does not seem to have been found among the Lovelace Papers; at least Malcolm Elwin cites a printed edition for the text he quotes.[3] The copy sent to John Murray is evidently the one (D) still among the Murray Manuscripts. Byron here adds the underline to "well" (line 4), changes "will live" to "shall live" (line 41) and "blessed" to "bless'd" (line 82), and revises the punctuation. The first proof (E) shows the printer taking over the punctuation but otherwise following copy D. Reading this proof, Byron corrected the one error, "love" for "lone" (line 75), changed "head" to "own" (line 10) and added two new quatrains to follow the third original stanza (line 20 above). The next extant proof (F) incorporates the revisions of E, with some tidying of the punctuation of the new stanzas; it was proofread by Gifford, who put "head" (line 10) back in place of "own," and changed "blessed" to "bless d" in line 82 and "upon" to "on" in the first new stanza.

This final proof was endorsed by Murray: "Correct & 50 Copies as early as you can tomorrow" (that is, make corrections and print 50

---

1. Thomas Moore is responsible for the tradition that this manuscript is "blotted all over with the marks of tears." See *Miscellanies of Lord Byron* (London, 1837), I, 136 n.; Thomas Moore, *Letters and Journals of Lord Byron* (London, 1830), I, 664. But this was perhaps simply Moore's attempt to persuade readers to believe — what he himself had confessedly doubted at the time — that the poem was an expression of "real feeling."

2. Augusta had just moved from Byron's house to her rooms in St. James's Palace; she may have seen Byron daily and could have made this transcript immediately. See Marchand, *Byron*, II, 590.

3. Malcolm Elwin, *Lord Byron's Wife* (London, 1962), pp. 448–449; p. 527, note.

copies on April 8, 1816). In apparently the same hand is written in the bottom left corner "Sunday Ap^l. 7. 1816." The printing of April 8 is apparently the source of most subsequent texts of the poem. A copy in the Pforzheimer Library is inscribed "As it was first privately printed— for distribution among his friends." The only change is a reversion to "a world" from "the world" in line 58. The final official text must be that of Lord Byron, *Poems* (London, 1816) ["printed for John Murray"], in which there are two changes in the punctuation of the two added stanzas and two other changes in the original lines: omission of the dash after the period at the end of line 76 and restoration of "blessed" in line 82.

There are two variants in the text printed in *The Examiner* of April 21, 1816; one is a change of "But" to "Yet" in line 70, the other a change of "one which once" to "soft one which" in one of the added lines — a substantive change not adopted elsewhere. Since the editor Leigh Hunt frequently called on Byron, he may have had authority for this revision, but Hunt's inclination to sentimentalize is the more likely source. The first public text, in *The Champion* of April 14, derives from the private printing of April 8, except for obvious typographical errors and some differences in punctuation, and appears to be the source of other newspaper texts, perhaps even including *The Examiner*'s.[4]

It should be noted that the dates inscribed on the two proofs, April 4 (E) and April 7 (F), are dates of correction not of printing — and that they may have been added at some later time when John Murray (in whose hand they appear to be) was putting his Byroniana in order. Murray's dates, however, though they may be recollections or deductions, seem more trustworthy than E. H. Coleridge's rubric "First printed as published, April 4, 1816," which he attaches to both "Fare Thee Well" and "A Sketch."[5]

---

4. A printing in the June 20 issue, for example, of the *Boston Weekly Messenger* of Boston, Mass. (vol. V, no. 36, p. 582) follows the newspaper text, or the private printing. Other London newspaper printings are: *The Sun*, April 15; *The Morning Chronicle*, *The Morning Post*, and *The Times*, April 16; *The Courier*, April 18; *The Star*, April 19; *The Anti-Gallican Monitor*, *The Independent Whig*, and the *Sunday News*, April 21.

5. Byron, *Poetry*, III, 540, 544. Manuscript copies may have begun to circulate before April 8, but the Coleridge statement that the 60-line text was "Printed and distributed, April 4, 1816" is plainly erroneous. *Ibid.*, VII, 233.

Byron sent "A Sketch" to Murray on March 30, made apparently final corrections of proof on April 2, on which date (we know from letters as well as from an inscribed proof) Murray gave orders to "print off 50 copies, and keep standing."[6] "Fare Thee Well" was first suggested for printing in Byron's letter of April 2,[7] which indicates that Murray already had the manuscript fair copy. "April 4" is a convincing date for the return of corrected proof E; "Sunday Ap¹. 7" is convincing for the revisions of the final proof (F), which must have been set and pulled on Saturday. Most probably both poems were printed Monday, April 8, in the requested fifty copies each, for the first time.

In the extant Murray account books there is nothing that appears to refer to this private printing. But in ledger folios 121, 137, and 247 are recorded the expenses and profits of the publishing of various pamphlet volumes featuring the Farewell poems. The first, apparently, appearing in the ledger as "Byron's Fare thee Well &c," was entered at Stationers Hall on May 22, 1816, with a copy ready "for B. Museum" by July 5. By 1818, 4,500 copies in demy octavo had been sold by William Bulmer of the Shakspeare Press, and 100 copies in quarto by Thomas Davison of Fleet Street, bringing Murray a profit of £220.[8] A cheaper edition, "Fare Thee Well!—A Sketch, etc.—Napoleon's Farewell.—On the Star of the Legion of Honour.—An Ode. By Lord Byron. London: Printed for Sherwood, Neely and Jones, Paternoster Row, 1816," had sold 2,200 of 2,770 copies printed, by August 18, 1818, when Murray received half the remaining copies and a profit of £79.4.0.[9]

"Fare Thee Well!" also circulated in sheet-music form, early versions including one with "music composed & arranged for the piano forte

---

6. Byron, *Poetry*, III, 544.

7. Byron, *Letters and Journals*, III, 279.

8. Murray ledger, folio 121. Bulmer paid for the 4,500 copies on "Heavy demy" at a rate of £7.4.0 per 100; Davison for the 100 quarto copies at £10. The Davison bill for printing the quarto copies was £1.16.0 (ledger, folio 137); the printing of the Bulmer copies cost £43.19.6. Total costs, including £12 for "Advertising," were £114.

9. Ledger, folio 247, "Byrons 'Fare thee Well' Sherwood & Co"; the dating is only generalized — "1816| May" in the "Dr" column and "1818| May" in the "Cr" column — and apparently derivative from the first date in folio 121. The 2,200 copies were "Sold at 3.12.0 pr 100." This Sherwood publication corresponds to the entry in E. H. Coleridge's list (Byron, *Poetry*, VII, 233) from which the full title is quoted.

by J[osiah] F[erdinand] Reddie, London" and one "Adapted to the beautiful air of Ah perdona, composed by Mozart."[10]

10. Items 7303 and 6223 in Richard J. Wolfe, *Secular Music in America 1801–1825* (New York, 1964), 3 vols.

THE LAST DAYS OF HARRIET SHELLEY

THE MARRIAGE of Shelley and Harriet had apparently begun to show signs of breaking up in the late fall of 1813 in Edinburgh. A few months later the signs were unmistakable. "In the beginning of spring," Shelley wrote to Hogg, I spent two months at Mrs. Boinville's [at Bracknell] without my wife. . . . I saw the full extent of the calamity which my rash & heartless union with Harriet . . . had produced. I felt as if a dead & living body had been linked together in loathesome & horrible communion."[1] Part of the reason for this feeling was the continuing presence of Harriet's older sister Eliza in the household: "It is a sight which awakens an inexpressible sensation of disgust and horror, to see her [Eliza] caress my poor little Ianthe. . . . I sometimes feel faint with the fatigue of checking the overflowings of my unbounded abhorrence for this miserable wretch. But she is no more than a blind and loathesome worm, that cannot see to sting."[2]

Shelley, alone at Mrs. Boinville's, found himself attracted by her daughter Cornelia Turner.[3] In May (1814), he wrote "To Harriet ('Thy look of love')," asking for a reconciliation. Harriet copied it out in her own hand. But the poem also contained a warning:

O trust for once no erring guide
Bid the remorseless feeling flee

The "erring guide" is clearly Eliza.

To the outside world the marriage continued to appear stable. Certainly it seemed so to Peacock and Godwin. And Shelley in spite of his doubts and growing anger was trying to hold it together. He told Godwin that he was planning to take Harriet and Ianthe to Wales.[4] He remarried Harriet on March 22 because there was some doubt of the legality of the Scottish ceremony. As their son Charles was born on November 30, and as Harriet regarded him as an eight-month baby,[5]

1. Shelley to Hogg, Oct. 4, 1814, Shelley, *Letters*, I, 401–402.
2. Shelley to Hogg, March 16, 1814, *ibid.*, p. 384. "Worm" here means snake (*NED*).
3. See Shelley, *The Esdaile Notebook*, pp. 293–299, on this and other aspects (some noted below) of the break-up of the marriage.
4. William Godwin to John Taylor, Aug. 27, 1814, *The Elopement of Percy Bysshe Shelley and Mary Wollstonecraft Godwin as Narrated by William Godwin*, ed. H. Buxton Forman, Privately Printed, 1911, p. 11.
5. Harriet Shelley to Catherine Nugent, Dec. 11, [1814], Shelley, *Letters*, I, 422 fn.

they must have been having sexual relations in March or April. But Shelley's feeling of alienation continued even though he did not let Harriet know of it or at least know the full extent of it. "It was no longer possible to practise self deception: I believed that one revolting duty yet remained, to continue to deceive my wife."[6]

In May Shelley began seeing Mary Godwin at her father's house. By the end of June they were lovers. Wrote Peacock:

He might well have said, after first seeing Mary Wollstonecraft Godwin, *Ut vidi! ut perii!*" Nothing that I ever read in tale or history could present a more striking image of a sudden, violent, irresistible, uncontrollable passion, than that under which I found him labouring when, at his request, I went up from the country to call on him in London. Between his old feelings towards Harriet, *from whom he was not then separated*, and his new passion for Mary, he showed in his looks, in his gestures, in his speech, the state of a mind "suffering, like a little kingdom, the nature of an insurrection."[7]

Harriet first became alarmed on July 6. She had left Shelley again by April 18; in early July she was in Bath. When she did not receive a letter for four days she enclosed a letter to Shelley in one to his publisher, Hookham: "Will you write by return of post and tell me what has become of him as I always fancy something dreadful has happened if I do not hear from him."[8]

By July 15 Harriet had returned to Bracknell. Shelley informed her of his love for Mary and that this love was of a kind that he had never felt for her. "Our connection," he wrote shortly afterwards, "was not one of passion & impulse. Friendship was its basis, & on this basis it has enlarged & strengthened. It is no reproach to me that you have never filled my heart with an all-sufficing passion — perhaps, you are even yourself a stranger to these impulses, ... Mrs. Boinville . . . predicted that these struggles would one day arrive."[9]

6. Shelley to Hogg, Oct. 4, 1814, Shelley, *Letters*, I, 402. By "deceive" Shelley does not mean that he was having an affair but only that he had not told Harriet of his true feelings.

7. Peacock, *Memoirs*, p. 91. Peacock's italics.

8. Harriet Shelley to Hookham, Shelley, *Letters*, I, 389 fn. The photostat of the manuscript shows that the letter is undated but it is postmarked with a London postmark, July 7, 1814, and docketed "Mrs Shelley| July 7.|1814."

9. Shelley to Harriet, undated but clearly written shortly after their first meeting in mid-July. Shelley, *Letters*, I, 389–390.

The following day Harriet came to London and saw Godwin and his wife. "She was very much agitated, and wept, poor dear young lady, a great deal, because Mr. Shelley had told her yesterday at Bracknell that he was desperately in love with Mary Godwin. She implored us to forbid him our house and prevent his seeing Mary . . . . We sympathized with her, and she went away contented, feeling, as she said, quite sure that, not seeing Mary, he would forget her."[10]

Mary, accompanied by Claire, then visited Harriet at her father's house in Chapel Street, and assured her that she would not see Shelley again.[11] But she did see Shelley again. Within two weeks she had run off with him. According to Claire, Shelley "succeeded in persuading her by declaring that Harriet did not really care for him; that she was in love with a Major Ryan; and the child she would have was certainly not his."[12] To this story Shelley added the persuasive power of one attempted and one threatened suicide.

While Shelley and Mary were on the Continent, happy in their love and youthful adventures — including a donkey that had to be carried instead of carrying — Harriet, pregnant and deserted, was at her father's house writing heartbrokenly to her Irish friend Catherine Nugent: "Mr. Shelley is in France. You will be surprised to find I am not with him."[13]

On September 13, on his arrival back in London, Shelley went to visit Harriet, leaving Mary, to her annoyance, "two long hours in the coach"; and he visited her on the succeeding two days also.[14] Harriet

---

10. Mrs. Mary Jane Godwin to Lady Mount Cashell, quoted in Dowden, *Shelley*, II, 543.

11. *Ibid.*, p. 544 and n.

12. Statement by Claire Clairmont, on the authority of Mary Godwin: "This Mary told me herself." Quoted in Dowden, *Shelley*, I, 424. White (*Shelley*, I, 346) comments — correctly, it seems to us — on the credibility of the story as follows:

> In no normal sense of the word does it seem possible for Shelley himself to have believed her unfaithful at this time. It had not been a fortnight since he himself had testified eloquently to Harriet's nobility and fidelity. In all subsequent references to Harriet's two children he plainly assumed paternity. Charles Clairmont, who drew his information from Shelley, later expressly exonerated Harriet from this charge while condemning her on other grounds. Either Shelley knew at the time that his argument was false, or else its truth was so utterly necessary to him that he believed it himself because he so intensely longed to do so.

13. Aug. 25, [1814], Shelley, *Letters*, I, 393 fn.

14. Mary Shelley, Journal, Sept. 13, 14, 15, 1814.

had begun to circulate rumors that Godwin had "sold" Mary and Claire to Shelley, and on September 26, Shelley expostulated: "You have asserted to various persons that Godwin favored my passion for his Daughter. This, Harriet, you know to be most false. It is wanton cruelty & injustice to circulate this report."[15]

In spite of her misery — as revealed to Catherine Nugent — and her growing spitefulness — as revealed in the story about Godwin — Harriet still appeared to hope that Shelley might return to her, that his passion for Mary would pass. On October 5 Shelley wrote to inform her that such hopes were vain. She was still legally his wife; but he considered her no longer so in fact:

I shall never cease to interest myself in your welfare — you were my wife, you are the mother of my child: you will bear another to me. But these are ties which only bind to worldly matters where sympathy in the great questions of human happiness is wanting. They produce mutual kindness, compassion & consideration . . . but the sacrafice [*sic*] & self devotion of an elevated friendship cannot exist when the causes have ceased to act.[16]

Following this, Harriet seems to have resigned herself, with growing bitterness, to the fact that her husband was lost:

Mr. Shelley is living with Godwin's two daughters — one by Mary Wollstonecraft, the other the daughter of his present wife, called Clairmont. I told you some time back Mr. S. was to give Godwin three thousand pounds. It was in effecting the accomplishment of this scheme that he was obliged to be at Godwin's house, and Mary was determined to seduce him. She is to blame. She heated his imagination by talking of her mother, and going to her grave with him every day, till at last she told him she was dying in love for him . . . . Eliza is at Southampton with my darling babe.[17]

In October, when Shelley was hard pressed by Charters, Harriet agreed to try to help him financially (as the debt was apparently partly

---

15. Shelley, *Letters*, I, 397. See also *Shelley and his Circle*, III, 338, and Charles Clairmont to Francis Place, Jan. 12, 1816, White, *Shelley*, II, 504: "Godwin, especially, though she knew his sentiments were inimical to Shelley's conduct, for he both wrote to her and called on her, was instantly the object of her blackest calumny and invective. I know of facts concerning her misrepresentations of Godwin, which place the weakness and treachery of her nature in a conspicuous light."

16. Shelley, *Letters*, I, 404.

17. Harriet Shelley to Catherine Nugent, Nov. 20, [1814], *ibid.*, p. 421 fn. Eliza had perhaps been in Southampton with Ianthe for more than a month. See Shelley to Harriet, Oct. 12, 1814, *ibid.*, pp. 406–407. Their second child, Charles, was born on November 30, 1814.

hers), but later her attitude hardened. On December 20 there arrived, as Mary noted in her Journal, "a letter from Harriet, who threatens Shelley with her lawyer." At the same time a mood of suicidal despair was reflected in Harriet's letters:

How I wish those dear children had never been born. They stay my fleeting spirit, when it would be in another state. How many there are who shudder at death. I have been so near it that I feel no terrors. Mr. Shelley has much to answer for. He has been the cause of great misery to me and mine. I shall never live with him again. 'Tis impossible. I have been so deceived, so cruelly treated, that I can never forget it. Oh no, with all the affections warm, a heart devoted to him, and then to be so cruelly blighted.[18]

The letter not only foreshadows the suicide nearly two years later, but it gives us further insight into the events of the spring and summer of 1814. Harriet was in love with Shelley — "with all the affections warm" — when Shelley told her in July of his love for Mary. Had she felt that her marriage was in danger she would certainly not have gone to Bath. One gets the feeling that the disclosure of Shelley's love for another woman was a complete, stunning shock. She had not, apparently, perceived Shelley's growing alienation or at least understood its seriousness. Nor had she seen how deeply he was shaken by his hatred of her sister or sickened by the household discord. Harriet, we have to remember, was very young and very inexperienced. When she eloped she was barely sixteen; in the spring of 1814 she was eighteen. Moreover she was, even for her age, unusually innocent. "Her whole aspect and demeanour," wrote Peacock, were "such manifest emanations of pure and truthful nature, that to be once in her company was to know her thoroughly."[19]

After a visit on December 7, 1814, following the birth of Charles, we have no record of Shelley's visiting Harriet until April 1815, when he saw her in order to get permission to take the infant Charles into court in connection with a Shelley family case in Chancery. It was at this time that Harriet had her lawyer send him a letter "that she meant (if he did not make a handsome settlement on her) to prosecute him for

18. Harriet Shelley to Catherine Nugent, Jan. 24, [1815], Shelley, *Letters*, I, 424 fn. See also Hogg, *Shelley*, I, 280 ("She spoke of self-murder serenely before strangers"), II, 12, 133 and Shelley to Elizabeth Hitchener, postmarked Oct. 28, 1811 ("Suicide was with her a favorite them{e and} her total uselessness was urged as its defence"), Shelley, *Letters*, I, 162.

19. Peacock, *Memoirs*, p. 95.

atheism."[20] In June 1815, when Sir Bysshe's estate was settled, Shelley granted her £200 a year out of his own annuity of £1,000; in June 1816 in his draft will, he willed her £6,000 and £5,000 to each of his children by her, and these bequests were retained in the legally drawn-up will in September.[21]

The court case involving Charles did not actually come up in Chancery until March 1816; at that time Harriet refused to allow him to appear and yielded only after being served a court order. The infant, however, did not actually appear in court but was represented by a temporary guardian appointed by the Lord Chancellor.[22] Whitton told Sir Timothy in a letter that Shelley was in court,[23] but he does not mention that Harriet was there as he certainly would had she been present. There was, in fact, no reason for Harriet to be at the trial (on Shelley family timber-cutting interests). The last recorded meeting of Shelley and Harriet, then, was in April 1815, more than a year and half prior to her suicide.

Sometime in 1815 Harriet was at the village of Stanmore near London. Just when she was there or why, or where she was staying is unknown. We know only that she wrote some verses in the Esdaile Notebook and dated them "Stanmore. 1815."

From April 1815 we hear little of Harriet until June 1816, when she wrote a letter from her father's house in Chapel Street to John Frank Newton on hearing of the illness of his wife:

If there is any thing which I can do for you pray let me know to the unhappy there is nothing so delightful, as being of use to others. if my presence would add in the least degree to yours or your childrens comfort I am very ready to leave Town & fly to give comfort to the distressed. which I am sure you would do for those you highly esteemed. I sincerely hope your usual illness will pass off slightly if there is any kind of Fruit I can send you do tell me at present there is but little variety owing to our cold Spring . . . . My Sister unites with me in kindest regards & best wishes to you all[24]

20. Mary Godwin to T. J. Hogg, April 25, 1815, sc 288.

21. See *Shelley and his Circle*, IV, 702–709, and Ingpen, *Shelley in England*, pp. 470–471.

22. *Shelley and his Circle*, IV, 680–682.

23. Ingpen, *Shelley in England*, p. 462.

24. From a photostat of the Ms., quoted by permission of The British Museum. The letter is postmarked with a London evening duty stamp, June 5, 1816.

In September, Mrs. Godwin was at Bracknell and heard that Harriet had been there spreading gossip about Shelley and Mary, gossip sufficiently damaging for Fanny Imlay to advise them to stay away from Bracknell.[25]

According to a story handed down in the Boinville family, Harriet visited Mrs. Boinville at Bracknell not too many weeks before her death, and this visit was probably that of the summer of 1816. Sometime after her return to London she wrote to Mrs. Boinville threatening suicide. The letter was delayed in the mails. On receiving it Mrs. Boinville hastened to London but "found that she was too late."[26]

If we exclude the evidence of the inquest — to be discussed presently — the next we hear of Harriet comes in the letter of Thomas Hookham to Shelley on December 13, 1816:

My dear Sir:

It is nearly a month since I had the pleasure of receiving a letter from you, and you have no doubt felt surprised that I did not reply to it sooner. It was my intention to do so; but, on inquiry, I found the utmost difficulty in obtaining, the information you desired relative to Mrs Shelley and your children.

While I was yet endeavoring to discover Mrs Shelley's address, information was brought me that she was dead–that she had destroyed herself. You will believe that I did not credit the report. I called at the house of a friend of Mr Westbrook. My doubt led to conviction. I was informed that she was taken from the Serpentine river on Tuesday last, apparently in an advanced state of pregnancy. All Little or no information was laid before the jury which sat on the body. She was called Harriet Smith, and the verdict was– *found drowned.*

25. Fanny Imlay to Mary Shelley, Oct. 3, 1816, Dowden, *Shelley*, II, 54. Fanny saw Shelley on September 10, 1816 (Shelley to Byron, Sept. 11, 1816, SC 341), but there was no mention then of Harriet's stories. When she saw him again (in London), on September 24 (Mary Shelley, Journal; Fanny to Mary, Sept. 26, 1816, Dowden, *Shelley*, II, 52) there was. Hence Mrs. Godwin's visit to Bracknell must have come between these dates.

26. Edmund Blunden (*Shelley*, p. 375) notes the following tradition in the Boinville family:

It is remembered that Harriet became exceedingly depressed, and Mrs. Boinville would take her for long walks to raise her spirits. At length Mrs. Boinville — at Bracknell, I take it — received a letter from Harriet asking her to come at once, and warning her that if she did not come by a certain date Harriet would end her life. This letter was delayed in the post, and although Mrs. Boinville set out at once she found that she was too late. The effect on her was to make her give up Shelley and Mary.

The walks must have taken place at Bracknell and presumably in the summer of 1816 for it was in September that Mrs. Godwin had heard of her being at Bracknell. (See fn. 25 above.)

Your children are well, and are both, I believe, in London.

This shocking communication must stand single and alone in the letter
which I now address to you: I have no inclination to fill ~~my letter~~ with subjects
                                                           it
comparatively trifling: you will judge of my feelings and excuse the brevity of
this communication.

> Yours very truly,
> T Hookham J^r

Old Bond Street
  December 13th 1816[27]

On December 11 *The Sun* had carried a brief and anonymous notice (repeated the next day in *The Times* and in the December 12-14 issue of the *St. James Chronicle and London Evening Post*):

> Yesterday [December 10th] a respectable female far advanced in pregnancy was taken out of the Serpentine River and brought home to her residence in Queen Street, Brompton, having been missed for nearly six weeks. She had a valuable ring on her finger. A want of honour in her own conduct is supposed to have led to this fatal catastrophe, her husband being abroad.[28]

On December 11 an inquest was held in the Fox and Bull tavern, Knightsbridge, in the parish of St. Margaret, Westminster, on the body of one Harriet Smith, which had been taken from the Serpentine on Tuesday, December 10, and brought to the receiving station of the Royal Humane Society located in the tavern.

Four witnesses testified as follows:

> JOHN LEVESLEY [*sic*] of No. 38 Dennings Alley Bishopsgate Street Without an Out Pensr. belonging to Chelsea Hospital being sworn saith as follows:
>
> About 10 o'clock yesterday Morning the 10th day of December instant I was walking by the side of the Serpentine on my way to Kensington and observed something floating on the River which conceiving to be a human Body I called to a boy on the opposite side to bring his Boat which after some time he did to the side of the bank of the River on which I stood. I got into the boat & found that it was the Body of the deceased quite dead, there appeared no sign of life and I have no doubt that the Body must have lain in the Water some days.
>
> (Signed) JOHN LEAVSLEY

27. Quoted from the Ms. by permission of The Berg Collection, The New York Public Library.

28. *The Times* is quoted in Ingpen, *Shelley in England*, p. 479. We have also looked at *The Courier*, *The Morning Chronicle*, and *The Champion* for November and December 1816 but have found no other notice of the suicide.

WILLIAM ALDER a Lodger at the Fox Public House aforesaid, Plumber, being sworn saith as follows:

I knew the deceased she resided at No. 7 Elizabeth Street Hans Place she was a married Woman but did not live with her husband — she had been missing as I was informed from her House upwards of a Month, and at the request of her Parents when she had been absent about a week I dragged the Serpentine River and all the ponds near thereto without effect the deceased having for sometime labored under lowness of Spirits which I had observed for several months before and I conceived that something lay heavy on her Mind. On hearing yesterday that a Body was found I went and recognized it to be the deceased — she was about 21 years of age and was married about 5 years.

(Signed) WM. ALDER

JANE THOMAS of 7 Elizabeth Street Hans Place, Widow, being sworn saith as follows:

The deceased occupied the second floor in my House she took them accompanied by a Mr. Alder, she stated that she was a married lady & that her Husband was abroad she took them from month to month — she had been with me about 9 weeks on the 9th of November last, she paid her month's Rent on the Thursday preceding — she appeared in the family way and was during the time she lived in my House in a very desponding and gloomy way — on the 9th of November last she left my House as I was informed by my servant Mary Jones I did not see the deceased that day.

(Signed) JANE THOMAS.

MARY JONES, Servant to the last Witness, being sworn saith as follows:

On Saturday the ninth of November last the deceased breakfasted and dined in her Apartments, she told me previously that she wished to dine early & she dined about 4 o'clock — she said very little, she chiefly spent her time in Bed. I saw nothing but what was proper in her Conduct with the exception of a continual lowness of Spirits — she left her Apartment after Dinner which did not occupy her more than 10 minutes — I observed she was gone out on my going into her room about 5 o'clock that day. I never saw or heard from her afterwards.

The x mark of
MARY JONES.[29]

The verdict was "Found dead in the Serpentine River."

---

29. Quoted in Ingpen, *Shelley in England*, pp. 648–650. The official papers relating to the inquest were discovered by Charles Withall. (*Ibid.*, p. vii.) The coroner who presided over the inquest was John Henry Gell, a solicitor and the coroner for the City of Westminster. (Pigot and Co.'s *Metropolitan New Alphabetical Directory* for 1828–29.)

That Harriet Smith was Harriet Shelley there can be no doubt. The identification is established by Hookham's letter, by a notation by Godwin in his Journal for November 9, "H.S. dies," and by the following passage in *The Memorials of the Hamlet of Knightsbridge* by Henry George Davis, published in London in 1859. The author is discussing, as a famous and then vanished landmark, the Fox and Bull tavern:

The "Fox and Bull" was for many years the receiving house of the Royal Humane Society: and here was brought the poor frame of the first wife of the poet Shelley, who had drowned herself in the Serpentine. She had lodged in Hans Place, a short time before, and was known to the landlord's daughter, Miss Mary Ann Phillips: hence, her remains were treated "tenderly," and laid out "with care." An inquest was held, and a verdict returned, which saved her the revolting burial then awarded the suicide.[30]

In the table of contents this anecdote is listed as a "reminiscence," and its contents show that it was based on material gathered in Knightsbridge from people who knew what had happened. No published work had by 1859 recorded that Harriet had lived in (or next to) Hans Place,[31] that her body had been taken to the Fox and Bull, that the name of the landlord at that time had been Phillips. These facts were not otherwise publicly known until the inquest proceedings were published by Ingpen in 1916.[32]

30. Davis also notes (p. 112): "for a long time was maintained [here] that Queen Anne style of society, where persons of 'parts' and reputation were to be met with in rooms open to all." Some of the judicial business of the locality was conducted there, "a magistrate sitting once a week for that purpose." (Edward Walford, *Old and New London*, London, 1892, V, 22.) The tavern is discussed also in John Timbs, *Clubs and Club Life in London* (London, 1872), pp. 478–479. Timbs notes that it dated from Elizabethan times and that its sign was once painted by Sir Joshua Reynolds but blew down in 1807. The tavern was itself demolished in 1836.

For Godwin's Journal entry see fn. 62. In a letter to William Baxter on May 12, 1817 (White, *Shelley*, I, 489), Godwin stated, "Mrs Shelley died in November." See also Shelley to Mary Godwin, Dec. 16, 1816; Shelley to Byron, Jan. 17, 1817; Shelley, *Letters*, I, 519–521, 529–530.

31. The address 7 Elizabeth Street, Hans Place, was just off Hans Place.

32. Since Ingpen's publication of the inquest material there had never been any serious question raised on the identity of Harriet Shelley and Harriet Smith until Edmund Blunden did so in his *Shelley, a Life Story*. Blunden argues (pp. 160–161) that the fact that Harriet committed suicide is but an "assumption" and that the inquest cannot be linked with "the name Shelley or Westbrook." He goes on to say that "A lady known as Smith is mentioned, and in one way and another is soon taken to have been Mrs. Shelley." These arguments were, as he notes (p. x), partly inspired by what turned out to be false reports "from over the Sea" of forgeries of Shelley documents. Even so, the statement that Harriet's suicide is merely an "assumption" is untenable. Even the most extravagant

Nor can there be any doubt that *The Sun*'s account of the "respectable female" whose body was taken from the Serpentine on December 10 refers also to Harriet Shelley in spite of discrepancies between this account, the inquest, and Peacock on the question of address. Peacock states that Harriet's body was taken to her father's house in Chapel Street.[33] The inquest gives her address as 7 Elizabeth Street, Hans Place. *The Times* states that the body was taken to "her residence in Queen Street, Brompton."

The contemporary maps of London, however, show that Queen Street and Elizabeth Street join. Elizabeth Street runs from Hans Place for one block to North Street; continuing across North Street for one more block to Brompton Row is Queen Street. They are both small, one-block streets and each is the continuation of the other. The Fox and Bull tavern is only a few blocks north of Elizabeth Street on High Row, bordering on the south side of Hyde Park; Chapel Street is diagonally across Hyde Park, perhaps ten minutes' walk away. Harriet's body was first taken to the Royal Humane Society receiving station at the Fox and Bull,[34] then, the inquest completed, it probably was removed to 7 Elizabeth Street, Hans Place[35] — the fiction of "Harriet Smith" still

claims of forgery — by Robert Metcalf Smith, Theodore Ehrsam, and their associates in *The Shelley Legend* (New York, 1945) — could not obliterate the large and diverse mass of evidence (some of it noted in this essay) on the fact of the suicide. (Possibly Harriet lived on to a ripe old age secretly hidden by Eliza? Or perhaps the bodies of two women, one called Harriet Smith and one called Harriet Shelley, were removed from the Serpentine on the same day, both twenty-one, married for five years and with husbands away, both having committed suicide, both brought to the Fox and Bull, and both having previously lived in or near Hans Place?)

33. Peacock, *Memoirs*, p. 106.

34. Davis' statement that the Fox and Bull — apparently more usually known simply as the Fox — was a receiving station of the Royal Humane Society is confirmed in the *Annual Report of the Royal Humane Society* for 1814, p. 73.

35. "Queen Street" was most likely simply a mistake. But it is possible that Harriet's body was taken to a house in Queen Street. *Boyle's Court Guide* for 1820 lists a Mrs. Thomas at 20 Brompton Row just around the corner from Queen Street. As Numbers 16, 17, 18 and 19 were occupied respectively by Mrs. Hooper, Mrs. Fuller, Mrs. Gattey, and Mrs. Rich this sounds like a row of boarding houses. Seven Elizabeth Street, then, may only have been one of Mrs. Thomas' hostels. And if so, she may have had another house in Queen Street. If this Mrs. Thomas of *Boyle's Court Guide* was indeed the same as Mrs. Jane Thomas, Harriet's landlady, then she must have been highly respectable, for otherwise she would not be in the rather select listing of the *Court Guide*.

being preserved. It might later have been taken to Chapel Street, or perhaps Peacock had been misinformed.

The three accounts — the inquest on Harriet Smith, *The Sun*'s report, and Hookham's letter — therefore, all deal with Harriet Shelley. And, if they all deal with Harriet Shelley, there can be no reasonable doubt that Harriet Shelley was pregnant when she committed suicide for all three contain statements to that effect. *The Sun*'s report was doubtless based on official sources — The Royal Humane Society, the coroner, or the police.[36]

The Royal Humane Society had reports made on all bodies taken to their stations.[37] The normal procedure for a person discovering a body was to report to the nearest station of the society; the society's rescue crew would then remove the body to that station and one of the medical staff would be called to make a report on it. The society maintained a central station on the north side of the Serpentine with full rescue and resuscitation equipment and a secondary station, with rescue equipment only, to the south of the Serpentine at the Fox and Bull, the back yard of which opened into Hyde Park. "On the outside of the other Receiving Houses are placed large and conspicuous boards, announcing their object. These houses are furnished with drags, poles, and other necessary apparatus . . . ."[38] Harriet's body was taken to one of these secondary stations and not the main station perhaps because it was found in Knightsbridge, "near Kensington," not in London proper, and there was obviously no hope of resuscitation.[39] As the society's employees removed and examined

36. Newman I. White — who did not know of the statement in Hookham's letter — was inclined to minimize the newspaper report as probably "founded only on the landlady's impression that she seemed 'in the family way' — an impression made plausible later perhaps by the appearance of a body that had been long under water." (White, *Shelley*, I, 485.) But in the early nineteenth century, before the days of large staffs of roving reporters, such news was more likely to be taken from official sources than from the interviewing of landladies. Reporters were sent to inquests. (See *The Sun*, Dec. 20, 1816.) For evidence that Harriet's body had not, in fact, been in the water for a long period, see below, pp. 793–794.

37. See *Annual Report[s] of the Royal Humane Society* for the early years of the nineteenth century for accounts of their activities and procedures. We have been informed by the society that their Hyde Park station was destroyed by German bombing in 1941 and many of its records lost.

38. *Annual Report of the Royal Humane Society* for 1820.

39. Leavsley stated that he was on his way to Kensington when he saw the body; the statement of the coroner and jury recorded that it was found "near Kensington." (Ingpen, *Shelley in England*, p. 651.) Kensington was beyond Knightsbridge, then an independent town to the southwest of London.

bodies daily from London's rivers and ponds they would presumably be able to recognize evidence of pregnancy. A report emanating from the coroner or the police would likewise be based on an examination of the body.

The source for Hookham's statement — "apparently in an advanced state of pregnancy" — was, as he informs us, "a friend of Mr. Westbrook." This friend must have had information other than that which appeared in the press because he knew of the inquest and of the alias "Harriet Smith."

And to these three statements we have to add Crabb Robinson's diary entry of November 2, 1817: "It appeared that Mrs. Shelley, being pregnant, threw herself into the river and was drowned."[40] Robinson's source was Basil Montagu, and Montagu's source was most probably Godwin or Shelley.[41]

And finally we have the statement of the landlady at the inquest: "she appeared in the family way."

It is true that the summarizing statement signed by the coroner and the members of the inquest jury does not specify that the body exhibited signs of pregnancy, but they were under no obligation to do so. The statement concludes: "that the said Harriet Smith had no marks of violence appearing on her body, but how or by what means she became dead, no evidence thereof does appear to the Jurors."[42] The inquest seems to have been a hushed-up procedure. Only one report seems to have gotten out, that of *The Sun*. Even then the name was withheld. The body — of "Harriet Smith" — was apparently first removed to Elizabeth Street. Yet the landlord of the Fox and Bull must have known whose body it was if his daughter knew; certainly William Alder knew.[43] One

---

40. Robinson, *On Books*, I, 211.

41. Montagu, long a friend of Godwin's, was one of Shelley's attorneys in the Chancery case for the custody of the children. Robinson had earlier heard the story from Mrs. Godwin. *Blake, Coleridge, Wordsworth, Lamb &c.: Being Selections from the Remains of Henry Crabb Robinson* (Manchester, 1932), p. 69.

42. Ingpen, *Shelley in England*, p. 651.

43. William Alder at the inquest gave his occupation as plumber and his address as the Fox and Bull tavern. Pigot's *Metropolitan New Alphabetical Directory* for 1828–29 lists a John Alder as proprietor of the Castle Tavern, Mark Lane; Robson's *London Directory* for 1837 lists a William Alder as proprietor of the George and Dragon, 17 Paradise Row, Chelsea. Perhaps William Alder

gets the impression that it is understood by the coroner, the jury and all concerned that this is a suicide — as indicated by the comments of the witnesses on despondency and pregnancy. What the coroner is apparently anxious to convey is that it is not murder (and this is perhaps the import of the notation on the valuable ring in *The Sun*). Murder they could not conceal; a probable suicide they could. Once it was shown that murder was out there was no legal need to go further and establish the fact of pregnancy in the official statement.

If, then, Harriet Shelley was "far advanced" in pregnancy on December 10, who was the father? It has been suggested that Shelley was. There is, however, no evidence to support this view,[44] and all the

<hr/>

belonged to a tavern-owning family, and, hence, the connection with Westbrook. Among the inquest jurors was a Thomas Holland; Johnstone's *London Commercial Guide and Street Directory* for 1817 lists a Thomas Holland, wine merchant, Cockspur Street, Charing Cross.

44. The theory that Shelley was the father was developed in Boas, *Harriet Shelley*. Mrs. Boas bases her case on two points. The first was that Shelley and Harriet had met in court in March 1816 when Harriet — she contends (p. 185) — took Charles to the trial. A romance then — hypothetically — bloomed (p. 215): "In their contact in 1816 she found traces of the Shelley she loved." But the child was not taken to court (*Shelley and his Circle*, IV, 680) and Harriet was almost certainly not present. What we know of the relations of Shelley and Harriet in 1815 — they had no meetings that we know of in 1816 — were those of bickering and discord (with lawyers going back and forth). The second piece of evidence (previously used in Smith, *The Shelley Legend*, pp. 114, 206) was that of an entry in Crabb Robinson's journal (Boas, *Harriet Shelley*, pp. 216–217; Robinson, *On Books*, I, 211). The entry was made in November 1817, about a year after Harriet's suicide, and is a kind of summary of previous events and conversations. It runs as follows:

> Montagu was employed by Shelley on the application to have his children taken from him by his late wife's father, on the ground that Shelley avowed atheism and lived in adultery with Godwin's daughter. The application was granted. It appeared that Mrs. Shelley, being pregnant, threw herself into the river and was drowned. It is singular that it was not suggested to Basil Montagu by Shelley that he was not the father of his wife's child. Mrs. Godwin has stated this to me as a fact. Basil Montagu thinks it improbable.

Beside this entry we have to place two others: first, that of December 15, 1816, i.e., just before Harriet's suicide became generally known (with Robinson's later comments added by his editor within wide-angle brackets; Robinson, *On Books*, I, 199):

> I dined with the Colliers, and in the evening took tea with Mrs. Godwin at her request, she wishing to speak with me *tête-à-tête*. ⟨The subject was the practicability of obtaining the divorce of Mr. Shelley from his wife, who, Mrs. Godwin says, was guilty of adultery before Mr. Shelley ran off with Mr. Godwin's daughter. In this case Shelley would certainly marry Mary Godwin.⟩

And in commenting in general on the events of 1816, Robinson wrote: "Mrs. Godwin accused Mrs. Shelley of being guilty of adultery & alleged this as an excuse for Shelley's conduct." (Robinson, *Blake, Coleridge . . . &c.*, p. 69.) On January 11, 1817 (Shelley, *Letters*, I, 528), we find Shelley writing to Mary: "I learn just now from Godwin that he has evidence that Harriet was unfaithful to me *four months* before I left England with you." Shelley and Mary eloped on July 28, 1814; Harriet

indications are against it. The last recorded meeting between Shelley and Harriet was, as we have noted, on April 22, 1815, when Shelley, as Mary noted in her Journal, had been "much teased" (i.e., harassed) by her in connection with the proposed appearance of their son Charles in Chancery court. So far as we know he never saw her again. On May 2, 1816, Shelley and Mary left London for Geneva and Shelley did not return to London until September 10. In November he wrote to Hookham that he had lost track of Harriet and would he make inquiries about her? Hence, if the child was conceived between May 2 and September 10 Shelley could not have been the father. If it had been conceived later Harriet could not have been "far advanced." If it had been conceived earlier than May 2 it is hypothetically possible that Shelley was the father — he and Harriet were both in England — but if he had been, Harriet would presumably have attempted to get in touch with him. As she was still Shelley's wife, she could have demanded that he support the child as well as Ianthe and Charles. Certainly there would have been no need for her to be living alone in lodgings if she had been pregnant by her husband.

There can, then, be no doubt that Harriet was pregnant when she drowned herself and that Shelley was not responsible for her condition.

What had happened? All the published accounts come from two sources: first, Shelley and the two men who were in daily association with him during the crisis, Leigh Hunt and Thomas Hookham; and, second, an informant of Godwin's. To these we can add a third, an unpublished account by Claire, based on information supplied by Eliza

and Shelley's child, Charles, was born on November 30, 1814. What Crabb Robinson was listening to, then, was the Godwins' gossip about the paternity of Charles. This, they thought, excused "Shelley's conduct." And by this they meant his eloping with Mary Godwin while married to Harriet. (There was no "conduct" in connection with the suicide.) It was the elopement that the Godwins were obsessed with for they naturally wished to make excuses for Mary. Robinson's reference, then, in his November 1817 summarizing entry to the "wife's child," goes back to his first sentence, which is his main subject, namely, the squabble over the children of the marriage. He is speaking of an actual child, not an unborn one. That Ianthe was Shelley's child there was no question, but the paternity of Charles had been called in question by Mrs. Godwin. It was this that Basil Montagu did not believe.

So far as we know, then, there was not even a rumor that Shelley was the father of Harriet's unborn child. But even if there had been such a rumor, by itself it would mean little or nothing. It would have to be supported by other evidence. There is, however, no such support. (See Kenneth Neill Cameron, "Harriet Shelley," *Times Literary Supplement*, March 23, 1962.)

Westbrook. If we put all these accounts together and compare them with the legal and other documents, the main outlines of the story can be made out even though some details remain hazy.

On November 9, the day on which Harriet disappeared from her lodgings in Elizabeth Street, Shelley was at Bath. Mary's Journal indicates that they had a quiet day. She had been reading Richardson's *Sir Charles Grandison*, and Shelley, *Gulliver's Travels*. A few days later he wrote to Hookham asking him to make inquiries about Harriet. He knew, therefore, that she was no longer living with her parents. And he may have heard that she was in need of help. If so, his informant was perhaps Mrs. Boinville, whom Harriet had apparently visited at Bracknell in the summer and who assisted him in his negotiations with the Westbrooks in the days following the discovery of Harriet's body.[45] But he cannot have received any really alarming news, for on December 5 he went off for a visit to Marlow and London. He was in Marlow with Peacock when Harriet's body was recovered on the morning of December 10, a morning marked, according to the *Annual Register*, by "much small rain." He was in London with Hunt on December 12 and 13 but he cannot have seen, or understood if he saw, the item in *The Times* on December 12, and he did not visit Hookham (as one can tell from Hookham's letter) on December 13. Hookham wrote to him of Harriet's death, not knowing that he was in London. He returned to Bath on the evening of December 14, presumably full of news of his new-found friendship with Hunt, who had published the first important tribute to him by a major journal in *The Examiner* on December 1. The next day's mail brought the "letter from Thomas Hookham with the news of the death of Harriet Shelley." "Walk out with Shelley," Mary's Journal continues. "He goes to town after dinner. Read Chesterfield."

Shelley must have arrived in London late in the evening of December 15. On December 16 he wrote to Mary:

It seems that this poor woman–the most innocent of her abhorred & unnatural family–was driven from her father's house, & descended the steps of prostitution until she lived with a groom of the name of Smith, who deserting her, she killed herself–There can be no question that the beastly viper her sister, unable to gain

45. Shelley to Eliza Westbrook, Dec. 18, 1816, Shelley, *Letters*, I, 522–523. Edmund Blunden, *Shelley*, p. 375 (see fn. 26, above).

profit from her connexion with me—has secured to herself the fortune of the old man—who is now dying—by the murder of this poor creature.

On December 18 he wrote to Eliza Westbrook:

... allow me to assure you that I give no faith to any of the imputations generally cast on your conduct or that of Mr. Westbrook towards the unhappy victim. I cannot help thinking that you might have acted more judiciously but I do not doubt that you intended well.[46]

On January 17 he wrote to Byron:

My late wife is dead.—The circumstances which attended this event are of a nature of such awful & apalling horror that I dare hardly advert to them in thought.—The sister of whom you have heard me speak, may be truly said, tho not in law yet in fact to have murdered her for the sake of her father's money.—[47]

In the same letter he refers to Eliza as "a libidinous & vindictive woman," who was attempting to deprive him of his children.

Where Shelley got the information that he relayed to Mary on December 16 we do not know. Hookham knew of the inquest on "Harriet Smith." Did Shelley visit the Fox and Bull or Mrs. Thomas at 7 Elizabeth Street, Hans Place? There is no record of such visits. Was Hookham his sole informant? Did he go with Hookham to see the friend of Mr. Westbrook from whom Hookham had originally derived his information? His letter to Eliza shows that he went to the Westbrooks' house on Chapel Street on December 17 but was refused admittance. He must have made some inquiries and felt that he had some basis for his story. But he did not later repeat the story. And perhaps when he saw Mrs. Boinville — whom he probably did not see until December 17 — he received a different version.

The story as it emanated from Leigh Hunt was essentially the same as Shelley's of December 16. Hunt himself did not print the story but he told it verbally, and it was repeated from three sources: Keats's friend, Charles Armitage Brown; Leigh Hunt's son, Thornton Hunt; and Thornton Hunt's friend George Henry Lewes, the lover of Mary Ann Evans (George Eliot). Harriet, according to Thornton Hunt, writing in 1863, was "driven from the paternal roof," then "deserted" by "a

46. Shelley, *Letters*, I, 521, 523.
47. From the Ms. in The Carl H. Pforzheimer Library. See Shelley, *Letters*, I, 529–530.

man in a very humble grade of life; and it was in consequence of this desertion that she killed herself."[48] Lewes's version was that "she first was taken up by a man, and, when abandoned by him, she took to any one."[49] Brown, writing in a personal letter in 1825, is more elaborate:

One evening she went to her own relation's house in London, where, on account of her bad conduct, the door was shut in her face, and her wants unrelieved, — on which she turned from that very door, and went and drowned herself.[50]

Godwin's account was contained in a letter to his Scottish friend, William Thomas Baxter, on May 12, 1817:

The late Mrs Shelley has turned out to have been a woman of great levity. I know, from unquestionable authority, wholly unconnected with Shelley, (though I cannot with propriety be quoted for this) that she had proved herself unfaithful to her husband before their separation. Afterwards, she was guilty of repeated acts of levity, & had latterly lived in open connection with a colonel Maxwel.[51]

When Trelawny was preparing material for his *Records of Shelley, Byron and the Author* (published in 1878), he wrote to Claire Clairmont to find out what she knew of Harriet's suicide. Claire, as it turned out, knew quite a lot:

I have forgotten to answer your question about Harriet Shelley. It was no fault of her's that S– quitted her–he fell desperately in love with Mary, ~~whos~~ who had great understanding and both knowledge and liking for the abstract subjects and high thoughts he delighted in–this, poor Harriet had not–she was only a beautiful accomplished school girl extremely ~~en~~ fond of her husband; she strove to adopt all his sentiments, and to attain to his intellectual height, but as that

48. "Shelley," *Shelley and Keats As they Struck their Contemporaries*, ed. Edmund Blunden (London, 1925), pp. 37–38.

49. William Bell Scott to William Rossetti, Dec. 2, 1868, *Rossetti Papers*, ed. W. M. Rossetti (New York, 1903), p. 373. Rossetti heard a similar story from J. Bertrand Payne (*ibid.*, p. 332), the managing partner of Moxon and Co., publishers of Shelley's works after his death; but Rossetti doubted the story and found Payne generally unreliable (*ibid.*, p. 386).

50. *The Letters of Charles Armitage Brown*, ed. Jack Stillinger (Harvard University Press, 1966), p. 203. On Brown see the same, pp. 1–33, and *The Keats Circle*, ed. Hyder Edward Rollins (Harvard University Press, 1965), I, liv–lxix.

51. Quoted from a photostat of the Ms. by permission of The Berg Collection, The New York Public Library, Godwin consistently uses "l" for "ll" at the end of names (e.g., Marshal, Cromwel).

was not in her nature, nor in her power, she often ~~made a~~ laid herself open to ridicule by the exageration [*sic*] of her expressions, and by talking dictatorially on subjects which it was evident to persons of cultivation she did not understand in the least. She did not form ~~a low~~ after S's leaving her, a connexion with some low man, as Mr Rossetti in his desire of making S a model of moral perfection hints and more than hints. Her lover was a Captain in the Indian or Wellington Army I forget which. _{and he was ordered abroad} ₳His letters did not reach her—with her sister's concurrence, she retired for her accouchement to live with a decent couple in a Mews ~~at the~~ ~~rear of~~ _{near} Chapel S^t her sister without telling either Harriett's or her own name, placed her there, saying she was her lady's maid, was married and that her husband was abroad as a Courier. The parents were told that H– was gone on a visit of some weeks to a friend in the country–it was of consequence in Miss W's opinion to conceal the affair from Shelley. ~~I~~ One morning Miss W– visited H– and the latter was very low at receiving no letters from her lover–and expressed a fear that he did not really love her and meant to abandon her–for she remarked I don't think I am made to inspire love, and you know my husband abandoned me–the Eg of that day, a dark November Eg–with rain–at eight o'clock she ~~drown~~ went into the park and ~~leap~~ threw herself into the Serpentine–Her body was not found till next Morning–was taken to St George's workhouse, an inquest held–and verdict returned–An unknown woman found drowned. Miss W– made no stir, nor any of the family appeared to claim her–and Harriet was buried at the expence of the parish in the small burial ground called St George's–which may now have disappeared, but which in former years was in the Bayswater road, opposite Hyde Park. To me it appears that Mr Rossetti has written his memoir to suit Lady Shelleys predilections–and she is a warm partisan of Shelley and Mary, and like all warm partisans does not care much about Truth. Miss Westbrook related all the above particulars to my Mother. Harriet's suicide had a beneficial effect on Shelley he became much less confident in himself and not so wild as he had been before.[52]

Trelawny in his *Records* combined this information from Claire with other information acquired over the years from Hogg, Peacock, and Hookham:

The father at last was confined to his room by sickness, and the sister refused her entrance there. Friendless, and utterly ignorant of the world and its ways, deserted by her husband and family, Harriet was the most forlorn and miserable of her sex–poor and outcast. It is too painful to trace her faltering steps. She

52. Aug. 30–Sept. 21, 1878, from the original Ms. (previously unpublished) in The Carl H. Pforzheimer Library.

made one effort to hold on to life. A man professed to be interested and to sympathise in her fate. He was a captain in the army, and was suddenly ordered to join his regiment abroad. He promised to correspond with her. Her poverty compelled her to seek a refuge in a cheaper lodging; her former landlady refused to forward her letters to her new address. In this deplorable state, fancying that no human being could take the least interest in her, and believing in Shelley's doctrine–that when our last hopes are extinguished, and life is a torment, our only refuge is death–blighted, benighted, and crushed, with hurried steps she hastened into the Park, and threw herself off the bridge into the Serpentine.[53]

That there must be some truth in these stories is shown by the fact that Harriet was pregnant and was living away from her family. But they cannot all be true and some of them are demonstrably false. The story that Harriet, in poverty, became a prostitute and lived with a "groom of the name of Smith" or any other "man in a very humble grade of life" does not make sense. She was not in poverty. Her family was well off. She had £200 a year from Shelley. She had rented a whole floor of Mrs. Thomas' rooming house. She was referred to in the press as "a respectable female" wearing a valuable ring. The maid, Mary Jones, testified at the inquest (on oath) that she "saw nothing but what was proper in her Conduct," and both Mary Jones and Mrs. Thomas spoke of her continuous melancholy and inactivity. She seems to have spent most of her time in bed, lonely and brooding. The picture is not at all that of prostitution.[54]

The story that Harriet was unfaithful to Shelley before he left her for Mary Godwin has no real evidence to support it and does not fit with what we know of the marriage of Shelley and Harriet or Harriet's character at the time. Harriet's statement — "with all the affections warm, a heart devoted to him" — should be allowed to stand as a true reflection of her feelings. Shelley, both in his letter to Harriet of October 5, 1814, and in his will and elsewhere, acknowledged Charles as his son.

On the other hand it is clear that Harriet had a lover in the spring or early summer of 1816 and the indication is that he was an army officer. Godwin heard that she was living with a Colonel Maxwell, Claire —

53. E. J. Trelawny, *Records of Shelley, Byron and the Author* (London, 1878), pp. 158–159. Trelawny gives his sources of information on page 156 (but without mentioning Claire by name).
54. The "groom of the name of Smith" story, of which Thornton Hunt's "man in a very humble grade of life" is apparently an echo, was — as Shelley heard it — part of the prostitution story.

indirectly via Eliza — that she had had an affair with an army captain. And the sources of both stories are apparently separate. Godwin's informant was someone "wholly unconnected with Shelley." This can hardly have been Eliza. Trelawny's main informant was Claire but he might have heard about Harriet's lover from one of his other sources.

To these we have to add Shelley's story to Mary in July 1814, that Harriet was in love with a Major Ryan. This story is almost certainly exaggerated, but there probably was a Major Ryan who was a friend of Shelley's and Harriet's in 1813. He is very likely, as White suggested, the Ryan mentioned by Harriet in two letters in that year. White came to the conclusion after examining the British Army Lists that he was probably Major Matthew Ryan, who in May 1814 joined the 30th Foot Regiment.[55] Further examination of the Army Lists shows that one of the lieutenant colonels of the 30th Foot was named Christopher Maxwell. This, of course, may be coincidence. But when we note that there were about 140 regiments in the British army in 1816 and that there were only three colonels named Maxwell and two majors named Ryan,[56] the laws of probability are strongly against the association's being pure chance. Godwin, furthermore, had never heard of Ryan,[57] so the two stories

55. White, *Shelley*, I, 675–676. White, however, may not be correct in identifying Major Matthew Ryan with the Ryan mentioned in Mary Shelley's Journal in January 1815 for Ryan is listed as being with his regiment in the Netherlands in September 1814, as having fought at Waterloo in June 1815, and as still being with his regiment in Paris in October 1815. (Lt. Col. Neil Bannatyne, *The History of the Thirtieth Regiment*, Liverpool, 1923, pp. 305–307, 352.) Ryan, however, could have been on leave in England between these various dates. He is noted in the Army Lists as having the Waterloo Medal. As for his later movements, he left France for England in December 1815 with a recruiting battalion. The battalion then proceeded to Ireland, arriving there in February. Some members, however, seem to have been stationed in England (*ibid.*, pp. 352–354) and some officers may have obtained leave. Previous to his joining the 30th Foot, Ryan had been on half-pay from the 85th Foot with the rank of captain. He had been on half-pay since at least 1810. When he was sent into active service in the 30th Foot he had the army rank of captain but the regimental rank of major. With Ryan as a captain on half-pay in the 85th Foot was Henry Shelley, who, according to *Alumni Oxonienses*, was Member of Parliament from Lewes, Sussex, in 1802, and who must, therefore, have been known to his fellow Sussex M.P., Timothy Shelley. Henry Shelley died on December 31, 1811. Timothy Shelley, one might note in passing, was also a lieutenant in the British Army on half-pay (with the 22nd Regiment, Light Dragoons).

56. *A List of the Officers of the Army and Royal Marines on Full and Half-Pay*, War Office, [London], Feb. 15, 1816. White apparently did not have the complete text of the letter mentioning Maxwell. He knew of the accusation but not the name. White, *Shelley*, I, 676.

57. Claire Clairmont states that she asked her mother about Ryan but that she had never heard of him. (Dowden, *Shelley*, I, 425.) And if Mrs. Godwin had not heard of him Godwin had not heard

must come from independent sources. We might note also that Knightsbridge, where Harriet was living, was a military neighborhood. A few blocks north of Elizabeth Street were two barracks, one for cavalry regiments, one for foot regiments, and to the south was the Chelsea military hospital with its 12,000 outpensioners, one of whom discovered her body. The city directories of the time show many army officers living in and near Hans Place. There is, therefore, some indication that the story Godwin heard was true and that Harriet's lover was an army officer named Maxwell[58] whom she perhaps met through her previous acquaintance with Major Ryan.

What of Shelley's story that Eliza was responsible for Harriet's death? This must be the same story as Thornton Hunt's and Brown's (both from Leigh Hunt) that "the door was shut in her face . . . on which she turned from that very door, and went and drowned herself." Unlike the prostitution story, which he did not again repeat, Shelley adhered to his accusation against Eliza. He repeated it to Byron on January 17, 1817. This story must be exaggerated but it may bear a germ of truth.

Early in June 1816 Harriet was still living at her father's house, and Eliza was there also — "my sister unites with me in kindest regards" — but whether Harriet had been there continually since April 1815 when Shelley saw her there, we do not know. Later in the summer of 1816 she

of him either, for such information would certainly be circulated in a household which was rife with gossip about Harriet. Charles Clairmont, however, writes to Francis Place on January 12, 1816 (White, *Shelley*, II, 504) that Harriet "associated (I do not at all mean what the world calls criminally) with an Irish adventurer whom she commissioned to take all possible legal advantage of Shelley."

58. Christopher Maxwell, the son of Sir David Maxwell, had been with the regiment since at least 1799. He cannot have been father of the child with which Harriet was "well advanced" in pregnancy on December 10, 1816, if the regimental records are reliable in regard to individual movements for officers because he is recorded as being with his regiment in India in March 1816 (Bannatyne, *The History of the Thirtieth Regiment*, p. 364), but if he did not leave England until late March he could have been the father. Furthermore he fits Eliza's story of the officer being called to Indian service. He was born in 1779 and so would have been thirty-seven in 1816. (*Burke's Peerage*, 1824.)

The two other Maxwells who were lieutenant-colonels were Charles William of the 21st Foot and Charles of the 67th Foot. According to the official regimental histories neither regiment was stationed in or near London between 1814 and 1817. (Richard Cannon, *Historical Records of the British Army, Comprising the History of Every Regiment*, London, 1849, XLIX, LXI.) Blunden (*Shelley*, p. 164) mentions a Colonel Maxwell who was "the commanding officer of the 7th Dragoon Guards," but this Maxwell does not appear to be in the British Army Lists and Blunden does not give the source of his information.

was in Bracknell and in touch with Mrs. Boinville (perhaps even staying with her). The next we hear of her is her appearance, accompanied by Mr. Alder, at the door of Mrs. Thomas at 7 Elizabeth Street, Hans Place, early in September. It cannot have been coincidental that Alder lived at the Fox and Bull and that Harriet was acquainted with Mary Ann Phillips, daughter of Thomas Phillips, proprietor of the Fox and Bull.[59] Presumably John Westbrook, owner of The Mount tavern in Lower Grosvenor Street, some ten minutes' walk across the park from the Fox and Bull, knew his fellow tavern keeper, Thomas Phillips, and Eliza must also have known the family. That Eliza was — as Claire stated — in touch with Harriet is implied in the suicide letter. She does not mention her lodgings or her situation but takes it for granted that Eliza has recent knowledge of her. It is clear, however, that Harriet did not feel that Eliza had treated her cruelly or unjustly. Her suicide letter shows the same strong affection for her as do her other letters. She addresses her (line 4) as "My dearest & much belo^d Sister"; "dear amiable woman." She wishes she had followed her advice (line 12): "it is not in your nature to be unkind or severe to any . . . that I had never left you" (presumably to live with her lover).

This is a very different picture of Eliza from that which we get from Shelley. Of the two there can be little doubt that Harriet's is closer to the truth. Shelley's initial statements about Eliza are the expression of his own guilt feelings in a period of emotional turmoil. The psychological necessity to transfer that guilt elsewhere converged on the person of a woman whom he had long hated. In his letter to Eliza — after he had perhaps learned more facts — he is more balanced: "I cannot help thinking that you might have acted more judiciously but I do not doubt that you intended well." A few weeks later when the Westbrooks were instigating the Chancery case for the custody of the children he wrote: "They do not tell Harriet's story: I mean the circumstances of her death, in these allegations against me. – They evidently feel that it make[s] against themselves."[60] What he has in mind in all these statements must be Harriet's pregnancy and her being secreted in lodgings by Eliza.

59. Alder or his family may also have been connected with the tavern and liquor business. See fn. 43 above.

60. Shelley to Mary, Jan. 11, 1817, Shelley, *Letters*, I, 527.

Of the various accounts of the last days of Harriet Shelley, that told by Claire seems to be closest to the truth. Not only does its general outline conform to the facts disclosed at the inquest — the pregnant girl put in lodgings to have her baby and avoid disgrace to the family — but some of its details ring true, for instance Harriet's pathetic cry that she was not made to inspire love. That Eliza would spirit Harriet away to have her child unknown to the parents or to Shelley fits in with what we know of her previous conduct. She had apparently always dominated and protected her younger sister, and she would not want to exclude the possibility that Shelley might at some time tire of Mary and return to Harriet. Other details, however, do not seem to tally with the evidence of the inquest. According to the inquest Harriet was not with a "decent couple" in a "Mews" near Chapel Street but with a widow who ran a boarding house across Hyde Park near Hans Place; her body was not found the next morning but some days later; it was not taken to St. George's workhouse but to the Fox and Bull. Mrs. Thomas stated that Alder accompanied Harriet to her lodgings whereas Claire stated that only Eliza knew of her whereabouts.

Are these inconsistencies real or only apparent? There are several pieces of evidence which indicate that both stories contain truth. In an affidavit sworn on January 13, 1817, for the trial for the custody of Shelley's children, Eliza Westbrook testified as follows: ". . . until a short time previously to her Death she [Harriet] lived with or under the protection of the said John Westbrooke her Father And that in the Month of December last she died. . . ."[61] Harriet's body was found on December 10; her suicide letter is dated "Sat. Eve."; the only Saturday in December prior to December 10 was December 7. The indication here that Harriet did not die until perhaps December 7 is supported by Leavsley's testimony at the inquest that the body had been in the water only for "some days" and by Alder's testimony that he "recognized" it. This does not sound like testimony about a corpse a month old. According to a standard work in the field, Cyril Polson's *The Essentials of Forensic Medicine*, a corpse that has been in the water for a month is unrecognizable.[62] Furthermore, a body would not normally stay under

61. Medwin, *Shelley*, p. 469.   62. (Springfield, Ill., 1965), p. 400.

water for a month but would surface within a week.[63] And if Harriet's body had surfaced in the Serpentine it would have been seen within a few hours. All this, of course, must have been clear to the coroner. It seems to be left as a silent implication at the inquest (perhaps to avoid involving the Westbrooks) that Harriet died on November 9 after leaving her Hans Place lodgings in spite of the statements apparently to the contrary by Leavsley and Alder. The coroner did not try to establish a date of death.

Eliza's story jibes also with Trelawny's (most likely from Hookham) that Harriet had had two sets of lodgings, in the first of which she had had a "landlady."[64] If, then, Harriet did not drown herself on November 9 when she left her Hans Place lodgings, shortly after four o'clock, where did she go? Where was she between November 9 and, say, December 7? In the register of burials for the parish of Paddington, Roger Ingpen found a record of a "Harriett Smith," age twenty-one, of Mount Street, who was buried on December 13, and a Benjamin Smith, age fifty-four, also of Mount Street, who had been buried two days previously.[65] Ingpen's contention that this Harriett Smith was Harriet Shelley seems certain: "She was accustomed at times to spell her name with the double *t*, she was twenty-one at the date of her death, and Mount Street was close to her father's residence and in the neighbourhood of *The Mount* coffee-house, where he had made his fortune." In Johnstone's *Commercial Directory* for 1816, corrected to August 31, 1817, Ingpen found no Benjamin Smith of Mount Street but he is in the directories for 1818 and other years up to 1824, and is listed as a "shopkeeper or painter and glazier" of 61 Mount Street. This Benjamin Smith seems most likely to have been a son or other relative of the Benjamin Smith who was buried on December 11, 1816, the day, in fact, of the inquest on Harriet Smith. The most interesting thing, however, is the address, for when we look at 61 Mount Street on Horwood's map of London it appears as part of or just behind "Reeves Mews."[66] A "Smith" in or

63. Polson, *Forensic Medicine*, p. 377.
64. Trelawny also stated that Harriet's landlady "refused" to forward letters. It may be, however, that the landlady did not know where to forward the letters to.
65. Ingpen, *Shelley in England*, p. 481.
66. See Area of the Elopement of Shelley and Harriet, *Shelley and his Circle*, II, 871.

near a mews near Chapel Street brings up both Shelley's "groom of the name of Smith" and Eliza's "decent couple in a Mews ~~at the rear of~~ near Chapel S^t." As Benjamin Smith was fifty-four at the time of his death the probability is that he had a wife. A mews was a converted stable with a courtyard. The indication is that Benjamin and Mrs. Smith were the "decent couple" and that Benjamin Smith was also Shelley's "groom." Apparently either Shelley or someone else, putting together rumors of Harriet's pregnancy, her living in lodgings, her association with someone called Smith, came up with the Smith-prostitution story. If Harriet was living with the Smiths, did her death have any connection with that of Benjamin Smith? The dates indicate that it probably did but what this could have been we can only guess. Perhaps the illness of Smith was a kind of last straw which, added to her pregnancy and her failure to hear from her lover, broke her spirit.

Several objections, however, can be raised to Eliza's story; for instance, Alder's statement that he had dragged the Serpentine and adjoining ponds at the request of Harriet's parents after "she had been absent about a week." Taken in conjunction with the other testimony at the inquest, "about a week" would be about November 16. On the Smith-mews hypothesis, however, Harriet on November 16 was not only alive but was living within a stone's throw of her parents' house. Furthermore, Eliza stated that she had told her father that Harriet was in the country with friends. Alder's testimony, of course, helps to establish the fact that Harriet was actually alive on about November 16 but it seems strange that a dragging would be ordered if she was, and it cannot have come after Eliza's friends-in-the-country story unless John Westbrook did not believe the story.

The explanation may lie in Westbrook's illness. Shelley had heard that he was dying, Trelawny (probably from Hookham) that he was "confined to his room," so he must have been seriously ill. (As for Mrs. Westbrook she was apparently quite ineffective. She seems to have played no active role in the household. Shelley never mentions her; Eliza is clearly in charge of Harriet; in all the events of the elopement and marriage Mrs. Westbrook seems to have taken no part.[67]) If John

67. Hogg, *Shelley*, I, 274.

Westbrook heard that his daughter was missing from Hans Place and had been "in a very desponding and gloomy way" — doubtless accompanied by threats of suicide, perhaps specifically of drowning — he could have ordered Alder to drag the Serpentine. Why, however, if he did so, did Eliza not stop him? We can only guess. Perhaps, in his condition, she could not. Perhaps she was not living at home and only learned of it later. Hookham implies that the children were not at Chapel Street, and wherever they were, they were probably with Eliza.

There are other problems also in Eliza's story. For instance it seems incredible that she could pass Harriet off as a "lady's maid" to people living in the next street. The curious thing about this story, however, is that Claire apparently accepts it. In telescoping the story for Trelawny in her letter perhaps she left out something that would make it plausible. Possibly Eliza never expected the Smiths to take the story seriously but felt that her father's illness would prevent anything from getting to his ears.

In considering the difficulties in accepting some aspects of Eliza's story, however, we have to remember that it is a story told to Mrs. Godwin and retold many years later by Claire. Some changes could have crept in during the transmission. For instance, the statement that Harriet had died in November, which is contradicted by Eliza's affidavit, probably came from Mrs. Godwin or Claire. Godwin believed that Harriet had died on November 9.[68]

The statement that Harriet's body was found "the next morning" may also have come in somewhere in the transmission. So, too, the statement that it was taken to St. George's workhouse. But if this latter story did come from Eliza the body must at some point have been taken to the workhouse, perhaps immediately prior to the burial. Perhaps the Westbrooks had it taken to the workhouse in their own parish (St. George's) where they knew the authorities and could arrange for a secret burial. True, Eliza also said that the Westbrooks did not claim

68. Notation checked in the manuscript of his Journal (in the possession of Lord Abinger and consulted by his permission). Godwin had made his normal entry for the day (in dark ink), leaving one blank line in the space assigned for the day. In the center of this line the words "H.S. dies" are written in reddish ink. In other entries Godwin used the same form for later additions, centering them on a final blank line.

the body. Clearly they did not do so at the inquest, but that they did intervene to some degree is indicated by the fact that Harriet's name was spelled with two "t's" in the Paddington Burial Record. The inquest also bears the marks of outside influence. Both Alder and the daughter of the landlord of the Fox and Bull knew that the body of "Harriet Smith" was that of Harriet Shelley and others must have known also, but the "Harriet Smith" fiction was preserved. It is curious also that the inquest was not reported in the newspapers, for such inquests were commonly reported.[69]

According to the parish records Harriet was buried in Paddington, and when in 1823 William Whitton was trying to find the location of her grave, he was informed by a lawyer for Shelley's executors that she "was buried, I understand, at Paddington."[70] According to Claire's account she was buried in St. George's cemetery on Bayswater Road opposite Hyde Park. If this statement came from Eliza, as it probably did, it is more likely that Harriet was buried in this cemetery than in Paddington parish, regardless of the records, for Eliza would have known where her sister was buried. That she was buried in the St. George's cemetery above Hyde Park is indicated also by the fact that as late as 1890 there was a tombstone in that cemetery bearing the comparatively rare name of Shelley.[71] One would expect that the Westbrooks would wish to have their daughter buried in their own parish, where she was born and married. That parish had two burial grounds, one near Chapel Street as well as the one above Hyde Park. If the Westbrooks wished to keep the facts of the suicide secret they could hardly have buried Harriet in a cemetery a few yards from their own house. They could, however, bury her in the cemetery above Hyde Park with

---

69. Between December 1 and 31 *The Times* reported four inquests. Four other London papers (*The Morning Chronicle, The Courier, The Sun,* and *St. James Chronicle and London Evening Post*), all of which gave greater play to legal items, recorded an average of eighteen inquests during the month of December. On the 12th *The Times, The Courier,* and *The Morning Chronicle* reported an inquest on an unknown man who had apparently starved to death and whose body had been found on the 10th. (He was judged to have "died by the visitation of God.") But there was no account of the inquest at the Fox and Bull.

70. Ingpen, *Shelley,* p. 482.

71. Boas, *Harriet Shelley,* p. x.

some hope of the secret's being preserved. If so, they must have arranged with the Paddington officials to register the burial as taking place in Paddington. This might have been legally a lie but, as the map shows, the St. George's cemetery across Hyde Park actually jutted into Paddington parish.

When all the evidence is weighed, Eliza's story seems to hold up in its main outlines: Harriet had a lover, was pregnant, spent the last days of her life with a married couple in a mews near Chapel Street. If we put it together with the other evidence, the indication is that she was first in lodgings near Hans Place, that she left there in the late afternoon of November 9, and that she drowned herself at about eight o'clock on a December evening prior to December 10, probably Saturday, December 7.

In assessing divergencies in various reports of the events leading up to and following Harriet's suicide we have to recognize also that such divergencies are usual in such situations. No two reporters see the scene alike, and this scene was a particularly hectic one. One gets the impression of an atmosphere of almost Gothic intrigue prior to the suicide and of a mad scramble to cover up tracks after it. Both are, of course, understandable. Harriet must have been very hard to handle, and Eliza doubtless did the best she could in a very difficult situation. Following the suicide, the Westbrooks must have been racked both by grief and by the panic of discovery.

It is against the background of these events and activities that Harriet's suicide letter has to be read. She was in lodgings, away from her family and her children, alone, pregnant, and desperate. The extreme, almost psychotic, depression that both Mrs. Thomas and Mary Jones commented on can be felt in the very penmanship, the cramped half-formed letters, the scrawlingly joined words, the incomplete words: "belo^d", "let^r", none of them characteristic of Harriet's normal script with its open, flowing characters. This depression is clear also in the content (line 7): "too wretched to exert myself." Compounding the depression is an obsessive guilt and self-recrimination. The guilt she admits (line 12): "that I had never left you oh! that I had always taken your advice. I might have lived long & happy but weak & unsteady have rushed on my own destruction." As a result (line 8) she is "lowered in the opinion of everyone." The blame is all her own (line 32): "do not regret me. I was unworthy your love and care." This turmoil of emotions is reflected also in the distracted state which caused her to begin the letter without salutation. The letter is signed "Harriet S——," which could be either Harriet Shelley or Harriet Smith; a tacit reference perhaps to her situation.

The question of Shelley's reaction to Harriet's suicide and the degree of his responsibility for it are not, strictly speaking, part of this narrative, but they have been so much discussed that some comment seems in order. In assessing his letter to Mary on December 16 with its charge of prostitution against Harriet, we have to remember that it was written in the shock of the first revelations in London of Harriet's terrible situation and death and arose out of a turmoil of emotions which had roots in previous attitudes. One of these was hatred of Eliza, with whom Shelley had been in bitter conflict for several years and was soon to be again (when she attempted to take his children away from him). Given Shelley's image of himself as a selfless and dedicated humanitarian it was virtually impossible for him consciously to accept any blame for Harriet's suicide. What he does, in effect, is to fling the guilt at Eliza. It was Eliza who had wrecked his marriage, turned Harriet into a useless member of society, and driven her to her death. These sentiments, we must remember, he expressed in a private letter to the person closest to him. Of the depth of his grief for Harriet and her "dark dreadful death" there is no question. Leigh Hunt, who was with him all day, tells us that "it tore his being to pieces."[72] It is apparently the motivating force for the following stark poem:

To ⟨   ⟩

Nov. 5. 1815

(~~And to me~~ The cold Earth slept below
            Above the cold sky shone
                And all around
                With a chilling sound
            From caves of ice & fields of snow
                    wind
            The ~~breath~~ of night like death did flow
              Under the sinking moon

72. Hunt, *Autobiography*, II, 33.

The Last Days of Harriet Shelley

The wintry hedge was black
    brown
The ~~green~~ grass was not seen
    ~~Bir~~ The birds did rest
    In the dark thorn's breast
Whose roots beside the pathway track
    sedge
    Had bound the hard soil; and many a crack
    The black frost made between

Thine eyes glowed in the glare
    Of the departing light
As a starry beam
On a deep dark stream
Shines dimly — so the moon shone there
And it shone thru the strings of thy tangled hair
    blast
    Which shook in the ~~wind~~ of night

The moon made thy lips pale beloved
    The wind made thy bosom chill
    The air did shed
    On thy dear head
Its frozen dew, and thou didst lie
    Where the bitter breath of the naked sky
    Might visit thee at will.[73]

73. The poem was first published in Leigh Hunt's *Literary Pocket-Book* with the title "November, 1815" in 1823. Medwin (*Shelley*, p. 181) first suggested that it might be misdated and refer to Harriet. Thomas Hutchison in *The Complete Poetical Works of Shelley*, Oxford, 1904, p. 1004, made a similar suggestion, and so too did Mrs. Boas, *Harriet Shelley*, p. 200 (both without reference to Medwin). We take our text (by permission) from the Bodleian Library manuscript notebook, adds. e.12. It is clearly a revised version. The poem was published from this same source in *Verse and Prose*, pp. 75–76, but without indication of cancellations and minus the reading "sedge" in the second stanza. As we indicate the poem is entitled simply "To ⟨   ⟩" with the following word or words crossed out. The first word following "To" could be "One" and the last three letters could be "ind." Running through the verses on page 29 of the Bodleian manuscript is the sketch of a woman's head with a fainter death-like head above it. On page 30 a new poem begins — "That time is dead forever, child" — which is dated "Nov. 5, 1817." That the poems were written into the notebook some years after their composition is shown by the fact that the previous pages contain lines from *Prometheus Unbound* (late 1818–1819), the sonnet "Lift not the painted veil" (1818), and the fragment "Alas this is not what I thought life was" (1820). (For other manuscripts of the poem see Boas, *Harriet Shelley*, p. 201.)

    That the poem "The cold Earth slept below" was on Harriet's suicide is indicated by the fact that it is addressed to a woman, by its content, and by its November date. The content fits with the events, season, and time of Harriet's suicide: the wintry landscape of grass and hedges in

Some four years later, in Italy, the image of Harriet and his lost children rose to torment him:

> For at her silver voice came Death and Life,
> Unmindful each of their accustomed strife,
> Masked like twin babes, a sister and a brother,
> The wandering hopes of one abandoned mother,
> And through the cavern without wings they flew,
> And cried 'Away, he is not of our crew.'
> I wept, and though it be a dream, I weep.[74]

What, finally, of the degree of Shelley's responsibility for Harriet's suicide? In any discussion of this question it is necessary — as is often forgotten — to take into account two different series of events, those leading up to the elopement of Shelley and Mary Godwin, and those leading up to the suicide. The second series of events followed the first by more than two years.

That Shelley was responsible for the final break-up of the marriage there can be no doubt. Harriet certainly did not wish to break it up. And while it is true that Harriet's retaining Eliza in the household undermined the foundations of the marriage — turning it from a union of two young people to that of a couple plus an overseer — nevertheless the marriage could have been saved if Shelley had been willing to save it.

the early evening, the frozen sedge (by the Serpentine?), the death at the end, which could refer to a drowning, with the wind stirring the water above the corpse. Furthermore they fit no other event that we know of in Shelley's life. (They could not, for instance, refer to the suicide of Fanny Imlay; Fanny took poison indoors.) The poem is clearly connected with the second poem, which is apparently commemorative of the events related in the first. (See Blunden, *Shelley*, p. 163.)

As to the date, Godwin, as we have seen, believed that Harriet died on November 9. He is most likely to have received this information from Shelley, who perhaps had heard that Harriet drowned herself on the day on which she left her Hans Place lodgings. That Shelley was later uncertain about the date of her death appears in his answer on January 18, 1817, to Eliza Westbrook's statement that she died in December: "this defendant admits that his said late wife died at or about the time in the said Bill." (Medwin, *Shelley*, p. 470.) Shelley when he came to write the poem could either have forgotten the exact date in November or deliberately changed it. That he changed the year date is indicated by the second poem. A commemorative poem would more likely be written one year rather than two years after the event. The weight of the evidence, therefore, indicates that the poem was on Harriet's suicide.

One more possible indication on dating may be noted. The phrase "caves of ice" in the second stanza occurs in "Kubla Khan," which was not published until 1816. Shelley, of course, might have hit on the phrase independently (he uses "icy caves" in *Alastor*, line 143), or he might have seen "Kubla Khan" in a manuscript version (though there is no evidence that he did).

74. *Epipsychidion*, lines 301–307.

But when Shelley met Mary Godwin he was carried away by a powerful passion that had no counterbalance in his feeling for Harriet.

The second series of events began when Harriet took a lover either in or before the spring of 1816. As a result, she ended up pregnant and alone in lodgings. Shelley was certainly justified in implying to Southey that he was not directly responsible for this situation.[75] Nor was he directly responsible for the fact that Harriet chose suicide as the way out. Harriet's obsession with suicide[76] was so strong that it seems probable that she would have attempted it in any apparently hopeless situation regardless of its nature or its cause. How strong it was is shown by the fact that she destroyed not only herself but her unborn child and left two children motherless. Nor was her situation, in fact, hopeless. She had two children, a wealthy father, and a devoted sister. The child with which she was pregnant could have been quietly placed for adoption. Many women have faced much worse situations without resorting to suicide. The indication is that Harriet was in a semipsychotic state (perhaps partly as the result of her pregnancy) which gave the suicidal tendencies full rein and broke down any conscious forces of resistance which she might have had.

75. August 17, 1820, Shelley, *Letters*, II, 231: "... the consequences you allude to flowed in no respect from me."

76. See fn. 18, above.

SC 345   HARRIET SHELLEY TO ELIZA WESTBROOK, P. B. SHELLEY, AND HER PARENTS, ?DECEMBER 7, 1816

AL signed *Harriet S*——, 1½ pages. Single sheet, 4to (9 x 7.2 inches). Laid paper. Watermark (Whatman cipher): [posthorn in crowned shield (lower portion)] |*JWJ*|.
Notations: 1. (page 1): *but as it is* copied above these words in the text (line 23); 2. (page 2): *unworthy your love & care* copied above these words in the text (line 32); 3. (page 2): *Mrs Shelley's Letter* in pencil below text and written vertically to it in the center of the blank lower half of the page.
Additions: 1. (page 1): two greasy spots, one following *none* (line 19), one below *za* of *Eliza* (line 21); 2. (page 1): two smaller spots, above *more* (line 21) and *I* (line 21); 3. (page 2): five small strokes, lower left edge.

PROVENANCE: George Suckling; H. Buxton Forman (The Anderson Galleries, March 16, 1920, lot 615); A. Edward Newton (Parke-Bernet, Oct. 30, 1941, lot 238).

To you my dear Sister I leave all my things as they more
properly belong to you than any one & you will preserve them
            Sat. Eve.
for Ianthe. God bless you both. . My dearest & much belo^d Sister

5   *When you read this let^r. I shall be more an inhabitant of this miserable*
world. do not regret the loss of one who could never be anything but a source
of vexation & misery to you all belonging to me. Too wretched to exert
myself lowered in the opinion of everyone why should I drag on a miserable
existence embittered by past recollections & not one ray of hope to rest on
10 *for the future. The remembrance of all your kindness which I have so*
unworthilily repaid has often made my heart ache. I know that you will for-
give me because it is not in your nature to be unkind or severe to any. dear
amiable woman that I had never left you oh! that I had always taken your
advice. I might have lived long & happy but weak & unsteady have rushed
15 *on my own destruction   I have not written to Bysshe. oh no what would it*
avail my wishes or my prayers would not be attended to by him & yet I
should he see this perhaps he might grant my last request to let Ianthe
remain with you always dear lovely child, with you she will enjoy much
happiness with him none   My dear Bysshe let me conjure you by the
20 *remembrance of our days of happiness to grant my last wish–do not take*
your innocent child from Eliza who has been more than I have, who has
watched over her with such unceasing care. – Do not refuse my last request–I
never could refuse you & if you had never left me I might have lived but
as it is, I freely forgive you & may you enjoy that happiness which you
25 *have deprived me of. There is your beautiful boy. oh! be careful of him & his*
love may prove one day a rich reward. As you form his infant mind so
you will reap the fruits hereafter Now comes the sad task of saying farewell
–oh I must be quick. God bless & watch over you all. . You dear Bysshe. &
you dear Eliza. May all happiness attend ye both is the last wish of her
30 *who loved ye more than all others. My children I dare not trust myself there.*

[261]

*They are too young to regret me & ye will be kind to them for their own
sakes more than for mine   My parents do not regret me. I was unworthy your
love & care. Be happy all of you. so shall my spirit find rest & forgiveness.
God bless you all is the last prayer of the unfortunate   Harriet S——*

line 4. *& much belo*ᵈ: run on; normally Harriet leaves a fairly long space between words and seldom joins them together; in this letter there are many run-on words.

line 5. *be more* (sic)

line 11. *unworthilily* (sic)

line 12. *or:* o written through *t.*

line 15. *on my* (sic).

    destruction: destruction is the last word on the line and Harriet uses the edge of the paper as a period; Shelley sometimes does this also.

line 16. *I should he see this* (sic). The sense is: I wish him to see this.

line 17. *he see:* h written through *?t.*

line 18. *always:* the last word on the line.

line 19. *none   My:* between *none* and *My* comes the first greasy spot noted in the Bibliographical Description; hence the space.

    me: m written through some other letter or part of letter.

line 20. *wish:* the h ends in a line apparently intended as a dash; so too does the *t* of *request* in line 22.

line 21. *Eliza:* za written through second greasy spot.

    have, who: who written through *?a ?m*; *who has* and the comma after *have* are in darker ink; Harriet perhaps began to write "who has been more than I have a mother to her," then changed her mind at *?a ?m*, added the comma after *have*, and converted the *?a ?m* into *who*.

line 22. *unceasing:* probable reading

    care. –: Harriet's pen lingered on the *e* of *care* turning it into a long slightly curling stroke ending in a dot; a short line like an acute accent following this stroke is apparently intended as a dash, as it is also on line 27 following *farewell.*

line 23. *but as it:* run together; as noted in the Bibliographical Description, someone has copied *but as it is* above the line.

line 25. *me of:* cramped below last full line on page 1.

line 27. *reap: a* written through *p.*

    hereafter: the *r* has an extra curl; Harriet's *r*'s are normally rather lavish; in this letter they are mostly plain.

line 32. *than:* Harriet's *a*'s sometimes look like *e*'s; so, here. *mine* is the last word on the line.

    unworthy your love & care: unworthy is a scrawl; the *th* goes up into the long ascender which marks some of Harriet's *th*'s in this letter; the *y* of *your* is written through *?of*; *& care* are run together. As noted in the Bibliographical Description, someone has copied the phrase above the line.

THE ABOVE letter was purchased by George Suckling, bookdealer, of 13 Garrick Street, London, in 1895[1] and sold soon thereafter to Harry Buxton Forman. The story of its purchase and sale is told by W. Courthope Forman, brother of Harry Buxton Forman, as follows:

The story of the re-appearance of Harriet's last letter is rather a curious one – It was told me by Mʳ George Suckling the second-hand bookseller, & print-seller in Garrick Street – One day a woman came into his shop & asked if he bought autograph letters– He said "Yes", & she produced a packet of letters

1. The date of purchase is given by Roger Ingpen in Shelley, *Complete Works*, X, 423.

written by William Godwin – These do not command a large price, but he made her a fair offer for them which she accepted– When she had gone (leaving her name & address) he went over the packet again, & found among the letters that one signed Harriet S– He came to the conclusion it was Harriet's last letter – "Your brother Buxton" he said to me "should have this I thought, so I went to the General Post Office & showed it to him"– He read it – How much he said, I answered £20– Too much Suckling, no I won't give it– So I took it away & walked back to my shop by Holborn in a leisurely way – On arriving there was your brother! I'll have the letter Suckling he said, & drew me a cheque for £20— I sent the woman on a proportion of my profit, & later much regretted my honesty – She worried me continually like the daughters of the horse leech crying out for more– At last I had to threaten her with proceeding if she bothered me any more – The purchase was a good one for my brother, or rather for his widow – When his library was sold in New York it realized some £350: for there is no doubt it was written by the despairing wife of the poet–[2]

The name of the woman from whom Suckling purchased the letter is not known nor is it known how it came into her possession, but the fact that it was in with a packet of Godwin letters indicated that its ultimate source was Shelley and not the Westbrooks. Of the persons — Shelley, Harriet's sister and parents — to whom the letter was addressed, then, Shelley and not the Westbrooks kept possession of the letter.

Where the letter then went we do not know. But there are two probable sources, namely, Claire Clairmont and Robert Madocks of Marlow.

Almost all the manuscript material left by Claire Clairmont, including a good deal of both Shelley and Godwin correspondence, was bought by H. Buxton Forman between 1879 and 1886. But no letter by Harriet Shelley is among the lists of that material prepared by Claire's niece Paola Clairmont. The only manuscript material from this collection that we know of as not having been acquired by Forman was that acquired by Edward A. Silsbee and brought to the United States. Silsbee,

---

2. Autograph memorandum, signed *W. C. F.*, obtained from Mrs. Elizabeth Forman, widow of W. Courthope Forman. The memorandum was perhaps intended for use in connection with W. Court-hope Forman's article, "Shelley's First Wife: The Unpublished Letter," in *The Cornhill Magazine*, LII (January 1922), 28–32. Forman did not, however, use the statement in the article but simply commented (page 21): "Before her death she [Harriet Shelley] wrote a letter to her sister, which is, however, in part addressed to her husband. This letter made a somewhat mysterious re-appearance many years after the writer's death. It has, I believe, never been published, but there is, I have reason to think, no cause to doubt its authenticity."

however, does not seem to have had any Shelley or William Godwin correspondence.[3]

When the Shelleys left Marlow in February 1818 for London and then for Italy they left behind a box-desk which included both Shelley and Godwin correspondence. It seems to have consisted largely of the letters received by Shelley and Mary during a period extending from a few months prior to their moving to Marlow in February 1817 to their leaving Marlow a year later. Furthermore, it contained material relating to the death of Harriet: Shelley's letters to Mary of December 16, 1816 (on Harriet's suicide), and of January 11, 1817. Hence, if Shelley received Harriet's letter, as Harriet requested (line 17), it would normally have been placed with the rest of this Marlow correspondence. Part of this Marlow material in the desk was retained by the Shelleys' landlord, Robert Madocks (some of it was in Marlow as late as 1870, some was sold to "Major Byron," who resold part of his purchase to Mary Shelley).[4]

Hence, of the two sources, the most likely is Robert Madocks. The woman who sold the letter to Suckling may have received it *via* Madocks or *via* "Major Byron." She either did not know that Harriet's letter was in the packet or if she knew that it was there she did not know what it was. (It is signed only "Harriet S——.") And the person from whom the woman received the packet can have known nothing of the Harriet letter or she would have been informed of its value. A packet of Godwin letters in the middle or later decades of the nineteenth century would not — as W. C. Forman correctly states — have been considered of much consequence and would normally have received but superficial examination. It may be that the letter remained undiscovered in the packet from the time that it was placed there by Shelley or Mary until it was found by Suckling. (We note below that the letter gives evidence of having long been in a folded state — perhaps inside another letter.)

As indicated in the Bibliographical Description, the letter is in Harriet Shelley's hand. This, however, was no easy matter to determine.

---

3. See "The Provenance of Shelley and his Circle Manuscripts," below, pp. 288–290, 298–301.

4. Kenneth N. Cameron, "A New Shelley Legend," *An Examination of the Shelley Legend* (University of Pennsylvania Press, 1951), pp. 99–101; Theodore G. Ehrsam, *Major Byron: The Incredible Career of a Literary Forger* (New York and London, 1951), pp. 57–59, 120–121, 144; see also "The Queen of the Universe," above, pp. 489–493.

The handwriting does not have the over-all appearance of Harriet Shelley's. Whereas Harriet's hand is normally open and flowing, with elegant flourishes to the tail of the "y" and the upward curve of the "d," the hand in this letter is cramped, narrow, and generally without flourishes. One other example of Harriet's hand, however, does have something of this appearance, namely, the poem "Late was the night" — especially the last stanza — which she copied in the Esdaile Notebook. Furthermore, they exhibit specific parallels. A comparison of the word "child" in both (sc 345, lines 18, 21; "Late was the night," line 24) shows the two to be essentially the same; so, too, with "misery" (sc 345, line 7) and "misery's" ("Late was the night," line 24). And a comparison of other words in the letter with the same words in other letters show certain basic similarities.[5] The explanation for the cramped appearance of the above letter must lie in Harriet's agitated state when she wrote it.

As we noted above in "The Last Days of Harriet Shelley," the indications are that Harriet was in a deep melancholia at the time of her suicide. What seems to have happened is that the elegant and rather flourishy aspects of the penmanship learned at Miss Hawkes's seminary for young ladies at Clapham vanished under the impact of her suicidal depression. We might note, too, the "ye" of lines 29–31, which may represent a return to an earlier dialectal pattern of speech.

The letter, as is also noted in the Bibliographical Description, is a single quarto sheet. Like all such it was at one time a double sheet (containing a complete watermark)[6] and a slight irregularity to the left edge shows that it has been torn along that edge. This missing portion of the sheet could have contained an address. If so, however, the letter was not sealed for there is no trace of a seal or seal tear on the remaining sheet as there would be had the letter been sealed. The letter, then, did

5. For instance, in Harriet's letter to John Frank Newton, June 5, 1816 (photostat in The Carl H. Pforzheimer Library from the manuscript in The British Museum) and her letters to Catherine Nugent of various dates (photostats in The Carl H. Pforzheimer Library from the manuscripts in the Henry E. Huntington Library). There are other parallels also to Harriet's writing in the Esdaile Notebook.

6. The watermark — a well-known Whatman watermark — is similar to the one illustrated in Thomas Balston, *William Balston: Paper Maker 1759–1849* (London, 1954), p. 167, figure 13. The paper is a thick rag paper typical of letters in the late eighteenth and early nineteenth centuries.

not go through the mails. Probably Harriet — in the way of suicides — left it behind in her rooms. If it was in the double sheet form when she left it the missing sheet probably contained only the name of her sister — and perhaps that of Shelley also — and was without address.

The words noted in the Bibliographical Description as copied above lines 23 and 32 are intended to elucidate the script, which, for these words, is difficult and run-together. These interlineations may be in Shelley's hand but since they are small, copied, and cramped between the lines it is difficult to be certain.[7] Shelley perhaps had the letter copied at the time of the trial for the custody of his children and either he or someone else might have been trying to ease the task of a copyist. The pencil notation "Mrs Shelley's Letter" gives the impression of being a later addition typical of the kind of comments put on by some book-dealers and collectors. The greasy spots also noted were on the letter when Harriet wrote: she has skipped over the first one and the pen has slipped on the "za" of "Eliza" on the second. The five small ink dashes on the lower left edge of page 2 are perhaps something left over from marks or writing on the now missing part of the sheet. They are not, however, the ends of letters because magnification reveals quite clearly that they do not extend quite to the edge. The letter has obviously been folded across the middle, with page 1 inside the fold. The lower half of page 2 is much darker than the upper.

The letter probably began: "Sat. Eve. When you read this . . . ." Page 1, from this point on, and page 2 were then completed and from "To you my dear . . ." to "much belo^d Sister" (lines 1–4) added last. If it had begun with the salutation "My dearest . . ." this would normally have been written from the left margin to the center, not from the center to the right margin. Nor would it have been written as close to "Sat. Eve." as it is. That the letter did not begin with "To you . . ." (line 1) is also indicated by the sense. The sentence grows out of the rest of the letter and is an addition to it.

7. Shelley's copying hand is different in appearance from his composition hand. There are differences again when he is interlineating. That Shelley had possession of the letter may be indicated in his letter to Eliza Westbrook of December 18, 1816 (Shelley, *Letters*, I, 522): "You will spare me & yourself useless struggles on this occasion, when you learn, that there is no earthly consideration which would induce me to forego the exclusive & entire charge of my child." This could be a reference to the above letter, line 20.

ANOTHER SHELLEY
FAMILY ELOPEMENT

S HELLEY EARLY made efforts to liberalize his sisters' views: "My Moth fancies me in the High road to Pandemonium, she fancies I want to make a deistical coterie of all my little sisters."[1] It has been assumed by Shelley's biographers that these efforts fell on arid ground, and the general impression conveyed is that of aging maidenly virtue at Field Place. One seed, however, seems to have taken root.

Three of Shelley's sisters, Elizabeth (the object of Hogg's affection), Hellen, and Margaret, remained unmarried. A fourth sister, Mary, however, married and left Field Place. It was Mary who in December 1811 had provided her brother with an introduction to her schoolmate, Harriet Westbrook. In spite of Mary's tender years — in 1811 she was but twelve years of age — Shelley thought she showed promise. He sent her books[2] and hoped to "add her to the list of the good, the disinterested, the free."[3]

With this comment, Mary drops from Shelley biography. Shelley doubtless saw her along with his other sisters on his later visits to Field Place — the last in 1815 — but we hear nothing particular about her. When she married, in June 1819, her brother, then in Italy and out of touch with his family, apparently heard nothing of it. At least we find no comment in his letters or in his wife's letters or journals.

But if Mary drops rather early from Shelley's biography, she did not drop out of sight. In 1829 — as apparently has not previously been known to Shelley's biographers or editors — she was the center of divorce proceedings in the House of Lords, having left her husband and eloped with another man, thus following in the footsteps of her brother and grandfather in what, as Shelley remarked on another occasion, was something of a "Shelley business."

---

1. To T. J. Hogg, Jan 11, 1811, *Shelley and his Circle*, II, 701.
2. "Will you write to Mary under cover to Miss Pigeon, Clapham Common, Surrey, where I wish you to send the books, also for Mary." Shelley to Edward Fergus Graham, May 29, 1810, Shelley, *Letters*, I, 12.
3. Shelley to Elizabeth Hitchener, Oct. 28, 1811, *ibid.*, p. 162.

Another Shelley Family Elopement

This elopement and its aftermath are interesting for several reasons, but perhaps most of all for the light which they indirectly shed upon the marital problems of Shelley himself. Today the marriage of Shelley and Harriet would have ended in the divorce court, and not in abandonment, social ostracism, and suicide. But when we see the barbed entanglements of divorce in early nineteenth-century England and specifically the hounding down and public pillorying that Shelley's sister had to go through we can appreciate more fully the dilemma that Shelley himself had faced.

The first we knew of Shelley's sister's elopement came when The Carl H. Pforzheimer Library purchased a copy of a parliamentary document entitled "An ACT to Dissolve the Marriage of *Daniel Franco Haynes*, Esquire, with *Mary*, his now Wife, and to enable him to marry again; and for other Purposes therein mentioned." Mary Haynes, the document informed us, was Mary Shelley. It was dated 1829 (the watermark bears the date 1828).

Why an Act of Parliament? The answer is that until the Matrimonial Causes Act of 1857 a marriage could be dissolved in England only by a special Act of Parliament. Such acts, as one can imagine, were exceedingly rare for Parliament was hardly equipped to handle a volume of divorce business. Until the accession of the House of Hanover, in fact, there were but five such acts. In the year 1829 there were seven.[4]

Following the introductory sentence given above the act proceeds as follows:

HUMBLY sheweth and complaineth unto Your most Excellent Majesty, Your true and faithful Subject, *Daniel Franco Haynes*, late of *Ashstead*, in the County of *Surry*, but now of *Barnfield*, in the County of *Southampton*, Esquire;

That on the Ninth Day of *June*, in the Year of our Lord One thousand eight hundred and nineteen, Your said Subject was married in *England*, to *Mary Shelley*, the Daughter of Sir *Timothy Shelley* Baronet:

That Your said Subject, and the said *Mary*, lived and cohabited together as Husband and Wife from the Time of their said Marriage, until the Time of her Elopement, as hereinafter mentioned, and there is Issue of their said Marriage One Son and Two Daughters:

4. *Encyclopædia Britannica*, 11th ed. (1910), "Divorce," "England."

[268]

That in the Month of *May*, in the Year of our Lord One thousand eight hundred and twenty-seven, the said *Mary* eloped from the said late Residence of Your said Subject at *Ashtead*, aforesaid, with *James O'Hara Trevor*, then or then late of *Millbrooke*, in the said County of *Southampton*, Esquire, and has since cohabited with and carried on an unlawful and adulterous Intercourse and criminal Conversation with him:

That Your said Subject hath not, since the said Elopement of the said *Mary* his Wife, lived, cohabited, or had any Intercourse with or Access to the said *Mary*:

That Your said Subject was unable to discover to what Place the said *Mary* and the said *James O'Hara Trevor* had gone after such her Elopement with him, until the latter End of the Month of *August*, in the Year of our Lord One thousand eight hundred and twenty-eight, when he discovered the Residence of the said *Mary*, and *James O'Hara Trevor*:

That Your said Subject in the latter End of the Month of *August*, in the Year of our Lord One thousand eight hundred and twenty-eight, brought an Action in His Majesty's Court of Common Pleas against the said *James O'Hara Trevor*, for such adulterous Intercourse and criminal Conversation with the said Wife of Your said Subject, and obtained Judgment by Default, and Two thousand Pounds have been assessed to Your said Subject, on a Writ of Inquiry, executed before the Sheriff of the County of *Surry*, and final Judgment has been entered up for that Sum and Costs, of *Hilary Term* last:

That Your said Subject has not been able to discover any Effects of the said *James O'Hara Trevor*, out of which Your said Subject could yet levy the said Damages by Writ of *Fieri Facias*, nor has Your said Subject been able to take the said *James O'Hara Trevor* himself in Execution, inasmuch as the said *James O'Hara Trevor* has, since the obtaining of the Judgment by Your said Subject against him, gone away from his Residence, near *Dover*, to some Place unknown to Your said Subject:

That Your said Subject exhibited a Libel in the Arches Court of *Canterbury* against the said *Mary* his Wife, and on or about the Fifth Day of *February*, in the Year of our Lord One thousand eight hundred and twenty-nine, obtained a Definitive Sentence of Divorce from Bed and Board, and mutual Cohabitation against her, the said *Mary*, for Adultery committed by her with the said *James O'Hara Trevor*.

That the said *Mary*, Your Subject's said Wife, has by her adulterous Conduct dissolved the Bond of Marriage on her Part, and Your said Subject stands deprived of the Comforts of Matrimony, and is liable to have a spurious Issue imposed upon him to succeed to his Estates and Fortune, unless the said Marriage be declared void and annulled by the Authority of Parliament.

[269]

From this we can gather, among other things, that Mary Shelley was married to Daniel Franco Haynes, had three children by him, a son and two daughters, and in May 1827 eloped with one James O'Hara Trevor, that her husband then instituted a search for the lovers and finally caught up with them at Dover in August of the following year.

Who was Daniel Franco Haynes? Little information is available in the standard biographical sources. He was presumably the author of a novel by "D. F. Haynes Esq." published in 1814 — the only work recorded by him — *Pierre and Adeline, or, The Romance of the Castle.*[5] But except for this one venture into literature, his life was apparently that of the country gentleman. He is noted in the act as coming from Ashstead, Surrey. Ashstead is about eighteen miles from the Shelley estate near Horsham, Sussex, and on the main road to London. In other sources we find Haynes listed also as the master of "Lonesome Lodge" near Wooton Hatch, Surrey, which is about twelve miles from Horsham. Both estates are recorded in Cary's *Roads* for 1819 as among the seats of the gentry. The Hayneses, therefore, were a landowning family in the same vicinity as the Shelleys.[6]

As the marriage was dissolved by an Act of Parliament, this indicated that some record of proceedings should exist among the parliamentary papers. In the *Journals of the House of Lords* for 1829 there was found, among other matter, the transcript of the divorce hearings before the Lords.

On March 3, 1829, the House heard a Petition by Haynes

praying their Lordships, "That he may have Leave to bring in a Bill to dissolve his Marriage with *Mary* his Wife, and to enable him to marry again; and to illegitimatise the Female Child born of the said *Mary Haynes* and *James O'Hara*

---

5. The novel was reprinted (as *The Romance of the Castle*) by William Hazlitt the younger in The Romancist and Novelists' Library in 1841. A cursory reading suggests that it was the work of a very young man. That Daniel Franco Haynes was indeed its author is almost certain because we find him referred to in other places as "D. F. Haynes, Esq.," for instance, in the note on his marriage in *The Gentleman's Magazine*, LXXXIX (June 1819), 578. We find no other work by him listed and no record of any other D. F. Haynes.

6. They cannot, however, have been landowners on the same scale as the Shelleys. We do not find them in *Burke's Landed Gentry*, and Daniel Franco Haynes does not appear in the alumni lists of Eton, Harrow, Oxford, or Cambridge.

Trevor in the Month of *September* last; and for other Purposes therein mentioned."[7]

One John Jennings, representing Haynes, was then called in and delivered to their lordships a copy of the divorce proceedings and "the Definitive Sentence of Divorce, in the *Arches Court* of The Archbishop of *Canterbury*, intituled, '*Haynes* against *Haynes*.'" (The reference to the Arches Court brings up an interesting point: although a marriage could be legally dissolved only by an Act of Parliament, divorce hearings could take place in courts and divorces be recommended, not, however, in civil courts but only in ecclesiastical courts, of which the Arches Court of the Archbishop of Canterbury was one.)

After presenting his documents, Jennings left and the Earl of Shaftesbury arose to present a bill to the House for the dissolution of the marriage.

The hearings on the bill took place on March 19[8] at a regular session of the House of Lords. A copy of the marriage register from the church at Warnham (where in an earlier day Thomas Jefferson Hogg had had his "peep" at Elizabeth Shelley) was produced in evidence and showed that the marriage had taken place on June 9, 1819. The officiating minister was Charles Henry Grove (who, some eight years previously, as a young medical student, had accompanied Shelley to his elopement rendezvous with Harriet Westbrook). These legal facts were confirmed by David Haynes, brother of Daniel Franco, and himself a clergyman. Their sister, Mrs. Catherine Bligh ("married to Captain *Bligh* of the Navy"),[9] was

7. *Journals of the House of Lords Beginning Anno Decimo Georgii Quarti*, LXI (1829), 100.

8. On March 5 it was moved that the bill be read a second time on March 19. On March 12 it was "*Ordered*, That *William Whitton, Thomas Aviolet*, The Reverend *William Samuel Parr Wilder, Catherine Arthur, Aaron Jones, William Sankey* the younger, *Samuel Sutton* and *Richard Gill*, do attend this House on *Thursday* the 19th of this instant *March*, in order to their being examined as Witnesses upon the Second Reading of the Bill, intituled, 'An ACT to Dissolve the Marriage of *Daniel Franco Haynes*, Esquire, with *Mary*, his now Wife, and to enable him to marry again; and for other Purposes therein mentioned.'" Whitton, the Shelley family lawyer, did not, however, actually appear as a witness.

9. Not Captain William Bligh of *The Bounty*. In the Navy Lists for 1829 we find Captain George Miller Bligh, and in the *DNB* Admiral Sir Richard Rodney Bligh (1737-1821), who had "a son George Miller Bligh, who was a Lieutenant of the Victory of Trafalgar, where he was severely wounded, and died a captain in 1835." Cary's *Roads* (1819) informs us that Admiral Bligh had a house near Southampton.

[271]

next called in. She testified that the Hayneses used to visit her mother (Mary's mother-in-law) near Millbrook, Southampton, for two or three months every year and that they appeared to her to be happily married ("I never heard an angry word").

Following her testimony Haynes's counsel announced that he wished to "call Evidence" to support the illegitimizing clause. He was, however, informed that such a clause had "not of late been introduced into Bills of this Nature, there being no Person in Attendance to watch the Interests of the Child." The clause does not appear in the act (as quoted above).

The next witness was Elizabeth Rice, servant in the Haynes family, who remembered the circumstances of Mary's leaving home.

"Do you remember Mrs. *Haynes* leaving *Ashstead Lodge; Ashstead Cottage?*"
"Yes."
"Did Mr. *Haynes* go from Home that Morning?"
"Yes; the Morning before."
"Did you hear from Mrs. *Haynes*, or in her Presence, where Mr. *Haynes* was going?"
"Yes."
"Where was Mr. *Haynes* going?"
"To *Southampton;* to his Mother's."
"For what Purpose was that stated?"
"It was to see his Daughter."
"On what Day do you recollect that Mr. *Haynes* went away?"
"On *Friday.*"
"Do you remember the Month?"
"No I do not; it was in *May.*"
"Towards the Beginning or the End of *May?*"
"Near the End."
"Mr. *Haynes* went away on the *Friday;* did Mrs. *Haynes* go any where about that Time?"
"Yes; they went on the same Day, both."
"Where did Mrs. *Haynes* go?"
"She went down to *Dorking* to meet her Mamma."
"Did Mrs. *Haynes* tell you that she was going to *Dorking* to meet her Mamma?"
"Yes."
"Did you see her leave the House?"
"Yes."

"What did she leave it in?"

"In her own Carriage."

"Did the Carriage come back empty?"

"Yes."

"Have you ever seen Mrs. *Haynes* since?"

"No."

"Are you acquainted with Mr. *Trevor;* with his Person?"

"No, I am not, very much; I have seen him."

"Did you ever see him near *Ashstead?*"

"No."[10]

The Hayneses, then, were in the habit of spending two to three months a year with Haynes' mother near Millbrook. And it was at Millbrook that James O'Hara Trevor lived. Trevor, we gather from later testimony, used to visit the Hayneses there;[11] and it was doubtless out of these visits that the romance between him and Mary sprang up. We learn from Elizabeth Rice's testimony that the elopement adventure began one May morning in 1827 with Mary's simply getting into her carriage and never coming back (after stating that she was going to meet her mother at Dorking — some six miles from Ashstead, on the road to Horsham). What happened after she reached Dorking, we do not know. But in June she was seen by the Reverend Samuel Parr Wilder of Millbrook walking "arm in arm" with Trevor in a "public street" in Paris. Haynes, it appears, had information of their whereabouts and had sent Wilder to Paris.[12] After that, however, he must have lost the trail, for he did not find them until August of the following year. Part, at least, of the intervening fourteen months were spent in a kind of hare-and-hounds chase, with Mary and Trevor moving from place to place and lodging to lodging.

Early in 1828 they were in London living at Portman Place near the Edgeware Road.[13] In July they were in lodgings in Hereford (near the Welsh border).[14] How long they had been there we do not know, but they made the mistake of hiring a servant, Martha Pember, with a relentless memory for the minutiae of bed-making. From Hereford they went back to London, and Martha went with them. Here again they

10. *Journals of the House of Lords*, LXI, 217–218.   11. *Ibid.*, p. 221.

12. *Ibid.*, p. 218.   13. *Ibid.*, p. 221.

14. *Ibid.*, p. 219.

sought lodgings in the Edgeware Road area (at Connaught Terrace, where they had five rooms).

But apparently they felt no security in London, for within a few weeks they left for Dover. After a month in lodgings they decided to take a house of their own in the country (as Mr. and Mrs. Trevor). It was there that the law (in the person of John Hovell Triston of Gray's Inn Square)[15] caught up with them, and it was there that a child was born to them (delivered by Mr. William Sankie, surgeon, of Snargate Street, Dover).[16]

The final major witness was one Thomas Powell.

Then *Thomas Powell* was called in; and having been sworn, was examined as follows:
(*By Counsel.*) "Were you Servant to Mr. *Trevor* at any Time?"
"Yes."
"How long did you live in his Service?"
"Between Nine and Ten Years."
"Where was he living at that Time?"
"At the *Hummums* Hotel."
"What was he; was he an Officer?"
"He was represented so to me."
"Did you live with him at *Milbrooke* near *Southampton?*"
"Yes."
"When you were living at *Milbrooke* near *Southampton*, did you see Mrs. *Daniel Haynes?*"
"Yes."
"How long did you live with Mr. *Trevor* at *Milbrooke?*"
"About Four Months."
"Did Mr. *Trevor* break up his Establishment at *Milbrooke?*"
"No, not quite."
"Did you leave Mr. *Trevor?*"
"I did."
"Why did you leave Mr. *Trevor?*"
"He told me he was going to *America.*"
"Did he give you any Directions what to do after he should be gone to *America*, about yourself?"
"To write to him, if I had no Situation, in a few Months."

15. *Ibid.*, p. 217; *Clarke's New Law List*, 1825.

16. *Journals of the House of Lords*, LXI, 221; Pigot's *Commercial Directory*, 1823–24.

Trevor, then, lived at the Hummums Hotel; and the Hummums Hotel was not — as one might at first think — in the Southampton region, where Trevor had his house, but in London. It was, in fact, a large and well-known hotel (commented on by Samuel Johnson and Leigh Hunt).[17] It would seem, from Powell's testimony, that Trevor kept up two residences, one in London, where he had been for "between Nine and Ten Years" and one at Millbrook, which is described as an "establishment," i.e., a house with servants. Trevor, therefore, must have been moderately well off, although what he did for a living is not clear. He was not, as Counsel is apparently hinting, an "Officer" in either the regular Army or the Navy, for a search of the Army and Navy Lists for the period fails to disclose him. He could, however, have been an officer in a county militia.

How long he had been at Millbrook is not clear. Powell had been there with him for only a few months prior to the elopement and it may be that Trevor was a fairly recent resident.[18] If so, his romance with Mary may have been of rather sudden development; for they seem to have first met at Millbrook. Trevor had apparently never been at Ashstead.[19]

We gather also from Powell's testimony that Trevor and Mary intended at first to elope to America. And it is possible that they were there between their sojourn in Paris in July 1827 and their residence in London in the early months of 1828, during which period we have no record of their whereabouts. Trevor had told Powell to write to him in America, and Powell does not indicate that this plan was changed.

Powell, in continuing his testimony, stated that he had returned to Trevor's service in London (apparently about eight months after the elopement) and lived with him and Mary in their various lodgings

---

17. Henry C. Shelley, *Inns and Taverns of Old London* (Boston, 1909), pp. 128–131. The hotel, which featured hot baths "in the Oriental manner," was said to have enjoyed a "lively reputation." (*Ibid.*, p. 127.) It was situated near Covent Garden, on the east side of the Piazza south of Russell Street.

18. The Reverend Samuel Parr Wilder (see fn. 8, above) testified that he had known Trevor "about a Twelve-month" and had lived "within Three or Four Miles of him." (*Journals of the House of Lords*, LXI, 218.)

19. As we have noted above, Elizabeth Rice, the Hayneses' servant at Ashstead, testified that she had never seen Trevor there.

(joined in July by Martha Pember), ending up with them at their house near Dover. He left them there in May or June 1828. The child was born in September.

The testimony concluded, it was "*Ordered*, That the further Consideration and Second Reading of the said Bill be put off 'till To-morrow; and that the Lords be summoned." On March 20, Haynes, through his attorneys, agreed to withdraw the illegitimizing clause (which, consequently, does not appear in the act). On March 25, a message having been received that the House of Commons had approved the bill, it was passed by the House of Lords. On April 13 the act was given "Royal Assent" and the marriage was officially dissolved.

This action in the House of Lords, however, was not the only one. As the act (quoted above) noted, Haynes had also brought action against Trevor in the Court of Common Pleas on the charge of "criminal Conversation with the said Wife of Your said subject" and had been awarded £2000 damages. But, as the act goes on to state, the "said Subject" had not been able to collect because James O'Hara Trevor was not to be found. (He had "gone away from his Residence, near *Dover*, to some Place unknown to Your said Subject.") Furthermore, the "said Subject" was unable to find any "Effects of the absent Trevor upon which he could "levy the said Damages."

Whether Haynes ever caught up with Trevor and got his pound of flesh we do not know; but financially Mary did not come out too badly. According to the divorce act Haynes was prevented from touching any of her effects or her possible inheritance from her father:

And be it further enacted, That the said *Daniel Franco Haynes*, and all Persons claiming or to claim by, from, or under him, is and are and shall be for ever barred and excluded of and from all Rights, Claims, Titles, and Interests of, in, to, or out of any Manors, Messuages, Lands, Tenements, and Hereditaments, and other Estates, Real, Freehold, Personal, and Mixed, and all Goods, Chattels, Personal Estate, and Effects whatsoever which the same *Mary* shall or may at any Time or Times hereafter acquire or become seised or possessed of, or entitled to by Descent, Gift, Devise, Purchase, or otherwise howsoever, during the Estate and Interest of the said *Mary*, her Heirs, Executors, Administrators, and Assigns therein respectively; and that the said *Mary*, her Heirs, Executors, and Administrators, shall and may hold and enjoy the same and every of them for all her and their Estate and Interest therein, for her and their own Use, Benefit, and Advantage, exclusive of the said *Daniel Franco Haynes*, his Heirs, Executors, and Administrators, and all and every other Person and Persons whomsoever claiming or to claim by, from, or under him.

What kind of settlement was actually made we can gather from some notations in ink on the outer leaf of our copy of the act. According to these, Haynes and Sir Timothy Shelley deposited jointly the sum of £10,000 with the trustees of the Shelley estate.[20] In his will, Sir Timothy left with the trustees a total of £10,000, the interest of which was for Mary's use, and, in addition left her £700 in cash.[21]

Both the divorce settlement and the will, one may remark, help to demolish the picture of Sir Timothy as a tyrannical father. His — and the trusty Whitton's — hands seem discernible in the protection given his daughter in the divorce settlement and he treated her in his will about as he did his other daughters. Whatever his intellectual limitations Sir Timothy was fundamentally honest and always attempted to be just. In his earlier dealings with his son he had been driven to distraction by that son's inflexible adherence to principles, moral and intellectual, which were beyond his comprehension.

What was the aftermath? We have also in our library an unpublished letter from Mary's sister Hellen, written after Sir Timothy Shelley's death in April 1844,[22] which provides part of the answer. It is to "Peggy and Flora:" and is signed "Your ever afte Aunt":

This a time of year that every one ought to hear of their friends even if they do not expect it & I should not have left my dear little girls so long in the dark concerning all our doings but that I know your Mama can tell you all that may interest you. . . . & now do you think you two can keep a little Secret? if I tell you that we propose before you leave Bath to pay it a visit if your Papas sojourn there Should be prolonged beyond that of the inhabitants of 12 Queen

20. Haynes put up £9425, Sir Timothy £575; a following notation records that Sir Timothy loaned £5000 "to Mr Haynes on his Bond to the Trustees" (i.e., the trustees of the Shelley estate).

21. Photostatic copy of Sir Timothy Shelley's will (dated Apr. 26, 1834), pp. 3, 4, 18 (codicil, May 13, 1843), 19 (codicil). Prior to her marriage Mary had been assigned £2000 (p. 2), perhaps her dowry.

22. The letter bears only the date "Dec — 27ᵗʰ" without a year, and the envelope is missing, but the watermark bears the date 1844 and the paper has a black border. As the date of the writing of letters is usually within two or three years of that of the watermark, and as two years was a customary span for a black border following the death of a close relative, the probability is that the letter was written on December 27 in either 1844, 1845, or 1846. See also fn. 23.

Square – for my Mama begins to think that She will not perhaps be able to take the long journey to Teignmouth, but I see no reason for the fear at present although y^r grandmama's health & strength varies very much – I hear that Florry is knitting Something in concert with her Mama and you may be Sure that we Shall value very much whatever you do. . . . I was called away in the midst of my letter to place the China on the old Oak Chest because so much consultation is required upon all these grave affairs Your Grandmama was half inclined not to send this parcel but I thought the old Sussex Fowls might taste very sweet although they are but poor Speciments of feudal tenure Do you not See My dear Children that I might run on for ever but I will conclude by wishing you increased happiness every Succeeding year as well as y^r dear Papa & Mama – Your grand mama & Marg^t unite too in every Kind wish and Eternal love.

Who were Peggy and Flora? Who was "Papa"? We find in *Burke's Peerage* for 1857 that Mary had a daughter named Flora-Brenda;[23] we find in a codicil to Sir Timothy Shelley's will a reference to "my Daughter Mary Trevor."[24] Mary, therefore, married Trevor and had two daughters by him, the first of them presumably the child born near Dover in 1828.

From the tone of Hellen's letter, with its references to "y^r dear Papa" and knitting "in concert" and so on, one gets the impression of a

23. As Flora-Brenda was married on December 5, 1848, and as she is clearly unmarried at the time of Hellen Shelley's letter, this sets an absolute terminal date on the letter of December 27, 1847.

24. Photostatic copy of will and codicils, p. 18 (May 13, 1843). In the will (Apr. 26, 1834) Sir Timothy refers to "her present or any future Husband"; hence, Mary and Trevor were married at least by April 26, 1834. The marriage, however, does not seem to have been publicized. *Burke's Peerage* in 1857 still refers to her as Mrs. Haynes. And the divorce proceedings seem to have been kept secret. We find no reference to them in the letters or journals of Shelley's wife, Mary Shelley, or in the letters of Leigh Hunt or Thomas Love Peacock. They are not mentioned by any of Shelley's biographers or editors; but perhaps Roger Ingpen knew something about the case, for, in his pedigree of the Shelley family at the back of his *Shelley in England* he lists Mary Shelley as having been married twice, first (mistakenly) to "David Francis Haynes" (Daniel Franco Haynes' brother was called David) and then to James O'Hara Trevor. He gives the date of her death as April 20, 1884.

The only other later references to Mary Trevor that we find in Shelleyian literature are by Trelawny. On June 19, 1869, William Michael Rossetti called on Trelawny and noted among other matters: "He dislikes Shelley's maiden sisters but likes Mrs. Haynes." (W. M. Rossetti, *Rossetti Papers, 1862 to 1870*, New York, 1903, p. 399.) We have in our library an autograph letter from Trelawny to Claire Clairmont, November 27, 1869, which contains the following sentence: "Your last letters were excedingly interesting to me every thing regarding S — is so — for I loved him from the first on the death of his son the present Percy the family will be extinct his three sisters are living; two unmarried the 3 married but no children and long seperated from her husband her name$_\wedge$Trever." (Mary)
From this we can gather that Claire Clairmont did not know of the elopement and divorce, and that Trelawny himself did not know very much. Apparently, however, he called Mary "Mrs. Haynes" when speaking to Rossetti.

happy family circle. Furthermore, the relationship between the Trevors and the Shelleys seems amiable.

One cannot avoid a final conjecture. What would Percy Bysshe have thought? Was there perhaps a wisp of ironical laughter in the air as Florry and her Mama knitted?

THE PROVENANCE OF SHELLEY AND HIS CIRCLE MANUSCRIPTS

O N FIRST seeing the original manuscripts of a great writer of a past century library visitors usually first ask "where did they come from?" and "how did they happen to be preserved?" The present essay is an attempt to answer these questions so far as Shelley is concerned and sketch in some of the facts for other members of the "circle" as well. Curiously enough, so far as we can ascertain, no similar study exists for the other major English poets.

In general the answer to both questions in regard to Shelley manuscripts is that they came from two main sources, his immediate family (his widow and his son), and from friends or business associates (publishers, lawyers, and so on). His literary manuscripts mainly stayed in the family; some letters stayed in the family but as we would expect, others were widely scattered. The family preserved manuscripts and letters because of their literary value and from a sense of family affection and loyalty. Others, as we shall see, preserved them for various reasons.

Let us consider the family material first. On the death of Mary Shelley in 1851 the family manuscripts passed to her son, Sir Percy Florence Shelley, then living at Boscombe Manor, near Bournemouth. Sometime following Sir Percy's death in 1889, the manuscripts were divided into three parts. One part his widow, Lady Jane Shelley, presented to the Bodleian Library at Oxford in 1893; one part went to the Shelley-Rolls family (descended from Shelley's younger brother John); and one part went to the Abinger family (the fifth Baron Abinger was the son of Sir Percy Florence Shelley's adopted daughter, Mrs. Bessie Florence Scarlett). As Sir John C. E. Shelley-Rolls presented his part to the Bodleian in 1946, two of the original three parts are now in that library. The third part is in the possession of the present Lord Abinger.[1]

By noting the main contents of these three parts we can see the extent of the family holdings.

The core of Lady Jane Shelley's gift to the Bodleian in 1893 was

1. For the Shelley-Rolls branch of the family see *Burke's Peerage*, "Shelley of Castle Goring," and the pedigree at the end of Ingpen's *Shelley in England*. For Abinger see *Burke's Peerage*. Mrs. Scarlett (née Gibson) was a niece of Lady Shelley (née Gibson).

made up of Shelley's literary manuscripts, including those of *Prometheus Unbound* and *A Defence of Poetry*. It contained also a number of letters by Shelley and Mary Shelley. Not all of these are letters within the family (for example, Mary and Shelley to each other); some, also secured by the family, are to such close friends as Leigh Hunt, Thomas Love Peacock, John and Maria Gisborne, and Thomas Hookham.[2]

Sir John Shelley-Rolls' gift also contained letters by Shelley and by Mary but its most important section consisted of 14 of Shelley's notebooks, 3 of which contain the manuscript of *Laon and Cythna* (*The Revolt of Islam*), and 1 of which contains parts of *Adonais*.[3] Shelley often did his first drafts in notebooks. As Lady Shelley's gift had contained 6 notebooks the Bodleian thus secured a total of 20.

The Abinger material, unlike the Lady Shelley (Bodleian) and Shelley-Rolls portions, contains little Shelley autograph material (5 letters and some journal entries), but represents that portion of the family papers which concerns William Godwin, Mary Wollstonecraft, and Mary Shelley. It contains the daily journal of William Godwin kept over a period of some forty-seven years, some of his literary manuscripts, a large number of letters to him (including some by Coleridge and Lamb), some of his own letters (partly copies made by Godwin for his own use); about 100 letters and notes by Mary Wollstonecraft; the diary of Mary Shelley (with a few entries by Shelley) from the time of her elopement with Shelley until after his death; the manuscript of part of Mary Shelley's *Frankenstein* and other literary manuscripts by her; a

---

2. For information on Lady Shelley's gift see *The Shelley Correspondence in the Bodleian Library*, ed. R. H. Hill (Oxford, 1926); C. D. Locock, *An Examination of the Shelley Manuscripts in the Bodleian Library* (Oxford, 1903); A. H. Koszul, *Shelley's Prose in the Bodleian Manuscripts* (London, 1910); Seymour de Ricci, *A Bibliography of Shelley's Letters* (Privately Printed, 1927); Shelley, *Complete Works*, X, 424–425 and *passim*. Hill lists the letters and prints some of them, lists the literary manuscripts (p. 46), and also notes the "Manuscripts Previously in the Library or Added Since the Shelley Donation" (p. 47). Locock examines the poetry, Koszul the prose. See de Ricci's entries for the Gisbornes, Henry Reveley (Mrs. Gisborne's son), Hookham, Hunt, Peacock, and Mary Shelley.

3. For information on Sir John Shelley-Rolls' gift see *The Bodleian Library Record*, II (July 1946), 144–145; *Verse and Prose from the Manuscripts of Percy Bysshe Shelley*, ed. Sir John C. E. Shelley-Rolls and Roger Ingpen (London, 1934); Ingpen, *Shelley in England*, pp. 659–691 (transcripts and facsimiles from the *Adonais* notebook); Neville Rogers in *The Times Literary Supplement*, London, July 27, Aug. 3, Aug. 10, 1951; July 24, 1953; Feb. 12, Nov. 5, 1954; Neville Rogers, *Shelley at Work* (Oxford, 1956).

large number of letters to Mary Shelley (including some from Thomas Moore).[4]

The literary manuscripts of Mary Wollstonecraft do not seem to have survived. Many, if not most, of them appear to have gone to her publisher, Joseph Johnson.[5] If they are still extant their present location is unknown.

Of the literary manuscripts outside the family the most considerable group consists of the works of Godwin. Although the Abinger collection contains some of Godwin's literary manuscripts, most of them were sold along with his library following his death in 1836[6] (many of them bought by the great Norfolk collector Dawson Turner[7]), and these manuscripts are now in various libraries. Three of them, *The Lives of the Necromancers* and the novels *Fleetwood* and *Cloudesley*, are in The Carl H. Pforzheimer Library (as are also the manuscripts of an *Enquirer* essay and a historical essay on Sir William Davenant, both published in the present volumes).

A number of Shelley's literary manuscripts are also outside the family collections. Shelley himself gave away some manuscripts — usually of shorter poems — and left others with publishers; Mary Shelley gave some away, and so, too, later in the century, did Lady Jane Shelley.

Shelley, for instance, gave away some manuscripts to Hogg and some to Miss Sophia Stacey, the ward of his uncle, Robert Parker.[8] Those to Hogg included the poem "Death! where is thy victory!" and

---

4. This information was gathered by an examination and tabulation of Lord Abinger's manuscripts made in the spring of 1954 in preparing these manuscripts for exhibition at The New York Public Library, and from a microfilm subsequent to that time. For a detailed survey see Lewis Patton, "The Shelley-Godwin Collection of Lord Abinger," *Library Notes*, No. 27 (April 1953), pp. 11–17, Duke University Library, North Carolina.

5. See *Shelley and his Circle*, I, 178 and n.

6. Sotheby and Sons, *Catalogue of the Curious Library of that Eminent and Distinguished Author, William Godwin, Esq., to which are added the Very Interesting and Original Autograph Manuscripts of his Highly Esteemed Publications*, June 17-18, 1838.

7. Puttick and Simpson, *Catalogue of the Important Manuscript Library of the late Dawson Turner, Esq.*, June 6 and following days, 1859, pp. 85–86. For Turner (1775–1858) see the *DNB*.

8. Edward John Trelawny also possessed some of Shelley's manuscripts. These were mainly copies of poems written to Jane Williams. How or when they came into Trelawny's possession does not seem to be known. W. M. Rossetti describes one of them — "With a Guitar, to Jane" — as "written out by Shelley with exquisite neatness." (*The Complete Poetical Works of Percy Bysshe Shelley*, London, 1881, III, 410. For a list of these poems, see H. J. Massingham, *The Friend of Shelley*, London, 1930, Appendix IV.)

the prose piece "The Wandering Jew" both given to Hogg at Oxford. Those given to Sophia Stacey comprised the lyrics partly written for her in Florence in 1819, including "The Indian Serenade."[9] Of the manuscripts of the poems left with publishers and subsequently placed on the market, the best known is that of *Julian and Maddalo*, a fair copy of which Shelley sent from Italy to Leigh Hunt for publication by his publishers, Charles and James Ollier. This manuscript remained in Hunt's possession and was discovered after his death by his friend, Samuel Ralph Townshend Mayer, and is now in The Pierpont Morgan Library.[10] (The Olliers, we might note here, had the manuscript of Shelley's prose work *A Proposal for Putting Reform to the Vote*, which was sold by their heirs in 1879.[11]) It is also possible that Hunt had at one time the manuscript of *Laon and Cythna* which was sent to the printers, for parts of this manuscript were among his papers. Some of these are at present in The Carl H. Pforzheimer Library, along with other Shelley manuscripts also once owned by Hunt.[12]

9. Shelley, *Complete Works*, III, 349; *The Poetical Works of Percy Bysshe Shelley*, ed. H. Buxton Forman (London, 1882), IV, 10–11; Helen Rossetti Angeli, *Shelley and his Friends in Italy* (London, 1911); pp. 98–99.

10. Forman, *Poetical Works of Shelley*, III, 102 (plus facsimile); Shelley, *Complete Works*, III, 332–333; George K. Boyce, "Modern Literary Manuscripts in the Morgan Library," *PMLA*, LXVII (February 1952), 21.

11. Shelley, *Complete Works*, VI, 351. This manuscript — a perfectly genuine manuscript — was declared a forgery in *The Shelley Legend*, by Robert Metcalf Smith, Theodore G. Ehrsam, *et al.* (New York, 1945), on grounds which were subsequently described by the bibliographical specialist of that work as follows: "The handwriting expert of *The Shelley Legend*, having designated the December 16 letter a forgery, used this letter as a touchstone to determine other forgeries. Such a procedure might have been perfectly proper had the touchstone actually been forged, but since the Wise letter, but for the signature, is a genuine Shelley manuscript, it cannot, obviously, be used as a sample of forgery. Thus the verdict that the manuscript of *A Proposal for Putting Reform to the Vote Throughout the Kingdom* is spurious must definitely be reversed." (Theodore G. Ehrsam, *Major Byron, The Incredible Career of a Literary Forger*, New York and London, 1951, p. 137.) On *The Shelley Legend* see Newman I. White, Frederick L. Jones, Kenneth N. Cameron, *An Examination of The Shelley Legend* (University of Pennsylvania Press, 1951).

12. That the *Laon and Cythna* fragments were part of a complete manuscript is indicated by their pagination. They were not, however, part of the first draft, for that draft, as we have noted, is in the Bodleian notebooks. Hence, they were probably part of the copy sent to the printer. The other Shelley manuscripts originating with Hunt include a draft of the dedication of *The Cenci* to Hunt, fragments of *Prometheus Unbound* and *The Masque of Anarchy* (all of which appear to have come from a notebook), and Shelley's translation of part of Moschus' "Elegy on the Death of Bion" (which is echoed in *Adonais*).

Provenance

Mary Shelley gave away at least 2 major manuscripts, that of *The Masque of Anarchy* (to John Bowring in 1826) and that of the first part of *Prince Athanase* (to John Chalk Claris in 1824).[13] The manuscript of *The Masque of Anarchy* came into the possession of Thomas J. Wise and passed with his library (The Ashley Library) into the British Museum. The present location of the *Prince Athanase* manuscript does not appear to be known.

Sir Percy Florence and Lady Shelley gave 4 of Shelley's notebooks to Richard Garnett. Three of these are at present in the Henry E. Hunt-

13. On *The Masque of Anarchy* see Mary Shelley to John Bowring, Feb. 25, 1826, *Letters*, I, 342; Thomas J. Wise, *A Shelley Library*, p. 72 (with photograph). Our information on the *PrinceAthanase* manuscript comes from a sales catalogue of Sotheby, Wilkinson & Hodge, sale of July 22–25, 1918, lot no. 701, which runs as follows:

SHELLEY (P. B.) ATHANASE, a fragment, 8½ pp. 8vo, THE MOST IMPORTANT POETICAL MS. OF SHELLEY SOLD BY AUCTION OF RECENT YEARS

At the back of the last page is the following, written in pencil and traced over in ink: "This Poem of Shelley's was given me by his widow, June 7th, 1824, Speldhurst St., Brunswick Sq., A. Brooke." The poem is in *terza rima*, like the unfinished Triumph of Life, and was dated by Mrs. Shelley 1817. At the beginning is the following autograph note: "The Author was pursuing a further development of the ideal character of Athanase when it struck him that, in an attempt at extreme refinement and analysis, his conception might be betrayed into the assuming a morbid character — the reader will judge whether he is a loser or a gainer by this diffidence."

The poem begins:

There was a Youth who, as with toil and travel
Had grown quite weak and grey before his time,
Nor any could the restless griefs unravel
Which burned within him, withering up his prime
And goading him, like fiends from land to land.
Not his the load of any secret crime, etc.

This MS. includes the whole of Part I, the only consecutive passage of any length which was written.

"Arthur Brooke" was the pseudonym of John Chalk Claris (1797?–1866), editor of the *Kent Herald* and author of poems on Shelley. (*DNB*; White, *Shelley*, II, 302, 356, 392–393.) In 1824 Mary Shelley was living at 14 Speldhurst Street, Brunswick Square, London.

A manuscript of *Prince Athanase* was among those given to the Bodleian by Lady Jane Shelley in 1893. C. D. Locock in *An Examination of the Shelley Manuscripts in the Bodleian Library*, pp. 50–51, wrote of it as follows: "From MS. evidence I am inclined to think that Shelley must have made another copy of the earlier Part; so that the numerous MS. variations in that Part will have no authority, except in one or two instances, and a simple categorical list of them will be sufficient." The manuscript given to Claris, then, must have been this other copy. Locock's deduction is of interest in view of the fact that he presumably did not know of the Claris manuscript. This manuscript has not, so far as we know, been used by Shelley's editors (except insofar as it may have been embodied in Mary Shelley's text in 1824).

ington Library[14] and one in the Library of Congress.[15] To another friend and Shelley enthusiast, the Reverend Stopford Brooke, Lady Shelley gave a manuscript book containing *A Philosophical View of Reform* and the short essay *On Life*. Brooke cut out the *On Life* section (now in The Pierpont Morgan Library) and sold it to aid the British Red Cross during World War I.[16] The manuscript of *A Philosophical View of Reform* is at present in The Carl H. Pforzheimer Library. There are thus, we might note, 25 of Shelley's notebooks extant, 20 in England and 5 in the United States. And in addition there is a manuscript book of poems, copied partly by Shelley and partly by Mary Shelley, in the Harvard University Library.[17]

14. Sotheby, Wilkinson & Hodge, *Catalogue of the Library of the late Dr. Richard Garnett*, December 6, 1906, lots no. 232, 233, 234, with the introductory notation: "These Note Books were given by Shelley's widow to her son Sir Percy Shelley, he and Lady Shelley gave them to Dr. Garnett." These notebooks passed into the library of W. K. Bixby in St. Louis and were published by him in 1911 (edited by H. B. Forman).

15. Frederick L. Jones, "Unpublished Fragments by Shelley and Mary," *Studies in Philology*, XLV (July 1948), 472–476; Parke-Bernet Galleries, *The Renowned Library of the Late John A. Spoor*, May 3–5, 1939, lot no. 745. Garnett gave the book to Miss V. E. Neale in 1904.

16. The manuscript of *A Philosophical View of Reform*, then owned by Sir Percy Florence and Lady Jane Shelley, was described by Dowden in *The Fortnightly Review*, November 1886: "The manuscript occupies upward of two hundred pages in a small vellum-bound Italian note-book. On the outer side of one of the covers is a pen-and-ink drawing by Shelley . . . At one end of the little volume is the fragment 'On Life' . . ." Dowden's comments were repeated the following year in his *Transcripts and Studies* (London, 1887), p. 42. In an autograph letter dated February 21, 1916, now with the manuscript of *On Life* in the Morgan Library, Stopford Brooke writes: "It may interest you to know that I have sent to Gosse's Red Cross Sale at Christies Shelley's MS of the Essay "On Life," published in Mary's *Essays & Letters*. Vol. I, p. 223. It is the first draft of this, taken out of one his Note Books, & given to me in 1894 by Lady Shelley." We have made a comparative examination of the manuscripts of *On Life* and *A Philosophical View of Reform*, placing the two manuscripts side by side, and it is apparent that the two were originally together in the notebook which now houses the latter only (paper, stitching holes, etc., are identical).

Brooke's comment, we might note, is ambiguous in one respect. He does not make it clear whether he or Lady Shelley divided the notebook. Brooke's son-in-law, T. W. Rolleston, however, informs us that the manuscript of *A Philosophical View of Reform* — "contained in about 200 pages of a small vellum-covered note-book" — was presented to Brooke by Lady Shelley. (P. B. Shelley, *A Philosophical View of Reform*, ed. T. W. Rolleston, Oxford, 1920, p. iii.) As Brooke later had the manuscript of *On Life* in his possession and as Rolleston makes no separate mention of it as part of Lady Shelley's gift, we can presume that she gave Brooke a whole notebook — as she did to Garnett — and not an incomplete notebook plus a separate manuscript cut out of it. Brooke's ambiguity is doubtless deliberate; he did not want to admit that he had cut up the book (for the Red Cross). On Brooke's death in March 1916, the notebook passed to his daughter, Mrs. T. W. Rolleston.

17. For the provenance of this book see below, p. 299. The book was edited in 1929 by George Edward Woodberry under the title *The Shelley Notebook in the Harvard College Library*. It is not,

Provenance

The curious thing about Shelley's literary manuscripts is not the number which have survived but the number which have disappeared. It seems almost incredible, for instance, that there should be no manuscript of his play *The Cenci* or of *Alastor* and but partial manuscripts for such other of his major works as *Adonais*, *Epipsychidion*, and *Hellas*.[18] Not that one would expect Shelley to keep such manuscripts for he seldom kept anything, including letters; but Mary Shelley seems to have inherited the hoarding instincts of her father, who methodically filed everything away, and as she kept so many manuscripts the loss of the rest seems strange.

Particularly is there a lack of Shelley's early manuscripts. None of these was preserved in the family papers because the family papers, so far as Shelley was concerned, began with Mary Shelley. Harriet seems to have had as little interest in preserving literary manuscripts as Shelley himself. The only exception, so far as is known, is a manuscript book of poems, which contained a dedication to Harriet herself and was presumably given to her by Shelley. The book has been preserved in her family and is at present in the possession of the heirs of Shelley's great-grandson, William C. H. Esdaile.[19] The only other major early manuscript is one of a revised version of *Queen Mab* (made in a copy of the first edition). This manuscript (at present in The Carl H. Pforzheimer Library) was among some papers which Shelley left behind in England

however, a regular Shelley notebook, in which Shelley jotted down ideas and drafts for poems, but is a book of fair copies.

18. For *Adonais* see Ingpen, *Shelley in England*, pp. 671–687; Shelley-Rolls and Ingpen, *Verse and Prose*, pp. 36–48. For *Epipsychidion*, see Locock, *An Examination of the Shelley Manuscripts in the Bodleian Library*, pp. 3–13, and Shelley, *Complete Works*, II, 428. A transcript of *Hellas* in the hand of Edward Ellerker Williams is at present in the Huntington Library and was previously in Frederick Locker-Lampson's *The Rowfant Library* (which also contained other Shelley material). Some *Hellas* fragments in Shelley's hand are in the Shelley-Rolls notebooks (*Verse and Prose*, pp. 47–52).

19. Ianthe, the daughter of Shelley and Harriet, married Edward Jeffries Esdaile of Cothelstone House, Somerset, who was connected with the well-known banking firm, Esdaile, Hammet & Co. of Lombard Street, and they had seven children. (See *Burke's Landed Gentry*.) Shelley's other child by Harriet, Charles, died in 1826 at the age of eleven (whereupon his son by Mary, Percy Florence, became heir to the Shelley estates). (See *Burke's Peerage*.) (This notebook was purchased by The Carl H. Pforzheimer Library in 1962 and was published in 1964.)

when he went to Italy in 1818. It was taken over with these papers by his landlord at Marlow, Robert Maddocks, and its transmission can then be traced in unbroken sequence.

Such, in brief, is the story of Shelley's major literary manuscripts. When we turn to the letters — with which we are mainly concerned here — the story is somewhat different, for whereas most of the manuscripts were in the possession of the family, most of the letters were in the hands of nonfamily correspondents. A few of these correspondents sold the letters themselves but usually they were either sold or given to an institution by heirs or legal executors.

Although there seems to be a common opinion to the contrary, there is probably no major difference in the patterns of letter preservation between the early nineteenth century and the present (although the telephone has cut down on the total number of letters). Letters sent to business or legal firms, for instance, are normally filed and often preserved for a long period. Some of Shelley's letters, as we shall see, were thus filed and preserved. In regard to personal correspondence, people tend to preserve the letters of authors and other prominent individuals, either for their intrinsic value or in the thought of eventually selling them.

Individual differences also play a part. Some people are natural hoarders, some are not. Some keep almost all letters; most keep some (from friends, lovers, or relatives); very few keep none.

If we put all these tendencies together we can see that there are certain general selective factors. There is, for instance, apt to be a larger proportion of business letters preserved than of personal letters; and among personal letters, a larger proportion of intimate than of nonintimate letters, a larger proportion of later letters (when an author is well known) than of earlier letters, a larger proportion of letters to some correspondents than to others. Some of these tendencies can, of course, be offset in individual cases by particular factors. For instance, as Shelley's genius became apparent early and he quickly developed intimate friendships, we have an unusually large number of his youthful letters.

It is important if one is using letters for biographical or critical purposes to see what particular selective factors are at work and to what degree they have rendered the existing body of correspondence unrepresentative of the total life. A person, for instance, writes differently to different correspondents, revealing different facets of his personality or thinking to each. Hence, a great number of letters to one person may reveal certain aspects of the writer and only a few letters show other aspects, but both may be equally important in attempting to get a balanced picture.

One does not work long with the letters and other manuscripts of Shelley and his circle without perceiving the constant recurrence of a small number of major sources. No matter how devious the later course of a letter through collections and sales rooms, the ultimate source is usually traceable to one of these.

Some groups of letters were early removed from circulation, for instance, the 46 letters which Shelley wrote to his friend, the Sussex schoolteacher, Elizabeth Hitchener, between June 1811 and June 1812. These were given to her solicitor, Henry J. Slack, when she left England for the Continent. On her death in 1822, Slack retained the letters. They later passed to his widow and from her to her nephew, who deposited them in the British Museum.[20]

Two other large groups of Shelley letters, also early removed from circulation, were those to Shelley's friends in Italy, the Gisbornes (and Mrs. Gisborne's son, Henry Reveley), and those to Shelley's publisher friend, Thomas Hookham. Most of the Gisborne-Reveley letters and apparently all of Shelley's to Hookham were given to the Shelley family and have now joined the letters in the Bodleian Library.[21]

Of sources for the letters of Shelley or those associated with him which have appeared on the open market, four great treasure-troves should first be noted: the Clairmont; the Whitton; the Byron-Murray; the Hogg family. Of these, all but the Byron-Murray contained extensive material by the Shelley circle as well as by Shelley.

When Claire Clairmont, stepsister to Mary Shelley, died in Florence in 1879 at the age of ninety-one, the letters and other manuscripts in her possession passed to her niece, Paola Clairmont. There then ensued the

20. De Ricci, pp. 105–106; *Letters about Shelley*, pp. 30–31 and *passim*.

21. De Ricci, pp. 57, 140, 221; Hill, *The Shelley Correspondence in the Bodleian Library*, pp. vii–xv. Three letters from Shelley to the Gisbornes and part of one to Reveley have come on the market. Many of John Gisborne's journals and notebooks are among the Abinger Manuscripts.

seesaw battle for possession between the English Shelley scholar, H. Buxton Forman, and the New England sea captain, Edward Silsbee, which formed the basis for Henry James's ironical novelette *The Aspern Papers*.[22] With one or two minor exceptions — for example, the Harvard copybook previously mentioned — the material was purchased by Forman. This material included 23 letters from Shelley to Claire Clairmont, 23 letters from Shelley to Godwin, 1 third-person note from Shelley to "Mr. Pike" (a lawyer associated with Godwin), 111 letters by Mary Shelley (5 of them "of old date"), "Shelley's will," 4 of Claire's notebooks, 1818–1820, her journal ("from 1825"), 8 or more letters by William Godwin, Godwin's "will, sermons, testimonial and other manuscripts," more than 50 letters from Edward J. Trelawny to Claire Clairmont, and 1 literary manuscript by Shelley, namely a section of *Notes on Sculptures in Rome and Florence*.[23] Part of this material was found in a box formerly belonging to William Godwin "with his name and address written in his own hand on the outside."[24]

Most of the letters by Shelley to Claire and Godwin Forman sold on the open market. (A number of them went into the great Shelley collection of Charles W. Frederickson in Brooklyn.[25]) Four letters to

22. See Leon Edel, "*The Aspern Papers*: Great-aunt Wyckoff and Juliana Bordereau," *Modern Language Notes*, LXVII (June 1952), 392–395.

23. See Appendix, below. A general account of Forman's purchases will be found in the introduction to his edition of the letters of Trelawny, pp. x–xi.

24. Paola Clairmont to H. B. Forman, Jan. 31, 1886 [misdated "1885"], The Berg Collection, The New York Public Library.

25. For Frederickson's holdings see Bangs & Co., *Catalogue of the Library of the late Charles W. Frederickson Sold by Order of the Administrator*, New York, May 24–28, 1897. Lots no. 2308 to 2370 consist of Shelley letters. As lot no. 2370 comprises 2 letters, this makes a total of 63. But one of the 2 letters in lot no. 2370 is a forgery and the other a copy. The first of them is one of the copies of Shelley's letter to Mary Shelley of December 16, 1816, the original of which is in the British Museum. The second is noted by de Ricci (p. 85; Shelley to Godwin, Nov. 13, 1816). It has now been safely removed from circulation. The Frederickson catalogue suggests that nos. 2339, 2341, and 2344 (to Ollier, Jan. 11, 1818; Dec. 22, 1817; Jan. 25, 1818) are in Shelley's hand. All of these letters are now in The Carl H. Pforzheimer Library; two are in Shelley's hand; one, December 22, 1817, is in Mary's hand; Mary wrote it for Shelley at the time. The catalogue states that lot no. 2342 (to Ollier, Jan. 22, 1818) is written by Mary. The present location of this letter does not appear to be known; but the probability is that the notation — which is unequivocal — is correct. In addition to these there is one letter (lot no. 2315, Shelley to Hogg, September 1815) which must be a copy (perhaps that in Mary Shelley's hand now in the Henry E. Huntington Library), whose history is traced by de Ricci (p. 131, no. 257) under the impression that it is a Shelley autograph, because the original is among the Abinger Manuscripts. Thus Frederickson had a total of 59 autograph Shelley letters. (There

Claire and 2 to Godwin were retained by Forman, and they were sold with his library in 1920 in New York.

Many of these letters thus preserved by Claire over the years — Shelley to Claire and Godwin, Mary to Claire, Trelawny to Claire, etc. — have come, by various routes, into The Carl H. Pforzheimer Library. The first item in these volumes, in fact, the testimonial for William Godwin, came from this source.

The story of the Whitton papers was told by Roger Ingpen in 1916:

It is now some years since an important discovery relating to Shelley was made by Mr. Charles Withall, of Messrs. Withall & Withall, the successors to Mr. William Whitton, who was entrusted more than a century ago with the legal business of Sir Bysshe and Sir Timothy Shelley. Mr. Charles Withall happened to find, among the papers preserved in his offices, some letters of Percy Bysshe Shelley, and also some pamphlets, including copies of *A Necessity of Atheism* and *An Address to the Irish People.* This discovery encouraged Mr. Withall to make a further search, which resulted in bringing to light other letters of the poet, besides a mass of correspondence, including numerous letters from various members of the Shelley family, as well as a large number of legal documents, pedigrees, Mr. Whitton's letter book and diaries and other papers.[26]

The papers were sold at Sotheby's two years later, and the sales catalogue shows their main contents as follows: 29 letters and 2 receipts by Percy Bysshe Shelley; 67 letters by Shelley's father, Timothy (from 1815 on, Sir Timothy) Shelley; 66 letters by Mary Shelley (4 of them signed jointly with Thomas Love Peacock).[27]

were no Shelley autographs sold at the earlier sales of his library — 1871, 1877, 1886, 1893. For some account of the 1897 sale see Harry B. Smith, *First Nights and First Editions,* Boston, 1931, p. 167.) We might note that lot no. 2335 ("Marlow, Dec. 3, 1817. No address") is to Charles Ollier and lot no. 2369 ("no address and no date") is to Claire Clairmont, dated in *Complete Works* as April 13, 1821.

　　Lots no. 2371–2394, 2399 contain Shelleyana, including letters by William Godwin, Mary Shelley, Horace Smith, Trelawny, and Peacock.

　　In addition to Frederickson the American collectors Harry B. Smith, Jerome Kern, Edward A. Newton, John A. Spoor, and W. Van R. Whitall had notable Shelley collections, all of which have been sold on the open market.

26. Ingpen, *Shelley in England,* p. v.

27. Sotheby, Wilkinson & Hodge, *Catalogue of Fine Books . . . Autograph Letters, MSS. &c. By or Relating to P. B. Shelley, discovered by and in the possession of the Solicitors to members of the Shelley family, Sold by direction of Sir John Shelley-Rolls, Bart.,* London, July 22–25, 1918, lots no. 712–756.

Of the 29 Shelley letters, 16 were to his father. Except for 2 letters from Oxford — apparently the only ones extant that Shelley wrote to his father from the university — these deal, in the main, with the two crises of the year 1811; the expulsion from Oxford and the elopement with Harriet Westbrook. These letters Timothy turned over to Whitton, whom he had appointed as his representative to deal with his son; and Whitton duly filed them in his office files where they lay undisturbed for a century. When he turned these letters over, Timothy also turned over the 2 earlier letters from Oxford, presumably because they discussed the philosophical views which had resulted in the expulsion. Other letters also dealt with these crises, for example, 2 from Shelley to his grandfather, Sir Bysshe Shelley; 6 from Shelley to William Whitton; 4 from John Hogg, father of Thomas Jefferson Hogg, to Timothy Shelley. Of particular interest is the presence among these papers of the letter from Eliza Westbrook to Shelley, June 11, 1811. It is in the new light shed on these events of the year 1811 that the main biographical importance of the Whitton papers lies. But the later letters tell us much that we did not know of the lives of Sir Timothy and of Mary Shelley following the death of Shelley.

Once these papers were sold, they were dispersed. Some are now at Yale, some at the Huntington, some — including Shelley's two letters from Oxford — are in The Carl H. Pforzheimer Library.

Shelley first met Byron in Switzerland in the summer of 1816 and the two poets made a trip around the Lake of Geneva; they came together again in the fall of 1818 at Venice, their meeting there being described in *Julian and Maddalo*; in the fall of 1821 when Byron's mistress, the Countess Guiccioli, and her family were being persecuted at Ravenna and Byron himself was under fire for his assistance to the Italian nationalists, he asked Shelley to visit him; shortly afterwards he joined Shelley at Pisa. These and other happenings are discussed in Shelley's letters to Byron, which are rich also in philosophical, literary, and political comments.

On Byron's death in 1824 a large portion of his correspondence — including 21 letters from Shelley to Byron — passed on to his literary executor, John Cam Hobhouse, later, Lord Broughton; on Lord Broughton's death in 1869 it went to his daughter, Lady Dorchester; on the death of Lady Dorchester in 1914 it went to John Murray, descendant of Byron's publisher. In 1926 all 21 of the letters from Shelley to Byron were purchased from Murray for this library. In addition to these 21, only 8 other letters from Shelley to Byron are known to exist, and these are now in various libraries and collections (one of them in this library).

Shelley met Thomas Jefferson Hogg at Oxford in the fall of 1810 (a meeting memorably described in Hogg's life of Shelley). When the two students parted for the Christmas vacation a vigorous (almost daily) correspondence ensued, dealing with personal matters, philosophy, and poetry. When Shelley was expelled, Hogg was expelled with him; when he eloped with Harriet Westbrook to Edinburgh, Hogg joined them. In the fall of 1811, as a result of Hogg's attentions to Harriet, they quarreled and parted; and again correspondence (of a somewhat agonized character) ensued. The following year, the quarrel was made up, and, although the two never became as intimate as formerly, they remained friends, and Hogg was a frequent visitor at Shelley's various homes until the departure for Italy in 1818. And from Italy the correspondence continued, the last letter being dated October 22, 1821.

Through Shelley, Hogg came to know Mary Shelley, Thomas Love Peacock, and Leigh Hunt. With Mary he had a curious epistolary "affair" in 1815; and after Shelley's death the two remained friends. When Jane Williams, widow of Edward Ellerker Williams, who was drowned with Shelley, returned from Italy to England in 1822, she bore a letter of introduction from Mary to Hogg. The acquaintance resulted in her marriage to Hogg, who thus achieved a new entry into the later Shelley circle, one further extended by the marriage of Jane's daughter Dina to Leigh Hunt's son Henry.

When Hogg died in 1862, the vast mass of letters and other documents resulting from these connections passed on to his younger brother John; on John's death in 1869 it continued in the family and later became the property of John's son, John Ewer Jefferson Hogg, who was born late in his father's life (1860).[28] In 1922 John Ewer Jefferson Hogg sold 7 letters from Shelley to Hogg and 3 literary manuscripts by

28. See "Hogg of Norton" in *Burke's Landed Gentry;* and John Ewer Hogg in *Walford's County Families of the United Kingdom* (London, 1920).

Shelley (all of which were acquired by this library).[29] On his death the rest of the material passed to his son, Major Richard John Jefferson Hogg, who sold it in 1948 at two sales. The Hogg family, we might note, had during all this time occupied the same house, at Norton-on-Tees, County Durham, and the material had remained in the house, except for a few of Shelley's letters to Hogg lent to Lady Jane Shelley, some of which remained in her possession and are now among the Abinger Manuscripts.[30] In addition we should note one letter from Shelley to Hogg which somehow came early into the open market,[31] a poem that Hogg himself gave in 1834 to Dawson Turner,[32] and a few letters the location of which we have been unable to trace.[33] Otherwise, apparently

29. Sotheby, Wilkinson & Hodge, *Catalogue of Valuable Printed Books and Manuscripts Comprising . . . Important Letters & Manuscripts of P. B. Shelley, the Property of John Ewer Jefferson Hogg, Esq.,* July 27–28, 1922, lots no. 326–335.

30. We know that Lady Shelley had at least the following letters in her possession because she corrected them in the margin of a copy of Hogg's *Life of Shelley:* Dec. 20, 1810; Jan. 2, 1811; Jan. 17, 1811; Apr. 26, 1811; June 2, 1811; Aug. 15, 1811 (Koszul, *Jeunesse,* Appendice II, pp. 405–418). Two of these letters, that of December 20, 1810, and most of that of June 2, 1811, are now among the Abinger Manuscripts (which, as we have noted, came from Lady Shelley). The final page of the June 2 letter was not among the Hogg family papers sold in 1948, nor, so far as we could discover, is now among the Abinger Manuscripts (although the whole letter was corrected by Lady Shelley). In addition there are among the Abinger Manuscripts a letter from Shelley to Hogg from Bishopsgate in September 1815 (the postmark appears to be September 23), the first four pages of a letter dated in Shelley, *Complete Works,* "[? November 14–18, 1811]," and a letter of May 8, 1817. Hence, Lady Shelley must have had other Shelley to Hogg letters in her possession than those which she corrected (as noted by Koszul). The letters of January 2, January 17, April 26, and August 15 were returned to the Hogg family and are at present in this library. (The only other Shelley letter that we have noted in the Abinger Manuscripts is one to T. L. Peacock, March 21, 1821.)

31. De Ricci, p. 134, No. 379, April 30, 1818, from Milan. This letter first came into the market in 1870. It is at present in The Carl H. Pforzheimer Library.

32. T. J. Hogg to Dawson Turner, May 30, 1834, Hogg, *Shelley,* I, 123–124. In the catalogue of the sale of Turner's library in 1859 (see fn. 7 above), we find the following among the autographs (p. 268): "Shelley, P. B., A.L.s., and an unpublished poem, partly in his autograph, 4 pages 8vo." The poem was presumably that given by Hogg for it is described by Hogg in his letter as "unpublished." (This poem, "A Dialogue," is also in the Esdaile copybook; Shelley, *Complete Works,* III, 315.)

33. The following letters were not among those sold by the Hogg family either in 1922 or 1948; nor are they, so far as we have discovered, among the Abinger Manuscripts. They were all, except for the last noted (No. 415), published in Hogg's *Life of Shelley* in 1858, so Hogg once had either them or copies of them in his possession. We give the de Ricci numbers (which are the same as in Shelley, *Complete Works*): No. 20, Dec. 26, 1810; No. 29, Jan. 16, 1811; No. 62, May 19, 1811; No. 64, May 26, 1811; No. 215, Apr. 5, 1813; No. 225, July 9, 1813; No. 415, July 25, 1819. No. 415 apparently exists only in transcript (one by Mary Shelley).

everything Hogg received from Shelley remained in the hands of the Hogg family until sold in the present century.

Of the two sales in 1948 the first (in June) was the larger and more important.[34] At this sale were sold 64 letters from Shelley to Hogg and 1 translation by Shelley, making, with the 1922 sale, a total of 71 letters, 3 literary manuscripts, and 1 translation. In addition there were 23 letters by Mary Shelley, 11 of them dealing with her relationship with Hogg in 1815; 6 letters from Timothy Shelley, 1 of them to Thomas Jefferson Hogg, 1 to P. B. Shelley, 3 to John Hogg, father of Thomas Jefferson Hogg, and 2 to John Hogg's legal adviser, Robert Clarke; 1 letter from Robert Clarke to John Hogg; 3 letters from Thomas Love Peacock to Thomas Jefferson Hogg. The Timothy Shelley, John Hogg, Robert Clarke letters and some of Shelley's own letters deal with the expulsion and elopement crises of 1811. Thus our most important sources of information on these two events are derived from letters which none of the correspondents expected to be preserved, those retained in his legal files by Whitton and those kept by Thomas Jefferson Hogg.

The letters of Shelley to Hogg sold at this sale cover the whole range of their friendship. The earliest of them is the second letter Shelley wrote to Hogg — December 23, 1810. (The first letter to Hogg — December 20 — was retained by Lady Jane Shelley.) The final letter is the last letter that Shelley wrote to Hogg, that of October 22, 1821, mentioned above.

In the second sale of the Hogg family material in 1948[35] there were sold 16 letters by Thomas Jefferson Hogg (2 to Shelley's mother;[36] 1 to Shelley's sister Elizabeth;[37] 1 to Shelley; 1 to John Frank Newton; 11 to Thomas Love Peacock); 5 letters from Peacock to Hogg and 7 from Leigh Hunt to Hogg; a group of letters from members of the Hogg family; 3 short literary manuscripts by Peacock and some Greek epigrams by Hogg.

34. Sotheby & Co., *Catalogue of the Correspondence of Thomas Jefferson Hogg (1792–1862) Consisting Principally of Letters from Percy and Mary Shelley, sold by order of his Great-Nephew, Major R. J. Jefferson Hogg*, June 30, 1948.

35. Sotheby & Co., *Catalogue of Valuable Printed Books and a Few Manuscripts, Autograph Letters . . . The Final Portion of the Correspondence to Thomas Jefferson Hogg (Sold by Order of Major R. J. Jefferson Hogg, M.C.)*, July 26–27, 1948.

36. July? 6–18, 1811, and Aug. 22, 1811, *Shelley and his Circle*, II, 820–823, 873–875.

37. May 25, 1811, *ibid.*, pp. 797–799.

Most of the material from these 1948 sales is at present in the Pforzheimer Library, which includes among its holdings more than 60 letters from Shelley to Hogg.

In addition to these four major sources, two other groups of Shelley letters should be noted, letters to his intimate friends, Thomas Love Peacock and Leigh Hunt, and to his publishers, Charles and James Ollier.

Some of Shelley's letters to Peacock were, as we have seen, acquired by the Shelley family; at least 15 are now in the Bodleian Library.[38] Seventeen were put on sale with Peacock's library following his death in 1866.[39] Thereafter wending their way through various collections (including that of Charles W. Frederickson) and sales rooms they are now scattered. Six are in this library.

Shortly before his death, Leigh Hunt gave several letters by Shelley and Mary Shelley to their son, Sir Percy Florence Shelley.[40] The 7 letters from Shelley to Leigh Hunt now in the Bodleian[41] presumably all came from the Shelley family. There was not, however, as there was for Peacock, any one sale at which the rest were put on the market. Some were retained by Leigh Hunt's son, Thornton Hunt;[42] at least 10 were in the possession of Leigh Hunt's grandson, Walter Leigh Hunt, as late as 1886, and some of these had been sold by 1890.[43] Some found their way into the Frederickson collection; some went to Thomas J. Wise. They are now scattered: the British Museum (via Wise), the Henry E. Huntington Library, the Stark Collection of the University of Texas, Texas Christian University, The Pierpont Morgan Library, The Berg Collection of The New York Public Library; 8 are in this library.

The Olliers became Shelley's publishers in 1817. Shelley's letters to them (addressed either to Charles or to the firm) extend from February of that year until April 1822, some two months before his death. Of Shelley's prose volumes the Olliers published *A Proposal for Putting*

---

38. Hill, *The Shelley Correspondence in the Bodleian Library*, pp. vii–xv.

39. Sotheby, Wilkinson & Hodge, *Catalogue of the Library of the Late Thos. Love Peacock . . . Some Highly Interesting Original Letters in the Autograph of P. B. Shelley*, June 11–12, 1866.

40. De Ricci, p. 146.

41. Hill, *The Shelley Correspondence in the Bodleian Library*, pp. vii–xv; Shelley, *Complete Works*, X, 424.

42. Hunt, *Correspondence*, I, vi.   43. De Ricci, pp. 146–158.

Reform to the Vote and *History of a Six Weeks' Tour*, both in 1817; and the following volumes of poetry: *Laon and Cythna (The Revolt of Islam)*, 1818; *Rosalind and Helen*, 1819; *The Cenci*, 1819; *Prometheus Unbound*, 1820; *Epipsychidion*, 1821; *Hellas*, 1822. Shelley's letters to them deal largely with these works, sometimes in business terms, sometimes in literary, for Charles Ollier was himself an author.

Ollier disposed of at least one letter before his death in 1859; a total of 43 others were preserved in his family and sold at two sales, one in 1877 and one in 1878.[44] Twenty-two of these letters went into the Frederickson collection and were dispersed at its sale in 1897. They are all now widely scattered. Nineteen are in this library, 8 at the Henry E. Huntington Library, 3 at the University of Texas, 2 at Harvard, and 1 each at other libraries.

Of Shelley's remaining correspondents, three should be noted in particular, as Shelley wrote a good many letters and other items to them and these continue to appear in the market. These are Brookes and Company, Shelley's bankers from the fall of 1815 until his death; his early friend and protégé of Timothy Shelley, Edward Fergus Graham; and the publisher of some of his juvenile novels and poems, John Joseph Stockdale.

Shelley wrote some 35 letters and notes to Brookes and Company (of Chancery Lane, one of the leading banking houses of the period), as well as about 130 signed checks.[45] Brookes and Company later became amalgamated with the Union of London Bank. Early in the present century these Shelley items were found in papers that had been preserved in the files of this latter firm. They were sold in 1916.

Shelley wrote some 30 letters to Graham, including one in verse, between April 1810 and July 1811. At least 12 of these were placed on sale as early as 1851 while Graham was perhaps still living.[46]

Shelley's 11 letters to Stockdale (also 1810 and 1811) were apparently kept in one group until 1872.[47] The earliest recorded sale is

44. *Ibid.*, p. 185.

45. *Ibid.*, pp. 20–25; Peck, *Shelley*, II, Appendix P, pp. 436–439 (list of checks); Walter T. Spencer, *Forty Years in My Bookshop* (Boston and New York, 1923), pp. 182–185.

46. De Ricci, p. 86. Graham seems to have died in 1852.

47. De Ricci, p. 261; *Stockdale's Budget of "all that is Good, and Noble and Amiable, in the Country,"* 1826–1827; Richard Garnett, "Shelley in Pall Mall," *Macmillan's Magazine*, II (1860), 100–110.

1877, which is for one letter only, but they may all have been sold privately by that date. The present whereabouts of most of them does not seem to be known.

As perhaps even the above brief summary may suffice to demonstrate, the history of the letters of few people is so well known as that of Shelley's. Almost every letter of the more than 600 extant can be traced back to its point of origin and usually from that point through an unbroken sequence into the present.[48]

A good deal of the provenance of the "circle" letters and manuscripts we have already noted in discussing Shelley: the great mass of Godwin and other material among the Abinger Manuscripts; the large number of the letters of Mary Shelley and Trelawny preserved by Claire Clairmont; the letters of Timothy Shelley and Mary Shelley in the Whitton papers; the letters of Peacock, Hunt, Mary Shelley, and others in the Hogg papers; the letters of Peacock, the Gisbornes, and

48. As Newman I. White pointed out, this fact affords "a protection against forgers enjoyed by the biographers of no other important English poet." (*An Examination of the Shelley Legend*, p. 14.) Yet, curiously enough, there has been in recent years a good deal of writing on forgeries of Shelley's letters. (Smith, *The Shelley Legend;* Theodore G. Ehrsam, *Major Byron;* Blunden, *Shelley,* pp. x, 162; Sylva Norman, *Flight of the Skylark, The Development of Shelley's Reputation,* University of Oklahoma Press, 1954, pp. 189–204; Edmund Blunden, *Selected Poems, Percy Bysshe Shelley,* London and Glasgow, 1954, p. 27; White, Jones, Cameron, *An Examination of The Shelley Legend;* Andreas Mayor, "A Suspected Shelley Letter," *The Library,* IV, September 1949, 144–145.) Now that the smoke of battle has cleared somewhat, however, one can see that there was not much to write about. As Professor White also pointed out, there has been a considerable deployment of the same letters repeatedly "like a stage army." (*An Examination of the Shelley Legend,* p. 7.) Actually only three Shelley letters were questioned: (a) the British Museum manuscript of Shelley's letter to Mary Shelley, Dec. 16, 1816, in which he tells of Harriet's suicide; (b) the Shelley-Rolls manuscript of Shelley to Mary, Jan. 11, 1817; (c) the John Murray manuscript of Shelley to Byron, Jan. 17, 1817. The questioning of these letters, we should note, was made without examining the manuscripts. Such examination has shown that they are all three genuine, as White, Frederick L. Jones, and other Shelley scholars had previously contended. (Mayor, "A Suspected Shelley Letter"; Ehrsam, *Major Byron.*)

The forgery discussion was partly set off by a curious circumstance, namely that Shelley's letter to Mary of December 16, 1816, was somehow remailed in 1859. We might note its subsequent history. In 1867 the Secretary of the Post Office sent it to Spencer Shelley, son of Sir John Shelley of Michelgrove. The letter then remained with this branch of the family until the year 1908 when Mrs. Spencer Shelley wrote to H. Buxton Forman about it. Forman, who was a post office official as well as a Shelley specialist, replied, offering to buy the letter. (ALs, draft, May 23, 1908; ALs, draft, June 1, 1908; both in The Carl H. Pforzheimer Library.) The negotiations were completed by Mrs. Shelley's daughter, Mrs. Dent. (June 19, 1908; ALs in The Berg Collection of The New York Public Library.) From Forman's library the letter passed to Thomas J. Wise and thence into the British Museum with Wise's library. (Wise, *A Shelley Library,* pp. 4–5, with photoduplicate.)

Provenance

Hookham preserved with the Shelley family papers and now in the Bodleian. In addition to these the following major sources should be mentioned: (a) letters from Mary Shelley to Leigh and Marianne Hunt preserved in the Hunt family and sold in 1922;[49] (b) letters from Leigh Hunt to Shelley and others (presumably secured from Mary Shelley) preserved in the Hunt family and sold in 1935 with the estate of Mrs. Beryl Dodgson, daughter of Leigh Hunt's grandson, Colonel C. Shelley Leigh Hunt;[50] (c) letters from Trelawny to Augusta White, who emigrated to Canada and married William Henry Draper, sold by her descendants in Montreal; (d) letters and manuscripts of Thomas Love Peacock, preserved in the family and sold in 1949 by Mrs. K. Hall Thorpe, Peacock's great-great-granddaughter.

APPENDIX

The Clairmont Papers

The actual battle for possession of the Clairmont papers, although fought with less psychological finesse than in *The Aspern Papers*, has, nevertheless, a certain rugged interest of its own. It can be reconstructed from a series of autograph letters by Forman and others, partly in The Berg Collection of The New York Public Library and partly in The Carl H. Pforzheimer Library. The following brief summary makes use of materials from both collections, designating them respectively as "Berg Ms." and "CHP Ms." The Berg letters are quoted by permission of The Henry W. and Albert A. Berg Collection of The New York Public Library.

Claire Clairmont died on March 19, 1879, in Florence (in *The Aspern Papers* the locale is shifted to Venice.) But before that date Captain Edward Silsbee had moved into the house with her and Paola. Silsbee fully expected to be able to purchase the letters and papers which she had left. But while the estate was still unsettled Forman moved into action, using two friends, Henry Roderick Newman and Charles Fairfax Murray, to negotiate in his behalf. On May 26 Paola Clairmont wrote, in answer to an inquiry by Forman, to describe the Shelley letters. By July 2 matters had gone so far that Silsbee saw the prize slipping from his grasp and wrote in mingled indignation and alarm to Murray (CHP Ms.):

---

49. Mary Shelley, *Letters*, II, 346. 50. Sold at Sotheby's, April 8, 1935.

Dear Sir,

I have been in treaty for the Shelly [*sic*] letters with Miss Clairmont the elder & her niece, & have always understood I should have the refusal of them if I would give more than any one else offered.

The matter has been delayed owing to the absence of the executor & could not be decided until within a few days.

I think the refusal belongs in honor to me & I will give more than has yet been offered for them or probably will be, & it would not be for Miss Clairmonts interest to sell them till they are offered to me.

I am vy truly

Your's E. A. Silsbee

P. S. It has been by a great misunderstanding they have been offered to another

By July 10 it looked as though Forman had the letters, for Paola had offered them for £150 and Forman was willing to meet this. Whereupon Murray (Berg Ms.) "locked the box and carried off the key which I have here with me (this that our friend Silsbee shouldn't go poking over them again as he was still in the house)." Paola still hesitated. On July 20 she informed Murray (CHP Ms.) that she did not feel herself "irrevocably bound to sell the letters to your friend." In the end, however, Forman won out, as he noted in his Introduction to *Letters of Edward John Trelawny* (Oxford, 1910), pp. x–xi: "An American who had been residing in the same house at Florence with the Clairmonts had been bidding against me for the collection; but, as his rather free bids turned out to be only in bills at long date, the executrix decided to accept my cash rather than his paper, in which she lacked confidence."

As a result Silsbee ended up with only the Harvard copybook (see fn. 17, above), a second smaller copybook, and a letter from Shelley to Claire (both now also at Harvard). (For some account of this second copybook, see Peck, *Shelley*, I, 477, and Smith, *The Shelley Legend*, pp. 43–44. On the letter — wrongly dated in Shelley, *Complete Works* — see Marion Kingston, "Notes on Three Shelley Letters," *Keats-Shelley Memorial Bulletin*, Rome, 1955, No. VI, pp. 16–17.) According to a letter from T. J. Wise (CHP Ms.) Silsbee secured the Harvard copybook manuscript by promising to marry Paola: "He recounted to us with glee how he had cheated Paola Clairmont out of the Manuscript."

On July 30 Paola sent to Newman (Berg Ms.) an inventory of the Shelley letters plus the 5 Mary Shelley letters of "old date," 106 other Mary Shelley letters, 11 letters from Sir Percy Florence Shelley, 4 notebooks by Claire, and "notes on Art etc." Paola also had letters by Trelawny to Claire but, in regard to these, Murray informed Forman on July 10 (Berg Ms.): "Trelawny wishes to have them himself & destroy them — He ret^d all miss Clairmont's letters just before her death & she burnt them he now wants his own ret^d (which is reasonable) to do the like." In April 1880, after the transaction was completed,

Provenance

Paola discovered that she had made some mistakes. On April 17 she wrote to
Forman that she had apparently given him only 56 Mary Shelley letters instead
of 106 and had given him a package of 8 Godwin letters in their place. "I have
furthermore been told that among the papers I sent you by Mʳ Newman a MSS.
of Shelleys was discovered containing his opinions of the Florence & other picture gallery which of course is of the greatest value." This, one might presume,
was the "notes on Art etc." of the inventory, which Paola did not recognize as
by Shelley, but Forman in reply (CHP Ms.) denied that this was so: "There
was no manuscript of Shelley's but the 47 letters named in the list: I wish there
had been." (Forman's edition of Shelley, *Prose Works*, the following year, gave
new readings — III, 42 — in the "Notes and Sculptures in Rome and Florence"
from "a MS. Notebook," but this may not have been in Shelley's hand.)

    Forman replied to Paola also on the Mary Shelley letters: "Of course, I
may be short in the number of Mrs Shelley's letters; but whether you choose to
send me those you name I must leave to your sense of justice." The Godwin
letters enclosed by error he airily dismissed as "unconsidered trifles" that no
one would buy. (As 90 Mary-to-Claire letters were sold with Forman's library,
presumably the appeal to Paola's "sense of justice" bore fruit and he received
the extra 50.)

    In May 1880 Newman wrote further to Forman (CHP Ms.) on the Tre-
lawny letters and other matters: "Ellis is to come in a day or two & will probably
carry off the rest of the plunder   Do you know the Trelawny letters were written while he was in Greece with Byron?" The reference to Ellis — of Ellis and
White, booksellers — produced a letter to him from Forman attempting to
stave him off, an effort which was successful. Trelawny's letters were not, as he
had requested, returned to him for burning. On October 22, 1881, Paola offered
them to Forman (Berg Ms.): "Trelawny is no more as you are aware. Would
his letters of old date that you once wished to have, & that I was then not at
liberty to give, be of any use to you?" On the blank pages of this letter Forman
has drafted his reply, stating that he was interested in Trelawny's letters "early
and late." In 1910 he published them (with some omissions).

    In 1886 Paola offered a final lot of material for sale. Writing to Forman on
January 10 (Berg Ms.), she listed the main "Contents of the box" as follows:
4 letters from Mary Shelley (3 of them to Claire Clairmont), "Godwin's will,
sermons, testimonials & other MSS," "Claire Clairmont's Journal 1825," a
"little Greek volume of Sophocles" and Shelley's inkstand. The story of the
inkstand and the Sophocles Paola relates as follows: "When the news of Shelley's
death became certain to Mʳˢ Shelley, Mʳˢ Williams & Claire who were then
staying at Lerici, Mʳˢ Shelley asked my aunt what souvenir she wᵈ wish to
have — & my Aunt begged for the inkstand & a little Greek book which Shelley
always carried in his pocket & which was found — either in the boat or in his
coat — after his death. These two things Mʳˢ Shelley gave my Aunt. This little

volume of Sophocles is from the year 1809 English edition. It is in my possession my Aunt wrote on the first leaf 'P. B. Shelley. This book was always in his pocket.' Signed Cl. Cl." This volume Forman must have purchased along with the manuscripts for it was sold with his library in 1920 (lot no. 719, p. 170).

In this connection we might note that Trelawny gave a water-stained Sophocles to Shelley's son, Sir Percy Florence Shelley, which he said had been found on Shelley's body. This volume was seen by Dowden in Sir Percy's possession in 1886 and was presented to the Bodleian by Lady Shelley in 1893. It is noted in Hill, *The Shelley Correspondence in the Bodleian Library*, p. 46, as follows: "Sophoclis Tragoediae septem. Two volumes in one. Oxon., 1809. The copy found in Shelley's hand at his death." (Mr. L. W. Hanson, Keeper of the Printed Books at the Bodleian Library has very kindly verified for us the correctness of this description.) The copy purchased from Paola is listed in the sales catalogue of Forman's library as follows: "Sophoclis Tragoedae Septem. Ex editione R. F. P. Brunck. Vol. II 32 mo, old half calf. Oxonii, 1809." And it notes the inscription by Claire. Leslie Marchand (in "Trelawny on the Death of Shelley," *Keats-Shelley Memorial Bulletin*, Rome, 1952, No. IV, p. 17) speculated that the Bodleian copy might be a "bogus relic" constructed by Trelawny. That the Forman copy cannot be bogus is attested by Claire's inscription and Paola's comments. Shelley certainly carried this book with him; and it was found after his death either in the boat or in his "coat." Marchand apparently did not know of this copy; and its existence further complicates matters. Perhaps Shelley had two sets of the 1809 Sophocles, one in two separate volumes and one bound in one volume. Mary's journals and letters show that Sophocles was a favorite author both with her and with Shelley.

SELECTED BIBLIOGRAPHY

Baker, Carlos. *Shelley's Major Poetry*. Princeton, 1948.

Blunden, Edmund. *Leigh Hunt, a Biography*. London, 1930.

——*Shelley, a Life Story*. New York, 1947.

Boas, Louise Schutz. *Harriet Shelley, Five Long Years*. New York, 1962.

Brown, Ford K. *The Life of William Godwin*. New York, 1926.

Byron, George Gordon. *The Complete Poetical Works of Byron*, ed. Paul Elmer Moore. Boston (reissue), 1952.

——*Lord Byron's Correspondence*, ed. John Murray. London, 1922.

——*The Works of Lord Byron, Letters and Journals*, ed. Rowland E. Prothero. New York, 1898–1901.

——*The Works of Lord Byron, Poetry*, ed. Ernest Hartley Coleridge. New York, 1898–1904.

Cameron, Kenneth Neill. *The Young Shelley, Genesis of a Radical*. New York, 1950.

Cline, C. L. *Byron, Shelley and Their Pisan Circle*. Cambridge, Massachusetts, 1952.

Dowden, Edward. *The Life of Percy Bysshe Shelley*. London, 1886.

Elwin, Malcolm. *Lord Byron's Wife*. New York, 1962.

Flexner, Eleanor. *Mary Wollstonecraft, a Biography*. New York, 1972.

Fuller, Jean Overton. *Shelley: A Biography*. London, 1968.

Godwin, William. *Enquiry Concerning Political Justice and Its Influence on Morals and Happiness*, ed. F. E. L. Priestley. Toronto, 1946.

——*Memoirs of the Author of a Vindication of the Rights of Woman*. London, 1798.

——*Memoirs of Mary Wollstonecraft Written by William Godwin ... with a Preface, a Supplement*, ed. W. Clark Durant. New York, 1927.

Grabo, Carl. *The Magic Plant, the Growth of Shelley's Thought*. Chapel Hill, North Carolina, 1936.

Grylls, R. Glynn. *Claire Clairmont, Mother of Byron's Allegra*. London, 1939.

——*Mary Shelley, A Biography*. New York, 1938.

Hogg, Thomas Jefferson. *The Life of Percy Bysshe Shelley*. First edition, London 1858. In *The Life of Percy Bysshe Shelley* .... ed. Humbert Wolfe, London, 1933.

Houtchens, Lawrence Huston, and Carolyn Washburn Houtchens. *Leigh Hunt's Dramatic Criticism, 1808–1831*. New York, 1949.

——*Leigh Hunt's Literary Criticism*. New York, 1956.

——*Leigh Hunt's Political and Occasional Essays*. New York, 1962.

Hughes, A. M. D. *The Nascent Mind of Shelley*. Oxford, 1947.

Bibliography

Hunt, Leigh. *The Autobiography of Leigh Hunt*, ed. Roger Ingpen. Westminster, 1903.

———*The Correspondence of Leigh Hunt* [ed. Thornton Hunt]. London, 1862.

———*My Leigh Hunt Library, the First Editions*, ed. Luther A. Brewer. Cedar Rapids, Iowa, 1932.

———*My Leigh Hunt Library, the Holograph Letters*, ed. Luther A. Brewer. Cedar Rapids, Iowa, 1938.

Ingpen, Roger. *Shelley in England: New Facts and Letters from the Shelley-Whitton Papers*. London, 1917.

Johnson, R. Brimley, ed. *Shelley-Leigh Hunt: How Friendship Made History and Extended the Bounds of Human Freedom and Thought*. London, 1928.

Jones, Frederick L., ed. *Maria Gisborne and Edward E. Williams, Shelley's Friends, Their Journals and Letters*. Norman, Oklahoma, 1951.

King-Hele, Desmond. *Shelley: The Man and the Poet*. New York, 1960.

Koszul, André. *La Jeunesse de Shelley*. Paris, 1910.

Kurtz, Benjamin P., and Carrie C. Autry, eds. *New Letters of Mary Wollstonecraft and Helen Maria Williams*. Berkeley, California, 1937.

Landre, Louis. *Leigh Hunt (1784-1859)*. Paris, 1935-1936.

Marchand, Leslie A. *Byron, A Portrait*. New York, 1970.

———*Byron's Poetry: A Critical Introduction*. Boston, 1965.

Marshall, Mrs. Julian. *The Life and Letters of Mary Wollstonecraft Shelley*. London, 1889.

McNiece, Gerald. *Shelley and the Revolutionary Idea*. Cambridge, Massachusetts, 1969.

Medwin, Thomas. *Conversations of Lord Byron: Noted during a Residence with his Lordship at Pisa, in the Years 1821 and 1822*. London, 1824.

———*The Life of Percy Bysshe Shelley*, ed. H. Buxton Forman. New York, 1913.

Moore, Doris Langley. *The Late Lord Byron*. New York, 1961.

Nitchie, Elizabeth. *Mary Shelley, Author of "Frankenstein."* New Brunswick, New Jersey, 1953.

Notopoulos, James A. *The Platonism of Shelley*. Durham, North Carolina, 1949.

Paul, C. Kegan. *William Godwin, His Friends and Contemporaries*. London, 1876.

Peacock, Thomas Love. "Memoirs of Percy Bysshe Shelley," in *The Works of Thomas Love Peacock*, Vol. VIII, ed. H. F. B. Brett-Smith and C. E. Jones (Halliford Edition). London, 1934.

———*The Works of Thomas Love Peacock*, ed. H. F. B. Brett-Smith and C. E. Jones (Halliford Edition). London, 1924-1934.

———*The Works of Thomas Love Peacock*, ed. Henry Cole. London, 1875.

Peck, Walter Edwin. *Shelley, His Life and Work*. New York, 1927.

Pollin, Burton Ralph. *Education and Enlightenment in the Works of William Godwin*. New York, 1962.

Pulos, C. E. *The Deep Truth: A Study of Shelley's Scepticism*. Lincoln, Nebraska, 1954.

Reiman, Donald H. *Percy Bysshe Shelley.* New York, 1969.

Robinson, Henry Crabb. *Diary, Reminiscences, and Correspondence of Henry Crabb Robinson,* ed. Thomas Sadler. London, 1869.

————*On Books and Their Writers,* ed. Edith J. Morley. London, 1938.

Scott, W. S., ed. *New Shelley Letters.* New Haven, 1949.

Scott, Winifred. *Jefferson Hogg.* London, 1951.

Shelley and Mary. For Private Circulation Only [London, 1882].

Shelley, Mary. *The Letters of Mary Shelley,* ed. Frederick L. Jones. Norman, Oklahoma, 1944.

————*Mary Shelley's Journal,* ed. Frederick L. Jones. Norman, Oklahoma, 1944.

Shelley, Percy Bysshe. *Complete Poetical Works,* ed. Thomas Hutchinson, corrected by G. M. Matthews. Oxford Standard Edition. New York, 1970.

————*The Complete Works of Percy Bysshe Shelley,* ed. Roger Ingpen and Walter E. Peck (Julian Edition). New York, 1926–1930.

————*The Esdaile Notebook, A Volume of Early Poems by Percy Bysshe Shelley,* ed. Kenneth Neill Cameron. New York, 1964.

————*The Esdaile Poems, Early Minor Poems from the 'Esdaile Notebook,'* ed. Neville Rogers. Oxford, 1966.

————*The Letters of Percy Bysshe Shelley,* ed. Frederick L. Jones. Oxford, 1964.

————*Shelley's Prose,* ed. David Lee Clark. Albuquerque, New Mexico, 1954.

Van Doren, Carl. *The Life of Thomas Love Peacock.* London. 1911.

Walling, William. *Mary Shelley.* New York, 1972.

Wardle, Ralph M. *Mary Wollstonecraft, a Critical Biography.* Lawrence, Kansas, 1951.

Wasserman, Earl R. *Shelley: A Critical Reading.* Baltimore, 1971.

White, Newman I. *Portrait of Shelley.* New York, 1945.

————*Shelley.* New York, 1940.

Wollstonecraft, Mary. *Letters to Imlay, with Prefatory Memoir,* ed. C. Kegan Paul. London, 1879.

————*Posthumous Works of the Author of a Vindication of the Rights of Woman,* ed. William Godwin. London, 1798.

————*A Vindication of the Rights of Men,* ed. Eleanor Nicholes. Gainsville, Florida, 1960.

————*A Vindication of the Rights of Woman,* ed. Charles W. Hegelman. New York, 1970.

INDEX

[307]

Index

Index